The Passion of Emily Dickinson

This transfiguration which all material objects undergo through the passion of the poet . . .

—Emerson, *Nature* (1836)

The Passion of
EMILY DICKINSON

Judith Farr

HARVARD UNIVERSITY PRESS

Cambridge, Massachusetts
London, England

First Harvard University Press paperback edition, 1994

Poem texts are reprinted by permission of the publishers and the Trustees of Amherst College
and Little, Brown and Company from *The Poems of Emily Dickinson*, 3 vols., ed. Thomas
H. Johnson (Cambridge, The Belknap Press of Harvard University Press), Copyright © 1951,
1955, 1979, 1983 by the President and Fellows of Harvard College; Copyright © 1929, 1935
by Martha Dickinson Bianchi; Copyright © renewed 1957, 1963 by Mary L. Hampson.
Quotations from *The Letters of Emily Dickinson*, 3 vols., ed. Thomas H. Johnson (Cambridge,
The Belknap Press of Harvard University Press), are reprinted by permission of the publishers,
Copyright © 1958, 1986 by the President and Fellows of Harvard College.

Publication of this book has been supported by a grant from the
National Endowment for the Humanities.

This book is printed on acid-free paper, and its binding materials
have been chosen for strength and durability.

Library of Congress Cataloging-in-Publication Data
Farr, Judith.
The passion of Emily Dickinson / Judith Farr.
p.   cm.
Includes bibliographical references and index.
ISBN 0-674-65665-2 (cloth)
ISBN 0-674-65666-0 (pbk.)
1. Dickinson, Emily, 1830–1886.   2. Dickinson, Emily, 1830–1886—
Aesthetics.   3. Dickinson, Emily, 1830–1886—Knowledge—Art.
4. Art and literature—United States—History—19th century.
5. Poets, American—19th century—Biography.   I. Title.
PS1541.Z5F27   1992
811'.4—dc20   91-28076
CIP

For George and Alec

Preface

It is now over a century since a small white book decorated with silver-gilt flowers, containing one hundred and sixteen poems by Emily Dickinson, was published in Boston in 1890. This volume, "Edited by two of her Friends," was reluctantly printed by Roberts Brothers. Its costs were paid by the poet's sister. Unexpectedly, it met with extravagant success, and the poet herself, dead four years, became the subject of widespread curiosity. Her distinctive literary style had been amended by conservative editors. Transcribing her poems from the fascicles or handwritten copies she herself had made, bound, and hidden, they regularized her spelling, altered her language, and normalized her punctuation. The result seemed to some readers the language of genius; to others, of eccentricity.

Much of the popular and even critical esteem her poems excited in the 1890s was the result not of their poetic style but of Emily Dickinson's "thoughts." (For the most part, it would not be until the 1930s; not until the intense scrutiny of the New Critics; not, certainly, until Thomas H. Johnson's restorative publication of her poems from manuscript in 1955, that Dickinson's style was paid homage.) Her thoughts were widely viewed as remarkable: the extraordinary richness and detail of her appreciations of nature; the probity and loftiness of her moral sentiments; her tough and delicate emotional perceptions; her daring investigations of that possibility, eternal life; and, most of all, her understanding of the many moods of love.

Emily Dickinson was a recluse for twenty years. Unmarried daughter of the redoubtable Edward Dickinson, once a member of the Massachusetts House of Representatives, she strayed from the family pattern of worldly engagement. Her father and brother distinguished themselves as philanthropists and civil servants. Her sister-in-law Susan thrived on entertaining. Even her timid mother could enjoy social life; Emily's sister Lavinia represented their mother's funeral as Mrs. Dickinson's "last party." After the early 1860s, however, the poet herself preferred solitude.

Confronted with the penetrating utterances of a woman considered an *isolata*, her public attempted to understand how Emily Dickinson had achieved all this knowledge. The divided Dickinson family supplied rival explanations, founded on differing versions of the poet's life. Susan Dickinson gave out that Emily had retired from society in thwarted passion for a married minister; if the poems were spiritual and aphoristic, they had derived much of their insight from suffering and from the comfort the poet found in nature. Sue's daughter, Martha Dickinson Bianchi, fostered this view, and she emphasized the sibylline precocity of an elfin aunt, associated with daffodils, cakes, children's games, and brilliant sayings, thus helping to create the Belle of Amherst. Lavinia Dickinson, her sister's life-long companion, contradicted the legend of Dickinson's forbidden love: by declaring that "Emily had to think," she innocently implied the truth that it is imagination which enables the true artist to transcend social limits. Nevertheless, Emily Dickinson's life continued—and continues—to fascinate scholar and general reader alike.

Although this book is not a biography, it attempts an inclusive vision of the poetry of Emily Dickinson, read in the context of her time, environment, and personal circumstances. I am interested in what became Dickinson's passion to lead a life in and through art—her own and that of others. I am concerned with her quest for honor, not fame, as a writer; with her aesthetic, supported by a Ruskinian image of herself as a painter; with her participation in the artistic modes of her day; and with her willingness—however ironic, enigmatic, and subtle—to transmute passages from her life experience, her special passions, into poetry. At the same time, I try to explore how richly she imaged her life in the poems by means of metaphors drawn from the arts she knew best: literature and painting.

Each chapter of this book addresses a theme central to Dickinson studies, by considering the poet's connection with literary or artistic works: her reclusion and self-description as a nun with the nuns of Tennyson and the Pre-Raphaelites, for example; her mysterious emblem of the white dress with scriptural Revelation and Rossetti's saintly maidens (known in Dickinson's New England through the activities of such painter-critics as William Stillman). Even as Dickinson's quotation of mid-Victorian literary texts was wider than has been supposed, she knew far more about nineteenth-century visual art than has usually been thought.

Although Dickinson once described the transcendent character of poetry by calling herself the mere "Representative of the Verse," she also wrote, "a Book, is only the Heart's Portrait – every Page a Pulse" (L 2.412; 3.756). Years of willful legend-making about Emily Dickinson the person, however, has discredited for some the classic function of literary biography in her case. Yet the prudent scholar should not ignore biographical evidence or even avoid informed speculation about biography if any illumination of the poems may result. For many poems there is the problem, as Jay Leyda says, of what might be called the "omitted center": "The riddle, the circumstance too well-known to be repeated to the initiate, the deliberate skirting of the obvious—this was the means she used to increase the privacy of her communication; it has also increased our problems in piercing that privacy" (I, xxi).

As a private poet who willingly published only a few poems and whose chief readership was sparse, intimate, or familial, Emily Dickinson was especially free to be allusive. Particularly in mysterious poem clusters about pearls, shells, and jewels; in letters and poems to the man called "Master," wherein she writes of daisies, suns, and voyages, Dickinson appears to be using a language suited with fine, systematic particularity to one subject or one addressee. That her language was probably drawn purposefully from specific "texts" in literature or painting is a premise of this book. When those texts—say Tennyson's *Maud* or Shakespeare's *Antony and Cleopatra*, Brontë's *Jane Eyre* or Thomas Cole's *Voyage of Life*—may be seen as associated with people about or to whom Dickinson repeatedly wrote, the result is a reduction in the puzzle of her "omitted center." Some Dickinson poems are difficult to read because they are what one might call coded. The coding was necessary, perhaps, not only because of her retiring nature and literate sensibilities but because rich evidence indicates that much of the riddlesome poetry of the 1860s and 1870s was written for a married man and for a married woman. With each she had a public relationship; but for each she felt a passion that transcended the relationship and could be expressed only in a private (sometimes shared) language. The beauty and the verbal/visual complexity of that language is the chief study of my book.

In reading and teaching the poems and letters of Emily Dickinson for over twenty-five years, I have always been freshly impressed with their intensity, with *her* intensity. The central radiance of her emotional life was her love for the woman she called "My Sue," her "precious Inn, where the Fair stopped" (L 2.498, 513). But this is not a connection that should be sentimentalized, for the poems and letters show it to have been charged also with disillusionment and uncertainty. Her love went out, as well, to "Master" with a related intensity; the looks of flowers, birds, or skies could be translated into a "Vision of Language" that was both shrewdly real and apocalyptic (L 3.748).

Dickinson preserved her honorable and courageous skepticism about Christian dogma from girlhood to the grave; but the same intensity with which she met creation characterized her address to the Infinite. Not death or nature or even love, but the idea of eternity was her central theme, as it was for painters like Thomas Cole and writers like Henry Vaughan, to whom she alludes. So symbolic was her imagination, so convinced her sensation of the transcendent, that many Dickinson poems which may be read for one addressee may also be read as intended for God. In calling her lover "Master," she immediately complicated eros with adoration. Some of the lyrics in the Master chapter of this book might be taken as songs of devotion, desire for, even anger against, another "Sire," God. As in many mid-Victorian poems and paintings, the divine and the human face often fuse in her art. For Dickinson's consistent apprehension is of "Eternity in Time."

In a poem about the distinction between experience and the memory of it, Dickinson writes,

> After a hundred years
> Nobody knows the Place
> Agony that enacted there
> Motionless as Peace   (1147)

One hundred years and more since the publication of her *Poems*, we continue to try to know Emily Dickinson's poetry in its careful design and full dimension.

Contents

1

The Hidden Face   1

2

Solitary Mornings on the Sea   48

3

The Narrative of Sue   100

4

The Narrative of Master   178

5

A Vision of Forms   245

6

Art as Life   314

Abbreviations   336

Appendix: Poems for Sue and Poems for Master   337

Notes   345

Acknowledgments   377

Index of First Lines   379

Index   383

Illustrations

Figures

Emily Dickinson (daguerreotype, ca. 1847). Amherst College Library, by permission of the Trustees of Amherst College   18

Margaret Aurelia Dewing (daguerreotype, ca. 1847). Courtesy of Richard Rudisill and the University of New Mexico Press   19

"Spriggins's Voyage of Life." *Harper's*, December 1859   72–73

Clementina, Viscountess Hawarden, *Two Girls: Hand to Bosom*. Courtesy of the Victoria and Albert Museum, London   102

Susan Gilbert Dickinson. Houghton Library, by permission of the President and Fellows of Harvard College   129

Samuel Bowles. Houghton Library, by permission of the President and Fellows of Harvard College   186

Frederic Edwin Church, *The Heart of the Andes*. Courtesy of the Metropolitan Museum of Art, New York, Bequest of Margaret E. Dows, 1909   237

Frederic Edwin Church, *Cardamum*. Courtesy of the Cooper-Hewitt Museum of Design, New York, Smithsonian Institution   277

Page from fascicle 11, "Just so – Christ – raps." Houghton Library, by permission of the President and Fellows of Harvard College   327

Plates
(following page 208)

Charles Allston Collins, *Convent Thoughts*. Courtesy of the Ashmoleon Museum, Oxford

Thomas Cole, *The Voyage of Life*. Courtesy of the Munson-Williams-Proctor Institute, Utica, New York

Elihu Vedder, *The Cup of Death*. Courtesy of the National Museum of American Art, Smithsonian Institution, Gift of William T. Evans

William Holman Hunt, *The Light of the World*. Courtesy of the City Art Galleries, Manchester, England

Thomas Cole, *Expulsion from the Garden of Eden*. Courtesy of the Museum of Fine Arts, Boston, M. and M. Karolik Collection

The Passion of Emily Dickinson

~ 1 ~

The Hidden Face

The real disadvantage of women has lain in being systemati-
cally taught from childhood that it is their highest duty to
efface themselves, or at least keep out of sight.

—Thomas Wentworth Higginson (1884)

When Emily Dickinson died at the age of fifty-five, most who knew her
had not seen her face for a quarter of a century. Even Dickinson's
physician, Dr. Bigelow, was expected to diagnose her final illness by
observing her fully dressed figure pass an open doorway, the face averted
in shadow. His remedies—quinine, belladonna, and digitalis—could not
avail against Bright's disease, which began in 1884 with exhaustion,
fainting spells, and edema and ended in paralysis and the "terrible
breathing" of coma while her brother Austin and sister Lavinia stood
sorrowfully by.[1]

Then Dickinson's long sequestration from Amherst eyes was necessarily modified as her family prepared a funeral for which she herself
had left some instructions. An old friend, Mrs. Phelps, assisted her
brother's wife Sue in washing and dressing the body in a white woolen
shroud. It was measured for one of the costliest caskets—five feet, six
inches long and lined in white flannel—provided by the Amherst funeral
director that year. Dickinson's courtly "Preceptor," Thomas Wentworth
Higginson, was summoned from Boston; an old neighbor, the Reverend
Jenkins, from Portland; and the Congregationalist minister, the Reverend Dickerman, from across the street. A few intimates (including
Mabel Todd, Austin's mistress and Dickinson's future editor) were
invited from the village. The current president of Amherst College,
Julius Seelye, and the former president, Edward Hitchcock (whose botanical studies had been Dickinson's textbooks), came to be honorary
pallbearers. And on the sunny afternoon of May 19, the family's six
Irish men servants carried Dickinson's coffined body down from the

1

upper room in which she had lived and written and placed it in the great parlor for a simple funeral service.

Though she had corresponded with her for years and played the Dickinsons' piano as the increasingly frail Emily listened in the dusk above stairs, Mabel Todd never achieved a meeting with this woman whose red hair and passionate intensity were said to be so like her lover's. Now at last (in an experience that seemed to her "beautiful" and "poetical"),[2] she could stare freely at the features of one she had come to call "The Myth." As Lavinia asked one after another guest to come forward to view the body, it was recalled, bees buzzed outside the open backdoor of the house while birds and even butterflies were seen in the air, as if they had come from a Dickinson poem. A neighbor, Mrs. Jameson, drawn to the casket, said that the face she too had never seen was "very spirituelle."[3] But it was Higginson who provided the most lyrical and reverent verbal portrait of Dickinson's last face. In life, on the first of only two occasions on which he was permitted to see it, he had pronounced it plain, "with no good feature."[4] Now, with pink cypripedium and violets at the throat, it seemed to him "a wondrous restoration of youth—she . . . looked 30, not a gray hair or wrinkle, and perfect peace on the beautiful brow."[5]

It was often the custom, especially among wealthy Americans in the Victorian era, to take a daguerreotype impression of the newly dead. Dickinson herself, who was always keenly interested in portrait photographs (which she called "Faces"), must have seen many such studies. They were usually of children and white-robed women, clutching flowers in a marble-like repose that could thenceforth be remembered as a portent of the lasting peace of their souls. Memorial daguerreotypes were especially prized, "the value attached to the subject of a picture . . . often transferred to the picture itself."[6] No photographer stepped forward at the Dickinson service, however, to record the lineaments of a face that had not been offered to the camera since girlhood. Instead, funeral guests were aware of their own efforts to commit its features— particularly the strangely long upper lip and profoundly white skin— to memory. They had feelings of transgression as they did so. For her sister-in-law explained in the obituary notice she composed for the *Springfield Republican* (May 18) that the dead woman had "screened herself from close acquaintance" because " 'the mesh of her soul,' as Browning calls the body, was too rare" to permit it.[7]

Colonel Higginson encouraged this explanation of Dickinson's hermeticism and implied that it was valiantly chosen when he selected as a funeral text Emily Brontë's "Last Lines" that begin "No coward soul am I." After Scripture readings and prayer, Higginson told the assemblage that his friend "frequently read the [poem] to her sister," and that Brontë's "poem on Immortality was a favorite of [her] who has put it on—if she could ever have been said to have put it off."[8] The lid of the coffin was then closed and covered with sprays of violets and ferns. But Lavinia first tucked two heliotropes in the poet's hand "to take to Judge Lord."[9] (Before his own recent death, that distinguished, elderly magistrate of Salem had asked Emily Dickinson to marry him.)

At last the poet's specific wishes were observed as the pallbearers carried her coffin through a rear door, then entrusting it to her father's servants who bore it across fields to the cemetery, keeping always in sight of the house. "When it shall come my turn for [funeral bouquets], I want a Buttercup," Dickinson had written to Mrs. Holland. "Doubtless the Grass will give me one, for does she not revere the Whims of her flitting Children?" (L 3.901). Higginson recalled that the fields were full of buttercups and wild geraniums that day. At the Dickinson plot where her mother and father's graves adjoined her own, the open ground had been lined with ferns and pine boughs. Cascades of flowers were heaped on the casket as it was lowered and this moment of her own burial, which the poet had envisioned in scores of poems and letters, was over.

Few of her mourners (excepting, I think, "Sister Sue") could have realized how long and how intently Dickinson had contemplated the grave that now finally, and completely, hid her face. Higginson was sent "Safe in their Alabaster Chambers" in her first letter to him in 1862. During the years that followed, he received "Step lightly on this narrow spot," "Ample make this Bed," "Not any higher stands the Grave," "She laid her docile Crescent down," and—as a eulogy for his infant daughter, Louisa—"The Face in evanescence lain." But by far the majority of poems she sent him in their twenty-four years of association were not precisely about death but about mysterious love and suffering. (Indeed, such lyrics as "Your Riches taught me poverty" [299], "A Death Blow is a Life Blow to Some" [816], and "I Have no Life but this" [1398] seemed to confide secrets of a vivid emotional experience that was far more extensive than he was ever piqued to surmise. That he was later shocked to discover her love poem "Wild Nights" seems improbable in view of the range of erotic perceptions contained in the poems he had already read.) But Dickinson's great poems about the advent of Death as a supportive and compelling suitor, like her many elegies for people and seasons, were still to be lifted by her sister Lavinia from the legendary locked box.

Therefore even Higginson, who remarked her otherworldly quality and attributed it to "an abnormal life,"[10] did not guess how deeply Emily Dickinson had meditated on the significance of death and, in particular, on the process whereby the living become the dead. Even in an age fascinated by its every manifestation and trapping, she showed exceptional curiosity about death; about whether the dying recognized their condition, and about where they "went" after the trip to the cemetery. (Once she advised a caller to go there immediately to save time.) In her last years she would call "the secret of Death" her central preoccupation (L 3.667). But it had always concerned her. Even as a schoolgirl at Mary Lyon's Female Seminary, she responded with more intensity than her classmates to sermons on the Last End, often preached on the Sabbath. The death of Sophia Holland when she and Emily were fourteen had the same destructive effect on Dickinson's physical and mental well-being as the death, thirty-nine years later, of her brother Austin's young son, Gilbert. She broke down. From Gilbert's death in 1883 she never recovered, becoming an invalid as much from sorrow (she said) as from illness. Her slow recovery from Sophia's death in 1844 had to be achieved with effort. She was sent away from Amherst to find new interests and distractions in Boston.

Two years later Emily Dickinson recalled this painful experience. Writing to an idolized new friend, Abiah Root, she mourned the pretty girl who had preceded Abiah as her intimate. Although her account contains some expressions common to sentimental Victorian death scenes, its drama and suffering are plainly rendered. Indeed, the awkwardness of some of the sixteen-year-old Dickinson's phrases provides a measure of her remembered anguish:

> I have never lost but one friend near my age & with whom my thoughts & her own were the same. It was before you came to Amherst. My friend was Sophia Holland. She was too lovely for earth & she was transplanted from earth to heaven. I visited her often in sickness & watched over her bed. But at length Reason fled and the physician forbid any but the nurse to go into her room. Then it seemed to me I should die too if I could not be permitted to watch over her or even to look at her face. At length the doctor said she must die & allowed me to look at her a moment through the open door. I took off my shoes and stole softly to the sick room.
> There she lay mild & beautiful as in health & her pale features lit

up with an unearthly – smile. I looked as long as friends would permit & when they told me I must look no longer I let them lead me away. I shed no tear, for my heart was too full to weep, but after she was laid in her coffin & I felt I could not call her back again I gave way to a fixed melancholy.

I told no one the cause of my grief, though it was gnawing at my very heart strings. I was not well & I went to Boston & stayed a month & my health improved so that my spirits were better. I trust she is now in heaven & though I shall never forget her, yet I shall meet her in heaven. (L 1.32)

Despite its stilted, formulaic expressions—"I trust," "Reason fled," "fixed melancholy"—the young Emily Dickinson's letter gives us a lively picture of her shock when the friend who was a second self was taken. A number of remarks in her letter anticipate ideas that appear in the mature poems. The woman "too lovely for earth" is (as in the works of other Victorian writers, sculptors, and painters) one of her chief themes. The meticulous authorial eye that would be depicted in "I measure every Grief I meet" (61) develops from the avid gaze of the fourteen-year-old girl, who fears she will herself die if not permitted to watch over Sophia. The child's desire to look at her face is multiplied over and over in the woman poet's desire to look at other faces; so poems like "What would I give to see his face?" (247), along with Dickinson's habit of perusing photographs (especially of the dead), seem related to this early need to keep Sophia's features before her. The gnawing of a grief that is suppressed and leads to depression would be the subject of many poems, such as 793. There "Grief is a mouse" whose wainscot is the breast. The girl who "told no one the cause of my grief" would write around 1863 that "Best Grief is Tongueless." It doesn't speak, even on the "rack." Finally, the young Emily's declaration that she will never forget Sophia and will meet her in heaven anticipates one of the central Dickinson tropes: profound love between two people, the terrible loss of one, and permanent reunion of both in heaven.

The reactions of others to Emily Dickinson's intensity may be inferred from her letter about Sophia. She is told to look no longer, led away, and sent to Boston. Although Victorian culture encouraged pious contemplation of death and eternity, Dickinson's absorption seems to have struck people as dangerously excessive. In later life she was often able to endure her own imaginative bonding with the dead and her yearning after them without falling sick. But sometimes the poet who wrote "A loss of something ever felt I" (959) could not tolerate loss without a violent response. "Does not Eternity appear dreadful to you," she asked Abiah in another letter of 1846. For she could not—like so many of the other girls that winter—become a Christian, formally, by "declaring for Christ" and joining the Congregational church. Being uncertain, therefore, of her reception "at the Bar of God," she temporarily repudiated another of the great themes she would write about as a mature artist: eternal life.

> I almost wish there was no Eternity. To think that we must forever live and never cease to be. It seems as if Death which all so dread because it launches us upon an unknown world would be a relief to so endless a state of existense [sic]. I dont know why it is but it does not seem to me that I shall ever cease to live on earth – I cannot imagine with the farthest stretch of the imagination my own death scene. (L 1.28)

What this youthful letter shows, of course, is that Dickinson had indeed begun to *try* to imagine dying even at age sixteen. She wrote many poems envisioning that divine country, Eternity. But what interested her primarily was the soul's passage there. This was what medieval theologians called the *transitus,* or transition. In nineteenth-century parlance it was sometimes called the "crossover." Souls borne aloft by angels to "meet Christ in the air" (1 Thessalonians 4:17), souls whom Death led by the hand into paradise or hell, had long been a subject for poets and painters. The poet Dickinson sometimes imagines the transitus as a homely genre scene: "I heard a Fly buzz – when I died" (465) or a cheery narrative about a "humble tourist": "Went up a year this evening!" (93). Once it was a balloon trip (1053) and once a buggy ride with a kindly gentleman (712). In one poem (160) it is a voyage on the sea without a ship, and eternity is a "disappointed tide" that recedes when the speaker is called back to earth. For this world and the next were to Emily Dickinson echoes and metaphors of one another, two stages of one existence as she developed her "Compound Vision" (906). The final evidence of this encompassing perception is her last letter, sent to her cousins, Louise and Frances Norcross. She had been reading a ghost story she thought her dead friend Samuel Bowles would have liked. Apparently with a presentiment of her own approaching death, she wrote the story's title as a farewell to the Norcrosses:

Little Cousins –
  "Called back" (L 3.1046)

The words echo her sentence about Sophia forty-two years earlier: "I felt I could not call her back." And Austin Dickinson seemed to share his sister's vision of life and life eternal as two adjoining realms. Later that week he wrote in his diary as she lay dying, "It was settled before morning broke that Emily would not wake again this side."[11] (On her tombstone he had the stonemasons carve "Born December 10, 1830. Called Back May 15, 1886.")

What the other side looked like invited Emily Dickinson's speculation throughout her life; for although Immortality often seemed to her "a member of the family" after Edward Dickinson's death, and though she could envision it riding with Death and herself for an afternoon drive, it had never had a distinct face (L 3.663). She was given to imagining the simple but apocalyptic rite whereby she would enter upon immortal life. And although on a few terrible occasions she imagined herself alone as she "traveled," Dickinson's poetry usually depicts her with an escort. "He" comes for her, lordly as a lover:

> It was a quiet way —
> He asked if I was his —
> I made no answer of the Tongue
> But answer of the Eyes —
> And then He bore me on
> Before this mortal noise
> With swiftness, as of Chariots
> And distance, as of Wheels.
> This World did drop away
> As Acres from the feet
> Of one that leaneth from Balloon
> Upon an Ether street.
> The Gulf behind was not,
> The Continents were new —
> Eternity it was before
> Eternity was due.
> No Seasons were to us —
> It was not Night nor Morn —
> But Sunrise stopped upon the place
> And fastened it in Dawn (1053)

"It was a quiet way," written when Dickinson was about thirty-five, reveals her audacious conviction as a poet of the transitus. The first two lines might be the opening confession of a betrothal poem or a poem of seduction. So might the next two lines, in which the speaker cannot speak but answers with her eyes. As the poem continues, however, the reader may return to these lines, realizing that Dickinson is not alluding to her shyness or sense of the decorous but to the fact that the dead do not talk. But they "answer" Death's summons with their eyes, for the eyes move up into the head after death (and someone may close the eyelids). The speaker might be being claimed for a moment of passion except that the "swiftness" of her companion has an impersonal, even abstract force. As is often the case in her poems about translation into eternity, she makes "his" actions and relation to herself indistinct. Thus "He" bears her from life—"this mortal noise"—with a swiftness that, though named, is still beyond calculation. It is "as of Chariots" (and one feels and hears the whoosh of those fleet old war carriages). The distance she traverses is "as of" wheels (and one imagines wheels turning for miles). But Dickinson's qualification "as of" reminds the reader that these wheels and this chariot are not earthly. In fact, they are her equivalents of the terrible conveyances of Revelation, while "He" appears with the awful ease of the Almighty in Psalms 18:9–10:

> He bowed the heavens also, and came down: and darkness was under his feet.
> And he rode upon a cherub, and did fly: yea, he did fly upon the wings of the wind.

She imagines herself in one of the balloons used for experimental flights in the 1840s, '50s and '60s; but again it is "As[if] Acres" of this world dropped away so that, leaning from the ether-filled balloon, she beheld "an Ether street." "The Gulf behind" her and between her dead soul and the life she left *might* be the "great gulf fixed" of Scripture (Luke 16:26). But she denies even that helpful placement in space. She says, instead, that there *was* no "Gulf behind" and the continents she sees are new. She is suddenly in Eternity before it was "due." (Her statement is another echo of scriptural passages such as "Ye know not what hour your Lord doth come" [Matthew 24:42] and "Thou are not far from the kingdom of God" [Mark 12:34].)

There is, finally, a "place" at the close of Dickinson's poem. It is Sunrise or Dawn, that Christian symbol of resurrection presented most dramatically in the gospels for Easter. Emily Dickinson would have read in Mark 16:2, for instance, "very early in the morning . . . they came unto the sepulchre at the rising of the sun." For it is at dawn that Mary Magdalene and the other women discover that Christ has risen. Dawn, therefore, in Dickinson's poem as in Mark's gospel, signifies passage from the grave into eternal life. Thus Dickinson's definition of the "place" in which her translated soul arrives is still paradoxical. For that grand moment Sunrise is made to "stop" and "fasten" the placeless place in another ephemeral time, Dawn.

Dickinson's sister Lavinia and her brother Austin (with whom she discussed "the Extension of Consciousness, after Death") were always aware of the facility with which their sister's contemplation moved between this world and an hypothetical other (L 3.667). But it was her sister-in-law Sue, to whom she addressed nearly a fourth of her correspondence, who probably perceived the degree to which this world was merely "the thrilling preface to supremer things" (L 3.683). The obituary notice Sue composed for her childhood friend shows that she knew Emily very well. Indeed, the obituary should be quoted in its entirety, for it reveals what Sue, as a family member, considered requisite to record about her sister-in-law. And, to some extent, it also shows some of the qualities in Sue that attracted Emily.

The obituary appeared, entitled "Miss Emily Dickinson of Amherst," in the newspaper once edited by Samuel Bowles, the *Springfield Republican* for May 18. It was reprinted in the *Amherst Record* the next day, when Dickinson was buried. Like so many nineteenth-century newspaper accounts, Sue's obituary has the thoughtful air of an essay or a character sketch. She is clearly trying to affect the public conception of her subject:

> The death of Miss Emily Dickinson, daughter of the late Edward Dickinson, at Amherst on Saturday, makes another sad inroad on the small circle so long occupying the old family mansion. It was for a long generation overlooked by death, and one passing in and out of there thought of old-fashioned times, when parents and children grew up and passed maturity together, in lives of singular uneventfulness unmarked by sad or joyous crises. Very few in the village, except among the older inhabitants, knew Miss Emily personally, although the facts of her seclusion and intellectual brilliancy were familiar Amherst traditions. There are many houses among all classes into which treasures of fruit and flowers and ambrosial dishes for the sick and well were constantly sent, that will forever miss those evidences of her unselfish consideration, and mourn afresh that she screened herself from close acquaintance. As she passed on in life, her sensitive nature shrank from much personal contact with the world, and more and more turned to her own large wealth of individual resources for companionship, sitting thenceforth, as some one said of her, "in the light of her own fire." Not disappointed with the world, not an invalid until within the past two years, not from any lack of sympathy, not because she was insufficient for any mental work or social career—

her endowments being so exceptional—but the "mesh of her soul," as Browning calls the body, was too rare, and the sacred quiet of her own home proved the fit atmosphere for her worth and work. All that must be inviolate. One can only speak of "duties beautifully done"; of her gentle tillage of the rare flowers filling her conservatory, into which, as into the heavenly Paradise, entered nothing that could defile, and which was ever abloom in frost or sunshine, so well she knew her chemistries; of her tenderness to all in the home circle; her gentlewoman's grace and courtesy to all who served in house and grounds; her quick and rich response to all who rejoiced or suffered at home, or among her wide circle of friends the world over. This side of her nature was to her the real entity in which she rested, so simple and strong was her instinct that a woman's hearthstone is her shrine. Her talk and her writings were like no one else's, and although she never published a line, now and then some enthusiastic literary friend would turn love to larceny, and cause a few verses surreptitiously obtained to be printed. Thus, and through other natural ways, many saw and admired her verses, and in consequence frequently notable persons paid her visits, hoping to overcome the protest of her own nature and gain a promise of occasional contributions, at least, to various magazines. She withstood even the fascination of Mrs. Helen Jackson, who earnestly sought her cooperation in a novel of the No Name series, although one little poem somehow strayed into the volume of verse which appeared in that series. Her pages would ill have fitted even so attractive a story as "Mercy Philbrick's Choice," unwilling though a large part of the literary public were to believe that she had no part in it. "Her wagon was hitched to a star,"—and who could ride or write with such a voyager? A Damascus blade gleaming and glancing in the sun was her wit. Her swift poetic rapture was like the long glistening note of a bird one hears in the June woods at high noon, but can never see. Like a magician she caught the shadowy apparitions of her brain and tossed them in startling picturesqueness to her friends, who, charmed with their simplicity and homeliness as well as profundity, fretted that she had so easily made palpable the tantalizing fancies forever eluding their bungling, fettered grasp. So intimate and passionate was her love of Nature, she seemed herself a part of the high March sky, the summer day and bird call. Keen and eclectic in her literary tastes, she sifted libraries to Shakespeare and Browning; quick as the lightning in her intuitions and analyses, she seized the kernel instantly, almost impatient of the fewest words, by which she must make her revelation. To her, life was rich and all aglow with God and immortality. With no creed, no formulated faith, hardly knowing the names of dogmas, she walked this life with the gentleness and reverence of old saints, with the firm step of martyrs who sing while they suffer. How better note the flight of this "soul of fire in a shell of pearl" than by her own words?—

> Morns like these, we parted;
> Noons like these, she rose;
> Fluttering first, then firmer,
> To her fair repose.[12]

Susan Dickinson composed this obituary at a time when she was somewhat alienated from Emily and Lavinia, a time when Austin was conducting a rather public romance with Mabel Todd. That Sue's husband and sister-in-law chose, or at least permitted, her to write the obituary probably indicated two things: their belief that, among them, she had the most skill with words and their probably reluctant respect for her long friendship with Emily Dickinson. Sue's account reveals as much about herself as about her subject. By its remarkable linkage of Dickinson's "worth" with her "work," her personal integrity and her art, it showed both perception and daring. Indeed, the obituary concludes by quoting an elegy written by Dickinson herself, thus calling attention to her as a poet.[13] Yet to be a Felicia Hemans, earning one's living by the pen, was not to be a proper lady in the nineteenth century; and thus Sue is careful to emphasize that Emily Dickinson was a gentlewoman, who believed as a Victorian lady should that "a woman's hearthstone is her shrine."

In this connection, it is significant to recall that when Dickinson first wrote to Higginson for a literary judgment, she enclosed her calling card. It proved that she was not one of the grubby race of women scribblers so hated by Hawthorne; for all her diffidence, she was the daughter of a member of the House of Representatives: "Miss Emily E. Dickinson." Clara Newman Turner, a ward of Edward Dickinson's, reported Emily's "remark that she did not deem it 'feminine to publish.' "[14] Since there is no evidence that Dickinson considered her revered Elizabeth Barrett Browning unfeminine—indeed, she once imagined herself that enchanting poet's "Bridegroom" (312)—her remark to Clara, if correctly recalled, is puzzling. Was it made to conceal her true ambition? To excuse her failure to comply with requests for poems made of her by Samuel Bowles or by Helen Hunt Jackson? Was it made to please Sue who, at the end of her life, showed ambivalence about women publishing—not only about Dickinson's poems appearing in print but her own daughter Martha's?[15] Sue did have a reputation in

Amherst as a snob, overly aware of her social position as the wife of Austin, a well-to-do lawyer and the treasurer of Amherst College. For all her interest in the arts, she also seems genuinely to have believed that the role of women was in the home.

In order to suggest the personal refinement she particularly valued in her friend, then, Sue spoke of her poetry in the obituary but associated it with delicacy of manner and with artistry in homemaking. One of Sue's favorite authors was Coventry Patmore. Her obituary envisions Dickinson as his heroine in *The Angel in the House*. It quotes Patmore's line "duties beautifully done," which appears in section 32 of that poem, entitled "The Cathedral Close." Once a poor and somewhat rootless girl attracted to Squire Dickinson's daughter, Sue illustrates Emily's unselfishness by saying that she sent fruit and flowers to "many houses among all classes." The vision she provides of Dickinson among her flowers and plants transcends Sue's obsession with social position, however. It is almost lyrical, and one glimpses for a moment the acuity of the bright young woman who served as the poet's confidante. There may be overemphasis on Dickinson's aversion to crudity or formlessness in Sue's account. Yet there is also true respect for her aesthetic sensibility in the allusion to Emily's "gentle tillage of the rare flowers filling her conservatory in which, as into the heavenly Paradise, entered nothing that could defile, and which was ever abloom in frost or sunshine, so well she knew her chemistries."

The phrase "nothing that could defile," like "the sacred quiet of her own home," however, helps to compose a portrait of Emily Dickinson as a respectable Victorian vestal virgin who kept to her own hearth. Susan Dickinson projects it, certainly, in order to dispel rumors of Dickinson's neuroticism or misanthropy or selfishness or ineptitude: reasons apparently advanced for her avoidance of Amherst society after the 1860s. Even the phrase "so well she knew her chemistries" reminds the reader that Dickinson was a clever and knowledgeable botanist. (The conservatory had been built to enable her to grow the exotic flowers—such as Bowles's gift of a white cape jasmine—that she particularly admired. Any horticulturist would realize that someone known for her conservatory, as for the half acre of ground she cultivated, was not helpless or without occupation.)

Sue focuses, finally, on Dickinson's singularity of spirit, her rarity—more like a strange bird's than a human being's. There is a faint tinge of awe as well in her phrase "who could ride or write with such a voyager?" (Considered closely, it might explain why Dickinson never married.) And that Sue coupled writing with voyaging in describing her friend's nature was wise; for there was, in both the subjects and the manner of Dickinson's poems, an ardor for flight. One of the many passages in the Dickinsons' books probably marked by Emily is a line from Matthew Arnold's "Maurice de Guérin" in *Essays in Criticism:* "So would I [like the birds] live, hovering round society, and having always at my back a field of liberty vast as the sky."[16] But Dickinson's retirement, Sue proposes, was gradual, occurring "as she passed on in life." And she concludes—having paid tribute to Dickinson as a scholar, versifier, housekeeper, botanist, friend—by seeing her as a quasi-saint of no sect. "She walked this life . . . with the firm step of martyrs who sing while they suffer." Here is one of the first allusions to some private cross taken up by the poet. It is also an allusion to one of Sue's favorites among Emily's poems, "Through the strait pass of suffering/The Martyrs – even – trod" (792).[17]

Sue was a churchgoer as Emily was not. But her sentence "To her, life was rich and all aglow with God and immortality" shows that—despite their partial estrangement at the end of Emily's life—she could put her finger unerringly on the poet's faculty of always perceiving eternity in the actual. Of course she had had much evidence of that habit of mind in the thirty years since they were children, especially in the poems and letters Emily wrote after little Gilbert's death. At what Dickinson called his "Rendezvous of Light," Emily began to decline (L 3.799). Or, as she herself might have put it, to "rise."

2

Emily Dickinson always showed care in composing poems and letters: the words themselves had unique, almost personal shapes ("Shall I take thee, the Poet said / To the propounded word?" [1126]). Her focus, despite a "thronging Mind," was on achieving an intense, comprehensive clarity of statement whose qualities of incision grew so acute by the close of her life that the letters to Sue about Gilbert read like proverbs or commandments. Her objective seems to have been to startle with bold, fresh observation. Yet it is well known that, though some of her tastes—for Shakespeare, the Bible, Dickens—were irreproachable, she was unimaginative and even recalcitrant in her attitude to many original geniuses of her time: Henry James, Hawthorne, Whitman, to name a few. And she had a marvelous appetite for pious, sentimental, or adventurous trash—books the younger Dickinsons read because they were fashionable. She seems from her twenties to her fifties to have been wholly sincere in commending works on mortuary or paradisal themes like her own. The books and magazines she read were full of death-bed scenes and poetic meditations on dying, commonly conceived as both the loss of earthly pleasures and the acquiring of heavenly ones.

In June 1862 the *Atlantic* published "Out of the Body to God," verses Dickinson probably read. Like many Victorian poems, it described a process of adjustment to being dead:

> Wearily floating and sobbing,
> Out of the body to God!
> Lost in the spaces of blankness,
> Lost in the deepening abysses,
> Hunted and tracked by the past:
> No more sweet human caresses,
> No more the springing of morning,
> Never again from the present
> Into a future beguiled
> . . . . .
> Home from thy wanderings weary,
> Home from the lost to the Loving,
> Out of the body to God!

Dickinson copied out the following (only slightly less maudlin) lines of one John Pierpont. They appeared in newspapers and anthologies throughout the 1840s:

> I know his face is hid
> Under the coffin lid,
> Closed are his eyes; cold is his forehead;
> My hand that marble felt—
> O'er it in prayer I knelt,
> Yet my heart whispers that, he is not there!

Dickinson quoted Pierpont's poem in a letter (2.325) to soothe her friend Mary Warner, who had lost a younger sister three years earlier. The poem ends comfortingly with the speaker meeting the dead child in heaven. But what is remarkable in Dickinson's choice of an anniversary message is her relish for recalling the events of death and burial as if they had just taken place. It might have been more merciful to Mary had Dickinson chosen a poem that was less obsessed, however clumsily, with rigor mortis. But it was characteristic of Victorians to study the appearance of death with great care.

In her journal entry of March 14, 1858, for example, Louisa May Alcott wrote stoically about the moments before and after her favorite sister's passing:

> My dear Beth died at three this morning, after two years of patient pain . . . Saturday she slept, and at midnight became unconscious, quietly breathing her life away till three; then, with one last look of the beautiful eyes, she was gone.
>
> A curious thing happened, and I will tell it here, for Dr. G. said it was a fact. A few moments after the last breath came, as Mother and I sat silently watching the shadow fall on the dear little face, I saw a light mist rise from the body, and float up and vanish in the air. [Mother saw] the same light mist. Dr. G. said it was the life departing visibly . . .
>
> So the first break comes, and I know what death means,—a liberator for her, a teacher for us.[18]

Alcott's account of the soul or mist rising visibly, the last look, and death as teacher and deliverer were standard elements of Victorian death-bed accounts. Just as the marvelous last speeches of those about to die in torment in Tudor times are so formal and polished as to suggest either incredible courage or ritual attribution—what they *might* have said, were they able; so Victorian accounts of death suggest that people "saw" what they were expected to. Alcott's fervent words, however, betray the commonplace interest in what became of the soul as the body grew cold. With the growing hardness of the flesh, did the spirit reveal itself as a mist on the air?

Her selection of the Pierpont poem reveals Dickinson's own interest in the discrepancy between the face, or soul, of the vanished boy that Pierpont imagines shining, still, upon the air in his chamber; the physical "face" "hid/Under the coffin lid"; and his transfigured "angel brow" in paradise. However trite Pierpont's poem was, it centered on the precise theme of the relation between body and soul that absorbed Emily Dickinson's energies all her life. As Richard Sewall says, her life was "metaphoric,"[19] the preoccupations of her poetry informing it so wholly that, as she aged beyond the twenty-sixth year that marked her condolences to Mary Warner, what Dickinson read and wrote seems more and more to have influenced her conduct.

The act most characteristic of that conduct is Emily Dickinson's retirement from general society. More than any other action—more than writing poetry or avoiding a revelation of its extent; more than a supposedly desperate love and renunciation; more than her habit of lowering baskets of cookies to children from her bedroom window (to list what the wider public has heard)—this hidden face has seemed paradoxically to be Dickinson's most flamboyant message to the world. The attentive Dickinson reader, moreover, may ponder a real connection between that gradual and final concealment—what one poem calls the "veil[ing of her] too inspecting face" (122)—and her concentration on the image, "Face," in scores of poems and letters.[20]

Writing letters that scan, enclosing poems in letters, composing poems that are letters, revising and rerevising both, Dickinson did not always sharply distinguish between the uses of her art. Indeed, as was often noted, the actual seemed, to her, easily metaphoric so that the puddings she prepared were as uncommon as comets.[21] Therefore, her elaboration in poems and letters of a series of conceits about disclosed and hidden faces, like her use of "face" as a pivotal image in many of her important poems, is related to an explicable pattern in her life. Dickinson's poems about eternal life and love establish the fact that for her the face symbolizes the quintessence of personality. It is the total and ultimate self. Thus, contemplating the rapture of heavenly union with her forbidden lover, she says "My face [will] take her Recompense – /The looking in his Eyes" (398). From what she came to call "sight's ineffable disgrace" (1429), she hid her "external Face" in order to model and perfect those of her inward nature and her art (L 2.508). This pattern of steady retirement was, I believe, at first hesitantly and then decisively adopted under the influences of her reading and of the catalytic events and perceptions of her first years as a writer.

Yet her reclusion might have been predicted long before it became habitual. Although lively, she had always been shy. If the Dickinsons hired no daguerreotypist to memorialize Emily's features at her funeral, their omission is attributable not only to good taste and aristocratic regard for privacy but to knowledge of Dickinson's old horror of being photographed. Her letters show an avid interest in photographic images, which often evoked a prophetic and heightened lyricism; and friends like Mrs. Holland, Higginson, Bowles, and James D. Clark (who sent her an impression of the Reverend Charles Wadsworth) were sometimes importuned for loved "faces." In her obsession with evanescence and loss, Dickinson was interested in the new camera's power to render the ephemeral permanent, to "transcend mortality."[22] She herself, however, had refused to sit to it ever since her only known daguerreotype was made at the age of seventeen. That experience seems to have been unpleasant and confirmed her increasing distaste for being seen. It probably also fostered the conviction that "To see is . . . never quite the sorcery that it is to surmise" (L 2.619). Or, more important, her view that "To disappear enhances," since those that "run away" are tinctured with immortality (1209).

In *Mirror Image,* his history of the daguerreotype in America, Richard Rudisill presents two plates in which two sitters, both photographed about 1847–48 by the same "Maker Unknown," assume identical positions. One is Margaret Aurelia Dewing; and the other, Emily Dickinson (fig. 1). Both have been seated slightly contrapposto to the lens, left hand loosely consulting the right, while two books have been placed (closed!) at their elbows. Both wear the dark colors Daguerre enjoined for women. Behind each was undoubtedly the iron headrest that "fixed" the sitter. As one commentator explained in writing an article on Daguerre for the New York magazine *The Corsair,* photography made it possible "by virtue of the sun's patent [for] nature, animate and inanimate, [to be] henceforth its own painter, engraver, printer, and publisher."[23] But this process, of consuming interest to Transcendentalists like Emerson, was a slow one, and subjects sat for long minutes while what some considered the camera's magic was wrought. Though scientists like Emily Dickinson's Edward Hitchcock praised it highly as the source of pictorial transcripts of history, the daguerreotype process often resulted in a rigidity of appearance.

This was not true in the case of Margaret Aurelia Dewing, a pretty woman in her twenties, perhaps, who smiles confidently at the camera. But it *was* so in the case of a quite plain Emily Dickinson, whose steady gaze implies forbearance, merely, and in whose nerveless hand the flowers (usually given to women who seemed anxious) dangle. Martha Dickinson Bianchi's recollection of an aunt who liked to throw up her hands in merriment, exasperation, or rapture, of a white-robed figure in whom even deep thought seemed motion,[24] is contradicted by the sullen daguerreotype image, which Dickinson herself disliked.

That she thought it unrepresentative we may deduce from a letter she wrote Higginson in July 1862, answering his apparent request for a photograph:

> Could you believe me – without? I had no portrait, now, but am small, like the Wren, and my Hair is bold, like the Chestnut Bur – and my eyes, like the Sherry in the Glass, that the Guest leaves – Would this do just as well?
>
> If often alarms Father – He says Death might occur, and he has Molds of all the rest – but has no Mold of me, but I noticed the

1a. Emily Dickinson, daguerreotype taken at Mount Holyoke
(December 1847 or spring 1848). "I noticed the Quick wore off . . . in a few days."

1b. Margaret Aurelia Dewing, daguerreotype, maker unknown (1847–48).

Quick wore off those things, in a few days, and forestall the dishonor – (L 2.411)

Edward Dickinson's desire to capture his family's images in molds, his
alarm when this brilliant daughter refused to be captured, implies natural affection and no more than natural possessiveness. Daguerreotypes
were regarded as aids to memory as well as "a means of self-definition
to each person, individually for himself and for his loved ones"; the
"limning [of] faces"[25] with the camera was an effort to outwit their
robbery by death. Emily Dickinson, however, had methods of her own
for making memorial portraits. Writing lovingly (indeed, with almost
Pre-Raphaelite sensuousness) to Kate Anthon around 1860, she demonstrates the vitality of her imagination: "you do not yet 'dislimn,'
Kate, Distinctly sweet your face stands in its phantom niche – I touch
your hand – my cheek your cheek – I stroke your vanished hair"
(L 2.222).

Dickinson's letter, together with her words to Higginson, shows her
preference for capturing images in the suggestive language of poetry
rather than by strict graphic means. Kate's hair is vanished, but present
to the imagination's touch; Dickinson's eyes are amber, evidently, but
of what specific hue Higginson is left to guess. They are the color of
sherry left in a glass. But her manner of description is provocative; for
sherry suggests conviviality and yet the guest's leaving implies memory,
loss, the moment gone. She makes her appearance flirtatiously elusive
in this way. Hers is the opposite of the kind of rude portraiture for
which American limners were known. It substitutes, for the awkward
realism of photography, the face that the heart wishes it might see.

Dickinson's phrase "I had no portrait" with its eccentric use of the
past tense *had* may merely be capricious; or, more probably, it may
allude to the lapse of fifteen years after the objectionable daguerreotype
was made. That stiff portrait of a girl could not serve, in any case, to
describe the woman of thirty-two to whom Higginson was writing. And
it did not convey that "Emily was handsome."[26] But what really offended Dickinson about the old daguerreotype is that, unlike a good
painting (either in words or, for that matter, in paint) it did not catch
"the Quick" of its subject. That is, in the scriptural terms whereby the
"quick and the dead" were always discriminated, it did not represent
her living spirit. Very different in appearance and (no doubt) personality
from Margaret Aurelia Dewing, she had been made to assume the
typical pose convenient to the daguerreotypist. The books and flowers

might actually have denoted her interests. But because they were standard props, they said nothing about her inner self. (Otis Bullard's painting of Emily as a child, rigid as it is, is more revealing than the daguerreotype. Her eyes are sharp, her book is open, her flower is clutched.)

Unlike the unknown photographer's, Dickinson's concern as person and artist is always for the "quick"—the vivid and singular—in persons, experiences, or poems. (Thus her first question to Higginson was "Are you too deeply occupied to say if my Verse is alive?" and her last, even more ultimate: "Deity – does He live now? My friend – does he breathe?"). It was well known that daguerreotypes not only failed to suggest the vital personality but frequently so depressed the sitter in the process that she or he looked "half-dead." Mrs. Anna Snelling, wife of *Photographic Art-Journal's* editor, complained

> What! put *her* in daguerreotype,
>   And victimize the pet!
> Those ruby lips, so cherry-ripe,
>   On lifeless silver set!

An undated daguerreotype of Susan Gilbert Dickinson, thought to represent her as a young wife,[27] depicts a dispirited, slant-shouldered waif whose dark hair and eyes are the sole possible indices of that Cleopatra figure who haunts Dickinson's letters.

In an effort to correct the devitalizing effects of the daguerreotype, the British photographer Julia Margaret Cameron began her career in 1863 declaring that her aspirations were to "ennoble photography" and to secure for it the character and uses of high art by combining the real and ideal by all possible devotion to "poetry" and beauty.[28] In the United States, however, poetry of representation in the early 1860s was still achieved by painting or in poetry itself. Emily Dickinson's tribute to portrait painting would be a poem in which what she (elsewhere) calls "the parting West – / The peace – the flight – the Amethyst – / Night's possibility!" (106) is equated to a representative portrait. Her quatrain regards a good portrait as more evocative of the inner self than the appearance of a subject in real life:

> Portraits are to daily faces
> As an Evening West,
> To a fine, pedantic sunshine –
> In a satin Vest! (170)

There was honor in doing such a portrait and honor in being its subject. Yet, Dickinson told Higginson, there was dishonor in being molded by such a photographer as the one for whom she had sat, one who—like some emissary from Death—stole the "quick" from her face. (The *Leipziger Anzeiger,* in an article published about the time of Dickinson's letter to Higginson, used an even stronger word. "Wanting to hold fast to transitory mirror-pictures is not only an impossibility," it said, but "blasphemy. Man is created in the image of God, and God's image cannot be captured in any man-made machine."[29])

Finally, by the close of her life Dickinson believed (as did Hawthorne) that verbal imagery was superior to limning. In 1883 she wrote to her old friend Elizabeth Holland (wife of Josiah Holland of the *Springfield Republican*) that she had received photographs of Mrs. Holland's son Theodore and her sons-in-law. They reminded Dickinson of Mrs. Holland herself. In gratitude she proposed to send the family her own portrait of Mrs. Holland. "If the Spirits are fair as the Faces," Dickinson said of the photos, " 'Nothing is here for Tears'" (L 3.761). Her "if" makes plain her feeling that a photograph could not reveal the inner self. Her poetic picture of Mrs. Holland would attempt to do so:

> To see her is a Picture –
> To hear her is a Tune –
> To know her an Intemperance
> As innocent as June –
> To know her not – Affliction –
> To own her for a Friend
> A warmth as near as if the Sun
> Were shining in your Hand (1568)

The first line proposes the art of painting, the second adds music, but it is poetry that articulates the whole impression. Elizabeth Holland is apparently pretty, charming, and good; her friendship provides a warmth for the poet that (in a characteristic appeal to Nature as a source of metaphor) Dickinson compares to sunshine. What she is, at last, is an inspiration to the writer who is fond of her. She is a sun "shining in your Hand": a muse. To some extent, Dickinson's poem conveys the comparative unimportance of physical looks. The same portrait of Elizabeth Holland was included, slightly altered, in a letter about another correspondent's little girl (L 3.766). It is the ideal self that concerns her.

The central Christian mystery, pondered both gravely and playfully in some of her poems, was the veiling in flesh of a divine being. Here was the foremost example of the primacy of the spirit over its bodily garment. The text of John 1:14, "The Word made Flesh and dwelt among us" also became an encouragement to revere the artistic use of language, itself a mysterious form of revelation. Christ who came to heal and reveal was the word made flesh, and even God made words his metaphors:

> A Word that breathes distinctly
> Has not the power to die
> Cohesive as the Spirit
> It may expire if He –
> "Made Flesh and dwelt among us"
> Could condescension be
> Like this consent of Language
> This loved Philology (1651)

For Dickinson as a maturing poet in 1862, there was a precise relation between quickness and poetry (the "consent of language" to the task of doing miracles); between honor and hiding the face from views that might distort; and between honor, art, and immortality. Daguerreotypes pretended to confer the latter. But Emily Dickinson knew that it was art—for her, the art of poetry—that led both to honor and immortality and that poetry was written alone, in seclusion.

3

In a thoughtful discussion of Dickinson as a religious poet, Jane Donahue Eberwein argues that the poet's "reticent habits . . . secur[ed] a privacy that liberated her for the artistic work to which she felt called."[30] This view is not a new one; it was held by Millicent Todd Bingham[31] and before her (if unsystematically) by Emily's sister Lavinia, who explained that the poet "was not withdrawn or exclusive really. She was always watching for the rewarding person to come, but she was a very busy person herself." Vinnie's definition of Emily's business as thought[32] was an indefinite way of saying that she was a poet, and not so secretive a poet after all. For she had her small public: Higginson, Sue, Bowles, the Hollands, Helen Hunt Jackson, nephews and niece, cousins, neighbors, and the many recipients of letters that enclosed poems. What *was* secret was the intensity of her professional commitment.

It is not necessary to think of Dickinson as the Nun of Amherst, however, in order to understand her choice of solitude as a *modus scribendi*. It was commonly believed in the early nineteenth century that the life of an artist should be a life apart. Emerson wrote in "The Poet" (1840), "O poet! . . . thou shalt leave the world, and know the muse only!" Had Dickinson read the *Atlantic*, as was her custom, in July 1860, she would have encountered these realistic but reverential "Words about Shelley":

> Shelley went entirely away from the ranks of society—farther away than Byron, and was a man harder to be understood by the generality of men . . . [He] was a sensitive, unaccommodating, and impulsive being, rebelling against the rules of life . . . and shrinking with a shy, uncomprehended pride from the companionship of society.

She undoubtedly read this advice from the author of "Our Artists in Italy," which had appeared in the *Atlantic* in January 1860:

> The foremost purpose of an artist should be to claim and take possession of self . . . Genius is exquisitely fastidious, and the man whom it possesses must live its life, or no life . . . Possession of self is the only condition under [which accomplishment] may be determined. It is only when a man stands face to face with himself, in the stillness of his own inner world, that his possibilities [as an artist] become apparent; and it is only when conscious of these, and inspired by a just sense of their dignity, that he can achieve . . . genuine success . . . He must be lifted away and isolated from worldly surroundings . . . from the pressure of all human relations . . . He must be alone.

And these words from "Individuality" were printed in the *Atlantic* for April 1862, the same issue that contained Higginson's "Letter to a Young Contributor," which was answered by Emily Dickinson:

> Each of us, wrapt in his opaque individuality, like Apollo or Athene in a blue mist, remains hidden, if he will . . . [Creative people must] guard frontiers. We must not lie quite open to the inspection or invasion of others . . . [Nature has] cast around each spirit this veil to guard it from intruding eyes, this barrier to keep away the feet of strangers . . . every one of us is . . . a celestial nature walking concealed.

The *Atlantic* articles reasoned that solitude promoted imaginative activity by encouraging the development of personal resources. But there was more than a hint of hermeticism for its own sake in their pages. From girlhood, Emily Dickinson enjoyed being alone, or alone with someone like Sue. Without Sue in March 1853, she found she needed "more vail [sic]," more protection from a world that "looks staringly" (L 1.229). There seems no doubt that her avowed love of silence and solitude may have arisen in part from a neurosis, an anxiety about being defenseless when "seen." Even when she was only twenty-three, Emily was confiding to Austin, "I sat in Prof Tyler's woods and saw the train move off, and then ran home again for fear somebody would see me, or ask me how I did" (L 1.254). Later what she called her "Cowardice of Strangers" made her relieved to be "HOME" (L 3.716; 1.58). Certainly her reactions to the visits or attempted visits of acquaintances or even friends were—as Susan Dickinson finally conceded—"peculiar."

But other nineteenth-century American artists had elected and recommended solitude. There was much in her culture to support Dickinson in a way of life that neurosis or artistic ambition or profound shyness or a combination of causes seems to have made attractive. She knew about the reclusive Hawthorne, wrote about Thoreau, and might have had said of herself these words that William James spoke of Emerson at the centenary celebration in Concord (1903):

> The duty of spiritual seeing and reporting determined the whole tenor of his life. It was to shield this duty from invasion and distraction that he dwelt in the country, that he consistently declined to entangle himself with associations or to encumber himself with functions which, however he might believe in them, he felt were duties for other men and not for him.

But James's remark, "Even the care of his garden . . . [Emerson] found 'narrowing and poisoning,'" was of course not true of Dickinson in her *hortus conclusus*. Nor could it have been said of her as of Emerson that "the faultless tact with which he kept his safe limits while he so dauntlessly asserted himself within them, is an example fitted to give heart to other . . . artists the world over."[33] For after the early 1860s, Dickinson was not usually tactful in refusing callers. Sometimes she quite literally ran to hide from them with a fear of personal contact that no artistic choice of "the buried life" can entirely explain.

Among the many stories of her escapes—when she left even old ladies to wait in her garden, sending a flower or a poem in her stead—is one that was later commemorated in verse by the disappointed caller. Emily Fowler Ford visited Amherst in July 1882, but her girlhood friend and correspondent Emily Dickinson refused to come downstairs. Dickinson's letters to Emily Fowler had been adoring when they were girls. As Jay Leyda says, they "sound like those of an enthusiastic, humble amateur writing to an older, wiser, more experienced writer."³⁴ Dickinson herself sent two poems to Mrs. Ford before her return to Amherst from her home in Brooklyn, where she had lived with her husband since their marriage in 1853. Not receiving her, Dickinson nevertheless later wrote to thank Mrs. Ford for the gift of her book *My Recreations*. After the appearance of *Poems* (1890), Emily Ford recorded her reactions to them—and to Emily Dickinson—in a sonnet published in the *Springfield Republican* (January 11, 1891):

> Oh, friend, these sighs from out your solitude
>   But pierce my heart! Social with bird and bee,
>   Loving your tender flowers with ecstacy,
> You shun the eye, the voice, the shy elude
> The loving souls that dare not intrude
>   Upon your chosen silence. Friend, you thought
>   No life so sweet and fair as hiding brought,
> And beauty is your song, with interlude
> Of outer life which to your soul seems crude,
>   Thoughtless, unfeeling, idle, scant of grace;
>   Nor will you touch a hand, or greet a face,—
> For common daily strife to you is rude,
>   And, shrinking, you in shadow lonely stay
>   Invisible to all, how'er we pray.

Emily Ford's words are interesting as an interpretation of the poet's reclusion. She attributes its cause to an aesthetic sensibility: a quest for the "sweet and fair," which might be found in hiding, and a repugnance for "common daily strife." (This hypothesis would seem especially creditable to the readers of the 1890s.) Dickinson, according to Mrs. Ford, had actually "chosen silence." And ironically her sonnet, which is fustily entitled "Eheu! Emily Dickinson," regards Dickinson's poems as sighs from a self-imposed, lonely world remote from the real one.

In 1882, Dickinson was not in truth "invisible to all," though even Sue had begun to complain of Emily's preference for her own society. Perhaps Dickinson merely shrank at last from the prospect of the conversation she would be likely to have with the writer of such verse as Mrs. Ford's. Perhaps—as in the cases of other girlhood friends—Dickinson was afraid to see how the years had changed Emily Ford; to be forced to "lift the lid to [her] box of Phantoms, and lay another in, unto the Resurrection" (L 2.330). Or perhaps Mrs. Ford's success as both a happily married woman and a writer daunted her, especially since her schoolmate's tone to her in the past had been condescending. In any case, Emily Ford regarded Dickinson's reclusion as willful. Although it seems to her a painful gesture, she sees it also as a shrinking from what was crude, a deliberate manifestation of personality.

In the journal she was keeping in September 1882, Mabel Loomis Todd recorded a somewhat similar view. She was just getting to know and appreciate Austin Dickinson. Describing him as "almost in every particular my ideal man," she remarks on his sensitivity to nature, "which made [her] sure he was a true, if silent, poet." That thought provoked another about Austin's sister Emily, "in many respects a genius," who "writes the strangest poems." Mabel confides what she has heard about the reasons for Emily Dickinson's withdrawal:

> I know I shall yet see her. No one *has* seen her in all those years except her own family. She is very brilliant and strong, but became disgusted with society & declared she would leave it when she was quite young. It is hinted that Dr. Holland loved her very much & she him, but that her father who was a stern old New England lawyer & politician saw nothing particularly promising or remarkable in the shy, half-educated boy, & would not listen to her marrying him . . . I have heard a great deal about Mr. Samuel Bowles who was the most intimate friend of both Mr. & Mrs. [Austin] Dickinson. How they did love him![35]

Not yet Austin's mistress, and not yet in possession of his own (unexamined) view that his sister retired because she was not beautiful,[36] Mabel flounders in her journal among current rumors.

Her word *disgust,* however, was strikingly anticipated in words written about Emily Dickinson by one who knew her as well as anyone except Sue. This was the same Samuel Bowles who had been an intimate of the entire Dickinson family from the 1850s until his death in 1878. Son of the founder of the *Springfield Republican,* its widely esteemed editor for three decades, and an influential writer on many topics, Bowles was lionized by the Dickinsons and became Emily's confidant. A letter from him to Austin in April 1863 is cited in Leyda's *Years and Hours of Emily Dickinson,* but it has not otherwise been much noted. In his letter Bowles reports that he is suffering from one of his intermittent periods of emotional unrest. (He was a temperamental and sensitive man, greatly strained by the Civil War which placed heavy burdens on him as a journalist.) Describing his feelings to Austin, he says

> I have been in a savage, turbulent state for some time—indulging in a sort of [illegible] disgust at everything & everybody—I guess a good deal as Emily feels,—I have been trying to garden, too. But I tire out

so soon, it is of small use,—& then I am gone for the day. I have to
wait for the morning to come again.

The letter suggests that he has been gardening as Emily does as a remedy
for this state of disgust. It then alludes to another garden, Gethsemane:
"Tell Emily I am here, in the old place. 'Can you not watch one
hour??[']."[37] Bowles's quotation—which paraphrases Christ's rebuke to
the sleeping Peter on the eve of his crucifixion—is histrionic in its
context. He compares his troubles to the Savior's and the poet, from
whom he has apparently not heard recently, to the chief apostle, who
repeatedly fails Christ. Since I believe Bowles was "Master," his avowed
vision of himself as a type of Christ is significant. What I will take up
at this point, however, is his choice of the word *disgust*.

By what could Emily Dickinson have been disgusted? "Everything &
everybody" points to dissatisfaction with life in general. But such Olym-
pian disenchantment usually begins with local setbacks and specific
disappointments. Mabel's phrase "disgusted with society" is much more
expressive and credible, judging from what Dickinson herself wrote—
with Sue in mind[38]—about "Cosmopolites" (1589); or gentlewomen
horrified by "freckled Human Nature" (401)—she had freckles; or
sophisticates who kissed your cheek and lied about you. For she liked
honesty, being "a rural man" (1466). She craved peace, she wrote, from
her schooldays to her last days; and society was clearly full of turmoil,
in the drawing room as on the battlefield. Yet in late 1859 Emily
Dickinson was writing of the *"Bliss"* she felt as "evenings open at
Austin's," where she was frequently entertained by her newly married
brother and his wife (L 2.355). Bowles himself was there frequently;
and so absorbed could Emily become in conversation, or reading poetry
aloud or playing the song she composed, called "The Devil," on the
piano, that on one occasion her grim father came to bring her home.[39]
Clearly she was not disgusted with society then.

Since the first publication of her poems in 1890, Dickinson's readers
have been puzzled by the mysterious love affair they seem to present.
Subsequently they have been challenged by her letters, which include
the poet's allusions (amid a rush of creative activity) to a "terror" or
to "so much [that] has occurred" or to her resolution not to leave
a home *"brighter* than all the world beside" (L 2.335; 1.151, 59). Each
remark seems related to her final reclusion. It was the poet's sister-in-
law who first spread the story that Dickinson had fallen in love with
the married minister Charles Wadsworth during a two-week visit to

Philadelphia in 1854. One note from Wadsworth, misspelling her name, is known to have been sent to Emily Dickinson around 1862.[40] He visited her in 1860 and 1880. Sue gave out, as Sara Colton Gillett later recalled, "that Emily 'had met her fate' when she went south on a visit, that the love had been instant, strong, mutual, that [Emily] would go no further for it would mean sorrow to another woman—his wife."[41] Presumably, then, those few days spent listening to Wadsworth's sermons and gazing at his somber visage inspired Dickinson with a sense of the world well lost. By 1861 (according to Thomas Johnson), Wadsworth's departure to Calvary Church, San Francisco, rendered her heartbreak complete; she began her "white election" and retired as "Queen of Calvary" to her "living entombment."[42] But why, in the late 1850s—five years after meeting the forbidden Wadsworth—did she say she was in paradise in Sue's drawing room, and what did Bowles mean by "disgust"?

Since Martha Dickinson Bianchi's espousal of her mother's account in *The Life and Letters of Emily Dickinson,* her aunt's readers have been offered many other explanations for the poet's semiretirement. They have been asked to consider the hermetic Dickinson as an agoraphobe; as reclusive to please her father; as a sufferer from separation anxiety or from the need to create a private religion in retreat; as a lesbian in love with a widowed friend of Sue's and guiltily hiding from that self-discovery; as a plagiarist afraid to be found out; as an anorexic for whom renunciation was better than food; as the damaged victim of a love affair, which included abortion.[43] In their eagerness to regard her as a professional poet, some scholars explain her reclusion as chosen. Lavinia's explanation that Emily had her own calling or "business"— which Dickinson herself called "circumference," one of her metaphors for poetry—and that the reclusion became "just a happen"[44] is regarded as the most commonsensical view of Emily Dickinson's retirement. But Lavinia's explanation, like Sue's, seems too simple. "Just a happen" is probably both myopic and loyal. On the other hand, Sue's story of the minister was, I think, intensely self-protective. It was a diversionary tactic, employed to distract people's attention from other loves of Emily Dickinson, much nearer home than Philadelphia.

While it can be dangerous to read the works of a lyric poet for their autobiographical content, it is certainly possible to discover in them the poet's habits of mind, anxieties, persuasions, and passions. Her poetry (like her letters) shows that the mature Emily Dickinson was personally drawn to solitude and to a hidden life. (Even the young Emily liked silence. Emily at fifty-three told Judge Lord "I love silence so," adding that she meant not just quietude but probity [L 3.786].) In my view, certain events of the late 1850s and early 1860s rendered her choice of reclusion irresistibly desirable. Her surrender of the adored Sue to marriage, motherhood, and a shared life with Austin (whom Emily resembled in looks and ambition, often a torture to her) seems to have prompted a thirst for prominence and position of her own. It clearly provoked a surge of desire for a life in art, a life for which she must have known herself suited. "Honor," she would write, was the "shortest route" to immortality (1366c). Honor obtained through Sue's life of marriage and motherhood, or Austin's profession of the law, could be transcended by the honor that accrued to a poet, even if one were a woman (as Dickinson's models, Barrett Browning, and the two Georges—Sand and Eliot—had proved). The knowledge that she too could be (as she called her models) both a woman and yet a "queen" (L 2.376) of language, and also that to be this queen might require great sacrifice, may surely have caused her secret "terror."

The evidence of her poems and letters, however, also shows that Emily Dickinson had indeed been in love—with the girlhood friend who became her sister-in-law; that later she was passionately drawn to the married Samuel Bowles, with whom Sue herself was sustaining a warm relationship; and that a good deal of disenchantment followed upon Sue's increasing detachment and upon Dickinson's growing understanding of Sue's real nature. To be the developed opposite of that brilliant but egotistical woman, to be powerful (however secretly) as an artist rather than like Sue—or even the masterly Bowles—a cosmopolite, became her steady aim in the 1860s. Whereas Sue and Bowles were in and of the world, Dickinson determined on a hidden life in art.

Though I do not think Dickinson is best defined as a religious poet but—because of her deep skepticism—as a poet for whom religion was a major theme, her acculturation through schooling and reading caused her to lead her life in art as a contemplative. To such a writer, Emerson said, solitude promised revelations about God and his creation. Among her favorite texts were 1 and 2 Corinthians in which St. Paul explains that "where the Spirit of the Lord is, there is liberty. But we all, with open face beholding as in a glass the glory of the Lord, are changed into the same image from glory to glory, even as by the Spirit of the Lord" (3:17–18). In emphasizing the relation of the human face to God's hidden face, 2 Corinthians insists upon the sacred vitality whereby the faithful see as in a magic mirror their perfected selves. By concealing the outward face from all influences that distract from God, the inward face or spirit, Paul teaches, was freed to achieve fulfillment in grace.

As the basis for the ideal of the monastic life, this principle of hiding the face is spoken of by Thomas à Kempis, a favorite author of Dickinson's, in his *Imitation of Christ*. It may be found especially in the recommendations on "Solitude," "Silence," and "A Retired Life." In the last of these he quotes 1 Peter 2:11: "If you will stand fast as you ought, and grow in grace, esteem yourself as an exile and a stranger upon earth."[45] Dickinson was no stranger to an earth she prefers in many poems to heaven: but she became an exile to most company. Calling herself, albeit whimsically, a "Wayward Nun" (722), she put herself in the presence of the unseen by turning the key in the lock of her bedroom door (which meant not punishment but liberty). In that way she avoided the strains imposed on her neurotic timidity in meeting others. In that way she became free to write poetry, to attempt to be "perfect" according to her gifts. By that ambition, all the other narratives of her life—her need for Sue, her yearning for Master, her craving for "size" or importance—were subsumed.

4

While her poems and letters variously develop her conceit of the hidden face, the early fascicles contain three poems about retirement which tease the reader to take them as apologia. These are "He put the Belt around my life" (273) in fascicle 12; "A solemn thing – it was– I said" (271) in fascicle 14; and "Not in this World to see his face" (418) in fascicle 15. One may discern in this poetic cluster a decided narrative: the speaker's invitation by divine authority to become a sequestered artist and the promise that the loss of her other freedoms will be rewarded by the vision of God's face in heaven. The speaker responds to this invitation with awe, delight, courage, and occasionally regret. She begins, as well, to fuse all faces that she loves with this divine one, and to imagine seeing it in her room or garden or dreams as well as in paradise.

In "He put the Belt around my life," the powerful He "snap[s]" what sounds like a medieval chastity belt (or a monk's cincture?) around the speaker's life so that she becomes "Henceforth, a Dedicated sort – / A Member of the Cloud." Fascicle 12 also contains "I taste a liquor never brewed" (214) and, immediately preceding 273, "Alone, I cannot be"

(298). These lyrics record both the poet's sensation of her own genius and her awareness that she is visited by "Hosts." It would not be necessary to associate these heavenly hosts, the "Recordless Company – / Who baffle Key," with any but angels except for the fact that she calls them "gnomes," her word for herself as poet. For this and other reasons,[46] they are *her* angels, who represent her quintessential spirit as artist and will "bustle" on the stair to take her to paradise in poem 461. Their advent is both a quasi-religious and a royal experience, and it is important that they are welcomed by couriers of her own:

> Their Coming, may be known
> By Couriers within –
> Their going – is not –
> For they're never gone – (298)

Because of the hosts and the belt, the speaker's life is altered most particularly with respect to social occasions. There are now limits to her intercourse with others. She meets household obligations and is

> not too far to come at call –
> And do the little Toils
> That make the Circuit of the Rest –

She is courteous enough to

> deal occasional smiles
> To lives that stoop to notice mine –

But she has ceased to engage in what Higginson would have called a normal human life, for if people "kindly ask [her] in," she says finally,

> Whose invitation, know you not
> For Whom I must decline?

In "He put the Belt around my life," Dickinson writes two six-line stanzas, a rare form for one who preferred quatrains with an occasional use of triplets. The "process" (as her alternate choice for line 3 calls it) of being belted or confined is divided from its consequence, her dedication, by a division between the stanzas. The effect, not often given in her quatrains, is of effortful scenario, time passing, and ironic emphasis. As in so many of her poems, the very form describes her experience.

Somewhat later in fascicle 14 the much-interpreted but rhetorically straightforward poem 271 seems to convey what I have already said about Dickinson as a reclusive artist by choice:

A solemn thing – it was – I said –
A Woman – white – to be –
And wear – if God should count me fit –
Her blameless mystery –

A hallowed thing – to drop a life
Into the mystic well –
Too plummetless – that it come back –
Eternity – until –

I ponder how the bliss would look –
And would it feel as big –
When I could take it in my hand –
As hovering – seen – through fog –

And then – the size of this "small" life –
The Sages – call it small –
Swelled – like Horizons – in my vest –
And I sneered – softly – "small"!

The second quatrain of 271 expresses its central theme: that it is a hallowed thing to drop a life into a mystic well; that is, to retire from the world and thereby relinquish one's life until it is restored in Eternity. (Dickinson's alternate choice for "mystic" was "purple," a royal color for her and the penitential color of the Christian church.) Mrs. Todd entitled this poem "Wedded" in the 1896 edition of the *Poems*. She was doubtless prompted to do so by Dickinson's image of the woman in white. If "Wedded" means married to a man, however, it is useful to point out that Dickinson's poem was probably written in 1861— brides did not customarily wear white in the United States until the late 1870s. It took almost forty years for Queen Victoria's white satin, lace, and orange blossoms, copied in England after 1840, to appear in American weddings. Conventual Victorian novices and postulants, however, almost always wore white. A nun about to take her final vows was usually presented in a wedding gown to her bishop and the community she was joining. Some nuns' daily dress or habit—the Dominicans', for example—was also white. There had been since the 1830s a spate of English and American portraits—in oils and journals—depicting nuns at the moment of their "marriage to Christ." Other pictures envision them enclosed by monastery gardens, surrounded by doves and white lilies as they gaze, brooding or transfigured, into the wells or ponds that implied the depths of their religious commitment. Wells or springs, moreover, are also traditional emblems of artistic inspiration. Dickinson's speaker in poem 271, therefore, may be compared to such meditative nuns as the one in Charles Allston Collins' *Convent Thoughts,* 1850 (see plate 1). Sacred *Book of Hours* in one hand and flower in the other, this nun stands at the edge of a pool that captures—imprisons—her image but also suggests her clarity and creativity of spiritual insight.

There is every reason to suppose that Emily Dickinson had in mind *not* Miss Havisham's failed white bridal in her woman-in-white poems but, rather, the nun's vocation as a bride of her master, Christ. That vocation is taken as itself a metaphor of the artist's calling. For despite Dickinson's eloquent ambivalence (in letters especially) toward marriage as a force for the subjugation of women, her use of "well" would have entailed crude exaggeration. One might add too that it is God who must count the speaker fit, not an earthly bridegroom; that brides, however virginal, are not necessarily blameless, nor is marriage itself a mystery. The mystic wedding of a nun, however, *is* blameless of physical passion, and certainly it is mysterious. Dickinson's speaker-nun in poem 271 will enjoy bliss, she says, but only through the fog of this life, the glass through which we see darkly.

Marina Warner sensibly observes that "the body is still the map on which we make our meanings; it is chief among metaphors used to see and present ourselves."[47] By donning her white dresses, Emily Dickinson the woman made a statement in the early 1860s. Emily Dickinson the artist appears to acknowledge that it was consciously made, not only in 271 but in other poems. In 388, for example, she admits that she has elected the divine marriage celebrated in 817 (in which she calls herself "Bride of the Father and the Son / Bride of the Holy Ghost"). Describing her indifference to someone who comes to call on her, she says imperiously

> Take Your Heaven further on –
> This – to Heaven divine Has gone –
> Had You earlier blundered in
> Possibly, e'en You had seen
> An Eternity – put on –
> Now – to ring a Door beyond
> Is the utmost of Your Hand –
> To the Skies – apologize –
> Nearer to Your Courtesies
> Than this Sufferer polite –
> Dressed to meet You –
> See – in White! (388)

It is clear that the speaker regards herself as a sufferer who has put on Eternity and whose "white" signifies renunciation and retirement from society. The caller comes looking, of course, for heaven—in Dickinson's time, as in our own, a synonym for love. The poet imagines telling him that, like some modern Beatrice, she is already there and remote now from his profane purpose. Samuel Bowles sent Emily Dickinson a tart message in 1863, giving "the Queen Recluse my especial sympathy— that she has 'overcome the world.'—Is it really true that they sing 'Old Hundred' and 'Aleluia' perpetually, in heaven—ask her; and are dandelions, asphodels, and Maiden's [vows?] the standard flowers of the ethereal?"[48] Bowles's phrase "overcome the world" was probably an allusion to 1 John 5:4–5:

> For whatsoever is born of God overcometh the world: and this is the victory that overcometh the world, even our faith.
>
> Who is he that overcometh the world, but he that believeth that Jesus is the Son of God?

The remark is rather tastelessly sarcastic. Not a conventionally pious man but, like Dickinson, something of a skeptic, Bowles was proclaiming what he considered the preposterousness of Dickinson's avoidance of society. He knew she was not a dogmatic Christian and had never even declared for Christ like the other Dickinsons. Her behavior implied a religious fervor and conventual commitment to which he thought her unentitled.

The scene Dickinson sketches in "Take Your Heaven further on," like her meditation in poem 29, has echoes in the Victorian literary and painterly tradition. She was probably entirely conscious of it. The scene is not wholly religious in character but vaguely erotic and even defiant. These qualities are also present in the tradition. There were many depictions of nuns visited (behind grates, in doorways, over garden walls) by angry or dejected lovers. Of these, John Everett Millais' *The Vale of Rest* (1858) was the most famous. It did not portray a lover, but Millais' beautiful young nun, seated in the convent cemetery, regards the viewer with defensive surprise. She is quite evidently, for all her voluptuousness, estranged from secular life. These conventual paintings were inspired in part by political and social currents, even as the Hudson River and Luminist paintings were stimulated by the voyages of Darwin and the theories of evolution published by Alexander von Humboldt and Louis Agassiz.[49] The Oxford and Tractarian movements had created an often critical interest in the Roman Catholic church. Increasing Irish immigration to the United States in the 1840s had familiarized many Protestant Americans with Catholic ritual. (At one time the Dickinsons had eight Irish servants. "Irish Maggie" Maher was no doubt partly responsible for the ease with which Emily could allude to the sacraments, the sign of the cross, and customs like "sealing the church" on Good Friday.[50] Susan Dickinson's father, Thomas Gilbert, was also of Irish Catholic descent; hence the I.H.S. and cross that Sue had carved on his tombstone. Though Sue joined the Congregational church in adulthood, she may have had some knowledge of Catholic ceremony and shared it with Emily.)

After the establishment of Anglican convents in 1845, painters like Charles Collins satisfied public curiosity about nuns with scores of canvases popular in England and America. Emily Dickinson probably saw *Convent Thoughts* or its like in the art books collected by Sue and Austin. Collins' pale, white-garbed nun might be an illustration of her poem "A solemn thing – it was – I said." The young nun looks appropriately starveling and anxious as she contemplates a passion flower, the symbol of Christ's crucifixion. But she seems also to be proudly considering the significance of her own vows. The nun is surrounded by lilies of three kinds. The painting's iconography, like that of Dickinson's poem, is of enclosure, celibacy, commitment to self-denial. Yet with its lilies and crystalline pond, it is also a lyrical celebration of the austere beauty of the cloister, the silence and ethereal composure of all who dwell there. What is absent from Collins' painting, though, are the qualities of fire and impudence in Dickinson's poem 271. For her nun seems, in part, to have elected to be "a woman – white" in order to prove herself to skeptical "sages," such as the one who calls on her in "Take your Heaven further on."

Dickinson's self-conception as nun is insistently developed in the early 1860s. It is part of her persona as divine bride, deeply related to her interest in the transitus, and an expression of her contempt for trivia and falsehood. Around 1864 Dickinson composed what can only be called a prayer to the Virgin Mary:

> Only a shrine, but Mine –
> I made the Taper shine –
> Madonna dim, to whom all Feet may come,
> Regard a Nun –
>
> Thou knowest every Wo –
> Needless to tell thee – so –
> But can'st thou do

The Grace next to it – heal?
That looks a harder skill to us –
Still – just as easy, if it be thy Will
To thee – Grant me –
Thou knowest, though, so Why tell thee? (918)

Here the poet's self-portrait as a nun recalls an arch early reference to herself as the "Wayward Nun," wayward because her service is to the "Sweet Mountains" who are her "Strong Madonnas," rather than to the Madonna herself (722). (There were far more wayward nuns in Victorian subliterature and pornography with which Dickinson probably never came in contact. But she always insists on her own unconventionality as a nun. She thinks too freely to be a nun; and, like the vestals in Pre-Raphaelite painting, her sexual feelings are not really forsworn.) To serve the sweet mountains, after all, was to be a vestal of Pan and of the romantic tradition in literature and painting. For the Hudson River and Luminist painters in particular, mountains represented what was permanent in nature and therefore revered. In poem 914, however, prompted by some "woe," Emily Dickinson adopts the language of Marian veneration with sincerity.

The culture of the 1860s, even in Calvinist New England, made that possible. To understand its heterodox character is to draw closer to understanding Emily Dickinson's white dress and her conventual allusions. In *Legends of the Madonna as Represented in the Fine Arts* (1864), a learned Englishwoman, Anna Jameson, exhibited the fascination with Madonna art that was typical of both the Catholic and Protestant bourgeoisie in the Victorian period. Anxious to create role models for the daughters they wished to keep at home, untainted by rude contacts, even some Calvinist fathers like Edward Dickinson presented girls with pictures of the Virgin Mary. While Roman Catholic daughters were educated by nuns in convents, their Protestant counterparts often felt like nuns in their own homes. In her *Legends,* popular in America, Mrs. Jameson explains that "by virtue of her perpetual virginity," Mary is "the patroness of single and ascetic life."[51] Such information was intended to explain the commonplace association of nuns or spinsters with the Virgin. Madonnas, with or without praying nuns at their feet, were often painted by Victorian artists, especially the Pre-Raphaelites. In writing her own Madonna poem, Emily Dickinson joined their company.

The fact of this tradition undoubtedly underlies not only Dickinson's poems like "A solemn thing – it was – I said" or "Only a Shrine, but

Mine"; it helps to explain the dress and attitudes she assumed as part of what she called her "White Election" (528). Pre-Raphaelitism had been introduced to the United States in many ways—newspapers, magazines, exhibitions—by the 1860s. For this, the painter William James Stillman was greatly responsible. Editor of the groundbreaking magazine *The Crayon,* Stillman was a friend of, and sometime model for, Dante Gabriel Rossetti. His magazine presented the theories, contained illustrations, and often reproduced the poems of the Pre-Raphaelites. Stillman's editorial successor, John Durand, printed Rossetti's "The Blessed Damozel" in 1858, recomending its "power of expression . . . depth of sentiment . . . force of imagination."[52] Rossetti was already known to American artlovers as the painter of the influential *Girlhood of Mary Virgin* (1849) and *Ecce Ancilla Domini* (1850). These three works by the painter-poet represented women garbed in white and associated with lilies. In *The Girlhood of Mary Virgin* the young Mary is embroidering a lily in the company of Saint Anne. An angel gazes at her devotedly, his hand around a tall lily that symbolizes her virginity and her holy separation from the world. The angel in *Ecce Ancilla Domini*—scene of the Annunciation—points his lily at Mary's womb, announcing her future as maiden-mother. In "The Blessed Damozel" the heavenly damsel—who, like the Dickinson of poem 640, is obsessed with her lover, even in paradise—has three lilies in her hand. (Like the Dickinson of "Because I could not stop for Death," she has lost track of time, thinking she has been dead one day instead of ten years.) It is Rossetti's blessed damozel as she is depicted in both poetry and paint that has been most famous for fusing the appeal of womanly purity and sexuality. But such a fusion was also consistent with Victorian literature. The nun as woman in white was a seductive figure, and the lily associated with her had an erotic perfume. Pre-Raphaelite emphasis on the lily as emblem of the Virgin or of those who devoted themselves to her—nuns or spinsters—antedated, while contributing to, the aesthetic fondness for lilies. Commenting on "Emily Dickenson's Rare Genius" in 1891, a reviewer (Mary Abbott) of her *Letters* for the *Chicago Post* reported Colonel Higginson's account of their first meeting in 1870: "She had a quaint and nun-like look, as if she might be a German canonness of some religious order whose prescribed garb was white pique . . . She came toward me with two day lilies [Abbott interjects, "and she had never heard of Oscar Wilde!"] which she put, in a childlike way, into my hand, saying softly under her breath, 'These are my introduction.' "[53] The referent for Emily Dickinson's lilies, however, was not the Wildean flower satirized by Gilbert and Sullivan but the emblem culled from traditional Christian iconography and made timely by the Pre-Raphaelites. So strong became the Pre-Raphaelite influence that young girls were often photographed in white, holding lilies.

In her allusions to herself as a nun, by her assumption of white and her repeated association of herself with lilies, Emily Dickinson was participating in a finely articulated iconographic tradition. It is telling, moreover, that Dickinson carried lilies that were often not white but orange-red, like her hair. In the Victorian palette, red was the color of passion and suffering. Dickinson once called herself a "cow-lily,"[54] consenting to the tradition whereby unmarried girls were associated with lilies but insisting on the distinction provided by her own coloring and—perhaps—nature: the wayward nun, the artist-recluse.

She may never have read about the scandal created in Paris in 1862 by James A. M. Whistler's "Symphony in White No. 1: The Little White Girl." Yet she created in herself a little white girl with some resemblance to Whistler's. As a portrait of his red-haired mistress, Jo Heffernan, in what appears to be a nun's or a wedding dress, limp flowers in her hand and a dazed look on her face, Whistler's shocking painting was a satire of the graceful Victorian portraits of white-clad virgins. Jo's hair streams down her back as if ravished from a proper coil and there is a bearskin, emblem of lewdness, at her feet. Whistler's painting, with its marked moderation of the white motif, like Dickinson's gesture in tendering cow or day lilies, suggests the power of the Victorian tradition wherein celibate girls proclaimed themselves by wearing white and carrying white flowers.

Tennyson especially shared in this tradition, writing of Elaine, the Lady of Shalott, and his nun "in raiment white and clean" in *St. Agnes* (1842) as she waits—like the speaker in Dickinson's master letters—for "the sabbaths of Eternity." In the Dickinson family's copy of Tennyson's *Poems*, volume 2 (Boston, 1853), "St. Agnes"—entitled "St. Agnes' Eve" after 1855—exhibits the light markings at the left side of the text which are characteristic of Emily Dickinson's hand. Like so many of these delicate pencil markings, the strokes by lines from "St. Agnes" seem to reveal her interest in the poem's sentiments. (Only occasionally does she annotate for style.) Tennyson's nun envisions the transitus in which she will be assumed by God into eternity, and Dickinson has marked all of Tennyson's passage:

> He lifts me to the golden doors;
>   The flashes come and go;

All heaven burst her starry floors,
  And strews her lights below,
And deepens on and up! The gates
  Roll back, and far within
For me the Heavenly Bridegroom waits,
  To make me pure of sin.
The sabbaths of Eternity,
  One sabbath deep and wide—
A light upon the shining sea
  The Bridegroom with his bride!

Dickinson's letter (1858) to the man she called "Master" confessed that she is writing on the Sabbath Day and that "Each Sabbath on the Sea, makes me count the Sabbaths, till we meet on shore" (L 2.333). Thus she associates herself with the nun of "St. Agnes," though her lover is human. She establishes herself, in one style, within the Victorian tradition of holy maidens. Yet she insists on the emotions of the woman confined within that tradition. For her orange-red lilies—like her poems of secular love—declared Emily Dickinson a more fiery nun, a more passionate virgin than Catholic rituals would ordain.

Sandra Gilbert and Susan Gubar assume that Dickinson, like an actress, wore white to play a role, "impersonating simultaneously a 'little maid' in white, a fierce virgin in white, a nun in white, a bride in white, a madwoman in white, a dead woman in white, and a ghost."[55] Is this a fair judgment? Dickinson seems to have had a characteristically ambivalent, paradoxical attitude toward theatrical behavior. If we are to trust people who observed her, she was certainly confirmed in it. Sending notes, flowers, and glasses of sherry on salvers in to your friends in the parlor (and keeping out of sight) is indeed theatrical. Introducing yourself by handing someone two lilies is a gesture and, like wearing a white dress, a dramatic act. Both suggest an effort to construct or assert a personality, to invoke and to share in a traditional and recognizable set of forms. Dickinson was far too sophisticated a Victorian not to know that by her actions she was "quoting" a whole tradition in religion as in poetry and painting. Whether these acts constitute impersonation, however, is a different issue: to impersonate is *really* to act, to substitute for the real self another identity. Genuinely shy, militant about telling the truth, opposed to anything she thought vulgarly ostensible, Emily Dickinson wore white to affirm her true nature and her membership in a spiritual company. That was the company of those who suffered for the sake of truth and thus overcame the world.[56] In her favorite Revelation 3:5 there is a text that fits very well:

He that overcometh, the same shall be clothed in white raiment; and I will not blot out his name out of the book of life, but I will confess his name before my Father, and before his angels.

It is this text that Samuel Bowles should have had in mind.

Indeed, Emily Dickinson's poem 325 (ca. 1861) is her rendering of that text. Revelation promises a great deal to the one who overcomes: "power over the nations" (2:26), for instance, a seat at God's right hand, and (Dickinson's loved planet) "the morning star" (2:28). It explains that such a spirit deserves these things, for those in white robes are "they which came out of great tribulation, and have washed their robes, and made them white in the blood of the Lamb" (7:13, 14). Now, clothed in their white robes, they stand "before the throne . . . palms in their hands" (7:9). In Dickinson's words:

> Of Tribulation – these are They,
> Denoted by the White.
> The Spangled Gowns, a lesser Rank
> Of Victors, designate –
>
> All these – did Conquer –
> But the Ones who overcame most times –
> Wear nothing commoner than Snow –
> No Ornament – but Palms –
>
> "Surrender" – is a sort unknown
> On this Superior soil –
> "Defeat", an Outgrown Anguish,
> Remembered – as the Mile
>
> Our panting Ancle barely passed –
> When Night devoured the Road –
> But we – stood – whispering in the House –
> And all we said – was
>   SAVED! (325)

Dickinson's poem establishes two kinds of victor and victory. There are those, like herself, in white or "snow"—a word she uses of her own nature in poems and letters; and there are those dressed in spangled gowns. The latter, she says decisively, are of "a lesser Rank / Of Victors." Spangled (sequined) evening dress was fashionable in the 1860s, and Dickinson surely has in mind cosmopolites like her sister-in-law, who was very fond of gowns and furs. Those given to swank, like the party-loving Sue, are victorious in the world. But those who are true victors accept defeat in secular terms, escape night—spiritual harm, confusion, possibly even eros— and stand "in the House," being "SAVED!" Here is Dickinson, the secular nun-artist, who follows her separate star and hopes to see her name confessed, as Revelation promises.

5

Three years before Emily Dickinson wrote "A solemn thing – it was – I said – / A woman – white – to be," she may have read an article in the March 1859 issue of *Harper's* entitled "Single Life Among Us." (By 1859, Dickinson had experienced bliss, she wrote Kate Anthon, at Sue and Austin Dickinson's parties. Kate had been there; Samuel Bowles was often there; and it was "unnatural" to be so happy [L 2.355]. But she had also come to recognize the fact of her single state. She was almost thirty and hastened to inform Kate, a widow, that though she had not married, she knew what love was: to be a "Millionaire" [L 2.365].) The *Harper's* article acknowledged the phenomenon that "vast numbers of noble women . . . prefer to be alone in what, comparatively speaking, is to them single blessedness." It added that

> not a few people remain unmarried because they cannot love any one whom they can win . . . When once the opinion, moreover, gains currency that certain persons are not in the marrying line, but are predestined celibates, the expectation not only acts upon others so as to discourage advances, but acts also upon the parties themselves, who quietly accept their destiny as much as if a ghostly ecclesiastic had given the black vail or cowl that makes wedlock impossible. We all soon fall into the habitudes of our profession.

The metaphor of the cloister leads the *Harper's* writer to continue with a meditation on the single person's opportunity to "pursue favorite studies without distraction," and on the fact that "in all ages, a portion of the noblest minds have been priests and vestals of God and humanity." Rising to new heights of conviction, he declares

> we are not, indeed, ready to say with our Oxford recluses and Roman devotees that single life is the highest spiritual state, yet we must confess that, when we think of the best specimens of this condition within our knowledge or observation, we shake a little in our predilection for marriage; and . . . we do take sides most cordially with the noble men and women who are single from a love higher than any that yet calls them to wedlock.

This higher love was mystical, a "cloister[ing] in Diana's cold and stately shrine." Cultivating refined tastes, "bringing the treasures of art and literature to enrich the whole coterie or village," the "maiden sister wears her modest robes with the inspiration and self-sacrifice of a priestess without waiting for ghostly hands to give her consecration." In this way the *Harper's* essay praises single life, especially for women, as a life of devout consecration. With remarkable aptness to the story of Emily Dickinson and her male friends—Bowles, Higginson, Holland, Lord—it recommends that "unmarried women of culture" be permitted "the society of intellectual and genial men." It ends, however, by associating celibacy with Minerva and the Muse.

Dickinson's poems "He put the Belt around my life" and "A solemn thing – it was – I said" may easily be understood within a tradition of conventual reclusion that, as a borrowed metaphor, emblemizes a life in art. But a third poem, "Not in this World to see his face," introduces a complexity that—rather delightfully—inhibits easy contentment with the poet's declaration of her divine and hermetic marriage. For just as she plays on the theme of androgynous or bisexual affection by interchanging "him" and "her" as objects of love in poems, so here she seems to be introducing the idea of an earthly lover whose face she cannot see in this life. At the same time, the poem may also be read by taking "his face" to mean God's:

> Not in this World to see his face –
> Sounds long – until I read the place
> Where this – is said to be
> But just the Primer – to a life –
> Unopened – rare – Upon the Shelf –
> Clasped yet – to Him – and me –
>
> And yet – My Primer suits me so
> I would not choose – a Book to know
> Than that – be sweeter wise –
> Might some one else – so learned – be –
> And leave me – just my A – B – C –
> Himself – could have the Skies – (418)

Emerson said that genius is religious and must "speak from within the veil."[57] The good artist, like the God perceiver, recognizes the superiority of heaven to earth, seen "through a glass, darkly"; or as Dickinson writes in 271, through the fog of this life. The attainment of the face of God, the "beatific vision" of his nature, was the Christian's proper end and certainly the end of the Christian artist. In one sense, it is the end of all artists, if the face of God is interpreted as the ultimate form of which all forms are expressions.

Thus *not* to see God's face in this world constitutes the primary deprivation of those who believe, or who want to believe. Dickinson's poem—another lyric written in two groups of six lines—offers it as primary in the first line. Its pain is nevertheless mitigated by thought of the unopened book of life (eternity) not "Clasped yet to"—really, "by"—"Him – and me." The reader may interpret "Him and me" to be God and the speaker (they have not yet communed) or the speaker and someone else. The second stanza, which corrects the first with "And yet," contains the frequent Dickinson theme of preference for paradisal fulfillment on earth. It is an ironic stratagem by which to express natural impatience with the speaker's chosen destiny.

On the other hand, there is no reason to dismiss the possibility that "his face" is an earthly lover's. Indeed, such a reading sets Dickinson's poem among the many poems known to her in which (as in the case of Tennyson's Guinevere or Elaine) a heroine laments being separated from a man's face; or the man, like Lancelot, is also tortured by "the bright image of one face" from which he is parted.[58] Like other Victorian writers, Emily Dickinson plays on the theme of the loved face that shines with its own integrity but also, as his image, reflects God's. In a number of poems she meditates on her godly lover's face and acknowledges it to be hidden, like her own. Sometimes it is hidden because he is a traveler, far away from her. Sometimes it is hidden because its "vision"—its semidivine apparition—has been offended by her (462). But in her most triumphal poems, the lover's face never fails. Like the divine Bridegroom's image for a saintly nun, it is present in her cloister, or "little Room" (405).

The first Dickinson poem to be transcribed from handwriting to typescript by Mabel Todd in 1887 was one that contradicted the sense of "Not in this World to see his face." This was what Higginson (titling some of the 1890 *Poems*) would call "Numen Lumen": "I live with Him – I see His face." (Not always perceptive about Dickinson's poetry, Higginson chose a title in this case that accurately focused on her association of the [divine?] lover's face with light.) This powerful poem, probably composed in 1862, is one of her most suasive yet elliptical accounts of the hidden life:

I live with Him – I see His face –
I go no more away
For Visitor – or Sundown –
Death's single privacy

The Only One – forestalling Mine –
And that – by Right that He
Presents a Claim invisible –
No Wedlock – granted me –

I live with Him – I hear His Voice –
I stand alive – Today –
To witness to the Certainty
Of Immortality –

Taught Me – by Time – the lower Way –
Conviction – Every day –
That Life like This – is stopless –
Be Judgment – what it may – (463)

As I have said, I do not think that the presence in her poems of tropes from Victorian literature and art demonstrates that Dickinson was writing out of what she read and viewed only, rather than from her experience with people. On the contrary, I think that she had poignant experiences drawn from life and that she sometimes made use of the imagery of her era in exploring them. The urgency of her voice in "I live with Him – I see His face," emphasized by spondees and the hymn meter on which her lines are built, does not suggest the activity of someone embroidering a trope. Rather, this conviction of a speaking "I" who sees what is never, and yet always, present—the lover's face— seems first to rise from rapt personal feeling. Some ingredients of the Pre-Raphaelite narrative of the enamored nun in her cloister are present, but the passion and the accents are Emily Dickinson's.

Her announcement that she no longer sees either visitors or sun- downs, although she certainly saw the latter to the end, and that Death has a prior right to the lover or that she has failed to obtain wedlock from him are especially Dickinsonian elements. Her speaker's affirma- tion "That Life like This – is stopless" mingles the themes of eternity and eternal love as do, somewhat differently, Dickinson's poems about death and resurrection. Finally, her assertion that no decree of God at the Judgment could interfere with the endurance of her love is present in many other poems. And in 463 she has also established the poles of Time and Immortality (or Eternity) by which she interprets all experiences. With her view that Time is "the lower Way" Thomas à Kempis would have concurred, for he writes of the "Day of Eternity," its height and majesty, and the "lowest place" and "way," the "low estate" of all who live in this world.[59]

Emily Dickinson's three poems—273, 271, 418—like many others in the early poetry, establish a narrative about hidden faces that is central to understanding her as a writer and a woman. She would not send Higginson a daguerreotype, but she sent him many pictures of her inward face. In "The Law of Beauty," the *Atlantic Monthly* feature writer for April 1860 told subscribers like the Dickinsons that "the highest beauty is doubtless that which expresses the noblest emotion. A face that shines, like that of Moses, from communion with the Highest, is more truly beautiful than the most faultless features without moral expression." If Emily Dickinson really considered herself "the only Kangaroo among the Beauty" around her, she seems also to have thought that by her singing she could please the cherubim (L 2.412, 413). As her poems continued to develop the trope of her buried life, they extended the possibility that, in the face of the mysterious lover, she also saw a divine face.

Emerson's conviction that great art is made in isolation and silence undoubtedly helped to convince Emily Dickinson in a way of life to which she was personally drawn. Certainly it helped to separate her from Sue and her other married friends. Her early letters show that Dickinson was never eager to be married (though she longed to experience the sort of burning passion Tennyson had his Fatima voice—she marked that poem in her copy of his *Poems* and may have been pleased by its lines, "I will grow round him in his place, / Grow, live, die looking on his face"). By her reclusion, she protected herself from such distractions as Sue enjoyed, however. And she adhered to a plan of self-reliance in working out her destiny as artist.

In her copy of Emerson's "Self Reliance," now in the Harvard collection, a page is turned down at the following passage, which is also marked at the right: "My life is for itself and not for a spectacle. I much prefer that it should be of a lower strain, so it be genuine and equal, than that it should be glittering and unsteady." Again, "What I must do is all that concerns me, not what people think." Genuine and equal, not glittering and unsteady: the antithesis seems to have been brought home to Emily Dickinson by lives near at hand to her own. But the gold and glitter to which she herself was dedicated was the great morning, artistic inspiration. Emerson said it rose out of that "sea of light," the East. One in search of it, he wrote, like "the soul that ascends to worship the great God, is plain and true; has no rose-color, no fine friends, no chivalry, no adventures; does not want admiration; dwells in the hour that now is, in the earnest experience of the common day."[60] Observing such mornings as she lived her hidden life, Emily Dickinson would strive to become what Emerson called one of the children of the light.

~ 2 ~

Solitary Mornings on the Sea

> I see the spectacle of morning from the hilltop over against
> my house, from daybreak to sunrise, with emotions which an
> angel might share. The long slender bars of cloud float like
> fishes in the sea of crimson light. From the earth, as a shore,
> I look out into that silent sea. I seem to partake its rapid
> transformations: the active enchantment reaches my dust, and
> I dilate and conspire with the morning wind.
>
> —Emerson, *Nature* (1836)

Although he had once been her brother's "royal guest" whom she
associated with Eternity "where dreams are born"[1]—and although her
own poem 67 would be attributed to him, implying the kinship of their
minds—Emily Dickinson never wrote to Ralph Waldo Emerson. Perhaps she feared to trouble or displease a seer so famous, so esteemed
by her family. Perhaps, because his *Poems* (1850) had influenced her,
Emerson seemed too daunting to approach. Or perhaps Dickinson perceived that Emerson's works were remarkably condescending to
women, and (though she often scoffed at silly women herself) she did
not wish to make herself vulnerable.[2] For whatever reason, it was not
her sister-in-law Susan's idol whom Dickinson approached for literary
advice in April 1862. It was to the prolific poet-essayist Thomas Wentworth Higginson (1823–1911) that she sent a cryptic message, asking
if her verse was alive (L 2.403). Dickinson had read Higginson's "Letter
to a Young Contributor" in the April issue of the *Atlantic Monthly*.
His severe but sympathetic words to aspiring writers probably appealed
to her. "Charge your style with life"; "remember how many great
writers have created the taste by which they were enjoyed, and do not
be in a hurry to publish": these lines were more suggestive of Dickinson's work and how it would be received than Higginson could have
known. And doubtless his comforting hypothesis that "the mute inglo-

rious Miltons of this sphere may in some other sing their Paradise as found"[3] reassured her that his soul had the necessary circumference to understand her own. As an ordained Unitarian minister, he too had his eyes on eternity.

She sent four poems to Higginson: "Safe in their Alabaster Chambers" (216), "The nearest Dream recedes unrealized" (318), "We play at Paste" (320), and "I'll tell you how the Sun rose" (318). She presented herself as a poetic ingénue with no mentors—"I have none to ask"—although, at Susan Dickinson's bidding, she revised 216 three times (L 2.403). Higginson was different from the conservative (if choleric) Dickinson men. He was a devoted liberal, an activist for women's rights. Though as a writer he lacked the stature of Emerson, he was artistic and cultivated. Too careful ever to recommend that she publish before she had corrected her "spasmodic gait," he was nevertheless fascinated by Emily Dickinson.[4] (He had a taste for spiritual—and spirited—women. One of his favorite women in history was not the Virgin Mary, as might befit a Victorian clergyman, but a favorite of Dickinson's, Cleopatra.[5]) Higginson never forgot taking Dickinson's letter from his postal box; he answered it immediately, and so began his career of twenty years as her "preceptor," whose precepts were never followed.

The prospect of what might have been Emerson's reply had *he* received "I'll tell you how the Sun rose" or that declaration of achieved artistic consequence, "We play at Paste," remains intriguing. Both poems reveal Emily Dickinson's commitment to the visionary ideals Emerson had set forth in his essays. They show that she was leading a poet's life that in outward form as in inner discipline accorded with Emerson's doctrine of the pursuit and creation of beauty through solitary contemplation.

I have said earlier that achieving honor—not necessarily fame—as a poet was Dickinson's central purpose. Had Emerson read the poems she was writing even in the early 1860s, he would have encountered a sensibility to admire. For it was firm in the aesthetic stratagems and philosophical insights on the intersection of eternity and time that he voiced in his essays. Emerson's precept that a poet's power was not comparable to, but above, "all that is reckoned solid and precious in the world,—palaces, gardens, money, navies, kingdoms"[6] was a "spiritual law" in which the otherwise skeptical Emily Dickinson could believe. And in her quest for honor as an artist, she was taking "real action" in "silent moments" (206); if he reasoned that to think is to act, Dickinson's understanding of that truth was acute. Furthermore, by the reclusion that afforded her heightened concentration, she was creating a world of measured and deliberate shapes. In their exactitude such shapes conveyed both her thirst for concretion and security and her desire to form a personal world in art. "Build therefore your own world," Emerson wrote. "As fast as you conform your life to the pure idea in your mind, that will unfold its great proportions."[7]

The proportions of Dickinson's world were both calculable and mysterious. Like the American landscape painters of the early nineteenth century, she observed and disposed the outlines of the real in order to suggest their evocation of the unseen. It was the tension experienced in perceiving both that inspired the paradoxes of her landscape poems. When a census taken in 1870 listed Emily Dickinson's occupation, it used the phrase employed for dependent daughters: "Without Occupation."[8] Apart from baking, gardening, sewing, nursing, canning, and other household duties, Dickinson had an occupation and defined it in terms any Luminist painter would have approved. It was that of poet-witness to the "mystical content"[9] as well as the hard outlines and deep colors of landscape: a word that implied the landscape of the human mind, heart, and soul as well as nature's. Furthermore, she did not inhabit a merely measurable house like reality's, which she compares, perhaps remembering her lawyer father's dark home, to prose. *Her* mansion is the numinous one that admits poetry:

> I dwell in Possibility –
> A fairer house than Prose –
> More numerous of Windows –
> Superior – for Doors –

Poetry, more open to the "natural light" that was, for Luminists and Transcendentalists alike, "the bearer of almost supernatural mysteries"[10] is also a safeguard. As her chosen vocation, it hides her as if in an impregnable forest from the intrusive eye yet opens her to infinitude:

> Of Chambers as the Cedars –
> Impregnable of Eye –
> And for an Everlasting Roof
> The Gambrels of the Sky –
>
> Of Visiters – the fairest –
> For Occupation – This –

The spreading wide my narrow Hands
To gather Paradise – (657)

Her poem makes the association frequent in Emerson between sky and paradise while her allusion to fairest visitors is to those transcendental emissaries, the muses, or sources of artistic inspiration to whom she alludes in a number of poems about the poetic process. Poem 657 describes the creative responsiveness Emerson praised in *Nature*: "Every spirit builds itself a house, and beyond its house a world, and beyond its world a heaven."[11] Dickinson herself figures in this tight declarative poem as an important presence: for she, or a distinctly characteristic speaker who appears in many other poems, is the slight ("narrow Hands") person rewarded with possession of the heavenly illumination from which art is made.

2

"I dwell in Possibility" is the eleventh of twenty-three poems copied by Dickinson into fascicle 22. Like each of the forty booklets, fascicle 22 presents lyrics that share themes, both with each other and with the other fascicles. Central to fascicle 22 and to "I dwell in Possibility," however, is the idea of the poet's nature, role, and development according to an aesthetic held by Emerson and conveyed to him by Wordsworth. In other lyrics, such as "I was the slightest in the House" (486), "Myself was formed – a Carpenter" (488), and "A Solemn thing within the Soul" (483), Dickinson confides the thoughts and characteristics of "a supposed person" (L 2.412) whose vital self-discovery as a poet invites her identification with the author. These poems describe Dickinson's understanding of the relation between life and art as well as the working patterns by which the speaker of this fascicle learns the secrets of the former to serve the latter. As Emerson enjoins poets in *Nature*, as Wordsworth describes his poet in *The Prelude*, Dickinson's speaker offers herself in solitude to nature's influence and predicates the sacramental connection between landscape and humanity, between landscape and the divine, which was the hypothesis of the romantics and a chief principle of Ruskin. Solitary, she surveys the scene outside her window, submitting it to a measured analysis that will link in language the magical frontiers of her street or garden with heaven's.

It is clear even from the early poems that like most nineteenth-century landscape artists—poets and painters—Dickinson studied dramatic

changes in day or season as evidence of sublimity. They were oppor-
tunities for an artist to record "the unity between [Nature's] outer
appearances and the ultimate forms of eternity."[12] Poems in fascicle 22
report that she usually writes in the early morning or works at night
until dawn. "I was the slightest in the House" (486), for instance,
discloses the guarded and secretive life of a persona embarrassed by the
noise and triviality of shared community; one who therefore depicts
herself living most enjoyably and creatively at night or just before
sunrise. (One of her models, Elizabeth Barrett Browning, spoke in
Aurora Leigh of writing accomplished during "long calm nights / From
which the silken sleeps were fretted out" (5.347–348). For women
writers in particular, who were and usually still are responsible for
household duties, the habit assumes importance.) Like "I dwell in Possibility," poem 486 contrasts the speaker, who is deliberately devoted
to a visionary artist's life, with others in her family's prosaic house.
Among them, she is "the slightest." This is probably an allusion both
to her physical size (as she conceived it[13]) and to her importance, "Least
Figure" (400). That she takes "the smallest Room" emphasizes the
irony that the reclusive speaker of 486 is identical with the triumphal
speaker of 298 who, visited by the company of gnomes or angelic hosts
that inspire art, cannot be alone. Thus she may be the least member in
the least choice room of the house; but 486's speaker has been chosen
to "catch the Mint / That never ceased to fall."

This allusion to the shower of gold in which Jove visited Danaë
forcibly (by recalling force) unites ideas of both the human and the
divine. The shower of gold is a shower of light that overwhelms the
speaker with inspiration; and though the story of Danaë is one of rape,
the speaker is reified by her experience. The author of poem 298 would
sign herself to Higginson "Your Gnome." So she identifies herself with
the spirits of art who, she said, stayed with her always, baffling the
keys of common doors and people. Seemingly a humble allusion to the
obscurantism of which Higginson accused her, the signature was a
proud acknowledgment of her calling. In poem 486, that calling is a
raison d'etre, for the poet-speaker dislikes exposure: "The Racket
shamed me so" and, were it not for fear, would welcome the noteless-
ness of death. Her existence is preserved and, like the poem itself,
literally formed by her nocturnal acts of composition:

> At night, my little Lamp, and Book –
> And one Geranium –

> So stationed I could catch the Mint
> That never ceased to fall –
> And just my Basket –

Emerson described himself waiting for morning to come so that its revelation of shapes and outlines might remind him of the relation between eternity and time, God and man. In sentences that serve as the epigraph to this chapter, he associated the concepts of morning, angel, sea, light, and mankind in the same paradigm of inspiration and destiny that informs Thomas Cole's *Voyage of Life* series (which, as we shall see, influenced Dickinson). Morning marked the miracle of a new day, metaphor for the imagination and its bright creation of new life. Dickinson's favorite magazine the *Atlantic Monthly* (in the same April 1862 edition that contained Higginson's "Letter to a Young Contributor") advised poets and painters to study the world in early morning when it was holy, full of the "awakening light" of Elysium.[14] Wordsworth had liked to sit "Alone . . . At the first hour of morning, when the Vale / Lay quiet in an utter solitude" (*The Prelude*, 2.362–364). It was then that he found the poetic consciousness and eye most lively and nature's spell most fresh.

Among the Dickinson books there were texts—frequently quite different in character—that showed the influence of the romantics in praising morning as the poet's hour. Dated 1867, Joseph and Laura Lyman's *Philosophy of House-Keeping*, for example, would not have especially affected Emily; it was a gift to Susan Dickinson from the authors. (Joseph Lyman had been Lavinia Dickinson's old beau.) The book includes a long passage, however, that reflects the "philosophy" of an era influenced by Wordsworth and Emerson (it also showed Lyman's anti-Byronic prejudice, which Emily Dickinson did not share):

> The most healthful as well as the most successful mental labor is always accomplished in the morning. Midnight, indeed, has its excitement; but it is hot and morbid. Don Juan, Manfred, Festus, and all those great labors of misguided genius, whose function it is to harrow the sensibilities, without either informing the mind or purifying the heart, are the product of late hours,—of false and wasteful excitement. But all the writings that we love to call immortal,—whose blessed office it has been to inspire successive generations of poets and thinkers, to elevate and instruct mankind or "charm their pained steps over the burnt soil of the world,"—were composed while the shadows of the trees all pointed westward, and the dew still sparkled in the meadow. In Homer and Virgil, in Shakespeare and Milton, we

seem ever to breathe the fragrance of the early morning, and catch a refrain from the inimitable trill of the heaven—soaring lark.[15]

A very different sort of text also imagined the importance of morning to the greatest of English poets. The ninth chapter of volume two in Edward Dickinson's collected works of Shakespeare shows signs of great use. This is a chapter called "Solitary Hours," an impressionistic conception of the Bard's private moments. The essayist, Charles Knight, comments on Shakespeare's descriptions of "morning under every aspect." That page has been folded in, probably by Emily Dickinson, who customarily creased and marked pages and enclosed flowers and ribbons in her books. Knight imagines that so great a genius as Shakespeare must have made actual observation of dawn and experienced "the coldness of the morning just before sunrise."[16] Such disparate texts as Lyman's and Knight's owe much to the celebrations of morning found in Emerson and Wordsworth.

Romantic exaltation in the morning, of course, is the heir of scriptural tradition in which each new day is like the Resurrection. In an early poem (58), Dickinson shows that she participates in this tradition:

> Morn is supposed to be
> By people of degree
> The breaking of the Day

She continues

> Morning has not occurred!
>
> That shall Aurora be –
> East of Eternity –
> One with the banner gay –
> One in the red array –
> *That* is the break of Day!

Thus, she says, the real morning or break of day occurs when the soul enters eternal life. Dawn, Aurora, will really happen "East of Eternity": a metaphoric place in which suns rise endlessly in a world that itself stands for sunrise or continued life. "East," "Eternity," and "break of Day" are linked here, and all connote life everlasting in paradise. Dickinson's conception of dawn flooding heaven like a "banner gay" in "red array" suggests her familiarity with other nineteenth-century nature poetry and painting. For example, she had read Tennyson's *Elaine,* with its story of the doomed lily maid who saw Lancelot's face from her lonely tower. So she knew the description of the woman "High in her chamber up a tower to the east" who watches for "morning's earliest ray" and on whose face "the blood-red light of dawn" flares like a torch announcing her death and passage into eternity.[17] The Hudson River and Luminist painters were well known to Dickinson and her family; they often imagined sunrise streaming victorious scarlet banners across the heavens. During the Civil War, the painter Frederic Edwin Church manifested his Union sympathies by painting a sunset composed of stars and stripes in *Our Banner in the Sky* (1861).

Emily Dickinson may have read the words of the Puritan divine, Jonathan Edwards, who quoted Psalms 130:6 to confess the inspiriting association he made between morning and the divine image: "'My soul waiteth for the Lord, more than they that watch for morning . . .' When the light of the day came in at the windows, it refreshed my soul from one morning to another. It seemed to be some image of the light of God's glory."[18] To Edwards (writing in *Images or Shadows of Divine Things*, ca. 1741) the rising of the sun was a type of the resurrection of Christ. In several other poems Dickinson avails herself of this traditional association of morning with divinity. "There is a morn of men unseen" (24), for example, in the first fascicle reveals her hypothesis of "the different dawn" while, in fascicle 35, poem 728 associates mornings with God's imaginative act in Genesis. That was the creation of light, itself the articulation of the world:

> Cunning Reds of Morning
> Make the Blind – leap –
>
> . . . . .
> the first Miracle
> Let in – with Light –

In "At last, to be identified!" (174), she longs to experience what a risen soul experiences. Addressing that soul, she says

> At last, the lamps upon thy side
> The rest of Life to *see*!
>
> Past Midnight! past the Morning Star!
> Past Sunrise!
> Ah, What leagues there *were*
> Between our feet, and Day!

Thus, anticipating her ride into the infinite world in "Because I could not stop for Death," Dickinson's speaker in poem 174 voyages past sunrise to reach the day that is eternal life. She imagines eternity as containing lamps that light "the rest of Life," so that this world and the next are connected, two sides of one reality. The provisional illumination of that reality is morning. For, she says in 250, "Morning [is] only the seed of Noon." Noon stands for passionate fulfillment in Dickinson's love poems, but it is also one of her emblems for eternal life.

Wordsworth wrote in *The Prelude* that

> the darkness and the light
> Were all like workings of one mind, the features
> Of the same face, blossoms upon one tree,
> Characters of the great Apocalypse,
> The types and symbols of Eternity. (6.567–571)

Like him and like her admired Emily Brontë,[19] Dickinson saw also in darkness a principle of fecundity so that it is possible to argue, as one critic does, that night was a "nourishing wellspring";[20] that darkness—a time she often associates with private activity, the inner self, exotic kingdoms of books and dreams, and fantasies of love—"felt beautiful" (593) to her. Indeed, with the facility usual in mythmaking poets, Dickinson is able to write of both night and day as symbols of confusion or enlightenment, peace or disturbance, productivity or waste, joy or deprivation. These darknesses or "Evenings of the Brain" (419), in which nights are linked to mental breakdown, appear in the same poetic canon that celebrates the raptures of passion or the effort to write poems:

> I made slow Riches but my Gain
> Was steady as the Sun
> And every Night, it numbered more
> Than the preceding One. (843)

Similarly "A Toad, can die of Light" (583) uses Dickinson's ubiquitous metaphor of light as welcome illumination, this time to express its challenging and perilous complexity.

Yet it is evident that Dickinson's prevailing attitude is to morning as the archetype of inspiration, immortality, revelation. This was the morning envisioned by the nineteenth-century American landscape artists. In Frederic Edwin Church's *Morning* (1848), for example, a small human figure, awed by what he sees, stands beneath high hills as a luminous dawn flows toward him like a tide of color over the lightening sea.

Church's teacher, Thomas Cole, rarely painted sunsets—even though it was customary among the Hudson River painters to depict both dramatic extremes of nature's day. Cole also wrote poems. "Before Sunrise" (1847) shows his religious associations with daybreak:

> Be still! For in this sacred, solemn deep
> Of silence all things mute do pray
> Amen!

He wrote essays about sunrise that recall Emerson's imagery of morning and anticipate Dickinson's:

> The mists were resting on the vale of the Hudson like drifted snow: tops of distant mountains in the east were visible—things of another world. The sun rose from bars of pearly hue . . . The mist below the mountain began first to be lighted up, and the trees on the tops of the lower hills cast their shadows over the misty surface—innumerable streaks.

In his poem "Morning" Cole notes the birdsong at dawn that Dickinson often described, seeing it as a type of prayer in which all should join:

> Like the Birds with cheerful voices
> When the morning lights the sky
> Our own simple songs should rise
> Unto God who dwells on high.[21]

And in such landscapes as *Sunny Morning on the Hudson River* (ca. 1827) or *A View near Tivoli (Morning)* (1832) he portrays morning as the dissipator of shadows and the bringer of serenity as light. For devout Christians like Cole, this new light also provided the opportunity for spiritual improvement and change, even for better fortune. Dickinson exhibited such an awareness, once sending her sister-in-law a note that said simply, "A Fresh Morning of Life with it's impregnable chances, and the Dew, for you" (L 3.733).

The Dickinson poems and letters again and again look for light. They disclose a persona searching for "dominion": whether it be in the house of art or of friends' hearts or in the "delinquent palaces" of self-esteem that she imagines and cannot quite attain (959). Though this persona who likes paradoxes declares, "In insecurity to lie / Is Joy's insuring quality" (1434), she returns over and over to the dominant quest for certitude, for a measurable landscape. Even the idea of God seems to her "much more friendly through a hearty Lens" (L 2.492). Therefore, while the conceit of night is richly useful to her as a vivid image of various states from misery to fulfillment, that of morning light is linked with the enfranchisement of clear sight. For her, "Dawn – knows how to be" and

> Sunrise takes us back to Scene –
> Transmuted – Vivider – (944)

Many of the poems, then, describe her fascination with the outlines, angles, and shapes of the landscape of this earth as they come into new being with the arrival of day. If her *"morning hours—*3 a.m. to 12 p.m.," as she describes them (L 2.344) were usually given to writing, they permitted her the silence and secret growth of nighttime composition together with the aesthetic and spiritual stimulus of dawn when "Mists – are carved away" (664). "Night," she says in poem 7, "is the morning's Canvas." Her own mission was the artist's—"Do I paint it *natural?*" (L 1.193); that is, her errand was that "of the eye / Out upon the Bay," the "Ether Sea" (1622) of light that for her as for Wordsworth and Emerson was the morning sky.

This light joined Dickinson's own provincial Amherst to other worlds and times. "I saw the sunrise on the Alps since I saw you," she once wrote Mrs. Holland, suggesting what was to her—who traveled only in literature, art, and longing—the relation between imagination and the real world (L 2.455). Perhaps reading Wordsworth or the Brownings or accounts in the *Atlantic Monthly* and *Harper's* of the Alpine subjects of the landscape painters gave her the fancied sunrise. The sentence may signify some experience of delight or enlightenment, the "solemn Alps – / The siren Alps" (80) connoting (like all mountains) a summit of feeling. And certainly, as "A Wife – at Daybreak I shall be" (461) shows most compellingly, "sunrise" in her letter shares some of the power and mystery of Eternity, East, Victory: her major symbols for romantic passion, poetic accomplishment, and everlasting life.

So her poems and letters provide throughout a portrait of the poet, awake "at night's delicious close" (1764) and measuring the moments and shadings which show that the sun will shortly "emerge / From His Amazing House" (888). In 304 she dramatizes the coming of morning, painting it with the ardent colors of Cole and the Hudson River School:

> The Day came slow – till Five o'clock –
> Then sprang before the Hills

Like Hindered Rubies – or the Light
A Sudden Musket – spills –

The Purple could not keep the East –
The Sunrise shook abroad
Like Breadths of Topaz – packed a Night –
The Lady just unrolled –

The Happy Winds – their Timbrels took –
The Birds – in docile Rows
Arranged themselves around their Prince
The Wind – is Prince of Those –

The Orchard sparkled like a Jew –
How mighty 'twas – to be
A Guest in this stupendous place –
The Parlor – of the Day –

Dickinson's concentration on gem colors here—Rubies, Purple, Topaz—
is characteristic of many of her landscape poems. It reminds us that
one of her favorite books of the Bible was Revelation, in which the
enthroned Christ is like a diamond and a ruby, surrounded by a rainbow
of emerald and separated from the viewer by a sea of crystal. Since she
thought this life the ground floor of the next, she often described it as
resembling the bejeweled paradise of Revelation. In poem 304 she
imagines the coming of day in homely as well as royal images. The
"Hindered Rubies" are able to spring as if animated (even as the thunder
and lightning of Revelation are individualized forces). The effect is
surreal. Yet the sunrise is also imagined as being unrolled by a Lady
like a bolt of cloth, an image related to the housekeeping images of
several other poems. And the speaker is a guest in a parlor: a final
conceit for sunrise that suggests the gentle domestic imagery of George
Herbert.[22]

Morning is a musical as well as a painterly event in poem 304, the
wind shaking its timbrels even, as in 888, the sun beats the drum of
the earth. The effect is one of "transport," says the speaker in 157,
who describes herself "waking – long before the morn" to experience
a "New Life," which she associates with the music of the spheres. In
poem 783, she records a humbler, though still ravishing, musical experience purveyed by dawn:

The Birds begun at Four o'clock –
Their period for Dawn –

> A Music numerous as space
> But neighboring as Noon

She emphasizes that she is alone, "Except for occasional man / In homely industry arrayed"—milkman, drover, farmer—to hear this aubade in which the Transcendental intimacy between infinitude ("numerous as space") and time ("neighboring as noon") is expressed. It is the eye of the poet that takes control of this scene, of course; and she is sensitized to it by solitary contemplation in precisely the fashion Emerson recommends, thus becoming the "transparent eyeball" that Luminist painters and landscape poets tried, under his influence, to be.

Emily Dickinson sometimes must have hoped that her chosen, hidden life in art would ultimately result in honorable disclosure, and fame. Morning, in this way, may have been specifically, personally meaningful. "Will there really be a 'morning'?" (101), for example, may easily be read as questioning both the possibility of eternal life and that of her own success as a poet. The Bible's promise of triumph in the elucidation of God's ways to humanity has morning as a prevailing metaphor. Morning makes clear that "nothing is secret, that shall not be made manifest; neither *anything* hid, that shall not be known and come abroad" (Luke 8:17). Working into and during the mornings of her poetic maturity, did Dickinson wonder whether her name would achieve its own ascendancy? Surely to one who had endured the threat of blindness, the renewed presentation of familiar shapes—her "faces"— must also have been welcome. She took "a Geometric Joy" (652) even in the "prison" of daily routine which, appearing also in fascicle 22, seems the bleak cognate of her luminous house of possibility. For she liked "to know the Planks" even of boredom or suffering. Her pleasure, then, at morning's defining light was also the confirming joy of recognition. Inspired perhaps by Ruskin's *Stones of Venice,* she describes herself waiting "Like a Venetian" (in that crowded city where light comes in at angles) for the first glimpse of a familiar apple tree:

> The Angle of a Landscape –
> That every time I wake –
> Between my Curtain and the Wall
> Upon an ample Crack –
>
> Like a Venetian – waiting –
> Accosts my open eye –
> Is just a Bough of Apples –
> Held slanting – in the Sky – (375)

3

The visionary, solitary speaker who gathers paradise from her house of possibility is associated in fascicle 22 with another writer who, as a true artist, understands the honest and "unpretending" nature of the labor by which the artifice or pretense of art itself is made. "Myself was formed – a Carpenter" (488) is related to "A Solemn thing within the Soul" (483) in insisting on the holiness of the poet's occupation. Both poems accord with Emerson's conception of the poet as "the man of Beauty," "isolated among his contemporaries by truth and by his art" who consoles himself that, as Christ says of himself, he "will draw all men sooner or later."

In "Myself was formed – a Carpenter" the speaker (again, like Christ, a craftsman) is confronted by a more worldly builder who comes to measure her attainments:

> Myself was formed – a Carpenter –
> An unpretending time
> My Plane – and I, together wrought
> Before a Builder came –
>
> To measure our attainments –
> Had we the Art of Boards
> Sufficiently developed – He'd hire us
> At Halves –
>
> My Tools took Human – Faces –
> The Bench, where we had toiled –
> Against the Man – persuaded –
> We – Temples build – I said – (488)

The Christ of Matthew, the gospel to which Dickinson alludes more than others, often utters his parables in plain-spoken architectural images. In Matthew 7:24–27, for example, he declares that the wise man builds his house on rocks and the foolish man, on sand. How and with what the spirit builds its house to receive the divine guest is a frequent biblical metaphor, as is the image of the "false prophet" (Matthew 7:15) or false builder. In Emily Dickinson's poems the speaker-carpenter has used Emerson's "materials" that enable a poet to redact "the world as [a] temple whose walls are covered" with emblems, pictures, and commandments of the deity. That she is offered hire at halves by the builder implies that, as neither architect nor craftsman, he is no artist but interested in an "Art of Boards," a facile technique rather than subtle construction. The speaker's techniques or tools, however, are those of Emerson's poet, "attache[d] . . . to nature and the Whole" [327]: they have "Human – Faces," even as her lonely chamber or "Bench" has the symbolic powers of human speech. Both declare her opposed to shoddy poems—dispensable buildings—and, like the poet-priest George Herbert in *The Temple* (quoted by Emerson in "Nature" [38]), determined to be the architect of *true* poems. Dickinson's use of the crucial symbol "face" clarifies the sanctity of the carpenter's calling.

Copied by Dickinson in fascicle 22 immediately after "I dwell in Possibility," poem 483, "A Solemn thing within the Soul," is also a dramatization of her identity as an artist, conceived here as spiritual growth. This poem, appropriately, is what Ruskin would have called a moral landscape and reflects both inner and outer weather:

> A Solemn thing within the Soul
> To feel itself get ripe –
> And golden hang – while farther up –
> The Maker's Ladders stop –
> And in the Orchard far below –
> You hear a Being – drop –
>
> A Wonderful – to feel the Sun
> Still toiling at the Cheek
> You thought was finished –
> Cool of eye, and critical of Work –
> He shifts the stem – a little –
> To give your Core – a look –
>
> But solemnest – to know
> Your chance in Harvest moves
> A little nearer – Every Sun
> The Single – to some lives. (483)

Biblical passages, such as the parable of the sower in which "he that heareth [God's] word . . . beareth fruit" and "the harvest is the end of the world; and the reapers are the angels" (Matthew 13:23, 39), are at the heart of Dickinson's poem. These texts were familiar to all nineteenth-century Christians; indeed, they would have been known even to the educated nonbeliever, in an era when great cultural documents— in history, science, or literature—commonly alluded to the Bible. The American landscape painters often depicted harvesting as a myth about the beauty of American enterprise; but under the hand of Thomas Cole or his follower Jasper Cropsey (*Harvest Scene* [1855] and *American Harvesting* [1864]) the myth assumed distinctly spiritual connotations. Behind the scenes of American farmers gathering wheat into barns was the spiritual discipline of gathering for God, of preparing for the Kingdom (Matthew 6:33). The landscape at harvest—Cole preferred autumn landscapes, rich in reds and golds—was Edenic, not because it was devoid of death but because harvest anticipated heaven, the reunion of God with his creation.

Dickinson's poem 483 may be read as an allegory about God's grace operative in the individual spirit to perfect it for its gathering into eternity. Certainly the speaker is a participant in a general experience; for God's ladders stop to pluck a more developed ("farther up") soul and send it below to be gathered. But the authority and immediacy of the speaker's voice qualify the experience as her own in which, like an apple core, her inner self is studied by a Sun, the Maker's assistant—Christ?—who is "cool of eye," critical of his own work and able to alter the position of her stem. The poem concludes, with biblical overtones of knowing not the day or hour of harvest, upon the Emersonian reflection: "Every Sun / The Single – to some lives"; every day might be the one of revelation in which the secret of life's meaning becomes clear through personal fulfillment, either on earth or after death.

Emily Dickinson's education at Amherst Academy and then at Mary Lyon's Female Seminary in East Hadley ensured her an extensive knowledge of the Bible. She never formally joined the Congregational church. Although her reactions to orthodox Puritan teaching and conventional piety were complicated and largely negative, she knew scripture extremely well. Her own King James Bible (1843), in green straight-grained morocco and gilt, is a small volume.[23] So minute is its print that she must have had to hold the book very close up; but Victorians liked bibles that were easy to carry or to tuck in a drawer. Like many of her books, Dickinson's Bible shows signs of much use. There is a pressed clover from her father's grave between pages 286 and 287 and another clover at Hebrews 11: "Now faith is the substance of things hoped for, the evidence of things not seen." It is characteristic, I think, of her rich and complex nature that she copied out on the back flyleaf some lines written by a neighbor, titled "The Bible." "Composed," she notes dutifully, "by Dr. J. Holt during his last illness," the verse was written in the mawkish tradition of "Out of the Body to God" and other effusions which (with that tolerance of sincere sentiment typical of most Victorians) Dickinson often excused:

It is a pure and holy word,
It is the wisdom of a God,
It is a fountain, full and free,
It is *the* book for you and me,
It will the soul's best anchor be,
Over life's tempestuous sea,
A guardian angel to the tomb,
A meteor in the world's dark gloom,
It is a shining sun at even
It is a diamond dropped from heaven.

Her own poem on the Bible, sent to her twenty-one-year-old nephew Ned in 1882, is three lines longer than Holt's, and it is also a definition. It was the final version of her earlier "Diagnosis of the Bible, by a Boy," begun about 1879. She probably sent the poem to Ned, sick in bed and unable to attend church, as a conspiratorial comment on puritanical orthodoxy. But it had been attempted—by the "Boy" Emily (1487), her outspoken, iconoclastic self—some years before this occasion. Opposite in feeling to Holt's poem, Dickinson's is a spoof of established doctrine, from the belief that Scripture is divinely inspired to the concepts of the fall and of hell. At the end she contrasts the captivating songs of the artist with the forbidding stories of the theologian:

The Bible is an antique Volume –
Written by faded Men
At the suggestion of Holy Spectres –
Subjects – Bethlehem –
Eden – the ancient Homestead –
Satan – the Brigadier –
Judas – the Great Defaulter –
David – the Troubadour –
Sin – a distinguished Precipice –
Others must resist –
Boys that "believe" are very lonesome –
Other Boys are "lost" –
Had but the Tale a warbling Teller –
All the Boys would come –
Orpheus' Sermon captivated –
It did not condemn – (1545)

Dickinson's witty terminology puts the old dogmas in relief. If ecclesiasts teach that the Scriptures are written by men under the inspiration of the Holy Spirit, she proposes with intentionally puerile bravado that the men are "faded" (dead as men, insipid as writers) and the Spirit is "spectres" (word play on "Holy Ghost"). The poem's intention as a literary confidence to a youth in her persona as the Boy Emily must be remembered, for she does not contemplate but merely *tags* the biblical characters: "Satan – the Brigadier" and "David – the Troubadour." Her slant rhyme underscores the impropriety (and yet the airy justice) of such epithets. Her Eden is an "ancient Homestead" where those first pioneers Adam and Eve lived. For her, "Sin – distinguished Precipice" has charm. As something "others must resist," it implies the delights as well as the dangers of disobedience and points up the hypocrisy of those who enjoy pleasures they forbid to others.

This roguish little poem has a brio that comes of its bald reduction of potent scriptural passages. "Boys that 'believe' are very lonesome," for example, is the fey equivalent of Christ's words, "Ye shall be hated of all men for my name's sake" (Matthew 10:22). And this is a poem whose history reveals Dickinson's earnestness as a poet. To achieve her adjective "warbling," she discarded thirteen alternatives: typic, thrilling, hearty, bonnie, breathless, spacious, tropic, ardent, friendly, magic, pungent, winning, mellow. Each in its way sought to suggest the humanity (and hence the beauty, energy, sympathy) of art by comparison with the strictures of Scripture. With *his* sermon, Orpheus captivated Pluto and recaptured Eurydice. The Bible, however, condemns so much that boys like Ned—and Emily—won't come to hear it. Since she worked over it for several years, this poem, however playful, seems to be making a statement whose cynicism she found as relevant as Dr. Holt's profession of faith.

It presents Emily Dickinson in one mood, however. For she was not immune to the captivation of many scriptural passages and paraphrased one of the noblest and most tender, Christ's words to the thief on the cross: "Verily I say unto thee, Today shalt thou be with me in paradise" (Luke 24:43). In one of her poems about faces she makes a modest prayer:

> Recollect the Face of me
> When in thy Felicity,
> Due in Paradise today
> Guest of mine assuredly –
>
> Other Courtesies have been –
> Other Courtesy may be –

We commend ourselves to thee
Paragon of Chivalry (1305)

Dickinson's autograph copy of Holt's lines on the Bible is accompanied by a newspaper notice from the *Hampshire and Franklin Express* (May 14, 1848), clipped and pasted into her own volume: "At Amherst, 14th inst., Jacob Holt, M.D., late of the firm of Hitchcock & Holt, dentists, of this city." Thus, at age eighteen, she sought to preserve a memento of a friend's piety. Always uncertain of her own convictions about Christian doctrine, she frequently sought encouragement from others. Her correspondence with the Presbyterian minister Charles Wadsworth doubtless concerned problems of faith and immortality. After he died, she asked his friend Charles Clark, "Are you certain there is another life? When overwhelmed to know, I fear that few are sure" (L 3.779). She asked the Congregational clergyman Washington Gladden whether he believed in eternal life. Her last lines to Colonel Higginson were written to an ordained pastor: "Diety – does he live now? My friend – does he breathe?" (L 3.905). Despite her religious doubts, however, Dickinson's knowledge of Scripture was impeccable.

Among the Dickinson books is the *Memoir of Mary Lyon* (1851) compiled by the president of Amherst College (1845–1854), Edward Hitchcock. Hitchcock had influenced the judicious scientific, literary, and ethical curriculum that Emily Dickinson undertook at Amherst Academy[24] and was thus Mary Lyon's colleague. His account of religious instruction at Lyon's seminary tells us much about the role organized religion played in the poet's early life. Although education at the school included training in vocal music, linear and perspective drawing, and ways to appreciate *Paradise Lost*, Lyon's principal purpose was, in her own words, to instruct "candidates for eternity."[25] The *Memoir* records:

> [Religion] was considered the most important object for which the institution was founded; and, therefore, everything else was held as subordinate to this. But such views did not make it necessary, save in peculiar exigencies, to interfere with the regular literary exercises . . . [Yet] the teachers really regarded religion, and especially personal piety, as of more consequence, a thousand times, than everything else . . . [To] advance religion was the grand ultimate object of all literary efforts, and, indeed, of every action.[26]

These words alone provide some justification for the young Emily's relief when she left Mary Lyon's. They also help to explain why she felt so isolated among her group of friends, fervently declaring for Christ at the Sabbath revivalist meetings there. In 1848 as in 1882, Emily preferred the sermons of Orpheus: "it is hard for me to give up the world," she tells Abiah Root, though by "the world" she means fragrance, spring flowers, mystery stories, romances—and poetry (L 1.67, 66). Though Dickinson held out against the evangelistic code of the seminary, however, she learned there to set the quest for eternal life above all other ends.

To Emerson, the vital force that forms "the poetry of the landscape" and of art was supplied by God.[27] To Wordsworth, "Our destiny, our nature, and our home / Is with infinitude, and only there" (*The Prelude*, 6.538–539). The slow growth and "seed-time" of the soul was for them, as for Dickinson in poem 483, dependent on God's "Nature." Dickinson's poem about harvest, "A Solemn thing within the Soul," metaphorically associates outer with inner landscapes, the developing soul with the maturing artist, her inspirational powers with Nature and Nature's God—and all, with the process that fascicle 22 stresses and that Wordsworth called "the growth of the poet's mind."

Emily Dickinson's vision of God was tortured. On one hand, his life was rare (338), and his paradise held infinite beauties for those who achieved it. On the other hand, he could be made of flint (1076). He stole away the looks and lives of all those one loved. She usually discriminates affection for the suffering, gallant Jesus from reservations about Jehovah. Like the painter Thomas Cole, she was unfavorably impressed by the Old Testament God who kept Moses from the Promised Land;[28] by the "Mastiff" who bullied Abraham into agreeing to kill his own son Isaac (1317). So she could not support any sweeping attribution to God of every benefit. She was "shrewd with" and wary of him (L 1.353, 193). Still her allusions to eternity, immortality, and infinity associate these abstractions with the godhead, which the majestic poem 871 identifies as the source of all power and light:

> The Sun and Moon must make their haste –
> The Stars express around
> For in the Zones of Paradise
> The Lord alone is burned –
>
> His Eye, it is the East and West –
> The North and South when He
> Do concentrate His Countenance
> Like Glow Worms, flee away –

Oh Poor and Far –
Oh Hindered Eye
That hunted for the Day –
The Lord a Candle entertains
Entirely for Thee –

In this splendid lyric, nature is symbolized by the agencies of light in this world—the sun, the moon, the stars—but they are urged to make haste, to be "express" in enjoying their power, since in the next world only the light of God burns. In the "Eye" of that light, the varied lights of the four poles fade. At last (in words that show trust in this awful divine power) the poem portrays God as a self-sacrificing host: he burns himself in paradise to entertain the poor, the hindered, and those far from him who have hunted for him in this life.

Underlying this poem is the trope of blindness and sight, darkness and light, which Paul establishes in 2 Corinthians and to which I have referred earlier in treating Dickinson's obsession with faces: "But we all, with open face beholding as in a glass the glory of the Lord, are changed into the same image from glory to glory, even as by the Spirit of the Lord (3:18). In one poem, "Like Eyes that looked on Wastes" (458), Dickinson described the despair of gazing into another face that mirrored her own misery. Her poetry often concerns itself with beholding "as in a glass" an image of fear or awe: a double, "Ourself behind Ourself concealed" (670). But, like the convinced Christian that she was not, Dickinson also imagined beholding God's face and molding her own as his reflection. In poem 871, the font of all light, actual and intellectual, is the Lord; though Dickinson's "Divinity dwells under seal" (662), his light goes abroad, tinting earth with "deep Eternity" (76).

4

There was a significant nineteenth-century American iconographic model for what Emily Dickinson herself considered the voyage of the soul on the seas of life and eternity. That was Thomas Cole's series of landscapes called *The Voyage of Life* (plates 2–5). It was commissioned in 1840 for a meditation room in the house of the New York banker, Luman Reed. (Finished in 1840, it is now in the Munson-Williams-Proctor Institute, Utica, New York.) Exhibited at the National Academy of Design in New York in 1840, it was so quickly and widely copied in steel engravings that Cole was encouraged to paint a replica (1842).

The second series was commissioned by Samuel Ward. His famous daughter Julia Ward Howe would remember that her father (who lost his wife in childbirth) intended it for the deprived Julia as a formative religious text. The series toured Boston and Philadelphia in 1843–44 and was, in turn, widely copied. (This version of *The Voyage of Life* is now in the National Gallery of Art.) More than 100,000 people queued to view the original *Voyage* when it was exhibited as a memorial to Cole on his death in 1848. The last panel, *Old Age,* with its vision of the human soul about to enter eternity, was thought to reveal Cole's firm Christian faith. What the crowds came to see, however, were the originals of pictures that had been turned out in copies by the "tens of thousands" in the 1840s.[29] Not only in parish houses but in homes, schools, hospitals, and even hotels and restaurants, Cole's *Voyage* was installed for the moral edification of the public. The paintings are exquisitely refined in color and draftsmanship, but that was often ignored. Throughout the nineteenth century, the series sometimes served as the metaphor of a dull devotional work. As late as 1905, Edith Wharton's aesthetic heroine in *The House of Mirth* summarizes "dinginess" as a house where engravings of Cole's *Voyage of Life* hang on the drawing-room walls.

Emily Dickinson no doubt saw copies of the *Voyage,* in one or the other version. The first version, illustrated in this book, is slightly more romantic and passionate in conception; for this reason and others[30] I have designated it as the painterly subtext for some of her own art. Dickinson acknowledged her identification with Cole in a note to Susan Dickinson in 1859. Though it is meant to be humorous—a joke about her skill in drawing—the note shows that, for her, "Cole" was synonymous with nature painters. She sent Sue a picture scribbled on a woodcut from the *New England Primer,* saying

> My "position"!
> Cole.

> P.S. Lest you misapprehend, the unfortunate insect upon the left is Myself, while the Reptile upon the *right* is my more immediate friends, and connections.
>
> As ever,
> Cole (L 2.359–360)

Since she alludes to a reptile and since she would also use the phrase "Expulsion from Eden,"[31] Dickinson may have thought of Cole because she had seen the popular *Expulsion from the Garden of Eden,* which was also widely copied in New England. By 1859 the art of Thomas Cole represented for most Americans the height of moral landscape, nature being translated into what he considered a new paradise. Barton Levi St. Armand mentions Cole (though not Dickinson's adoption of his name) in his valuable *Emily Dickinson and Her Culture*. He concludes that "the spirit of such series as . . . *The Voyage of Life* . . . lived on in the very personal and much more elaborate correspondences that Dickinson made of her passion of the mystic day."[32] However, not only the spirit but also the iconography of the *Voyage* is alluded to in Dickinson's work. Moreover, Cole's own imagery is more complex than St. Armand implies.

Since 1980 (after hearing a set of lectures on *The Voyage of Life* and American education at the National Gallery in Washington) I have thought it likely that Emily Dickinson saw engravings of the *Voyage* during her sojourn at Mary Lyon's seminary in 1847–48, when Cole's influence on the American public was at its height. In 1843 there was an exhibition of the second *Voyage* at Harding's Gallery, Boston, sponsored by the Boston Artists' Association. Like another at Clinton Hall in New York City (1843–44), it once again resulted in the sale of thousands of copies, especially to churches and schools. So established was Cole's *Voyage* as a metaphor of life's journey that there were even caricatures and burlesques of it throughout the 1850s and 1860s. If Emily Dickinson read the family's copy of *Harper's* for December 1859, she would have encountered "Spriggins's Voyage of Life" (fig. 2) a cartoon depicting the alcoholic hero from his "launch[ing]" to his "Wreck" and Death's "Destruction of the Hulk." The cartoon assumed the function of a cautionary tale, and the lyrical beauty of Cole's paintings was scarcely suggested by its buffoonery. But the cradle with "Sun Rise" around it; the panel entitled "Manhood—The Marriage"; "Low Tide on the Rocks"; and "Sun Set" follow the course of Cole's series. "Spriggins's Voyage of Life" was yet another indication of Cole's influence, even after his death. William Cullen Bryant's sonnet "To Cole, the Painter, Departing for Europe" is checked on the table of contents in Susan Dickinson's copy of Bryant's *Poems* (1849); the page on which it appears is folded over. Bryant's sonnet, written before Cole's trip to England in 1839, begged him to be faithful to the wild image of America; it was further proof of Cole's symbolic importance as an American artist and was doubtless familiar to Emily Dickinson.

We cannot know for certain, but in her religious fervor Mary Lyon may have hung on the seminary walls copies of Cole's series, wherein platonic highmindedness, Christian faith, and romantic delight in nature were fused in an admirable text for her pupils. Though Dickinson never says she saw *The Voyage of Life,* it was this series that was most identified with Cole. Moreover, Cole's name was especially famous in New England: one of his most influential paintings, *View from Mt. Holyoke, Northampton, Mass., after a Thunderstorm—or The Ox-Bow* (1836)—was a study of the sublime in a landscape well known to Connecticut River Valley dwellers like Mary Lyon or Emily Dickinson. Like the *Voyage* paintings, it revealed Cole's pious perception of the divine in American scenery, which led him to say, "We are still in Eden."[33] (Such a perception of course was also Emily Dickinson's. She liked to write of her home and garden that they were a new Eden; she did so from girlhood until death.[34])

In *The Ox-Bow* Cole included himself as painter, reverent amid the stillness following a storm. This was an act suggestive of both the poetic and the painterly traditions on which Cole chiefly drew. He was well acquainted with the way artists included themselves in their canvases, for reasons ranging from devotion to contempt for the subject. Salvator Rosa and Claude (Lorrain), Cole's masters in the landscape tradition, improvised a kinetic and highly personal relationship between their landscapes charged with light and the human beings within them. Furthermore, "in nineteenth century aesthetics, [it was] assumed that new compositions would often include references to earlier works by other artists."[35] Allusions on Cole's part to Rosa, Claude, or Domenichino; by his student Frederic Church to Cole; and, finally, by Dickinson to Cole would have been thought both learned and natural.

A young Emily Dickinson might have inferred from either the *Voyage* series or *The Ox-Bow* the special relation between nature, the artist, and eternity in which Cole devoutly believed. Like his depiction of a solitary viewer—Wordsworth?—in the painting *Tintern Abbey* (ca. 1836), Cole's representation of himself in *The Ox-Bow* was a celebratory act. It suggested the disclosure of divine secrets through nature and meditation. In the same way, Dickinson's assertive, magisterial speaker learns "The Soul's distinct connection / With immortality" by studying "Lightning on a Landscape" (974) and remarks, "sudden intimacies with Immortality, are expanse – not Peace – as Lightning at our feet, instills a foreign Landscape" (L 3.661).

Cole had been dead eleven years when Emily Dickinson assumed his name in writing to Sue in 1859. Yet his fame was undimmed, in part because his student Frederic Church and his friend Asher Durand were

2. "Spriggins's Voyage of Life." This cartoon from *Harper's* (December 1859)
indicates the fame of Cole's series.

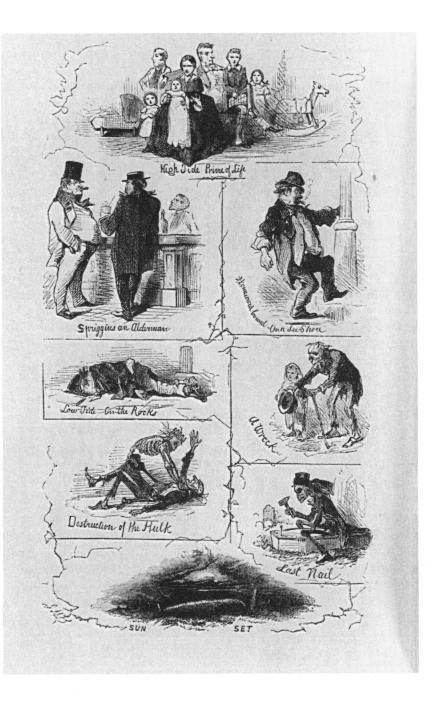

keeping his memory vivid, both with painterly tributes (Church's *Ox-Bow (after Thomas Cole)*, 1844–1846) and by espousing Cole's philosophy that a painting becomes great by revealing God's glory in his creation. Dickinson's knowledge of Cole's work could only have been enriched as Susan and (particularly) Austin Dickinson developed an interest in acquiring paintings by Cole's successors.[36]

All of Cole's paintings would probably have appealed to Emily Dickinson since all in various ways are designed to demonstrate the belief that "the 'Supernatural' [is] only the Natural, disclosed" (L 2.424). *The Voyage of Life* is an allegory on that favorite evangelical topic of the Victorians, a Christian's progress through this world to the next. Combining so many motifs and images for which Dickinson shows preference, the *Voyage* had to have special appeal for her. Cole provided an explanatory gloss for the four paintings of the *Voyage,* but this would not be needed by a viewer acquainted even in general terms with Genesis. Its narrative of the expulsion from Eden, sin and suffering through pride and ambition, trial by the waters of the flood, and God's covenant with humankind signaled by attending angels was well known to Victorian readers. The sequence was thought to be repeated in every human life; and, as the myth passed into the general language and iconography of western culture, almost everyone acknowledged the image of life as a river on which one's boat or soul sailed serenely or dangerously until death. (As Dickinson said, "the sea is ordained," so that it was important to have courage in "Life's Mysterious Boat" [L 3.709, 760].) For the viewer who was also a believer, the *Voyage* would be particularly comforting, with its angels descending from God to welcome the voyager at journey's end.

The first painting in the *Voyage* is called *Childhood,* the first of four stages in the human career. It depicts a tiny skiff, its golden prow supporting a carven angel holding an hourglass, which issues from a cave (a platonic archetype) into a lambent landscape. On the gentle, glassy river there are islands of water lilies (flowers that open at dawn) and primroses. On its banks receding into dim stretches that ultimately blend with the sky, more passionately colored red flowers mingle with ivies and ferns to suggest awakening. In the skiff itself an infant sits up in excitement, arms out, and behind him we see the protective figure of a guardian angel as pilot.

Youth, the second painting and the most copied (as might be expected in an age that valued adventure and optimism), discloses a changed landscape. The infant is now a boy who takes the boat's rudder himself and—as the viewer ought to note with alarm—has his back to the guardian angel, who waves to his departing figure from the shore. The vegetation in the painting is exotic, palms and eucalyptus blending with what appear to be maples and elms in a mixture of eastern and western trees, suggesting both the Garden of Eden and the American landscape. The youth's arm, aloft in a gesture of hope and enthusiasm, imitates the upheld arms of the angel-image carrying the still full hourglass. In the distance, like a mirage, floats a Moorish castle, and the river winds through a lovely passage that—the youth might see if he turned his head in the angel's direction—opens, however, into a rocky sea at the far right of the painting.

In the third of the series, *Manhood,* Cole exercises his mastery of the techniques of painting *terribilità,* the "timeless combat between heaven and hell or light and darkness."[37] In this sort of dramatic painting, the Hudson River School and many of the Luminists sought to excel. Cole explained what he intended to portray here:

The swollen stream rushes furiously down a dark ravine, whirling and foaming in its wild career, and speeding toward the Ocean, which is dimly seen through the mist and falling rain. The boat is there, plunging amid the turbulent waters. The Voyager is now a man of middle age: the helm of the boat is gone, and he looks imploringly toward heaven, as if heaven's aid alone could save him from the perils that surround him. The Guardian Spirit calmly sits in the clouds, watching with an air of solicitude the affrighted Voyager. Demon forms are hovering in the air.[38]

In his misery the man clasps his hands, and the hourglass is almost empty.

The series completes its mission as a landscape of exalted moral purpose with *Old Age.* Light in varying gradations of strength assumes great significance here. In *Manhood* demon faces in the sky recall Christ's allusion in Luke 22:53 to the "hour, and the power of darkness," evil. Conversely, the light coursing from heaven in *Old Age* is the "light [that] shineth in darkness," the "true Light, which lighteth every man that cometh into the world" (John 1:5, 9). The voyager, now an old man in a boat from which the masthead has been broken away, holds open his arms in wonder before angels descending from the sky, God's throne. In *Childhood* and *Manhood* his figure faced east, to the right of the painting; that is, it faced away from the opening heavens of *Old Age.* Now the placement of the voyager's figure, gazing left, makes clear that the false illusion of *Youth*'s castle in the sky is to be supplanted by the true palace of the Lord in paradise. The bright figure of the guardian angel again takes charge. He pilots the old voyager away from the grim, barren rocks of life toward the welcoming rays of heaven. Other angels descend to the old man from above, so that he can mount—in Dickinson's words—"By routes of ecstasy / To Evening's Sea," paradise (L 3.712). Cole's *Old Age* was, then, a lambent vision of the transitus.

The common concerns and images of Cole's *Voyage* and many Dickinson poems about life's voyage reflect a common cultural heritage. Art historians variously attribute the sources of Cole's series. Matthew Baigell writes:

> The immediate source for [*The Voyage of Life*] might have been a sermon by the Reverend Reginald Steber [1783–1826], its central allegory referring to "life [which] bears us on like the stream of a mighty river." In addition, Cole drew on the heritage of religious dissent in England and America, best epitomized by John Bunyan's *Pilgrim's Progress,* one of the most popular books of the nineteenth century. Cole also used several images derived from popular emblem books . . . a rare instance of an important artist of the period using popular, rather than fine, art sources for a major work.[39]

It is true that Bunyan's "metaphors / To set forth truth" include a wilderness, a tree of life, a pleasant river, and finally a celestial gate to a heaven full of seraphim and cherubim. But the more precise imagery of Cole's *Voyage* is not in Bunyan. Cole himself wrote a long poetic version of the *Voyage* which he finished at Catskill, New York, in 1844. Prolix, Miltonic in fervor if not in art,[40] it is also indebted for some phrases to Wordsworth, whom Cole regarded as his chief teacher. But Cole's poem largely describes the voyager's feelings rather than the scenes and events of the voyage. Those are, remarkably, to be found in Wordsworth's *The Prelude.* That great poem, however, was not published until after Wordsworth's death in 1850, ten years after Cole finished his series. Still Cole seems to have been familiar with the poem.

Like other American painters seeking education abroad, Cole returned to England (his birthplace) in 1829, remaining there until 1832. Lionized by the London literati as that rare species, an American painter-bard, he was befriended by Samuel Taylor Coleridge and Thomas De Quincey. It is possible that he met Wordsworth; his painting *Tintern Abbey* (1836) was later done in homage to him. The evenings he spent with Coleridge may have included some conversation about Wordsworth. Possibly Coleridge recited some parts of *The Prelude* for Cole; he was often known to read aloud from Wordsworth's manuscript-in-progress.

In any event, many lines in *The Prelude* bear reference to *The Voyage of Life.* There is, for instance, Wordsworth's famous account in book 1 ("Childhood and School-Time") of taking a skiff from within a rocky cave upon a shining lake that was surrounded by a craggy ridge that gave upon gray sky (lines 375, 398, 400). There is his allusion in book 4 to a sense that "a blessed Spirit / Or Angel" (228–229) within himself directed his actions, which in youth were filled with sensations of "beauty . . . love / Enthusiastic," delight and joy (245, 246). And he compares himself to

> one who hangs down-bending from the side
> Of a slow-moving Boat, upon the breast
> Of a still water, solacing himself
> With such discoveries as his eye can make (247–250)

These are at first "weeds, fishes, flowers, / Grots, pebbles, roots of trees" (261–263) as in Cole's *Childhood,* which then become "vanities" as in Cole's *Youth.* Wordsworth's adventurer "in Araby, Romances, Legends" (521) resembles the boy gazing in Cole's painting at the Moorish mirage; and Wordsworth's "blasts of water-falls," "black drizzling crags," and "the raving stream" (558, 563, 565) call to mind Cole's iconography in *Manhood.* There are many other such parallels, but Wordsworth's closing summary of his voyage could easily serve as a description of Cole's:

> we have traced the stream
> From darkness, and the very place of birth
> In its blind cavern, whence is faintly heard
> The sound of waters; follow'd it to light
> And open day, accompanied its course
> Among the ways of Nature, afterwards
> Lost sight of it bewilder'd and engulph'd,
> Then given it greeting, as it rose once more
> With strength, reflecting in its solemn breast
> The works of man and face of human life,
> And lastly, from its progress have we drawn
> The feeling of life endless, the great thought
> By which we live, Infinity and God. (13.172–184)

Like Cole's vision of the life voyage, Wordsworth's is grave, his lines composing a quiet fugue that ends on Emily Dickinson's favorite theme, Infinity. Though her mature style is very different from his, we know that Dickinson read Wordsworth. Her letters quote the "Elegaic Stanzas" and "We Are Seven" (L 2.449, 510; 1.215), and for years she has been thought "well qualified as a potential disciple of Coleridge, Wordsworth, and the Romantic Movement."[41] To her have also been attributed a Victorian sensibility, a metaphysical mind, and a preference for medieval conceits, each of which may be documented by examples from the poems.[42] Her vision and style are unique and wholly recognizable, as rhetorical studies show,[43] but there are many instances of quotation and allusion in Dickinson. Some texts—*Jane Eyre, Aurora Leigh, Antony and Cleopatra* (and, as we have seen, Revelation and 1 and 2 Corinthians)—are vital to an informed understanding of her art.

The fact is that Emily Dickinson experienced her books—"these Kinsmen of the Shelf" (604)—as if their "countenances" made up another world on whose lineaments and accents she could draw. Like many other painters and writers, she is a highly instructed artist whose incorporation in her works of narrative and stylistic elements from the works of others does not reflect "massive rummaging"[44] but a cultivated and scholarly imagination. Literature and art, and to a lesser extent music, were to her living realities: an ethereal sky reminds her of Vaughan (L 3.669); Mrs. Sweetser's crepes recall Don Quixote (L 2.506); heaven, to one for whom food often signified love, is "Da Vinci's Supper" (L 2.452); God is the "perfect Mozart" (503). She yearned to join the company of living artists and dreamed that her sister-in-law (her surrogate in adventure) met Tennyson at the bookseller's, Ticknor and Fields. So she would not have overlooked the major work of her great contemporary, Wordsworth. That helped to form the imagination of Emerson; more relevantly (because of the weight of Dickinson's personal feeling for a sister artist), Wordsworth influenced Emily Brontë. It is most likely that Dickinson's preoccupation with the visionary gleam of eternity in time, with solitude, and with morning as a fresh contemplative hour for artistic reverie and composition was strengthened by reading *The Prelude*.

Evidence from the poems and letters, however, indicates that it was *The Voyage of Life* upon which Dickinson drew directly in creating a (Wordsworthian) narrative about human progress through time to immortality. Dickinsonians may recognize in Cole's paintings certain images that recall hers. There is, first of all, the central image of the boat;

there are the guardian angel and the youth, both of whom figure in Dickinson's oeuvre; there are the tempests, cliffs, and falls of mankind, portrayed as afflicting voyagers who sail "Down Time's quaint stream" (1656); the ascending angels in poem 461 who conduct her to eternity, "a Child no more," recall the angels of Cole's *Old Age*. Finally, the masculine figure of the youth, embarking on a dramatic journey, is an image that may help to explain Dickinson's frequent references to herself as a boy. (A woman's journey was of lesser consequence, at least in Victorian iconography, it seems. Dickinson's friend Josiah Holland wrote the novel *Miss Gilbert's Career* in which, patterned perhaps on the strong Sue Gilbert, the frustrated heroine cries, "I wish to God I were a man!")

Into the very first fascicle, Emily Dickinson copied two poems whose iconography suggests Cole's. The first is poem 30, "Adrift! A little boat adrift!" and the second, copied with three poems intervening, is "On this wondrous sea / Sailing silently" (4). Johnson hypothesizes that the first was written about 1858, near the time Dickinson signed herself with the painter's name:

> Adrift! A little boat adrift!
> And night is coming down!
> Will *no* one guide a little boat
> Unto the nearest town?
>
> So Sailors say – on yesterday –
> Just as the dusk was brown
> One little boat gave up its strife
> And gurgled down and down.
>
> So angels say – on yesterday –
> Just as the dawn was red
> One little boat – o'erspent with gales –
> Retrimmed it's masts – redecked it's sails –
> And shot – exultant on!

This unaccomplished poem, in the purposely naive style that Dickinson never entirely dropped and that she seems to have associated with charm and new-minted sincerity, describes a shipwreck, a subject always of interest to her. Her many wrecks or ships in distress do not only imply her view of life as tragic; they place her in an age whose thinking was shaped by the paintings of Turner and the aesthetics of Ruskin, to whom a wrecked ship was quintessentially sublime. The little boat, personification of the soul, might have its antecedent elsewhere than in

Cole's series, but other aspects of the poem—the brown dusk, the raining down of night, the red dawn, the angels—appear in *Manhood* and *Old Age*. The counterpoint established between the sailors who see only shipwreck and the angels who recognize that it leads to eternal life on another sea is implicit in Cole.

Poem 4 is even more allusive:

> On this wondrous sea
> Sailing silently
> Ho! Pilot, ho!
>
> Knowest thou the shore
> Where no breakers roar –
> Where the storm is oer?
>
> In the peaceful west
> Many the sails at rest –
> The anchors fast –
> Thither I pilot *thee* –
> Land Ho! Eternity!
> Ashore at last!

Here the first two stanzas seem to pose the desperate question of an endangered voyager like Cole's in *Manhood,* while the last is the answer of a speaker like the angel pilot, who returns to guide the voyager's skiff in *Old Age*. The poem is an immature effort, but it shows Dickinson working with key images: the seas of life and eternity, the storm and shore, the west (as opposed to east). These images were probably etched in her imagination by *The Voyage of Life*. She would eventually employ them with authority in the Master letters and poems.

Other youthful efforts continue this pattern. Fascicle 3 contains both poems 52 and 94. Poem 52 declares that Dickinson's concern is with her soul's progress:

> Whether my bark went down at sea –
> Whether she met with gales –
> Whether to isles enchanted
> She bent her docile sails –

and whether it had found the "mystic mooring" that Cole's voyager desires (and that Dickinson eventually describes in later poems like "Wild Nights"). Poem 94 depicts ubiquitous angels who guide human beings both in the morning and "when the sun is hottest," protecting both bud and flower. Dickinson's speaker meets such an angel in 231 (fascicle 10), forsakes her schoolmates for him, and laments his return to God "at the setting sun." In fascicle 6, angels see "a tattered heart" in the "Ebbing Day" that "Flowed silver to the West," "Intent upon the vision / Of latitudes unknown":

> Tenderly [they] took it up from toil
> And carried it to God –
> . . . . .
> There – gathered from the gales –
> Do the blue havens by the hand
> Lead the wandering Sails (78)

Other poems, such as "Will there really be a 'Morning'?" (101), use Cole's imagery of mountains, water lilies, exotic countries, and envision the speaker as a Bunyanesque voyager from this world to the next:

> Please to tell a little Pilgrim
> Where the place called "Morning" lies!

A zealous Christian (who inspired in his student, Frederic Church, a passion for religion as well as art), Thomas Cole attempted to ennoble landscape painting by associating it with faith. The early *Expulsion from the Garden of Eden* (ca. 1827–28), like *The Pilgrim of the Cross (The Vision)* (ca. 1846–47), proclaimed his belief that earthly life was essentially a struggle to attain purity of spirit and a preparation for life after death. Even in his use of chiaroscuro and gradations of light and dark, Cole meant to describe the battle between good and evil in the human soul. *The Voyage of Life* was his most vital and poignant moral landscape. *Childhood* and *Old Age* made clear his conception of grace, emblematized by the protective guardian angel. "The angel begins in the morning in every human life," Emily Dickinson wrote to Maria Whitney (L 3.777). Speaking in "No Man can compass a Despair" of a traveler, she calls "His ignorance – the Angel / That pilot Him along" (477). And she may have been remembering *Youth* (with its lesson on the imprudence of forsaking one's angel) when she wrote, possibly in 1864,

> Never to pass the Angel
> With a glance and a Bow
> Till I am firm in Heaven
> Is my intention now (895)

Cole, who like Wordsworth and Emerson preached the virtues of silence, solitude, even isolation to aspiring artists, found the best emblem of eternity to be the wide stillness of the sky at morning. In his *Voyage* paintings, that grand and peaceful light is twinned in *Childhood* and *Old Age* when the dawn of life is echoed by the dawn of eternal life. Dickinson would make that association too, around 1884:

> Morning that comes but once,
> Considers coming twice –
> Two Dawns upon a single Morn,
> Make Life a sudden price. (1610)

But in her depiction of the landscape of the human mind and heart in the poems and letters of the 1860s and 1870s, Dickinson incorporated the emblems of sea, sky, mountains, shores, angels, and the solitary artistic "eye" which show her to be, herself, one of the ablest iconographers of major nineteenth-century themes.

5

Emily Dickinson was probably referring to *Modern Painters* in listing "Mr Ruskin" as favorite reading in her letter to Higginson on April 25, 1862 (L 2.404). That book, with its celebration of the art of Joseph Mallord William Turner, would have acquainted her with the continued importance in the 1860s of Edmund Burke's *Philosophical Inquiry into the Origin of Our Ideas of the Sublime and Beautiful* (1756). Like the art of Turner himself, Burke's aesthetic had a great influence on the painters of Dickinson's time. Cole's *Expulsion from the Garden of Eden* (plate 8), for example, illustrates Burke's concept of the beautiful in the right half of the painting: Eden's waterfall, fair gardens, and lush trees suggest the delicacy and grace Burke associated with the principle of beauty, founded on pleasure. The left side of the canvas, however, depicts Burke's principle of the sublime, founded on what he called "terror" and "the idea of bodily pain . . . labour, anguish, torment."[45] There, bent against a storm that has blasted the trees and turned the skies into whirlpools of murky light, Adam and Eve creep away from the cavelike entrance to Eden, doomed now to exile and suffering.

In Dickinson's continual recourse to the image of Eden, she often makes use of Burke's aesthetic alternatives. Her landscape poems about sunrise and sunset, storm and snowfall, record moments of sublimity or beauty, as in some contemporaneous paintings of the Hudson River

School. Burke's pages on the sublime include the precept that "Infinity has a tendency to fill the mind with that sort of delightful horror, which is the most genuine effect and truest test of the sublime."[46] Dickinson's many poems about the transitus were—when their mood and imagery were solemn—exercises in sublimity.

A set of related Dickinsonian themes reveals both her powerful originality and the positioning of her art in its time. Burke had called "privation" a sublime idea: "all *general* privations are great, because they are all terrible; *Vacuity, Darkness, Solitude,* and *Silence.*"[47] Emily Dickinson, who could say sweepingly, "A loss of something ever felt I," chose loss as one of her central themes; she saw herself like Adam (or Milton's Satan, whom she admired) "The only Prince cast out" (959). But solitude and silence and emptiness were also important themes. In most of her poetry about morning, they are developed in harmony with Burke's concept of the beautiful. A considerable portion of Dickinson's poems, however, is devoted to examining not only the sublime subjects but the "soul admitted to itself / Finite Infinity" (1695). That theme was usually seen to be "terrible." Dickinson speaks of the *soul* or *souls* 141 times in the poems. She addresses her own soul; has funerals in her soul; tells her soul to sing when it is deserted; feels dread like a spur on her soul; finds that her soul has its own art. Seven poems begin as declarative sentences about "The Soul," which is conceived as the quintessential self or, as in Emerson, the inner spark attuned to the divine. Like the brain (considered 26 times in the poems) or the mind (79 times), the soul is subjected to careful study as Dickinson analyzes the relationship between herself and all external powers.

Although Dickinson wrote poems in which, through inspiration or reverie, she felt herself at one with the creator, she also experienced fearful moments when she was reduced to "A Speck upon a Ball," who

> Went out upon Circumference –
> Beyond the Dip of Bell – (378)

This was a voyage into space during which, she says, "I touched the Universe – / And back it slid – and I alone." In these surreal poems, she uses visual and auditory techniques that emphasize the struggle, and usually the failure, to grasp the infinite in the real. The solitary soul, a speck upon the ball or globe, moves outward "upon Circumference," beyond sound (everything earthly and communicative); yet it is forced to return, to come back to her isolation in the finite. Dickinson always conceives a connection, however diffuse, between the soul and the celestial powers. Describing a "Funeral, in my Brain"—the death of joy or a mental breakdown akin to losing consciousness—she hears the heavens as a bell in her brain ("Ear") while "I, and Silence"—her sanity—are "wrecked." Finally she "Finish[es] knowing" (280). These efforts made by the soul to understand its place in the universe are related to the poems of the transitus. Often the sublimity of the effort results in suspended consciousness or despair.

Emily Dickinson's willingness to write about "the Soul" may have been prepared by her knowledge of the sermons of Jonathan Edwards or the essays of Emerson. In both, the comprehensive rational, volitional, and emotional faculties of the human being are expressed by that term; most important, though, "the Soul" underscores the relation of the human spirit to God. Thus, when Dickinson writes

> The Soul selects her own Society –
> Then – shuts the Door –
> To her divine Majority –
> Present no more –

she is reporting on an election of suitable fellowship, made by that quintessential spark, the anima, composed in God's image and therefore divine. This best known of her poems about the soul seems to crystallize her personal attitude to society, the world outside the self. Readings of this poem have usually stressed the adamant fastidiousness and exclusivity of the speaker; she is made out to be the archetypical cool Puritan. It is important, however, to note the *kind* of society the Soul rejects here; she will not receive the potentates of time and this world, having chosen instead the One—a private lover/friend/Christ or Christ figure—who represents the sum of value, the mystical number 1:

> Unmoved – she notes the Chariots – pausing
> At her low Gate –
> Unmoved – an Emperor be kneeling
> Upon her Mat –
>
> I've known her – from an ample nation –
> Choose One –
> Then – close the Valves of her attention –
> Like Stone – (303)

The heart has valves, and they are turned to stone against all but the beloved. The Soul's basic humility, not her pride, is emphasized; for her gate, the entrance to her inmost nature, is "low" and the mat before it is not the crimson or purple rug that might be appointed to receive an emperor. Nevertheless, this gate, however modest, is related to the gate of heaven that Jacob recognizes as leading to the house of God in Genesis 18:17; and it is the same gate that Dickinson will write of to Master in the first of her three famous letters to him. (Thus she exults in her choice of such a lover by saying, "Indeed it is God's house – and these are gates of Heaven": her life has been made heavenly by having admitted him at her gate [L 2.333].)

"Society" is, then, nearly an ironic word in the poem. For Dickinson's speaker has selected the sweet society of her godly beloved rather than the worldly company of persons in chariots, to whom she refers elsewhere as "cosmopolites." Those persons travel continually, expect hospitality, and are promiscuous in their demands for love and favor. To them, doors must continually be opened:

> Cosmopolites without a plea
> Alight in every Land
> The compliments of Paradise
> From those within my Hand
>
> Their dappled Journey to themselves
> A compensation fair
> Knock and it shall be opened
> Is their Theology (1589).

Written on the back of a draft of a note to Sue, about to go on a journey, poem 1589 is in a group of poems related both to the theme of the soul and to the theme of open and shut doors. Each theme is developed to explore the idea of supernatural grace in accord with the message of Christ's words in Matthew 7:7, "Ask, and it shall be given you; seek, and ye shall find; knock, and it shall be opened unto you." The cosmopolites ask admission by alighting everywhere; but they are too arrogant to plead, as God expects. Instead, they are so used to sycophancy that they expect the "compliment of Paradise." "Dappled" is probably related to "spangled," the adjective Dickinson may be using for Sue as the victor of the "Spangled Gown" in poem 325. To such persons, the journey is itself a compensation; they have not understood the message of Matthew's Christ that the manner of arrival must be prized above the journey itself. It is important to get inside, to "shut the Door" (of heaven or her own room), as Dickinson says in 303, "Because strait is the gate, and narrow is the way, which leadeth unto life, and few there be that find it" (Matthew 7:14).

Underlying the conceit of the open and closed doors of the soul, of the open or shut gate, there is usually a sexual as well as a religious and ethical reality. The issue of choice extends to both human and divine love, so ample is Dickinson's "compound vision." They are frequently related, and her human lovers are tested by their ability to vie with God in rewarding her. The narrow gate, open to but one, is a brilliantly erotic and yet maidenly and even Puritan image. Dickinson's poems about the soul, however, address the question of moral conduct (including sexuality) in a way that also relates it to artistic endeavor. She seems to be describing artistic inspiration as well as grace:

> The Soul should always stand ajar
> That if the Heaven inquire
> He will not be obliged to wait
> Or shy of troubling Her
>
> Depart, before the Host have slid
> The Bolt unto the Door –
> To search for the accomplished Guest,
> Her Visitor, no more – (1055)

Here the poet acknowledges that a door "ajar"—still maintaining privacy but slightly open—is necessary if "the accomplished Guest" or visitor from heaven is to find her. That he is "accomplished" suggests his kinship with the hosts "Who baffle Key" (298) and are her muses. Again, this poem about the soul has scriptural overtones; in Isaiah 60:11–13, for example, the people of Israel are given an order, "Thy gates shall be open continually [so that] the glory of Lebanon shall come unto thee." And they are told, "Open ye the gates, that the righteous nation which keepeth the truth may enter in" (26:2). These solemn biblical echoes are, of course, wittily complicated by Dickinson's light hand: she imagines her God as shy of her.

The upright character of the speaker Dickinson so often empowers appears in most of her poetry about the soul. Like some of her poems about a shattered brain or the torture of the mind that "lives on the Heart" (1355), many of her lyrics characterizing the soul reveal a sensibility acutely familiar with guilt and the terrors of self-punishment:

> The Soul unto itself
> Is an imperial friend –
> Or the most agonizing Spy –
> An Enemy – could send –

Secure against it's own –
No treason it can fear –
Itself – it's Sovereign – of itself
The Soul should stand in Awe – (683)

Poems such as this one construct an adjoining house to the "house of possibility": the home of the soul that is secure against insurrection and attack when it is honest. The emperor, forbidden access in "The Soul selects her own Society," now resides within the Soul when she is faithful to her moral convictions. Thus Dickinson redirects her metaphor of the Kingdom and the imperial Sovereignty, establishing both as attributes of the speaker when she resists the temptation to treason. Treason would come from violating one's integrity. Dickinson found lying or dissembling, for example, among the worst of sins; in many texts she says so, perhaps most winningly in an affectionate note to her niece Martha in 1884:

> Be true to yourself, Mattie, and "Honor and Immortality" – although the first will do – the last is only inferential, and I shall be prouder of you than I am, which would be unbecoming – (L 3.845)

This piece of advice was sent by the same aunt who also told Martha, "Be sure to live in vain."[48] Thus met in Emily Dickinson two paradoxical and productive currents, the passion for intellectual honesty and the passion for romance.

Finally it was, of course, the soul that would undertake the eternal passage, not the body. Around 1864 Dickinson contemplated the awful fact of the endlessness of selfhood. The soul could never escape its "polar privacy" like a "solitude of space" (1695), for such privacy would travel as a companion of the Soul as it attempted translation to another world:

This Consciousness that is aware
Of Neighbors and the Sun
Will be the one aware of Death
And that itself alone

Is traversing the interval
Experience between
And most profound experiment
Appointed unto Men –

How adequate unto itself
It's properties shall be

Itself unto itself and none
Shall make discovery.

Adventure most unto itself
The Soul condemned to be –
Attended by a single Hound
It's own identity. (822)

Once again the poet meditates on the central mystery of her house of art: the persona she will be as she travels into the infinite, alone. With dignified perplexity, the first three lines set out an incredible thought, that the same mind which meets ordinary experience must ultimately confront death. She realizes that she will need "properties" to withstand such a test; yet it is also an adventure. Just as "Belief is unconsciously to most of us Ourselves – an Untried Experience" (L 3.920), so death is untried, the test of belief and, in the proof, a condemnation. Yet Dickinson ends her poem with a subtle irony: the self is never alone. It is always attended—like royalty—by "Its own identity," a persistent hound that can comfort or afflict. Dickinson's exact rhyme "be / identity" stresses that it is the "columnar self" (789) on which one must rely in this last, as in every, crisis. Since "You cannot take itself / From any Human soul," she imagines it finally as an "indestructible estate." Even on its flight in air unto infinity, the Soul will be "Impregnable as Light" (1351).

6

There were two nineteenth-century American painters whose evocations of the suffering mind or soul evoke Emily Dickinson's. Different from Thomas Cole's, their works were probably unknown to her; but their exploration of similar themes is remarkable. In his dreamscapes and moonlit seascapes, Albert Pinkham Ryder (1847–1917) attempted to disclose "the ideal world that lay behind the illusory screen of the physical real world."[49] He was an admirer of the works of Edgar Allan Poe, and his *Temple of the Mind* (1885) was an illustration of Poe's verse-allegory "The Haunted Palace." Like so many of the American painters of his day, Ryder chose literary subjects from Chaucer, Shakespeare, the Bible, Byron, and Tennyson; for the spirit of the age was philosophic, synthetic, quotational. Ryder's late painting *Death on a Pale Horse* (ca. 1913) was more often entitled *The Race Track*. There, in an ordinary racing setting, Death as a skeleton with scythe is the jockey. Everyday life fuses with the terrible scene from Revelation 6:8,

"And I looked, and behold a pale horse; and his name that sat on him was Death." Ryder's vision of death, unlike Dickinson's, was never homely or intimate, but in his mystical studies of the self he too tried to place the real in the infinite. (He was also a recluse and showed—as she did, toward the end of her career—diminishing interest in the fate of his work. The *act* of creation was what interested him; one might say, the "honor" of it.)

Even closer analogues to the art of Emily Dickinson are furnished by the paintings of the poet-artist Elihu Vedder (1836–1923). Only six years younger than Dickinson, Vedder had a career that was on one hand quite public: he made the powerful murals and impressive mosaic for the Library of Congress (1896–97). At the same time, his sensibility was intensely private and most of his compositions were visionary. His chief theme might be described as the soul's struggle in a crass and indifferent universe.

Vedder's introspective, fantastic paintings, such as *The Questioner of the Sphinx* (1863), caused him to be numbered in the company of Church, Bierstadt, Winslow Homer, Gifford, and Kensett when he showed his work at the Metropolitan Fair, New York, on April 4, 1864. Susan Dickinson owned J. J. Jarves' book *The Art Idea* (1864) in which the author calls Vedder an excellent colorist. Vedder began to illustrate for *Harper's Magazine* and, responding to the late nineteenth-century cult of Egypt and oriental luxury, did a voluptuous portrait for *Scribner's* (December 1888) called *The Lion of the Nile, Anthony and Cleopatra*. Many of his paintings or drawings, such as *Soul of the Sunflower* (1868), *Memory* (1867), and *Weirdness* (1868), show a fascination with the domination of one mind by another or with the powers of mental illness and recollection. Vedder also wrote poems like "Identity" (1880?) in which he imagined faceless ghosts realizing each other anew in space. He knew Melville, Mark Twain, Josiah Holland, T. W. Higginson, and Whitman, and assumed new importance in the literary establishment as the illustrator of Edward Fitzgerald's *Rubáiyát of Omar Khayyám* (1884). An illustration once intended for the *Rubáiyát* (quatrain 49) became a masterpiece in oils: *The Cup of Death*.

In 1864–65 Vedder painted *The Lost Mind,* wherein he conceives the brain under siege as Dickinson does in "The first Day's Night"; there, as her "Brain keeps giggling," she wonders "Could it be Madness – this?" (410). Barbara Novak observes that in the nineteenth century "American culture stressed Mind—Mind raised to the level of divinity, a 'mental power with which our own is akin'."[50] Dickinson's explorations of the experience of madness or unconsciousness were in harmony with those of her age: dramatizations of the importance of intellect fully felt through its destruction or suspension.

Like Vedder's *The Lost Mind,* Dickinson's "I felt a Funeral, in my Brain" is a narrative, staged to describe the sensations of lost perception:

> I felt a Funeral, in my Brain,
> And Mourners to and fro
> Kept treading – treading – till it seemed
> That Sense was breaking through –
>
> And when they all were seated,
> A Service, like a Drum –
> Kept beating – beating – till I thought
> My Mind was going numb –
>
> And then I heard them lift a Box
> And creak across my Soul
> With those same Boots of Lead, again,
> Then Space – began to toll,
>
> As all the Heavens were a Bell,
> And Being, but an Ear,
> And I, and Silence, some strange Race
> Wrecked, solitary, here –
>
> And then a Plank in Reason, broke,
> And I dropped down, and down –
> And hit a World, at every plunge,
> And Finished knowing – then – (280)

Cleverly, Dickinson's story here of a fainting spell that ends sensation begins with the strong "I felt." As she so often does in her landscape poems, she undertakes a description of process by which, through a series of minute translations and shifting scenes, a final yet still inconclusive vision is achieved. The poem is a mindscape, so that its depiction of events suits the central "event" of intellection and its lapse. With almost rustic simplicity, its first setting—"a Funeral, in my Brain"— establishes the subject, the death of consciousness. But not until the tenth line, when the mourners are decidedly identified as interior, "creak[ing] across my Soul," does the poem make clear that this funeral records the steady failure of the various sentinals of perception. The vivid and even stark equations between physiological sensations and ceremonial ritual point up the experience of the speaker as she moves from feeling to not "knowing." It is Dickinson's clinical accuracy that pleases, together with the device that she is recording the act of fainting (syncope) in syncopated language.

Thus "treading – treading" and "beating – beating," the numb mind and the boots of lead, suggest the throbbing and dizziness that announce a fainting spell, while the lines "I dropped down, and down – / And hit a World, at every plunge" convey the reality of sinking out of consciousness and, indeed, to the ground. Perhaps the most brilliant sequence describing her experience is that synaesthetic one of tolling space—the ringing in the ears that precedes fainting—the bell of the heavens and her own Being, an ear to hear it. (In 1890 the symbolist Odilon Redon would paint *Silence* as a giant ear; Dickinson's description here of the wreck of silence as an ear anticipates his surreal conceit.) Finally, reason is the foundation of knowledge so that, when its plank breaks in the last stanza, understanding is finished for the speaker. To describe such a condition carefully is to insist on the consequence of everything cerebral in an era whose scientists, such as Louis Agassiz, were debating the connection between the individual mind and the manifestations of Mind in the universe. This poem does not necessarily come about because Dickinson herself had some acquaintance with fainting, not necessarily because she knew the symptoms of mental breakdown. It may reflect the fact that American pragmatism, empiricism, and Darwinism led to a concentration on intellectuality, its biological origins and meaning, and that many artists were exploring the connection in words and paint. In "I felt a Funeral, in my Brain" it is remarkable that the last "then," followed by its dash, suggests the continuity of intellect. At one time—*then*—the funeral took place, but the speaker is still alive to think and record it.

Often, for the nineteenth-century artist, "brain," "mind," and "soul" were interchangeable. (Dickinson's first choice for the word "Soul" in line 10 of poem 280 was "Brain.") Vedder, like Dickinson, created dramatic visions of the soul in a state of deliberation or reaction. His painting *The Soul in Bondage* (1891) was the fruit of acute religious doubt, influenced by William Blake. Yet he attempts a characteristic balance between melancholy and hope. Like Emily Dickinson, he conceives the butterfly as an emblem of Resurrection (her butterfly in poem 18 alludes to the risen Christ). His serpent, curled round the distressed soul's feet, is the old one from Genesis. The painting captures the soul in a moment of indecision and stasis; she has the right to choose evil or good. In the background the whirling light of space and chaos

dramatizes her friendlessness and isolation. This vision of lonely suffering appealed to art reviewers in the Aesthetic period of the 1890s; it
was the same theme that the first reviewers of Dickinson's *Poems*
welcomed as "the special and serious revelation of a soul apart."[51]

Just as Ryder's *Death on a Pale Horse* shows a fascination with death
as the ultimate moment of sublime terror, Vedder's best-known painting
The Cup of Death (plate 6) interprets it as a moment terrible and yet
serene. No single painting mentioned in this book better approximates
the visionary power of Dickinson's most famous poem about the passage into eternity than this one. "Because I could not stop for Death"
(712) imagines the poet, dressed in gossamer and tulle, overtaken on
life's road by Death as a courtly suitor, who conducts her out of this
world. She is not at all afraid of him. The real landscape is translated
under their carriage wheels into a grave placed out of time, a "ground"
that—though the word is repeated twice in one quatrain—is really
groundlessness, nowhere. Still the speaker is "passed" and has passed
into this nowhere without apparent pain.[52]

Similarly, Vedder's *Cup of Death,* the first version of which he completed in the year of Emily Dickinson's death, depicts the Angel of
Death escorting a lovely woman down from the fields of life to the
banks of the River Lethe; there she will be borne into eternity. Unlike
Dickinson's alert speaker, Vedder's lady suffers death passively. Yet,
like Dickinson, Vedder envisions Death itself as both suitor and sur-
cease, kidnapper and killer; and his emphasis is on the former. Although
the angel's dark skin, muscular arm, and great feathered wings are
contrasted with the pallor, limp grace, and nerveless feet of the woman
descending into unconsciousness, he appears to be her chevalier, careful
as he half-carries her down the incline into unconsciousness from the
high hill of waving grass that is life. She sinks downward without
evident pain; the angel's intense hold about her waist is almost loverlike;
and his head is bowed as he offers the cup, as if it were a chalice and
he, a priest at a sacred rite. The garb of the two figures is reminiscent
of the tunics of Greece and Palestine in the time of Christ, so that a
hint of scriptural authority is imported to sacramentalize the painting.
In the background is the setting sun, by 1885 a classic metaphor for
dying (as it is in Dickinson's own "Because I could not stop for Death").
There is impressive harmony in the sculptural folds of the angel's garment and the lady's veil and robe, which mirror and answer each other's
draping, left to right and right to left. Like the clothes of Dickinson's
dying woman, these do not resemble a shroud (which was tied under

the chin and sacklike) so much as an evening dress beneath a wedding veil, the former Grecian but the latter, with its suggestion of a bonnet, oddly Victorian. (Queen Victoria was buried in a wedding dress and veil, announcing her second marriage to Albert, in heaven.) Only the looseness of the folds over the left breast, so that the breast spills slightly above the angel's hand, implies unpreparedness and burial clothes, albeit of an indeterminately classical nature. The painting is peaceful and so seems the woman's deathly passage.

At the same time, however, Vedder has made clear that death is a relinquishment. There is still a suggestion of pink, being vanquished almost as we watch, in the woman's face. Her lips bent above the cup as if inhaling, rather than drinking from it, are invitational. Her lustrous hair, a traditional motif of sexuality, curls upon her beautiful shoulder. Why must she die? Vedder's painting is a summary articulation of the Victorian fascination with death: it led to hundreds of human *natures mortes,* especially in oils and daguerreotypes of dead women and girls. The view of Edgar Allan Poe that no subject was more poetic than the death of a beautiful woman was illustrated during this period by a whole tradition of sleeping or dead ladies borrowed from literature, such as the American painter Tobias Rosenthal's *Elaine* (1874), or drawn in the death chamber of one's wife or daughter. Significant is the fact that, like many of Dickinson's important poems on the transitus, Vedder's painting does not commemorate a death. Rather it attempts to record—and to "poetize" with both romance and regret—a dying.

7

When Emily Dickinson's *Poems* were first brought before the public in 1890, her own version in poem 712 of the story of a lady conducted into eternity would be regarded as original in imagery but also wonderfully expressive of a favorite nineteenth-century theme. Dickinson herself imagined the passing of both men and women. By far the majority of her poems, however, whether they envision the process of dying or lament its occurrence, place a woman at the center of this experience of the sublime. Even when her poem is an elegy, it is the tension between life and death, two worlds, that she prefers to explore:

> Today or this noon
> She dwelt so close
> I almost touched her –

Tonight she lies
Past neighborhood
And bough and steeple
Now past surmise (1702)

At a death watch, the poet observes that "'Twas comfort in her Dying Room / To hear the living Clock"; "Diversion from the Dying Theme / To hear the children play" (1703). This is so, not because she fears to see death, precisely, but because the disappearance into the void of someone who once *lived* threatens her sense of safety in the actual. The world of the living, with the sights and sounds necessary for poetry, is symbolically jarred and diminished each time a loved spirit departs. Dickinson often desires a balance between having and losing, keeping and letting go; the vision of death on the horizon while the beloved remains. This was the sort of equipoise that would permit the contemplation of the hereafter without the savage experience of parting. When her father died—that stern and rational gentleman who lived forty-four years with a genius for a daughter and chiefly praised her baking—the poet's behavior often frightened her family. She would roam through the large, quiet rooms of "my Father's House" (824), one after the other, for days after Edward Dickinson was buried, crying "Where is he? Emily will find him."[53] Such an act was related to those of receiving callers with a lily in her hand or letting down cookies from a bedroom window like some plain New England Rapunzel: it was, indeed, an *act,* the enactment of an inner need to proclaim herself and her concerns— beauty, love, life after death.

And while Dickinson the woman said, near her life's close, that she was ill and dying because other people's "Dyings have been too deep for me," the poet Dickinson continually described them (L 3.843). Using the image of woman as bird that she employed in many love poems, she wrote of her dead mother:

To the bright east she flies,
Brothers of Paradise
Remit her home,
Without a change of wings,
Or Love's convenient things,
Enticed to come.

Fashioning what she is,
Fathoming what she was,
We deem we dream –
And that dissolves the days

> Through which existence strays
> Homeless at home (1573)

Mrs. Emily Norcross Dickinson had been too unintellectual and possibly too unresponsive to attract her brilliant daughter, who told Higginson in 1870, "I never had a mother" (L 2.475). Then, in 1875, she was placed under Emily's care after a stroke. "We were never intimate Mother and Children while she was our Mother," Dickinson wrote to Mrs. Holland, "but Mines in the same Ground meet by tunneling and when she became our child, the Affection came" (L 3.754–755). Her daughter's elegy for Mrs. Dickinson remembers her fussy practicality, her bustling solicitude: she hopes the angels will get her mother straight to heaven with no need for a change of clothes ("wings") or any of the conveniences ("things") Mrs. Dickinson always took with her on trips to Monson, Massachusetts, or Washington, D.C. The word "Fashioning," which gently suggests Mrs. Dickinson's interest in Paris fashions, is set off against "Fathoming." To make or decide what she now is as a spirit and to understand what she was as a human being are so difficult that "We deem we dream," the poet acknowledges with wonder. In the absence of the mother who had once kept house for them all, she is "Homeless at home." What Dickinson describes here—the dissolving of days—is not merely "grief of wonder at [Mother's] fate," her phrase to Maria Whitney (L 3.771). Rather, it is her own painful sense of the known world dissolving around her with the loss of someone loved. That Dickinson essayed the terrifying subject of death so often in poetry was extraordinarily brave of her; at the same time it was, as her way of capturing the experience, an effort to achieve equanimity, peace of mind. In poem 1573, interestingly, death becomes the euphemistic, religious "bright" flight to paradise. Thus her mother's spirit was in air, "vanished" (L 3.771). But all the alliteration of the second stanza—fashioning, fathoming; what, what, was; deem, dream, dissolves, days; homeless, home—acts to stiffen the poem as a formal and permanent entity. It thus reassures the reader—and the writer—that Mrs. Dickinson is going to some firm place; perhaps to the new home that has replaced the old one.

Most of Dickinson's lyrics on death and dying act as memorials and thus keep hold of the dead by art and memory. One poem recalls a woman's vitality, which Dickinson imagines continuing in the spirit world, and yet regrets her ready compliance with death's summons:

> This docile one inter
> While we who dare to live

> Arraign the sunny brevity
> That sparkled to the Grave
>
> On her departing span
> No wilderness remain
> As dauntless in the House of Death
> As if it were her own – (1752)

"The Dead," Dickinson wrote, were "exhilirants . . . Lures – Keepers of that great Romance still to us foreclosed" (L 3.919). So her departed women seem to beckon, Dickinson says, with information about eternity. Their graves become shrines, images of all creation:

> She dwelleth in the Ground
> Where Daffodils – abide –
> Her Maker – Her Metropolis –
> The Universe – Her Maid –
>
> To fetch Her Grace – and Hue –
> And Fairness – and Renown –
> The Firmament's – To Pluck Her –
> And fetch Her Thee – be mine – (671)

Here the graves that make up the Metropolis, the city of the dead, merge in the poet's mind with the Maker: God is himself a town in which "she" now dwells. And the dead woman is waited upon by the Universe. Of course she is buried like, and with, daffodils. As perennials, they "abide." (Even as the flowers will come up from bulbs when spring arrives, the departed will rise again.) In a second quatrain that contains both elision and a sudden apostrophe, Dickinson imagines the woman's final life, after the resurrection, in eternity. She has grace, hue, fairness, like a daffodil; and as one who is still loved, she has renown. All those related qualities will be fetched, finally, by and into the firmament. But Dickinson demands that *she* be allowed to "Pluck . . . and fetch" the actual body of the flower, the woman, herself: "Thee – be mine." As another elegy makes clear, she may "borrow" immortality at a woman's grave; but it never stops her from "famishing" for "The Might of Human love" (1648).

Some of Dickinson's poems for the dead are, it has been said, so necrophilic as to seem disgusting or even mad. Condemnations have been made[54] of poems such as this one, where the beloved's body becomes an "it":

> If I may have it, when it's dead,
> I'll be contented – so –
> If just as soon as Breath is out
> It shall belong to me – (577)

They are misplaced, however, for Dickinson is being consciously and conscientiously bitter and ironic in such poems. She cannot lay claim to, cannot possess, the desired body until it is a person no longer: *that* is the cruel pass to which she has been brought, she complains. (And, since she has a habit of writing poems that could be intended either for a man or a woman or both, she may be playing on the concept of androgyny and on its opposite, sexlessness.) Dickinson's was an age in which the dead "lived" in mausoleums, where—as in the case of Queen Victoria visiting Albert entombed at Frogmore—their survivors might come to sit awhile or even brew a cup of tea. This was an age in which the young Emerson, who could stand his loneliness no longer, dug up his wife Ellen's body by lantern light so that he might hold it in his arms again. Presumably the emotions of Emerson or Victoria were not too unlike the speaker's in poem 577, who says

> For tho' they lock Thee in the Grave,
> Myself – can own the key –

As an elegy for her eight-year-old nephew, Thomas Gilbert Dickinson, his frequent playmate and correspondent Aunt Emily wrote a letter to the stricken Sue. Gilbert or "Gib," named after Sue's feckless father, was the last fruit of the Austin Dickinsons' disintegrating marriage and was precious to the entire family. He died of typhoid fever very suddenly on October 5, 1883. Mourned by many in Amherst as an especially winning child, Gilbert had brought Emily and Sue close again in the late 1870s. Townsfolk recognized that the Austin Dickinsons—who, some chortled, had "lived only for pleasure"[55]—were now truly overwhelmed. Not including Austin, Dickinson sent her sister-in-law these words, appropriate to Sue as mother, the gate to Gilbert's earthly life:

> The Vision of Immortal Life has been fulfilled –
> How simply at the last the Fathom comes! The Passenger and not the Sea, we find surprises us –
> Gilbert rejoiced in Secrets –
> His life was panting with them – With what menace of Light he cried "Dont tell, Aunt Emily"! Now my ascended Playmate must instruct *me*. Show us, prattling Preceptor, but the way to thee!

He knew no niggard moment – His Life was full of Boon – The Playthings of the Dervish were not so wild as his –
No crescent was this Creature – He traveled from the Full –
Such soar, but never set –
I see him in the Star, and meet his sweet velocity in everything that flies – His Life was like the Bugle, which winds itself away, his Elegy an echo – his Requiem ecstasy –
Dawn and Meridian in one.
Wherefore would he wait, wronged only of Night, which he left for us –
Without a speculation, our little Ajax spans the whole –

> Pass to thy Rendezvous of Light,
> Pangless except for us –
> Who slowly ford the Mystery
> Which thou hast leaped across! (L 3.799)

In some lines this letter slips into poetry; thus we may read

> He knew no niggard moment –
> His Life was full of Boon –
> The Playthings of the Dervish
> Were not so wild as his –

Once again we are reminded of the interwoven tapestry created by Dickinson's letters and poems. This letter is ordered by some of Dickinson's central images and explores with great unselfconscious brilliance that central theme of hers, the voyage into eternity. Here, as in Cole's emblematic *Voyage*, the passenger is on the sea; and the sea is once again not only life but heavenly life. Associated on earth with the light of childhood's innocence and energy, Gilbert is now a preceptor. Like all the dead, he can instruct; for he has become one with nature: "I see him in the Star." Thus he inspires the very words she writes as an echo of his presence; and he is full—"no crescent" but a full moon, the moon that she identifies with the poetic imagination, "circumference."

Her letter was a celebration of Gilbert's entrance into morning, the dawn of eternity. As he once supported the Dickinsons and kept them together, now he is the Ajax who "spans the whole," or connects heaven with earth. It ends in a quatrain that is a prayer as well as a farewell. Death as a mystery is the river (like Lethe in Vedder's *Cup of Death*) which must be forded—her word *ford* sounds the difficulty of the venture.

In other letters Emily Dickinson would attempt to comfort Gilbert's mother with heavenly visions. To Dickinson herself, however, he remained more than any of her dead as a living presence: "The little boy we laid away never fluctuates, and his dim society is companion still" (L 3.827). She thought of Gilbert, her parents, and Samuel Bowles together in Eden, her word for joy.

The Narrative of Sue

Art thou the ghost, my sister
White sister there
Am I the ghost, who knows?

—Algernon Charles Swinburne,
"Before the Mirror: Verses Under a Picture"

If Thomas Cole sought to inspire American landscape artists by saying "We are still in Eden,"[1] Emily Dickinson often alluded to Eden to describe her own circumstances, and not always happily. In her erotic poem "Wild Nights," a fantasy of union with an unidentified lover, she rows in Eden so that its sea fuses with eternity's. But just as often, Dickinson's Eden, a place of perfect natural happiness, is guarded by angels brandishing flaming swords; it is a kingdom of lost, remembered bliss.

Eight years before she died, she equated Eden with Sue, in one of the scores of notes, letters, and provocative lyrics that establish the fact of her lasting and troubled love for her sister-in-law: "Sue – to be lovely as you is a touching Contest, though like the Siege of Eden, impracticable – Eden never capitulates" (L 2.631). Her tone is resigned, her words unmistakably, if wittily, sexual in implication. It will not surrender to an invading power (even, we must infer from "Eden" as emblem, to one who is a former inhabitant). Her note, written during the years of their partial estrangement, shows the dignified continuance of Dickinson's love; that, as she told Sue, "Though the Great Waters sleep, / That they are still the Deep, / We cannot doubt" (L 3.828). It was a love that enjoined flattery — "to be lovely as you" — of the most abject and caressive kind, as well as loyal support: "You asked would I remain? Irrevocably, Susan – I know no other way" (L 3.803).

Dickinson's feeling was founded on memory. In poems and letters full of oriental and eastern imagery, she associated it with the remembered Eden.[2] It triumphed over familial bitterness occasioned by Sue's unhappy marriage to Austin. It survived what seem to have been Sue's betrayals of Emily herself. "Susan – I would have come out of Eden to open the Door for you if I had known you were there," Dickinson writes in 1880, long after she had stopped opening doors to anyone (L 3.672). Sue, she explains, is to her "Infinity" (L 3.830). Since it is the nature of infinity, however, like Eden, to be forbidden to those on earth, Dickinson's tones — though maturely subdued — recall her youthful voice: "Oh my darling one, how long you wander from me, how weary I grow of waiting and looking, and calling for you . . . [I] try hard to forget you because you grieve me so, but you'll never go away" (L 1.175–176). Both voices, early and late, express piqued but unsatisfied desire, disenfranchisement, and mourning.

Dickinson's passionate addresses to her "Only Woman in the World" leave no doubt about Sue's absolute importance in her life (L 2.546). Increasingly couched in the lavish and sinuous cadences of the Elizabethans (by one who thought Shakespeare the sum of all books), these apostrophes frame a trope carried out in poems and letters whereby Sue becomes Cleopatra and Emily is Antony. Sue taught her more "about Life" than anyone except Shakespeare, Dickinson told her, adding soberly: "To say that sincerely is strange praise" (L 3.733).

Were they "carnal" lovers?[3] Did Susan Huntington Gilbert Dickinson — whose cruelties reportedly "shortened Emily's life"[4] and who spent the years after Emily's death reading her poems at dinner parties but doing nothing to get them published — love her sister-in-law in *any* sense? Was she merely loved *by* her? Finally, can one hypothesize the nature of that (true or failed) love? Lillian Faderman argues that Dickinson's letters to Sue, even in girlhood, were erotic and clearly different from those addressed to other friends.[5] (But Faderman posits a tradition of romantic friendship and love among nineteenth-century women which would justify all such epistles.)

There was, indeed, a cult of fond sentimentality among Victorian girls. By including encomiums to cheeks, hair, and bosoms, it acquired an ambiguous eroticism. The obliquely sensuous daguerreotypes—such as *Two Girls: Hand to Bosom* (fig. 3)—made of her two daughters by Clementina, Viscountess Hawarden (1822–1865), illustrate the subtle sexuality of this social phenomenon. In that collodion study, made in 1862, one girl gazes at the camera while pressing the left breast (over

3. Clementina, Viscountess Hawarden, *Two Girls: Hand to Bosom* (1862).
Lady Hawarden presents her daughters as lovers or mirror images of each other.

the heart) of the other. Her posture is almost suppliant, as if she were
kneeling to her sister who, in turn, clasps the hand on her bosom.
Looking down on what appears to be the younger girl, the long-haired
girl on the right has the carven profile of a statue, while the flowers
and flowing dresses of both contribute to the photographer's subject: a
moment of courtly, but feminine, love. In *Hand to Bosom,* as in other
vaguely homoerotic daguerreotypes, Lady Hawarden disposes the lines
ordering her figures so that the impression they make is circular. (The
two girls' arms and the gaze transferred from one girl to the other to

the viewer make a circle.) Bram Dijkstra writes of the late nineteenth-century fascination with Sapphism that "woman was thought [by the Victorians] to have much less of a capacity for individuation than man"; that therefore artists, especially after 1885, frequently represented love between women by visions of similar faces meeting or kissing in a glass.[6] The effect was once again circular, as in Fernand Khnopff's portrait *The Kiss* (ca. 1887).

Emily Dickinson called her love for Susan Gilbert an "endless fire" (L 2.305). The circle is the foremost symbol of endlessness or continuity, and her love poems for Sue sometimes employ circular images or construction. In the early and mid-Victorian period, such a statement as hers might—almost—have passed without notice. There was a general emphasis on the sweetness and social benefits of affection among women and little organized suspicion of the possibility of passion between them. (Mary Lyon's strictures against exclusive friendships at her seminary, however, may have been watchful.) In many popular Victorian texts, young girls romanticized older ones, played the game of love—wooing and being wooed with gifts and letters—and were given (again, like Lady Hawarden's many pictured ladies) to open caresses that were considered innocuous and charming. Usually, as with Meg and Jo in *Little Women* (1862), the coming of the final, true suitor—a man—broke up the little preliminary circle of feminine tenderness. With the circular wedding ring came the Victorian girl's wedding vows, so often contemplated with mingled interest, aversion, or admiration by Emily Dickinson. This was the ultimate form of love: marriage, delicately foreshadowed in sentimental friendships at school. And since, of course, the Victorian bride's life could end in childbirth not so very long after the wedding, the goodbyes given her by her intimates were a farewell to girlhood "peace," as Dickinson put it, and poignant indeed (L 1.210).

Emily Dickinson had several cherished schoolfriends, with whom she carried on what was then, as now, called a "hot" correspondence (L 1.171). The word meant frequent, not ardent. But Dickinson enacted the girlish rituals of love pledges and shared dreams with characteristic intensity. To her girlfriends, she wrote about love, death, and immortality with the excitement and relish for language of a developing writer. Though her notes to young men she liked (John Graves or Henry Emmons) could be affectionate, her letters to old schoolmates were often rapturous. Jane Humphrey received the following from "Your Emilie Dickinson" in 1855, while teaching at Groton Academy:

Jennie – my Jennie Humphrey – I love you well enough tonight, and for a beam from your brown eyes, I would give a pearl . . .

How I wish you were mine, as you once were, when I had you in the morning, and when the sun went down, and was sure I should never go to sleep without a moment from you. (L 2.320)

Dickinson also wrote in this style to her other schoolmates. She uses the popular courtship language of her day, found in Ik Marvel's (Donald Grant Mitchell's) *Reveries of a Bachelor* (1851) and Longfellow's *Kavanagh* (1849). But she was twenty-five when she wrote this letter. Even in the 1850s, such amorous tones to another woman would have provoked remark. Eliza Coleman wrote of Emily to their mutual friend, John Graves, in 1854, "I know you appreciate her and I think few of her Amherst friends do. They wholly misinterpret her, I believe."[7] (Eliza's comment could allude to a number of qualities, even Emily's preference for staying at home. But it follows this sentence: "Emilie . . . sends me beautiful letters & each one makes me love her more." Eliza had clearly decided to dismiss as enthusiasm what was, doubtless, Dickinson's intensity in letters to herself.) When Jane Humphrey married in 1858, however, she abruptly stopped answering Dickinson's letters.

Jane's defection, as Emily regarded it, had been anticipated by that of another girlhood friend, Abiah Root. Abiah's image as adorable woman prefigured Sue Gilbert's, and Dickinson wrote her in the tones of a lover. The daughter of Deacon Root of West Springfield, Abiah Palmer Root was born in 1830, as Emily was, and attended Amherst Academy when she did. Judging from her daguerreotype, Abiah as a teenager was far more womanly in appearance than Emily Dickinson (or Susan Gilbert, for that matter). Full-bosomed with shapely shoulders, glowing complexion, and shining hair, she also seems to have had—besides beauty—a fun-loving though dutiful nature. After only one year, Abiah left Amherst Academy in 1845, but Dickinson wrote steadily to her at Miss Campbell's Academy in Springfield. Indeed, she wrote until 1854. The correspondence ended when Abiah ceased writing back.

A letter from "Emilie"—as she then styled herself, a Gallic flounce—to Abiah at twenty-one mourns that "you and I have grown older since school-days." Superficially an exercise in Dickinson's typical mortuary themes—the brevity of life, the death of the loved, and so on—this message is really a lament for the infrequency of Abiah's letters. As if to jog Abiah's memory and thus (she hopes) evoke in her an equal sentimentality, Emily Dickinson recalls their first meeting. Since she feels snubbed, her letter is barbed:

> You were always dignified, e'en when a little girl, and *I* used, now and then, to cut a timid caper. That makes me think of you the very first time I saw you, and I can't repress a smile, not to say a hearty laugh, at your little girl expense. (L 1.105)

(Three years hence, Abiah was married. Even at this time—as her picture makes abundantly clear—she was no "little girl." But fearing she herself is gone and forgotten by Abiah, Dickinson reminds her of their childhood.)

> I have roused your curiosity, so I will e'en tell you that one Wednesday afternoon, in the days of that dear old Academy, I went in to be entertained by the rhetoric of the gentlemen and the milder form of the girls – I hardly recovered myself from the dismay attendant upon entering august assemblies, when with the utmost equanimity you ascended the stairs, bedecked with dandelions, arranged, it seemed, for curls. I shall never forget that scene, if I live to have gray hairs, nor the very remarkable fancies it gave me then of you . . . Oh, Abiah, you and the early flower are forever linked to me; as soon as the first green grass comes, up from a chink in the stones peeps the little flower, precious "leontodon," and my heart fills toward you with a warm and childlike fullness! (L 1.206)

There is much warmth after some cattiness here, but to call it "childlike" is reductive and inaccurate. (That Abiah was "always dignified" in childhood, by the way, is utterly undercut by Dickinson's vignette. The story is a clever way of making love to her and of romanticizing differences between them.) Richard Sewall quotes this letter in the first "Early Friendships" chapter of his noble *Life*. He then says (of their schooldays), "Abiah soon became one of 'the five,' an honor, perhaps."[8] Dickinson's account of her reaction to first seeing Abiah deserves more attention, I think; for what it reveals is that Emily was smitten with the *sight* of Abiah. With dandelions arranged as curls, Abiah looked madcap in that severe setting, but she must also have seemed like a maenad or wood sprite, the sort of nubile maiden John Everett Millais painted as *The Bridesmaid* (1851) in the same year Dickinson was writing.

Emily Dickinson's recollection is no mere tribute to one of her chums. (What were "the very remarkable fancies it gave me then of you"?) Now, Dickinson relates, Abiah is forever associated for her with spring flowers. Like Tennyson in "Flower in the Crannied Wall," she would like to "pluck [Abiah] out of the crannies" and, like him, sees her as a "little flower"—her phrase, in fact, is Tennyson's. By the concept of littleness, she links Abiah with children, thus achieving that desexualizing spiritualization Dickens, Thackeray, and other Victorians sought when treating their good heroines—Agnes Wickfield of *David Copperfield* or Amelia Sedley in *Vanity Fair*. Emily's true feelings for Abiah, which are tinged with eroticism, may thus hide behind this pious tribute to a shared girlhood.

Dickinson's longing for Abiah—not the distance between them or the years since Abiah left Amherst—was what undoubtedly deprived her, at last, of Abiah's correspondence. Abiah's letters, as Dickinson's complain, were becoming less frequent as the girls approached their twenties. "We are growing away from each other, and talk even now like strangers," Emily laments at twenty (L 1.104). She wants to bind Abiah to her—can they be "a pair of decayed old ladies" together? (L 1.103). Suddenly Abiah is not answering her letters at all. She comes to Amherst for the commencement ceremonies in August 1852. Emily catches a glimpse of her—"a sacred thing to me"—but from a distance, for Abiah does not call upon the Dickinsons (1.166). Emily writes to her in some torment. Her tone, which is certainly more ardent and abrasive than was customary among affectionate Victorian women, indicates why Abiah drew back: "Why did you not come back that day [Commencement], and tell me what had sealed your lips toward me? Did my letter never reach you, or did you coolly decide to love me, & write to me no more?" (L 1.71). These are the remonstrances of a cast-off suitor, not a schoolmate. But so were Dickinson's words on many occasions. Here Abiah is in Philadelphia, and Emily complains from Amherst:

> Very likely, Abiah, you fancy me at home in my own little chamber, writing you a letter . . . Hard-hearted girl! I don't believe you care . . . I will not forget your name, nor all the wrong you did me!
> Why did you go away and not come to see me? . . . I did want one more kiss, one sweet and sad good-by, before you had flown away. (L 1.166, 167)

Abiah is given concert tickets by a Mr. Eastcott. Emily upbraids her sourly: "He is a young man I suppose. These Music teachers are always such high souled beings that I think they would exactly suit your fancy" (L 1.118). Because Abiah had joined the church and Emily had not, religion was frequently a subject of Emily's letters to her. Of this one,

Sewall says, it shows Abiah to be "the dignified one, proper and pious, while Emily posed as the scapegrace."[9] Mr. Eastcott's error, however, lay in being a man, not a music teacher; a man interested in Abiah. And Emily is accusing Abiah not of piety but faithlessness.

A conventional Victorian woman in her twenties might have found it discomfiting, boring, absurd, or even threatening to be plagued by such as: "Your image still haunts me, and tantalizes me, with fond recollections" (L 1.71). This last was Dickinson's outcry to Abiah when both were fourteen. Almost a decade later, however, her accents are the same. Thomas Johnson writes that Dickinson's friendship with Abiah Root came "to have little meaning for either" after Abiah's marriage.[10] Sewall observes that Emily was learning from Abiah "who she was not. Even from the first, there is a slight sense in her letters that the two are functioning on different planes."[11]

I think that the difference between them was not in Abiah's simplicity and interest in the Christian faith and Emily's genius and skepticism. It was in the girls' sexual development. By twenty, Abiah Root was clearly heterosexual. She had moved from the girlish world of best friends, shared secrets, and crushes on the headmistress (represented by Dickinson's breathless allusions to Miss Woodbridge of the "witching eyes" at Mary Lyon's [L, 1.45]). In 1854 she made a happy marriage with the Reverend Samuel W. Strong of Westfield. Absorbed in love for a new husband, why would Abiah wish to continue answering Emily's letters, which rebuke her for not caring enough, not writing? (Curiously, a later daguerreotype—published by Mabel Todd in the *Letters* [1931]—shows the new Mrs. Strong to be sternly coiffed and astonishingly masculine and lantern-jawed, quite unlike the pretty Abiah whom Emily mourned.) Emily herself, as Abiah drifted away, worried that "some knight [would] arrive at the door" for her sister Vinnie (L 1.175). As she had said to Jane Humphrey of men, "this is an *enemy's* Land!" (L 2.321). But, in fact, by 1854 she had found a new Abiah: Sue. This friendship was far more serious, more devout. Emily was at first so possessive that she urged Sue not to go to church but to "come with me this morning to the church within our hearts, where the bells are always ringing, and the preacher whose name is Love – shall intercede there for us!" (L 1.181). With metaphors of true passion but also of marriage, Dickinson would court this new friend, her "Precious Susie." So, not long after, did Emily's brother Austin, triumphantly. That Emily's "endless fire" for Sue was indeed lasting, there can be no doubt. It endlessly complicated her life, and Sue's. Its special character is important to understand. For Emily Dickinson, despite the poignant gravity of her love, did not finally seek to bind Sue to herself alone. Rather, in an example of triangulation (which she later repeated with Sue and Samuel Bowles), she welcomed Austin's interest in Sue and sought to join Sue with the Dickinson family.

On one hand, this solution—for such it was—to the problem of her love was, I think, as instinctively and generously chosen as it was dangerous. On the other, it may have been subliminally advanced, as some poems imply, in desperation. To encourage Sue in marrying Austin was to keep her permanently in Amherst; to give her to the only Dickinson who might legitimately take her; indeed, to give her to Emily herself, in masculine form. That Austin (who resembled Emily) was dear to her, Emily's youthful letters make clear. There was, on Emily's part at least, covert rivalry: Austin fancied himself a writer at one point, had a Harvard degree, was their father's favorite. But in lines like "Prithee, my brother, / Into *my* garden come!" (2), Emily's fondness for him is obvious.

This pattern whereby one yields the person one loves to another one loves, or comes to love the lover of the person one loves, is certainly circular. It is also commonplace. Dickinson seems sometimes to have found comfort in Sue's proximity and in their legal sisterhood after the marriage. But evidence shows that she also found, in both, torment. As Dickinson's love poems make clear, ecstasy in love is always followed or even accompanied by anguish. In her copy of Emerson's "The Sphinx"—Sue's sphinx-like qualities were often her theme—Emily Dickinson marked these lines:

> Eterne alternation
> Now follows, now flies;
> And under pain, pleasure,—
> Under pleasure, pain lies.

In the triangular relationships she sustained with Sue and Austin and (to some extent) with Sue and Bowles, Dickinson was forced to suffer. Hers was always the least share of the shared love. Furthermore, each experience taught her more about Sue's complex and untrustworthy nature. After her mother's death in 1913, Martha Dickinson Bianchi brought out an edition of her Aunt Emily's poems entitled *The Single Hound* (1914). In an introduction she observed, not quite accurately, "The romantic friendship of my Aunt Emily Dickinson and her 'Sister Sue' extended from girlhood until death." Her book, she said, was "a memorial to the love of these 'Dear, dead Women.' "[12] Austin Dickinson's mistress, Mabel Loomis Todd, had published an edition of Emily Dickinson's *Letters* in 1894. Reissuing it in 1931, when all the Dickinsons but Martha were dead, Mabel recalled that Austin and Lavinia had insisted that she "omit certain passages, references to a relative then living, in some of the early letters"; and she would "continue to respect their wishes" in the present volume.[13]

The relative was of course Susan Dickinson. For, by 1894, Sue had become—in Mabel and Austin's cruel epithets—"The Power" or "The Great Black Mogul,"[14] feared by Lavinia and avoided by Austin. So Emily's youthful letters to Sue were suppressed. Early poems to Sue such as "One Sister have I in the house" (fascicle 2) were scribbled over and obscured—probably by Austin—in the materials Mabel was given to edit after Emily's death. Because, as Austin and Lavinia agreed, Sue had changed, and changed toward Emily, it was evidently impossible for them to contemplate, or to see recorded, how close the two women had been in youth.

By using the phrase "romantic friendship," however, Austin's daughter Martha (who detested her father) sought to establish the fact of Sue's ascendancy over Emily. Dickinson's niece was evoking the sentimental Victorian tradition of mutual feminine attraction captured by Lady Hawarden's daguerreotypes of the 1860s. She also prepared a context in which some of Emily's extravagant letters and poems for Sue might be read. Though she repeated her mother's story of Emily's passion for Charles Wadsworth, Mrs. Bianchi indirectly tried to give Sue the crown she deserved: a crown as Emily's best-beloved. In disseminating the legend of the minister, Sue had most likely attempted to provide a motive for her sister-in-law's embarrassing reclusion. She may even have been trying to deflect attention from herself. Since broken hearts were a continual theme of Victorian art, Sue's story was easily believed. Again, though, Mrs. Bianchi's use of "romantic"—like the weighty evidence of her aunt's poems and letters—empowers a different interpretation of Dickinson's life.

All this is important, or more specifically Emily's love for Sue is important, because it helps to explain consistent images and tropes in her art. Dickinson's passion for her sister-in-law resulted in a body of poems and letters that is as eloquent and complex as any written to "Master." Furthermore, since Sue outlived both of the men Dickinson came to care for—Samuel Bowles and Judge Otis Lord—the literature devoted to her is more vast and describes a broader arc of emotional development. As Sue's character and personality became clearer to her over the years, Dickinson tried to become her opposite. If Sue was given to frivolity, snobbery, and ruthlessness, Dickinson became increasingly gentle and private. While Sue grew into a proud "cosmopolite," Emily became the intimate of birds, plants, and children. As Sue became more and more busy "with scintillation," Emily Dickinson busied herself with thought (L 2.575). Sue's appetite for power as a New England aristocrat led her to write "Annals of the Evergreens," an account of her well-known soirées at the Austin Dickinson villa. Emily Dickinson's contempt for such "fame" emerged in unpublished poems:

> Some – Work for Immortality –
> The Chiefer part, for Time –
> He – Compensates – immediately –
> The former – Checks – on Fame – (406)

Nevertheless, while (as Dickinson said) the tie between them became very "fine," it was "a Hair" that never dissolved (L 3.893). "Susan, I dreamed of you, last night," writes Dickinson at forty-eight, enclosing a carnation (to recall their girlish sentimentality about flower-poems?) and echoing the voice of the young girl who longed to be with Sue as she falls asleep and to awaken in her sight (L 2.632, 317). "There *are* no others," Dickinson reassures her "momentous" sister-in-law in 1878, though she was being courted at that time by Judge Lord (L 2.631, 632). So instinctive was her conviction that they somehow belonged to each other that, in 1864, she wrote Sue from Cambridge (where she was under treatment for her eyes), "Should I turn in my long night I should murmur 'Sue' " (L 2.434). So the image of the lover asleep and calling out the name of the beloved is commuted into a vision of the buried, sleeping away the "long night" of death and still able to say the lover's name.

If we are to believe the persuasive evidence of the poems, this intense romance of the heart was never physically consummated. Therefore, when Dickinson speaks magisterially about "denial" (965) or—more frequently—"renunciation" (745), she is probably alluding to her experience as the frustrated lover of Sue. To this sorrowful deprivation was added the knowledge imparted by her thwarted experience with Master. Furthermore, if one is to credit the powerfully plainspoken testimony of such poems as 631, it is the anger and pain occasioned by being jilted by her female lover (who marries) that drive the speaker to accede to Master's rescuing love. What I shall call the "Sue cycle" of poems for and about a beloved and inaccessible woman is thus related to, and sometimes overlaps with, the Master materials themselves.

One could, of course, regard both bodies of writing as etudes in poetic or compositional form and dismiss the question of their relevance to biography as a distraction from the text. This strategem is advantageous in avoiding the risk of censure by future revision. Severely formalist, it focuses attention on the (rewarding) articulations of the literature itself. Applied to the Dickinson oeuvre, however, it seems a solipsistic avoidance and even unhelpful in studying an art that is so clearly post-romantic.

Some scholars are understandably fatigued by the overwhelming interest in possible romances that has always attended (and often obscured) Dickinson study. Robert Weisbuch, for example, eschews the biographical; announces that the Master letters were fictions; and says that even if they are not, the identity of the addressee is unimportant.[15] In strained efforts to avoid the obvious, other critics regard such poems as "Ourselves were wed one summer – dear" (631), with its tone of bitter and familiar intimacy, as written for the celebrated and distant Elizabeth Barrett Browning.[16] In both instances, effort has been made to remove the poet's art from the immediate circumstances of her life. "Master" becomes an imitative persona, dependent for his shape on the books she knew. The woman of the hot, anguished love poems must be the wife of the famous Robert Browning rather than a woman Dickinson lived with or knew. In this way, fantasy and inaccuracy are presumably avoided. But another fantasy is substituted: that great artists write without directly experiencing what is called "life." The addressees of Emily Dickinson were her intimates, and the possible subjects of her work must be considered: their nature directed her choice of language.

Dickinson included willfully mysterious and highly revealing, pointed lyrics in letters, whose recipients were thus pressed to intuit the private significance. She seems frankly to have regarded her poems as products of a shaping personality. Her remark to Higginson—that the poems were the work of "a Supposed Person"[17]—disclosed her awareness of the distinction between Dickinson as woman and Dickinson as artist. It recognized the process of translation and distancing by which art is made. It may also have been a protective personal strategem, since Dickinson would send her "Dear Preceptor" several fraught poems about love. Her habit of enclosing poems to correspondents, however, joins woman and artist in one utterance.

I intend to read the poems and letters that I judge (or that Dickinson indicates) to be inspired by Sue with an assumption of the importance of biography in illumining a rich imagination. What is known of Sue's life, especially through Dickinson's account of it, proffers a powerful and intelligible narrative. It sheds light on the mystery that has surrounded Dickinson and her poems for a beloved woman, and also for Master. Most important, it offers insights on the form and meaning of Dickinson's art.

2

Susan Huntington Gilbert was born nine days after Emily Dickinson on December 19, 1830, in Greenfield, Massachusetts. Although Dickinson disparaged her own mother's timid simplicity by saying "I never had a mother," Susan Gilbert actually lost hers to tuberculosis at the age of seven. One of the chief similarities between Emily and Sue, so different in other ways, was the desire to be mothered. Dickinson's craving for stability and nurturing affection may have arisen from Mrs. Dickinson's inadequacies, as some writers maintain.[18] Certainly Sue's loss of her mother, who was loving and gently bred, pained her for years. To her brother Dwight, Sue wrote twelve years later, "I do feel so lonely at times dear brother, I [feel] so keenly the loss of a mother's love, and influence, and that sympathy our Mother alone could give." Interestingly—for one who would become the friend of Emily Dickinson (devoted to seeing daguerreotype "faces")—Sue lamented, " I have often wished, we had Mother's [miniature] for I have quite lost her expression."[19]

Sue was the youngest child of an alcoholic tavern and stable keeper named Thomas Gilbert, who had been born poor and died listed in the county records as an insolvent debtor. His reputation for dissoluteness and his "dying upon charity" were—as Polly Longsworth records[20]—a theme of gossip in Amherst until the 1880s. (After Sue married Austin and acquired the cachet of the Dickinson name, she tried to rehabilitate her father's reputation, moved his remains to a plot near the Dickinsons' in West Cemetery, and called her youngest son Gilbert. But when she first knew Emily she was still ashamed of Thomas Gilbert and for a few years after her marriage dropped the name Gilbert, signing herself Susan Huntington Dickinson.) Sue spent her childhood being shuttled back and forth from her father's tavern to the home of her Aunt Sophia in Geneva. Orphaned entirely in 1841 at the age of eleven, she lived partly in Geneva and partly in Amherst, with her sister Harriet Cutler, who had married the prosperous owner of a dry-goods store.

William Cutler despised Sue and her sister Martha for having been forced on him as dependents. One of Sue's earliest cravings was for a home of her own. She attended both Amherst and Utica academies, preparing to seek her independence by teaching school. (In this way Sue fulfilled the purpose for which Dickinson's seminary, Mary Lyon's, had been founded.) She rejoiced in the success of her favorite brother Dwight, who became a banker and millionaire; who paid for her clothes and medical bills and generously gave her five thousand dollars when she married Austin Dickinson. But Sue's teenage life was bleak and precarious. Her family considered her fearful at heart, if buoyant in manner. While Emily was the privileged daughter of Squire Dickinson, Susan Gilbert did housework for her keep and worried about holes in her shoes and refurbishing her dresses.

During Susan's first year (1847) at Amherst Academy, Emily was at Mount Holyoke. They were probably introduced by Lavinia or by other academy girls. By their late teens and early twenties, Dickinson considered Sue her best friend. There were several sides of Sue's nature that would have quickly interested Emily. One was, simply, Sue's ability to *feel* and to feel deeply on topics important to Emily. Which of the two girls, one might legitimately wonder, wrote the following lines?

> These sabbath nights have been sad, thoughtful hours to me, since our dear Mary was lain in her grave, for each successive Sabbath brings her image, and the scene of her burial, before me with a painful vividness and reality . . . How little we thought when we stood by her side, on the morning of her marriage, that she would be first-called to the "spirit-world," or that the first anniversary of her bridal-day would come to us fraught with bitter memories and unavailing tears. At times I cannot realize that Mary is really buried from our sight.[21]

These words from Sue to Dwight on the night before her dead sister's first wedding anniversary rehearse the burial scene of a well-loved woman, one of Dickinson's best subjects. They reveal the writer's willingness to remember—no matter at what emotional cost—the person she has loved. They disclose Sue's belief in the spirit world, which (like Emily in the poems and Master letters) she experiences as especially close to her on Sabbaths. Finally, they show the same longing to restore what has been and to bring back a "buried" face that one finds in

Dickinson's elegies. Sue's lines lack the pungency of Dickinson's writing, which usually has a measure of wit or irony or grotesquerie to break up the lugubrious tone. But they are the voice of one who has been sufficiently afflicted by grief to be able to pen a set piece on it.

Sue loved books and had a vivid imagination. Seeking to break free of the Cutlers, she left Amherst to teach school in Baltimore in 1851. Dickinson sent pages of praise and love to her, complaining that, in her absence,

> All life looks differently, and the faces of my fellows are not the same they wear when you are with me. I think it is this, dear Susie; you sketch my pictures for me, and 'tis at their sweet colorings, rather than this dim real that I am used. (L 1.229)

Dickinson needed no one to sketch her pictures. Here Emily characteristically pays Sue an excessive compliment by attributing to her an artistic talent that is really hers. So woebegone is she that she even makes a sentence, "dim real[ity]" or "dim real [world]," that is grammatically confused. What she missed was an appreciative yet creative collaborator, one whose mind was venturesome, whose wit could be daring, whose reading was wide. It was well known that Sue found delight in books. When Sue left Utica Academy, her schoolmistress "J.E.K." gave her an edition of Tennyson's *Princess*. (It must have been chosen for the theme: women's right to an education. She would read it closely with Emily, who marked many lines salient to their thoughts on the subject.) Twelve Utica Academy classmates gave Sue in 1848 Rufus Griswold's *Sacred Poets of England and America*. When she left teaching, Sue's pupils gave her the *Poems* of Ossian. Finally, her brother Frank offered as a wedding present two hundred books of her choice. During the forty years in which she knew Emily Dickinson, Sue's usual gift to her was a book. Often her choices seem intended as comments: thus Sue gives Emily *The Imitation of Christ* in an edition of 1876, shortly after Samuel Bowles died. It was an inspiriting text for a recluse, perhaps, though Emily had already read the *Imitation*. At Christmas in 1880 her present was, one thinks, almost wholly inappropriate: Benjamin Disraeli's novel of society, *Endymion*. Sue's inscription in that book alluded to their near estrangement: "Emily, Whom not seeing, I still love." Other gifts were straightforward: novels like *Adam Bede* (in 1860) because Emily much admired George Eliot. But sometimes, as in the case of *Endymion*, Sue seems to be describing the difference between their lives at that moment—Emily's as the so-called Shadow Lady of Amherst and hers as, in Bowles's phrase, the Queen of Pelham.[22]

Since Edward Dickinson—according to his impatient daughter—read only "*lonely* and *rigorous* books" like *Pilgrim's Progress* and the law journals, Emily read Sue's books for the most part (L 2.473). She would especially associate two texts—*Antony and Cleopatra* and Tennyson's *Maud*—with Sue and her complex feelings for her. But Sue's library, both before and after marriage, afforded Emily a broad choice in reading. A bold hand wrote either "S H Gilbert," "S H Dickinson," or "Mrs. Wm A. Dickinson" in Ruskin's *Sesame and Lilies*, Burns's *Complete Works*, Michelangelo's *Sonnets,* the *Works of Sir Thomas Browne* (cited by Emily to Higginson as a favorite text), Browning's *Sordello,* various treatises on art and artists such as James Jackson Jarves' *Art Thoughts* (1869) and *The Art Idea* (1864), and indeed a great many of the most important books of the Victorian age. Sue also shared in reading Emily's books, bought for her with some hesitation by Mr. Dickinson. In fact, it is Sue's hand that frequently inscribes Emily's name in her volumes—in an 1850 edition of *Wuthering Heights,* for example, or even the *Complete Concordance to Shakespeare,* which Dickinson received in 1877 from Judge Lord. In the latter, the inscription reads "Emily Dickinson from Judge Otis P. Lord." Unlike other inscriptions, it may have been entered after Emily's death, and even after Austin's and Lavinia's; it indicates Sue's assumption that the poet's affairs were somehow hers to keep account of, even as she kept a record of Aunt Emily's sayings for her children. In fact, if Dickinson regarded Sue and herself as mysteriously sharing a single, or scarcely differentiated, identity as girls, Sue ultimately presented herself as knowing Dickinson's thoughts, even in heaven. When *Poems* (1890) were about to appear, she defended her decision not to edit them by writing Higginson, "I am told Miss Lavinia is saying that I *refused* to arrange them. Emily knows that is not true." And Sue ends her letter with the picture of herself going "in the snow to-morrow to put a wreath of her own mountain laurel on [Emily's] grave."[23] The letter shows the same confidence that the poet and she know each other perfectly which Dickinson manifests in words about Sue from first to last.

Because "Susie" seemed to her—in her earnestness and privation—a "dear child," Emily Dickinson's tenderness was more roused for her than for any schoolmate (L 1.250). Sue's absence when they were girls prompted one of her allusions to 1 Corinthians 13:12, in a favorite metaphor for earthly frustration:

Susie, will you indeed come home next Saturday, and be my own again, and kiss me as you used to? Shall I indeed behold you, not "darkly, but face to face" or am I *fancying* so, and dreaming blessed dreams from which the day will wake me? (L 1.215)

In these letters Susan Gilbert constitutes Dickinson's heaven, though her dreams of her in sleep are, like her words, ardently physical: "I will not shut my eyes until you have kissed my cheek" (L 1.223).

Evidence shows that all the Dickinsons, including Emily's stern father, were infatuated with Sue. Her dark handsomeness, her pitiable history, her spirited joy in nature and society, her gratitude for their kindness and her willingness to work for her own support, appealed to their chivalry and their Puritan admiration for self-reliance. Sue herself, however, was far more fearful than she appeared, especially to Emily who saw Sue as fearless and herself as often "vanquished" (L 1.312). Sue particularly avoided the final commitment to a person or a place that might actually bring her the repose she desired. Thus, while Emily was writing to Sue of her love, Sue was casting about for ways to leave teaching and for the means to avoid returning to Amherst. Unlike Emily, she regarded "plain humdrum old Amherst among the hills" as wholly depressing, ugly, and dull. Years later she would recall her girlhood distaste for it:

> As the snow lay two or three feet on the level in those Wintry days, Amherst, with no street lighting, no trolleys, no railroads, seemed to my youthful and perverse mind, animal spirits and vigorous habit, a staring, hopeless place, enough to make angels homesick. The lugubrious sound of the church bell still rings in my Winter dreams.[24]

What Sue enjoyed were trips to what she called "the great *Gotham*, alias New York"[25] to which she went unescorted, so keen was her need for excitement.

By the spring of 1853, Emily's brother Austin—then a law student at Harvard—had known Sue Gilbert for three years. He was courting her with increasing, if clumsy, assiduity and with Emily's encouragement. Letters sent to Austin from Emily urge him to write Sue more often. On one occasion in 1851, she rebuked him: "Susie asks in every letter why she dont hear from you" (L 1.138). Sue had no need to reproach Emily for not writing, of course. From Emily she was receiving every reassurance—often hysterical—that, even more than Austin, she had pledged herself to Sue:

> I have but one thought, Susie . . . and *that* of you . . . I need you more and more, and the great world grows wider, and dear ones are

fewer and fewer, every day that you stay away . . . Susie, forgive me Darling, for every word I say – my heart is full of you, none other than you in my thoughts, yet when I seek to say to you something not for the world, words fail me. If you were here – and Oh that you were, my Susie, we need not talk at all, our eyes would whisper for us, and your hand fast in mine, we would not ask for language. (L 1.211–212)

That there was a certain competition going on for Sue's affection, it is likely to suppose. Austin's letters become more and more eager and earnest and prosaic. (They never reached the emotional height of his letters to Mabel in the 1880s.) Sometimes he and Sue share a joke at Emily's expense, as when Austin is visited by his two sisters in 1851: "The girls stayed with me till last Monday morning and had some capital times together – Vinnie enjoyed herself, as she always does among strangers – Emily became confirmed in her opinion of the hollowness & awfulness of the *world*."[26]

Austin's emphasis (which he expected Sue to appreciate) on Emily's horror of the "*world*," as represented by the staid city of Boston, points to the crucial difference between Emily and Sue; indeed, between Emily on one hand and Austin and Sue on the other. Austin and Sue liked the world, and it was, at first, a tie between them. Austin would later become burdened with care, as Emily thought, and given to a certain poetry of spirit through his love for art, landscape, and Mabel Todd. Even when he met Sue, he was a sensitive young man. But he and Sue first appealed to each other by being practical and fun-loving. Each enjoyed parties and travel; each was proud, ambitious, and high-spirited. Sue was accused of a rather mannish determination to better herself by means other than marriage. Austin had to be brought to heel by Edward Dickinson's paternal demands before he agreed to settle in Amherst rather than seek his fortune in Chicago. Both worked as pupil-teachers in the public schools—Sue, because she needed money, but Austin because he wanted to do some good for society. This was an aspect of their worldliness that would make the Dickinsons important in Amherst, indeed in western Massachusetts. Sue forced Austin to join the First Church. She welcomed the power and influence that came from his wealth and, liking finery, created an elegant home. That Austin could meet Sue on this ground far more easily than his sister is shown by a note he sent Sue: "I have a sort of land of Canaan letter from Emily yesterday—but she was too high up to give me any of the monuments on earth."[27]

Although Sue's coldness—in person, in letters—was a source of complaint, Austin finally persuaded her to become engaged to him in March 1853. Aware that she was not much drawn to marital lovemaking, he at first promised Sue that she could live quite as a girl with him if she wished. While he was imploring her to set a date for their wedding, however, Sue was writing fondly to the Reverend Samuel Bartlett, a bachelor friend in New Hampshire for whom she seems to have felt a far keener attraction, which lasted as late as 1861. Sue's nature was remarkably complex, as we learn from the tone (and words) of her letters of this period. She was ill for a year before marrying Austin on July 1, 1856; her brother-in-law Cutler accused her of making herself ill to avoid her duties and to avoid marrying. Sue herself remarks—using a word frequent with Emily—that she is such a "child"[28] she cannot believe she is to be a wife. Yet in a letter to her brother Frank about the marriage, she shows both the romanticizing faculty that attracted Emily and the cool calculation all Amherst would attribute to her before long:

> Why don't you write to me Frank and congratulate me, that I have found someone who is going, by and by, to encumber himself with me? . . . I have wanted very much to know how you were looking on this new phase of my life . . . I see no reason, viewing the subject as I try to, without prejudice, why you won't like Austin and find in him all you could desire as the companion of your sister. He is poor and young and in the *world's* eyes these are great weaknesses—but he is strong, manly, resolute—understands human nature and will take care of me . . . We shall have a cozy place some where, where the long-cherished wish of my heart to have a home where my brothers and sisters can come, will be realized. I have no *extravagant* ideas of life. I expect to forego a great many enjoyments that wealth could procure, and that no one loves more than I—but I can do it very cheerfully and happily if the man I love well enough to marry is unable to give them to me.[29]

Two impulses are evident in this letter. One is Sue's need to succumb to Victorian sentiment by describing Austin, and their love, as straight out of *Kavanagh* or *Little Women*. (Thus Alcott's heroine Meg says of her John to wealthy Aunt March: "John is good and wise; he's got heaps of talent; he's willing to work . . . energetic and brave . . . I'm not afraid of being poor . . . because he loves me."[30]) The other is Sue's clear-sighted desire to communicate to Frank her satisfaction at having found a source of economic support. That Emily Dickinson could envision her as Cleopatra seems implausible in view of Sue's simple picture of a home of her own, "a cozy place." But Sue knew perfectly well that she was marrying the son of Squire Dickinson—who, in fact, would build for them as his wedding present the Italianate villa she called the "Evergreens," the first house in Amherst to be titled. There is a degree of hypocrisy and sophistication in her letter that is quite at odds with qualities attributed to her by Emily Dickinson, the "girl with a large, warm heart, earnest nature and delicate tastes"[31] who could write with such candor: "I love you as dearly, Susie, as when love first began, on the step at the front door, and under the Evergreens, and it breaks my heart sometimes" (L 2.315).

Sue married Austin, with none of the Dickinsons present, at her aunt's home in Geneva. Her attitude toward the ceremony was blasé: "a little cake — a little ice cream and it is all over — the millionth wedding since the world began."[32] The approbation of the Dickinson family— and particularly of Edward—was well known. Sue reserved her own compliments for the imposing figure of her father-in-law. She never described her husband so admiringly as she did Squire Dickinson, astride one of "the finest horses in the country."[33] Sue and Austin went to Niagara Falls on their honeymoon. Then the orphaned daughter of Thomas Gilbert came home to wealth and—to all appearances—security.

3

Dickinson's second fascicle contains a poetic tribute, really a love poem, for Sue. It begins as the sweet compliment of a sister-in-law and ends— swinging from the quatrain unit into first a six- and then a five-line stanza—as a personal declaration of feeling. Charmingly and comfortably, the poem first emphasizes the differences between Sue's nature and the smitten Dickinson family's. Then it "takes" Sue forever more as the poet's own:

> One Sister have I in our house,
> And one, a hedge away.
> There's only one recorded,
> But both belong to me.
>
> One came the road that I came –
> And wore my last year's gown –

The other, as a bird her nest,
Builded our hearts among.

She did not sing as we did –
It was a different tune –
Herself to her a music
As Bumble bee of June.

Today is far from Childhood –
But up and down the hills
I held her hand the tighter –
Which shortened all the miles –
And still her hum
The years among,
Deceives the Butterfly;
Still in her Eye
The Violets lie
Mouldered this many May.

I spilt the dew –
But took the morn –
I chose this single star
From out the wide night's numbers –
Sue – forevermore! (14)

A recollection of youthful days when Susan Gilbert had indeed "Builded [their] hearts among," this poem was later distasteful to Austin and Lavinia. So it appears, scribbled over and effaced, in the *Manuscript Books;* but Martha Dickinson Bianchi published her mother's copy in *The Single Hound.* Important to an appreciation of their relationship is Dickinson's identification of Sue with a bird, who nests in all their hearts. She had used this bird image ten years earlier in writing to Abiah Root: "I caught one glimpse of your face, and fondly anticipated an interview with you . . . but . . . 'the bird had flown' " (L 1.71). It was employed even more pointedly for Sue: "I pray that such summer's sun shine on my Absent One, and cause her bird to sing!" (L 1.201).

Dickinson's poems for Sue often rest on the courtly tradition in which admired women are compared to birds. Mingled in that tradition were both pagan and Christian conceptions of woman as a bird, often as a dove. In picturing Lesbia with her pet sparrow, for example, Catullus expresses desire cunningly by wishing he might take the bird's place at her lips. But in her indifference to him, Lesbia is herself a sparrow, a bird associated with promiscuity. She can soar above and away from the beholder. Depicting Lesbia in the company of a bird—like Venus with her doves—Catullus indirectly attributes to his callous sweetheart qualities that birds typically possess: a soft body, a musical voice, an appearance of harmony with their surroundings. Yet her nature is such that she resembles a bird, too, by eluding his grasp. Dickinson's poems for "singing Sue" as a bird reveal the same fascination and fear: Sue is lovable in her vitality and especially so when confiding herself to be cherished. But she sings a different tune from the Dickinsons, a music of which she herself is maker and measure. So she may never be willing to rest in that nest or enclosure Emily is eager to offer.

In *Maud* (1855), a poem Dickinson associated with Sue, Tennyson's speaker calls the heroine "My bird with the shining head, / My own dove with the tender eyes." (Indeed, so frequent was the comparison of women to doves in the Victorian period that Robert Browning in "Too Late" satirized a love poet who "Rhymed you his rubbish nobody read," "Loved you and doved you.") Such painters as Walter Howell Deverell brought out in *A Pet* (1853) or *The Grey Parrot* (1853) representations of pretty young women holding or feeding caged birds whose domestic enclosure suggested their own. In these representations, as in Sue's favorite *Angel in the House,* little survived of the lecherous, cruel bird of Catullus. Instead, the overtones were of the Song of Solomon in which the Bridegroom (Christ) addresses the Bride (the Church) as "my sister, my love, my dove, my perfect one." In this biblical canticle, comeliness is the reflection of holiness. The beautiful spouse, like the Victorian domestic "angel," is contented as a dove in the garden of her husband where lilies grow.

This is the sort of gentle, sociable, abiding bird for which Dickinson's heart wants to be a nest. In the letters addressed to Susan Gilbert during their young womanhood, Emily Dickinson sees the two as birds, mounting together in an exultation of love like that depicted on Victorian valentines: "I move on wings now, Susie, on wings as white as snow, and as bright as the summer sunshine—because I am with you." There is even a scriptural echo in her longing: "Be patient then, my Sister, for the hours will haste away" (L 1.216). And the desired conclusion is ever the same: to "see you home" with "my mother and my sister – *thy* mother and *thy* sister" (L 1.222). Within these accents of familial welcome, however, a lover's tones barely conceal themselves. (Sometimes the speaker reacts with surprise to acknowledge the fact: "Why, Susie, it seems to me as if my absent Lover was coming home so soon – and my heart must be so busy, making ready for him" [L 1.216].)

Sue is also likened to a bumblebee that makes its own singular natural music. For Dickinson, bees are emblems of sexuality but also of faithlessness. Bees of course sting, as does the unnamed "friend" of the poems. In one poem, probably for Sue, this friend is both bird and bee, both faithless and stinging:

> My friend must be a Bird –
> Because it flies!
> Mortal, my friend must be,
> Because it dies!
> Barbs has it, like a Bee!
> Ah, curious friend!
> Thou puzzlest me! (92)

Though Dickinson finds Sue's caustic tongue astonishing, she always sees her as rare (although Sue too must die: itself a "curious" thought here). Thus the Dickinsons walk roads, wear clothes, remain unexcitingly stable. Sue, a natural force (attractive but self-regarding), impels them forward or condescends to sojourn among them.

"One Sister have I in our house," a staid declarative statement in the early quatrains, kindles rhythmically with "and still." The luxuriantly rhymed fifth stanza is remarkable for presenting, however positively, an image of deception, since that would be attributed to Sue by many factions in later years. Its allusion to Sue's eyes full of moldering violets suggests time's passage and a dusky blue color that recalls Barrett Browning's apostrophe in a "A Flower in a Letter" to "Deep violets, who liken to / The kindest eyes that look on you." Written probably around 1858, Dickinson's poem divides itself—even the stanza form is not consistent—between private and familial feeling. It is followed in the later fascicles by other poems that mask as friendship or sisterhood but actually reveal love and desire. The imagistic thread that begins to bind them, as in poem 631, is one of eastern opulence and royalty or northern cold, beggary, and want. Dickinson's earliest language for Sue, however, rises out of the sentimental Victorian tradition of birds and flowers. It is decorated with allusions to wounded hearts and bows and arrows that, in turn, survive from the Elizabethan sonnet tradition.

Thus in a famous letter to Sue, written about 1854, Dickinson included another poem about a bird and a flower. But she states that the bird—unlike Sue now–stands for a former love and an old dream of security and serenity. The original of this letter in the Houghton collection at Harvard is noteworthy for being in a firm and careful script. It appears to be the fair copy of an earlier draft, and the letter's tone of vibrant sorrow and forced optimism are remarkably at odds with its even hand. (That Dickinson made drafts of her letters, remnants show. It is moving to find her making three or four efforts to send a few words to Sue.) Thomas Johnson in a note to this letter (L 1.307) observes, "There is nothing in other letters to indicate a rift between the *girls* [emphasis mine] at this time." But, however fond she was of pleading childlike, in images a child might understand, Dickinson was a woman of twenty-four, and so was Sue, when she sent this letter. And the woman speaks forth clearly and boldly:

> Sue – you can go or stay – There is but one alternative – We differ often lately, and this must be the last.
>
> You need not fear to leave me lest I should be alone, for I often part with things I fancy I have loved, – sometimes to the grave, and sometimes to an oblivion rather bitterer than death – thus my heart bleeds so frequently that I shant mind the hemorrhage, and I only add an agony to several previous ones, and at the end of the day remark – a bubble burst!
>
> Such incidents would grieve me when I was but a child, and perhaps I could have wept when little feet hard by mine, stood still in the coffin, but eyes grow dry sometimes, and hearts get crisp and cinder, and had as lief burn.
>
> Sue – I have lived by this. It is the lingering emblem of the Heaven I once dreamed, and though if this is taken, I shall remain alone, and though in that last day, the Jesus Christ you love, remark he does not know me – there is a darker spirit will not disown it's child.
>
> Few have been given me, and if I love them so, that for *idolatry,* they are removed from me – I simply murmur *gone,* and the billow dies away into the boundless blue, and no one knows but me, that one went down today. We have walked very pleasantly – Perhaps this is the point at which our paths diverge – then pass on singing Sue, and up the distant hill I journey on. (L 1.305–306)

Dickinson's letter concludes in a poem. Whether artfully or instinctively, the poem (as if deciding between the letter's opening alternatives "you can go or stay") ends with the command, "Return." Before noting the poem's iconographic pattern, however, it is helpful to notice that of the letter. Its images are of solitude, the grave, a bleeding (indeed hemorrhaging) heart, burst bubbles, the coffin, a burning heart, heavenly emblems, Jesus Christ and the devil, waves, the sea, and the road or hill of life. Each image occurs frequently within the tradition of Victorian poetry of love or religion. (One of the causes of the usual, ultimately misplaced comparison between Dickinson and Christina Rossetti stems, in fact, from their employment of these images.[34])

Yet this imagery tells much about Emily Dickinson, establishing patterns to which she later adheres. The solitary mourner, parting with a beloved at the grave, like the bereaved observer watching as someone drowns (or becoming the drowner), frequently appears in the poems. Dickinson's absorption in the concept of eternal life was merely heightened by love, and she seeks baroque equivalents of the courtly or religious image—mingling the two—to express the fact. In her, Crashaw sometimes meets Tennyson, though her overwrought, plangent intensity is usually defined by brisk meters. There is, of course, a decidedly inherited cast to her language here. She is wholly participating in the language, verbal and graphic, of her day. Her images may be seen on the mourning pictures in paint and crewel or engravings of the 1830s–1860s: shattered hearts, sinking ships, Bunyanesque mourners climbing the hills of life alone. This letter also revises Dickinson's earlier vision of herself holding Sue's hand "up and down the hills" by challenging singing Sue to pass on while she herself climbs up "the distant hill"— into Eternity?—alone. Most important, the view of her sister-in-law that the poem affords is of a person who can sing (with the indifference of a bird?) while someone who has idolized her grieves, and grieves because through her idolatry she has lost her. Dickinson once called herself "Susan's Idolator" (L 1.265). Surely she expected Sue to remember and take account of her reference. (This is an early admission of what seems to have been the truth: that Emily's idolatry sometimes bored Sue. Both Emily and Vinnie were for her "the Girls"[35]: never quite grown up and Emily, at least, too apt to fawn, to overwhelm her with sentiment.)

The letter opposes to the idea of religion the burning reality of love. Dickinson imagines herself on the last day, the Day of Judgment, claimed by the devil ("darker spirit") while Sue, who loved Jesus Christ, is saved. A version of this vision will reappear in the haunting and brilliantly constructed poem 640 (usually assumed to be written to Master), "I cannot live with You." As is the case in poem 640, the implication in her letter is that Dickinson's excessive love for Sue is a sin against the first commandment, "Thou shalt have no other gods before me," and costs her heaven. Sue had joined the Congregational church in 1850 during the revivalist frenzy that permeated the Connecticut River Valley. Emily Dickinson did not, being unable to declare confidently for Christ. Some argument about religion may underlie this letter. Sue regarded belonging to a church as fitting in a well-bred woman. To have her pew at First Church and serve Christ were, for her, related. Though the Congregational minister once declared Emily Dickinson a sound Christian, she was always afflicted by doubts. Certainly, as she once did in writing to Abiah Root or Jane Humphrey, she creates a wildly exaggerated image of herself as the child of Satan, presumably because she has not yielded to the revival mania and set down her name on the church rolls. To some extent, Dickinson seems truly to have felt guilt for this nonconformity; yet it is prompted mainly by her lifelong recognition that she can love people (her friends, Sue, Master) more than God.

The poem that concludes the letter to Sue unites the underlying religious motif, in its association with eternity, and the love motif, represented as the Bird:

> I have a Bird in Spring
> Which for myself doth sing –
> The spring decoys.
> And as the summer nears –
> And as the Rose appears,
> Robin is gone.
>
> Yet do I not repine
> Knowing that Bird of mine
> Though flown –
> Learneth beyond the sea
> Melody new for me
> And will return.
>
> Fast in a safer hand
> Held in a truer Land
> Are mine –
> And though they now depart,
> Tell I my doubting heart
> They're thine.
>
> In a serener Bright,
> In a more golden light
> I see
> Each little doubt and fear,
> Each little discord here
> Removed.

> Then will I not repine,
> Knowing that Bird of mine
> Though flown
> Shall in a distant tree
> Bright melody for me
> Return (L 1.306–307)

Before her marriage—to Emily Dickinson's dismay, as we know—
Sue frequently traveled from Amherst. Is she the Robin who initiates
the spring of the speaker's love but leaves her "as the Rose appears,"
the rose conventionally emblematic of summer wooing and weddings?
Is Dickinson suggesting here, as she does elsewhere, that Sue's marriage
(by which she serves heaven) causes her to fly from her first beloved,
Emily herself? As the decoy of spring, the robin is linked with the birth
of feeling and song, love and poetry. With the coming of summer and
roses (Victorian brides often carried roses), the robin is "flown."[36]

But the speaker cannot bear to concede her own pain and announces,
"I [do] not repine." She imagines that the bird leaves her to learn in a
truer land beyond the sea,—a motif from works like Cole's *Voyage of
Life*—a new "melody for me." She assures herself that the bird still
belongs to her in eternity, "a serener Bright," where any discord between
them will be removed. The second and last stanzas echo and modify
each other. The bird, like "singing Sue," herself a kind of heartless
artist, has indeed gone. But such is the speaker's ardor and her yearning
for possession of the beloved that she cannot help imagining her returning the poem's song in paradise (a "distant tree").

The effect of letter 173 of 1854 is to say, "Go, but I know you
can't." And, "I know you *have* gone as a lover but you will love me—
sing for me–in another life." It shows the complex, knowing, *literary*
quality of Emily Dickinson's relationship with Sue. Until the end of
their lives, they communicated with each other in coded language. Or,
more precisely, we know that Emily wrote Sue in privately allusive
terms. By making Sue "Maud" or "Cleopatra" through quoting Tennyson and Shakespeare, she could overstep their public relation as
sisters-in-law and remind Sue of her secret feelings. Letter 173 establishes a predicament that underlies other letters and poems. Dickinson
has been called "a great poet of erotic bereavement."[37] Founded on
several causes (the deaths of friends, her vague and unsatisfactory mothering, and so on), Dickinson's sense of loss was sharpened by the real
loss of Sue: to her brother; to motherhood; to "scintillation" and the
whole "kingdom" (or queenship) of marriage, social prominence, and

householding. Although she encouraged Sue's marriage to Austin, the evidence of her letters and the narrative presented in the poems from 1858 to 1863 suggest that it cost Dickinson a great deal. It also gave her much: an experience of privation and sublimation that became one of her chief poetic themes.

4

Dickinson's letters of summer 1854, when Austin was pressing Sue to become engaged, include an effusive one to Sue's near counterpart, Abiah, on the subject of a mysterious illness:

> Susie is better now, but has been suffering much within the last few weeks, from a Nervous Fever, which has taken her strength very fast . . . [She] just begins to trudge around a little – went as far as her garden, Saturday, and picked a few flowers, so when I called to see her, Lo a bright boquet, sitting upon the mantel, and Susie in the easy-chair, quite faint from the effort of arranging them – I make my story long, but I knew you loved Susie (L 1.298)

It is possible that Abiah Root "loved," was fond of, Sue Gilbert. Even in 1883, when Sue was accused throughout Amherst of being an alcoholic, a snob, a flirt, and a destroyer of reputations (even when she herself was in love with Sue's husband), Austin's mistress was charmed by Sue. Mabel Todd told Austin, "Can you see how I can still love her very much? But I do—she stimulates me intellectually more than any other woman I ever knew."[38] She too had responded to one whom Emily called "the Susan who never forgets to be subtle" (L 3.831). Apart from her wit, Sue was also a fascinator; and with her dark good looks—one man called her "some punkins"[39]—she was what the Pre-Raphaelites thought of as a "stunner." In Emily's imagery, she is physically strong and emotionally reserved or "spotless": "Sinew and Snow in one" (L 3.733). A pastel portrait of Sue by Clara Lathrop gives her brown eyes, a down-turned mouth, a low forehead, and makes her appear big and imposing (fig. 4). But there is no evidence that, for all Sue's appeal to others, Abiah would care particularly if Sue were ill. It is Emily who cares.

Sue's illness, a "Nervous Fever" that keeps her from wanting to smile (Emily explains) or get out of bed, sounds like depression. In scores of brilliant poems, Dickinson anatomizes depression, to which she herself was susceptible and to which she may also have succumbed in the late

1850s. A well-known letter to her Uncle Sweetser describes a manic sadness that mars her conviction of order and both blunts and sharpens her poetic perceptions:

> Much has occurred, dear Uncle, since my writing you – so much – that I stagger as I write, in its sharp remembrance. Summers of bloom – and months of frost, and days of jingling bells, yet all the while this hand upon our fireside. Today has been so glad without, and yet so grieved within . . . I cannot always see the light – please tell me if it shines. (L 2.335)

Her allusion to "this hand upon our fireside" has already been taken as an image of depression.[40] (I am told that such expressions are often used by sufferers from "endogenous" depression, the experience of being kept by some force within from enjoying external conditions perceived to be pleasant; the experience may not necessarily last very long.) This letter, by evidence of the handwriting, was written two years after Sue's marriage to Austin, just as Dickinson was beginning to compose as a serious artist, and just as she was drafting letters to Master. Everyone supposes that something happened to her around this time that helped form her into the recluse-poet. In my view, what happened was her recognition that she *could* be a poet. But it was related to her feelings for Sue.

Sue's depression before agreeing to marry Austin and Dickinson's depression in 1858 were, I think, similar in character. Each was probably attributed to the decision to take a "road" — Dickinson's conventional metaphor in poem 14 and elsewhere — that is simultaneously threatening, exciting, frustrating, promising, but dislocative. For Sue, the decision (Dickinson calls it in 631 her "Vision") was to marry. For Emily Dickinson, the vision also meant commitment and sacrifice: she would fulfill herself, "in Vision – and in Veto!" (528), as a poet but could not (as she had fantasized) have Sue to herself. That fantasy never lapsed, and as late as 1877 she wished "To own a Susan of my own"; but by then it was only a courteous dream, a gesture, a faithful acknowledgment of their amorous past (L 2.598).

Susan Gilbert's attitude toward her marriage in 1856 was pragmatic and cool. Perhaps she thought a restrained manner would appeal to the well-bred Dickinsons, though it sometimes chilled Austin, and Emily too. Her private nature was by all accounts turbulent. She was subject, in particular, to rages. (Dickinson's allusions to her "torrid Spirit" as akin to Cleopatra's epitomized her volatility [L 3.791]). If Mabel Todd's report is to be credited, Sue waited many months to consummate her marriage; had a keen distaste for sexual relations, which she called "low practices," a condemnation on moral grounds; and, in her terror of childbirth, sought several abortions despite the birth of three children.[41] One remembers that Sue's sister Mary died in childbirth. A subject of considerable horrified fascination for both Emily and Sue as girls was

4. Susan Gilbert Dickinson (1870?). "Egypt – thou knew'st."

the perilous fate of the married woman, who is "yielded up" to the "man of noon," her husband (L 1.210), and after him, possibly, to death.

Mabel Todd's memoir of Sue, later called by her daughter Millicent "Scurrilous but True," was an effort to explain her adultery with Austin. Its accusations against Sue include not only frigidity but violence: Mabel claims that Sue drank, gave wild parties in which furniture was broken, and sometimes threatened to kill Austin. She also wrote of Sue's pride, ambition, and deceit. "Her neighbors," claimed Mabel, "told of [Sue's] flirtations with delightful Sam Bowles, and of how she sent her husband off for a few hours occasionally in order that she might pursue her foolishness with him, untrammeled." Sue's "unutterable superiority" of attitude in Amherst made certain that her humble origins were always remembered: Lavinia Dickinson later liked to recall that the "lofty" Sue's father had "died in the gutter." Mabel attributes to Austin complete "disenchantment" with his wife, as early as their wedding journey: "the story was told me, first by indifferent persons in town, and later more in detail by Lavinia, with a few comments by Emily in her curiously interrogative voice from the next room." A relative of Austin's is said to have called Sue the "serpent" in their home, which was otherwise in all its loveliness "a Paradise."[42]

As the partner in Austin's adultery, however, it was in Mabel's interest to blacken Sue. Mabel's own life as a woman who regularly slept with her husband's employer (it was Austin who hired David Todd to be the Amherst College astronomer) might seem to many, then and now, less savory than Sue's. Millicent Bingham remembered her childish grief at seeing her father's wedding ring replaced on her mother's left hand by a ring of Austin's. Mabel called Austin her "King."[46] Though he apparently agreed to his wife's love affair with Dickinson, Mabel's husband ended his days in a mental asylum. There he was said to cry whenever the Dickinson name came up. If Sue had not wanted children, moreover, Mabel was glad to have only one child (until she met Austin, with whom she tried to conceive as an "experiment").[47] And there is evidence that not only Sue but Austin as well wanted no children at first. In an unpublished letter in the Harvard collection, Bowles urges both to rejoice when their son Ned is finally born in 1861. Though he is himself, Bowles says, not fatuous about infants, he thinks parenthood worth the sacrifices it entails. Finally, among the Dickinson books is Sue's copy of Patmore's *Angel in the House*. Austin had inscribed it as a gift for their first Christmas as husband and wife: "Some one has been watching us, Sue, Dec 23rd [18]57." The serpent had once, it seems, been an angel.

Sue's loyal children, Ned and Martha, came to think of her as an excellent and attentive mother, yoked to a man who openly betrayed her. Even in his will, Austin recorded his children's absolute preference for their mother. One of Ned Dickinson's most anguished memories was of Sue on her knees before his father, begging him to speak to her. All this sorrow, disorder, and scandal lay ahead when Sue and Austin married in 1856. But the seeds were sown through Sue's ambivalance toward Austin and Austin's evident failure to perceive it during their courtship of three years.

Austin's sister, however, had chosen Sue "forevermore." By 1858, that choice became fraught. The complexity of those events by which Emily lost Sue to marriage yet gained her as a sister, by which she had to confront her own singleness and (the poems show) angry jealousy together with her desire for a vocation of her own, made her development as a poet crucial. Dickinson would have come to poetry in any case. She had already, even before meeting Sue, demonstrated a passion for words and the wit to use them well. But the narrative presented in the Sue cycle suggests that her emotions were deeply stirred in the late 1850s and early 1860s. They required what she called the "balm"— the solace, pleasure, and healing powers—of composition. What might have been "A Death blow . . . to Some" became a "Life blow" to her as an artist (816).

In a poem probably written in 1862, a year of acute emotional crisis, she made a characteristic association between poets and painters. Each turned to art as a secret remedy for unspeakable distress:

> The Martyr Poets – did not tell –
> But wrought their Pang in syllable –
> That when their mortal name be numb –
> Their mortal fate – encourage Some –
>
> The Martyr Painters – never spoke –
> Bequeathing – rather – to their Work –
> That when their conscious fingers cease –
> Some seek in Art – the Art of Peace (544)

Dickinson's last line in this poem may be read in two ways: artists work to record their suffering so that others may find peace through their art, but they themselves seek peace in their work. While she sometimes regarded love as a balm for the suffering that sprang from the human condition, she thought art more lasting and less "mortal" than love. Stimulated by the complex circumstances of her life, Emily Dickinson turned to her art.

5

The forty fascicles, together with a few unbound poems, talk about the beloved woman in a fashion inconvenient to facile deductions about the chronology of events. For example, long after the beloved has been claimed by another, Dickinson's speaker rehearses heightened moments of their love as if these had just occurred. Meanwhile another lover has also entered her life, and there are similarities in the language Dickinson uses for each. The Dickinsons had a well-thumbed copy of the sonnets of Shakespeare; and one is reminded by Dickinson's poems of his speaker's ambivalence in that sequence toward one "too dear for my possessing" (87)—the "better angel is a man"—and his "worser spirit a woman colored ill" (144). Sometimes the speaker declares the dark lady his "dear love" still, though she is "black as hell" (147). Sometimes the young man, "my saint," seems a devil under her influence. Because he loves both, the speaker's "sensual feast" is not always shared with one person (141), and his lovers occasionally blend. Shakespeare's sonnets record a well-known story of triangulation. As she turned the pages of the family Shakespeare, did Dickinson herself see the similarity? Since she came to love two people—"just two 'Heart[s]'" (495)—her poems for the woman and those for Master sometimes share imagistic and thematic motifs. Furthermore, some poems include the figure of another man, the one who marries the beloved woman; and when, by the early 1860s, all characters are on stage in her drama, the poet feels free to express what she has experienced, is experiencing, or fears to experience in loving her. Chronologically, then, Dickinson's story is random. Nevertheless, taken in their entirety, the poems for the beloved woman constitute a distinct narrative.[48]

Dickinson's speaker admires a charming, intelligent, exotic, but vulnerable girl who, becoming a woman, is also physically lavish and more opulent of gesture and enthusiasm than she. They share an uncanny empathy of feeling and taste, but Dickinson is often surprised and stung by the girl's treacherous acts and cutting remarks. Tortured by her, she also understands and pities her. She is aware too that although her beloved woman ultimately acquires an apparently fortunate position— a rich kingdom or queenship—Dickinson is wiser than she. Indeed, in the teaching experience that becomes one aspect of their relationship, Dickinson's speaker is imaginatively superior. The beloved woman can "teach" Dickinson envy (if she chooses to feel it) or loss (which she must accept) or joy and anguish. At last she teaches her betrayal of the heart. But Dickinson is able to show *her* beloved "Heights she never saw" (446): extents of passion and caring, extensions of awareness to which by nature she is not privileged.

Although in one poem (458), which I shall discuss, Dickinson depicts herself and the woman in a crucial moment of shared physical attraction, her beloved deserts her for one who is not "poor" and whose "cottage" is not, like Dickinson's, surrounded by oceans and the north (631). In a number of poems, Dickinson deplores her own lack of persistence in wooing this "jewel," this "pearl" (452), who only slipped through her fingers because, as she admits, she lacked courage. In a group of resentful poems, she disparages the male who has seized the jewel: for so stupid is he that he has no idea she is his rival. (He succeeds only because he can "swim" (452)—her Freudian image for the biological and social authority of men.) Discarded by the beloved woman, the speaker permits herself to be chosen by someone else:

> overtaken in the Dark –
> Where you had put me down –
> By Some one carrying a Light –
> I – too – received the Sign. (631)

Now the dimly realized but admirable figure of a man holds the stage of the poems simultaneously with the beloved woman. As the speaker recognizes her dwindling importance to the woman, however, "he" is celebrated increasingly. She continues to compliment and serve the beloved woman insofar as she can, but, finally, the beloved's defection turns the speaker increasingly to a life in art. This is supported through the last of the fascicles: poem 538 ("'Tis true – They shut me in the Cold"), which complains of being excluded from the beloved's happiness, is followed by two poems, "The Province of the Saved" (539) and "I took my Power in my Hand" (540), which argue that one overcomes despair through action.

The beloved woman is at first associated, like Sue, with birds and flowers, a pairing that suggests the "ecstasy" and "transport" (as Dickinson puts it in 137) of spring and young love. As early as fascicle 5, however, there appear eastern and oriental motifs that will connect her with Shakespeare's Cleopatra and Egypt. Strains of what has been diagnosed as Dickinson's "anxiety of gender"[49] also appear:

> Her breast is fit for pearls,
> But I was not a "Diver" –
> Her brow is fit for thrones
> But I have not a crest.
> Her heart is fit for *home* –
> I – a Sparrow – build there
> Sweet of twigs and twine
> My perennial nest (84)

This revealing youthful effort[50] sets up a central theme of the Sue cycle: the deserving and sensuous beauty of the beloved woman, so rare that it merits the accoutrements of royalty. The speaker acknowledges the fact warmly, with allusions to breast and brow, pearls and thrones, which have a vaguely amatory quality. The woman's loveliness is itself a proof of royalty, but like Queen Victoria she is also associated with domesticity. Dickinson's speaker longs to "nest" in her heart, a girlish equivalent of the lubricious desire of Catullus.

Although the beloved woman merits queenship, Dickinson declares that she cannot provide it. Interestingly, she gives the reason in the past tense: "I was not a 'Diver'," that is, she is (and long has been) of the wrong sex. The received approach to Dickinson's poetry, ever since Higginson fretted about the manifest erotism of "Wild Nights," has often been to deny her metaphors any more than an errant and unconscious sexual intent. But both Dickinson's sense of humor (fully exercised in letters to Sue) and her country girl's knowledge of country matters seem in play to me here. She says she is neither king-nobleman nor rooster ("crest") nor, in short, any form of "Diver," in quotes—a code word shared by them? — or *man*.

Among the young Dickinsons, Austin's nickname was "Rooster."[51] And Austin had a "crest" for another reason too: he was Edward Dickinson's heir. This is one of the first of Dickinson's poems to regard men as more fortunate in wooing than women. For men can dive to bring back pearls to adorn the beloved. It is men who confer pearls and thrones. Indeed, men can also dive into that "sea" of love, the beloved herself, and bring *her* back to their home, herself a pearl. This dark phallic power of the male, a "Negro" like Othello or (looking ahead) the heroes of D. H. Lawrence, Dickinson's speakers come to envy, make fun of, fear and admire (452).

"Her breast is fit for pearls," however—though a lament that her gender is female—suggests one of Emily Dickinson's tender solutions to love between women. In a circular form that begins by considering the beloved and ends by picturing herself, she depicts as in a mirror the need of each for a home. In place of the dangers of diving (heterosexual passion) and the gorgeousness of thrones (aristocratic station), she proposes the simple, unchallenging intimacies of girlish love. She would give Sue a *home*. In the turnabout that reflects their sameness of sex, she claims a home herself in Sue's heart. Each, then, becomes both bird and nest, the circularity of her poem's imagery and form rising from the fact of the sexual equation, and the nurturing roundness of *nest* symbolizing the feminine intimacy and insularity of her theme.

The Sue cycle makes plain that Dickinson's beloved has deep emotional needs—but so does the speaker. Her constant yearning, like Sue's, is for stability. The beloved woman, however, shocks her continually by affronting their established affection for each other. In fascicle 9, poem 156 presents the speaker's doubts about the beloved's constancy and her apprehension and conviction of being cheated by her. "Dollie" was a pet name for Sue:

> You love me – you are sure –
> I shall not fear mistake –
> I shall not *cheated* wake –
> Some grinning morn –
> To find the Sunrise left –
> And Orchards – unbereft –
> And Dollie – gone!
>
> I need not start – you're sure –
> That night will never be –
> When frightened – home to Thee I run –
> To find the windows dark –
> And no more Dollie – mark –
> Quite none?
>
> Be sure you're sure – you know –
> I'll bear it better now –
> If you'll just tell me so –
> Than when – a little dull Balm grown –
> Over this pain of mine –
> You sting – again! (156)

Like other Sue poems, this one creates sympathy for the nervous and clever speaker, who makes her childish need for nurturing reassurance very plain. On the other hand, if one reflects on the terms of their bargain of sentiment — Dickinson speaks of cheating — one might not like to be Sue. For the speaker identifies being loved with feeling the effects of the sunrise and coming home to find lighted windows and Dollie there – a nominative reduction ("Dollie") of any grown woman's desire for adult identity. The last stanza, of course, clarifies the problem: Dickinson fears that Dollie will not be faithful or loving. But she has asked of her a momentous, impossible competency: to overcome night or death. She has asked her to become a vast and magical mother, always at home for her to run to. Sue's "stings" may have come, in part, from fear.

Poem 158 is a more explicit exploration of such imagery. Dickinson demands light—the comfort of love—as she dies and, as is also usual with her, she wants it from a human lover, not Christ:

> Dying! Dying in the night!
> Wont somebody bring the light
> So I can see which way to go
> Into the everlasting snow?
>
> And "Jesus"! Where is *Jesus* gone?
> They said that Jesus – always came –
> Perhaps he does'nt know the House –
> This way, Jesus, Let him pass!
>
> Somebody run to the great gate
> And see if Dollie's coming! Wait!
> I hear her feet upon the stair!
> Death wont hurt – now Dollie's here! (158)

Though she will eventually write poems that treat Jesus tenderly as a chevalier, fellow sufferer, or magnanimous savior, Dickinson alludes to him scornfully here. His name is in quotes at first, suggesting doubt that he is real. Next it is underscored. Finally she associates it with "they," who are clearly untrustworthy. It is left to Sue, Dollie, to come past "the great gate"—the gate of heaven conflated with the Dickinsons' gate—to comfort Emily. Around 1862, at the height of her creativity, Dickinson composed "A Wife – at Daybreak I shall be" (461). As we have seen, that poem ends as her "Future climbs the Stair" of the Dickinson house (one of its more prominent architectural features, by the way, and a ready metaphor of sexual feeling, poetic elation, and supernatural fulfillment). When Eternity climbs the stair to fetch Emily Dickinson, she concludes, "I've seen the face – before"; indeed, so she has. The Sue cycle (like Dickinson's letters to her) instructs us that Sue is her Eternity. By comparison, Christ himself pales. And the Dickinson who knew the narratives of Browning's *Dramatis Personae,* conducting a colloquy in stanza 2 between "them" ("this way, Jesus") and herself, chooses Sue over Jesus.

How does one react to being loved with such avidity, such dependency? There is evidence that Sue shrank from it or started arguments or lashed out or snubbed Emily, perhaps to bring her to her senses: Austin's love, after all, must come first. Sue was a married woman when most of the Sue cycle was probably written. Dickinson broods that she always knew Sue would fail her, and the nest image turns into a coffin:

It did not surprise me –
So I said – or thought –
She will stir her pinions
And the nest forgot,

Traverse broader forests –
Build in gayer boughs,
Breathe in Ear more modern
God's old fashioned vows –

This was but a Birdling –
What and if it be
One within my bosom
Had departed me?

This was but a story –
What and if indeed
There were just such coffin
In the heart instead? (39)

Here the bird Dickinson has wed during their girlhood romance "stir[s]," she imagines—the word looks ahead to poem 518—flies away, forgets her, and marries one more "modern." "God's old fashioned vows" are the same, interestingly: there is no hint of wrongdoing about the girl's first marriage with the speaker. But she has wanted a "broader," "gayer," "more modern" life, a life with someone different from the speaker, who later describes herself in a number of poems as a "dull Girl" (704), a "rustic" (373). In poem 39, "This was but a story" and those who flew away were birdlings (Abiah? Jenny?). Yet she knows that "One within my bosom"—Sue—also has pinions, mature wings, and a thirst for fulfillment that will finally call her away.

Dickinson's speaker later fantasizes, however, that some day when she becomes a nobleman—a change in sex as well as status—the girl will regret having refused to notice her:

No matter – now – Sweet –
But when I'm Earl –
Won't you wish you'd spoken
To that dull Girl?

Trivial a Word – just –
Trivial – a Smile –
But won't you wish you'd spared one
When I'm Earl? (704)

"Earl" and "Duke," Dickinson's epithets for her ennobled speaker, are joined in the Master sequence by "Queen"; thus she uses appropriately gendered titles for herself as lover of a woman or a man. In her love poems for the woman, however, Dickinson does not make clear how she proposes to become an Earl in order to impress her. In some of the Master poems, she is a queen because Master's love crowns her. One short and moving poem suggests that art will make her royal to both lovers. Although her sister-in-law Sue loved gems, Emily Dickinson once announced, "I never wear jewels."[52] In this sad lyric, she adorns herself with the jewelry of metaphor, organic as the flowers she grows in her garden. Though she is rankless, her art can be all that Sue admires, both rustic and royal:

> When Diamonds are a Legend,
> And Diadems – a Tale –
> I Brooch and Earrings for Myself,
> Do sow, and Raise for sale –
>
> And tho' I'm scarce accounted,
> My Art, a Summer Day – had Patrons –
> Once – it was a Queen –
> And once – a Butterfly – (397)

During their early relationship when Sue is Dollie, Dickinson's speaker is never really content. She often describes herself as "weary." Fatigue is frequently a Dickinson euphemism for sexual longing and the despondency it brings. "I got tired," she tells Master in 1861 (L 2.373); "how weary I grow," she writes Sue in 1852 (L 1.175). In poem 51, she imagines embracing Dollie in the only place convention might allow, a grave. Even then two women were not usually buried in the same plot unless they were mother and child. Dickinson's paraphrase of Ruth 2:16–17, sent to Sue in 1852, gives the scriptural "Where thou diest, will I die, and there will I be buried" a nuance evocative of *Wuthering Heights:* "my father will be your father, and my home will be your home, and where you go, I will go, and we will lie side by side in the kirkyard" (L 1.201). When the speaker is dead in poem 51, she will receive Sue's corpse. It is a necrophilic (yet, in view of the addressee, thoroughly understandable) version of the act of love:

> So when you are tired –
> Or perplexed – or cold –

Trust the loving promise
Underneath the mould,
Cry "it's I", "take Dollie",
And I will enfold! (51)

Here sexuality masks as sisterhood once more. The diction adheres to the Victorian language of sentiment as it appears in Dickinson's poetry of girlhood romance. Apart from its cute but stark ending, this poem resembles "One Sister have I in our house" or poem 20, the fourth to be copied into the fascicles (fascicle 1). This poem, "Distrustful of the Gentian," leaves a dash for a name in the first stanza. Did Dickinson feel some need to conceal the name in question? (Mrs. Todd later wrote next to the blank, "a man."[53]) "Susie" should appear in the blank, not "Dollie," since Dickinson probably intended alliteration preceding the s's in her following words. The poem reveals what Dickinson wanted from Sue—everything, in fact—which she knows she cannot have:

Distrustful of the Gentian –
And just to turn away,
The fluttering of her fringes
Chid my perfidy –
Weary for my——
I will singing go –
I shall not feel the sleet – then –
I shall not fear the snow.

Flees so the phantom meadow
Before the breathless Bee –
So bubble brooks in deserts
On Ears that dying lie –
Burn so the Evening Spires
To eyes that Closing go –
Hangs so distant Heaven –
To a hand below (20)

Sue is "heaven" for the poet as well as a "phantom meadow" and church "spires": three of Dickinson's important images. As in poems such as 245, "I held a jewel in my fingers," the speaker's is the hand that either reaches for or loses the beloved. Giving the hand in marriage is a sacramental conceit that may underlie these images of taking, holding, and keeping. Marriage becomes the royal experience that finally separates the beloved woman from Dickinson's speaker.

6

In 1862 Emily Dickinson sent a note—a poem—beyond the hedge and across the lawn to her sister-in-law in the Austin Dickinson home adjoining the homestead. (Some of these poems as notes, once folded into small rectangular packets, may be seen in the Harvard and Amherst College collections. The effect they have is wholly different from any produced by printed texts; viewed in manuscript form, these poems are clearly messages created by one person to be read by another.) The note, now poem 299,[54] was followed by three prose lines: "Dear Sue— You see I remember—Emily." As if emphasizing the poem's character as a note, Dickinson also wrote *above* it, "Dear Sue." When it was sent, Susan Dickinson was not only a wife of four years but a new mother; and Master was on the scene. Here are the words to Sue:

> Your Riches – taught me – Poverty.
> Myself – a Millionaire
> In little Wealths, as Girls could boast
> Till broad as Buenos Ayre –
>
> You drifted your Dominions –
> A Different Peru –
> And I esteemed All Poverty
> For Life's Estate with you –
>
> Of Mines, I little know – myself –
> But just the name, of Gems –
> The Colors of the Commonest –
> And scarce of Diadems –
>
> So much, that did I meet the Queen –
> Her Glory I should know –
> But this, must be a different Wealth –
> To miss it – beggars so –
>
> I'm sure 'tis India – all Day –
> To those who look on You –
> Without a stint – without a blame,
> Might I – but be the Jew –
>
> I'm sure it is Golconda –
> Beyond my power to deem –
> To have a smile for Mine – each Day,
> How better, than a Gem!

At least, it solaces to know
That there exists – a Gold –
Altho' I prove it, just in time
Its distance – to behold –

Its far – far Treasure to surmise –
And estimate the Pearl –
That slipped my fingers through –
While just a Girl at school. (299)

We are often reminded about the Dickinson homestead that Emily's writing desk faced Main Street but was placed so that she could look westward to the Evergreens.[55] Letters reveal that she watched Sue on the street outside. She could see people arriving at Austin's parties or Sue leaving to attend one. "Your Riches – taught me – Poverty" is a love poem—of loss and regret—to a woman she once loved, indeed studied, when both were girls. The woman was rich then, as now, because of her very nature. (Sue's real poverty, Emily's wealth, are transposed.) This poem, like "Ourselves were wed"—631 in fascicle 26—establishes the themes of wealth/poverty, east/north, opulence/restraint, rank/beggary that Dickinson traditionally uses to cope with the image of Sue as queenly beloved. From these poems it was but a step to the elaboration of the Antony-Cleopatra trope, which, as I shall show, was surely a code language between them. Poem 299 expresses, quite straightforwardly, a farewell to adolescent romance: the speaker has lost this "pearl," her "gold," just as she comes to know its value. Now others have her "treasure" and also claim her "smile," while the speaker must be poor and "behold" her at a "distance."

The setting for this experience of failed love is, in retrospect, a "school." And though Sue and Emily were in different classes at Amherst Academy, it is appropriate if one recalls their long conversations about the duties and misfortunes of marriage. Fittingly, in view of the school setting, Dickinson's allusions are to the far-off places—Buenos Ayre, Peru, India—that she once found described in *Woodbridge's Larger Geography*. (The desirable Sue is always associated with warm tropical climes: not because she is herself given to passion, but because she arouses it.) In the 1860s as Dickinson was writing this poem, *Harper's,* the *Atlantic Monthly,* and *Scribner's* were running articles about South America. *Harper's* issue of September 1859 had already featured "something about Diamonds" with an illustration, "Diamond Washing in Brazil," which may have given Dickinson some of her imagery. *Harper's* described the Indian mines of Raolconda, five days' journey from the fortress of Golconda. The Golconda mines "formed the first, and for many years the most important, spot known for the production of diamonds."

Dickinson's poem says, then, that it would be like being in a diamond mine, surrounded by diamonds, to have one of Sue's smiles "for Mine" (a pun?). *Harper's* reporter, however, added that the miners are "held in a slavery of the most abject kind, their lives being entirely at the mercy of their masters." "Golconda" referred to the mine; yet it was, more properly, a fortress and prison. The primary meaning of Golconda is the limitless wealth of the beloved woman's person. But in Dickinson's circles and to Sue, who knew that Golconda was also a prison-fortress, the word would have implied misery and deprivation. Dickinson's frequent image for her emotional life was Byron's conceit of imprisonment in "Chillon" (L 2.393). In poem 299, Golconda is Chillon. To gaze at Sue is to be in prison.

These specific images eloquently blend to support the estimate of her beloved as a glorious Queen like Victoria, while Dickinson contemplates what must be the wealth of those who can look on her all day "without a blame." That last phrase is of course revealing; for nothing in the poem but the speaker's poverty could be cited as worthy of blame (unless it be the fact that her pearl slipped through her fingers). Though it is pathetic, poverty is not blameworthy. The poem's last lines imply that Dickinson was simply too young to value her pearl, too inexperienced, too "simple." Such innocence, now viewed as carelessness, is still not culpable. Some aspect of the speaker's nature, however—her gender?—makes it a "blame" to want such gold.

Two related poems, 801 and 245, employ similar situations and images to consider blame in relation to craving love or wealth. In 245 the speaker "held a Jewel in my fingers –/ And went to sleep." When she awakes, it is gone because her fingers were too "honest." In 801 "she play[s] at Riches – to appease / The Clamoring for Gold" and declares that she has often been "overbold / With Want, and Opportunity" and "could have done a Sin" and been freed of her imprisonment: "An independent Man." It is clear in these poems as in 299 that to keep *some* jewels is wrong. The speaker's candor is very striking. Other "men" would not have had her "opportunity" to take the jewel; for she is a secret wooer—only secretly a man—and thus Victorian restraints on social intercourse between the sexes do not include her. In "Your Riches – taught me – Poverty," the beloved woman is a queen who also teaches Dickinson as a female that she herself is *not* queenly, *not* desirable. The speaker's poverty does not only result from rejection but from feelings of inadequacy. (This is in one way the worst effect on Dickinson of the Sue affair: she becomes apologetic about her own nature, her own femininity.) Finally, it is clear that the beloved woman does not reciprocate the speaker's passion in kind. For she has "drifted [her] Dominions" and wants "A Different Peru," a different country of love: a man's love.

Into fascicle 36, which contains poems about Sue's coldness (727) or faithlessness (788), Emily Dickinson copied "Let us play Yesterday" (728). Using the imagery of birds and eggs that she has already established for Sue and herself as girls, she describes herself as having been born only when the beloved woman enters her life. Although this is another "school" poem, it is significant for two reasons: it declares that Sue, as Love, was Emily's first muse; and—written in 1863, when the experience described is past—it voices the poet's assumption that loving Sue has freed her from the imprisonment of childhood. Dickinson's tone is direct, self-aware, and even slightly cynical until at the end it becomes anguished. There the reality that she still may be a prisoner of a different kind colors her lines:

> Let Us play Yesterday –
> I – the Girl at school –
> You – and Eternity – the
> Untold Tale –
>
> Easing my famine
> At my Lexicon –
> Logarithm – had I – for Drink –
> 'Twas a dry Wine –
>
> Somewhat different – must be –
> Dreams tint the Sleep –
> Cunning Reds of Morning
> Made the Blind – leap –
>
> Still at the Egg-Life –
> Chafing the Shell –
> When you troubled the Ellipse –
> And the Bird fell –
>
> Manacles be dim – they say –
> To the new Free –
> Liberty – Commoner –

Never could – to me –

'Twas my last gratitude
When I slept – at night –
'Twas the first Miracle
Let in – with Light –

Can the Lark resume the Shell –
Easier – for the Sky –
Wouldn't Bonds hurt more
Than Yesterday?

Wouldn't Dungeons sorer grate
On the Man – free –
Just long enough to taste –
Then – doomed new –

God of the Manacle
As of the Free –
Take not my Liberty
Away from me – (728)

The poem has two time frames, then and now. It presents, as well, two characters: the speaker as she was, and is, and the beloved woman. The latter, as Sue usually does, represents eternity; like eternity, and because she is sexually unknown, she is also for the Dickinson who loved books, the "Untold Tale." The speaker is hungry and thirsty and tries to appease her hunger with study: words (Lexicon) and figures (Logarithm). But she finds them insufficient: "Somewhat different – must be." In her dreams she imagines the colors of morning, the reds of sexuality. While she is still thus blind as an unhatched chicken, still in her egg or "Ellipse" (in equilibrium), the beloved woman comes to "trouble" her, to awaken and arouse; "and the Bird fell." By an adroit reversal of the meaning implicit in the comfortable nesting imagery of earlier poems, Dickinson says here that Sue startled her into adulthood. She freed her from childhood, for which she still feels "gratitude." The experience, however, was a "doom" and not altogether pleasant.

So the seventh stanza with its pointed question, "Can the Lark resume the Shell," is not without a suggestion of nostalgia for the "Egg-Life." Such an embryonic existence meant bonds and dungeons, and Dickinson does not want to resume it or them. But her last lines, rhyming couplets to create emphasis, are a prayer for her liberty, which still seems endangered. The beloved woman has liberated Dickinson's sexual feelings, even her imagination; but now Dickinson's speaker is a free "Man" who remembers the old manacles too vividly. As other poems of the Sue cycle show, moreover, she has only been freed into a different imprisonment.[56]

The beloved woman herself, whose charm imprisons the speaker, is a jailer or jail. Dickinson spends her life, she once suggests playfully, laying siege to her who "never capitulates" (L 2.631). As Susan Dickinson became more despotic, more given to tantrums in middle age, Emily began alluding to her knowingly, forgivingly, as a tyrant: "Cherish Power – dear," she writes in 1878, "Remember that stands in the Bible between the Kingdom and the Glory, because it is wilder than either of them" (L 2.631). Sue was in her heart; there, she told Maria Whitney, one must expect to find wildness (L 3.793). Since Sue never "capitulated"—never loved her unreservedly—the speaker sees her in one set of epithets as a giant or "Golia[t]h." (She uses the misspelling "Goliah," especially commonplace in seventeenth-century prose.) Sue is the creature of "Sinew and Snow" (L 3.733). The poet herself is "David – the Troubadour" (1545), who tries to lay her low with song. The figure of Goliath, puzzling to many,[57] is associated, like the social Mrs. Austin Dickinson, with "the World." Poem 540, at the heart of the Sue cycle, pits the poet and her poems against the world's champion, Sue as giant:

> I took my Power in my Hand –
> And went against the World –
> 'Twas not so much as David – had –
> But I – was twice as bold –
>
> I aimed my Pebble – but Myself
> Was all the one that fell –
> Was it Goliah – was too large –
> Or was myself – too small? (540)

There is black humor at Dickinson's own expense here; a resumption of the imagery of size that she likes to use in evaluating lovers; and a brilliantly bitter imaging of love as rage ("I aimed my Pebble"—a poem?) and love as disgraceful death. In 1873, when Sue was making many trips to the middle west, Dickinson writes to someone called Goliah who has forgotten to write to her. The pleading accents are the same as those of her letters to Sue in Baltimore when they were girls:

The most pathetic thing I do
Is play I hear from you –
I make believe until my Heart
Almost believes it too
But when I break it with the news
You knew it was not true
I wish I had not broken it –
Goliah – so would you – (1290)

Sue, who "breaks many commandments," keeps one: "do it unto the Glory" (L 2.652). With her appetite for sensations and pleasures of an artistic (if not a sexual) sort, she is seen as exotic. Representing erotic desire and the "East," she is Cleopatra. Living west of the homestead, she is dazzling as sunset. Since she *is* eternity, images of sunset become her. Among the many poems-as-notes Emily sent her sister-in-law is one that survives in the Harvard collection. Penciled, folded in a little packet with "Sue" on top, it is written in the sort of code language Dickinson used to address her. Ostensibly about the peak of Tenerife, a dormant volcano on the largest of the Canary Islands, the poem is a love letter to Sue, the ice maid/mountain/jailer/queen:

Ah, Teneriffe!
Retreating Mountain!
Purple of Ages – pause for *you* –
Sunset – reviews her Sapphire Regiment –
Day – drops you her Red Adieu!

Still – Clad in your Mail of ices –
Thigh of Granite – and thew – of Steel –
Heedless – alike – of pomp – or parting

Ah, Teneriffe!
I'm kneeling – still – (666)

It is probable that Austin, had he intercepted this message when it was delivered to the Evergreens, would have thought his sister was continuing her lyrical salutes to volcanoes, far-off islands, and the mysteries of nature. But Vesuvius was one of Emily's nicknames for Sue,[58] and "Teneriffe" is its analogue. That she was "retreating," growing more aloof toward Emily, time had shown. She was "Still"—important word—unyielding. The code here is explicit: her thighs are "Granite." The last lines with their last "still" are as servile as any Sue could wish. As she will do for Master, Emily Dickinson makes the beloved woman master-mistress of Nature. Time stops for her; the armies of the sky march past for her pleasure; the day itself is her lover. She of course is "heedless" of them all, as of the poet.

In 1858, when Emily Dickinson began copying and binding her poems into packets, her beloved woman had been her beloved brother's wife for two years. The challenge to her good will, the complications for her already surcharged psyche, were obviously immense. A few poems about the theft of her pearl by a black Malay appear in the fascicles around 1863. They are a vision of Austin's courtship and marriage of Sue as a kind of rape and of the poet-speaker as triumphed over by one braver, because cruder, than herself; by a man who can swim—in fact, the diver of 84:

> The Malay – took the Pearl –
> Not – I – the Earl –
> I – feared the Sea – too much
> Unsanctified – to touch –
>
> Praying that I might be
> Worthy – the Destiny –
> The Swarthy fellow swam –
> And bore my Jewel – Home –
>
> Home to the Hut! What lot
> Had I – the Jewel – got –
> Borne on a dusky Breast –
> I had not deemed a Vest
> Of Amber – fit –
>
> The Negro never knew
> I – wooed it – too
> To gain, or be undone –
> Alike to Him – One – (452)

There have been many discussions of this poem. In 1951 Rebecca Patterson acknowledged the sexual rivalry and triangularity of its theme by identifying the Earl, the Malay, and the Pearl as Dickinson, John Anthon, and Kate Scott Anthon.[59] Patterson's hypothesis—notorious in its time—was that Dickinson's love poetry was largely devoted to Sue's friend, Mrs. Anthon. (I well remember the indignation of the man who taught Dickinson at my girls' academy about such allegations of "Sapphism.") Theodora Van Wagenen Ward claims that the pearl's "spherical form represents the wholeness that Emily was reaching for."[60]

Eleanor Wilner writes that Dickinson is the Earl: "with her Puritan idea of renunciation necessary for this aristocratic election . . . she cannot dive into the 'Unsanctified' sea, into the realms of instinct and sensuality, to claim the pearl, an image that combines body and soul."[61] Robert Weisbuch argues that the poem refers to no subject but is "the moral recommendation of certain attitudes, the 'teaching' function of traditional allegories, without referring to extrapoetic codes of conduct. The poem gracefully transforms material to spiritual gain to illustrate a forceful moral: that nothing will come to the man who waits in selfish fear . . . [The poem's] recommendation of risk does not derive from any particular sphere of action."[62] Vivian Pollak observes that Weisbuch may "in one sense" be right, but then she says of the poem: "The pearl need not be Sue, the Malay need not be Austin, and the Earl need not be Emily. Yet however generalizable the situation depicted, the poem is informed by the sexual temptations of Dickinson's experience." And, she adds, "I have seen no discussion of this poem that adequately explains it. Perhaps the Sea represents the speaker's unconscious or female sexuality or an alien environment or nature or death. Probably the Sea represents the unknown."[63]

Like the poetry of Yeats, Emily Dickinson's poetry may be profitably read by regarding individual lyrics as contributing to a continuum in which imagery is often repeated, thereby gathering new or differentiated power. Dickinson imagines herself an Earl, as we have seen, in poem 704, impressing a woman who would not notice her earlier. Taken together, Dickinson's poems and letters establish Sue as her "Pearl," her "Jewel." The Earl does not seem, as Weisbuch says, to "wait in selfish fear"; for he is not selfish at all but thinks himself unsanctified to touch his pearl. While he is praying to be worthy of her, he is defeated. Why and whence comes the Malay? Should he be identified with Austin? Jack Capps associates the imagery of this poem with Browning's "Paracelsus," where "a prince," a "diver," "rises with his pearl."[64] The more helpful imagistic source is Thomas De Quincey's *Confessions of an English Opium Eater,* which Dickinson was trying to borrow in 1858 and then obtained for the family library. Any number of lines in the *Confessions* might have appealed to her, so crowded were they with fantasies about spirit messengers and ladies who could dance though they had been in the grave for two centuries. While in the Lake Country, however, De Quincey writes that he is bothered by "a Malay" who, though pacific, has a disconcerting aspect: "small, fierce, restless eyes, thin lips, slavish postures." He speaks no English. De Quincey bribes him to leave by giving him a large amount of opium. Later, he "festered . . . upon my dreams, and brought other Malays with him":

> The Malay has been a fearful enemy for months. I have been every night, through his means, transported into Asiatic scenes . . . I had done a deed . . . which [Isis and Osiris], the ibis and the crocodile trembled at. I was buried for a thousand years in stone coffins, with mummies, and sphinxes, in narrow chambers at the heart of eternal pyramids. I was kissed . . . amongst reeds and Nilotic mud.[65]

In De Quincey's passage, the imagery of Egypt and the Nile, which Dickinson will use for Sue and Cleopatra, is also associated with sexuality—"I was kissed"—and slime. It is the Malay who makes that so by conducting De Quincey in dreams to exotic places where he is punished for some "deed" by being buried alive or drowned. Two themes in De Quincey—the unspeakable deed and the living burial—are related to those of Dickinson's love poems for Sue in which she regards herself as guilty or in which she and the beloved woman are together in death. It is the Malay who, ugly himself, convicts De Quincey of a past crime. Though he is ignorant of everything De Quincey thinks (they cannot converse), he is his enemy. Giving the Malay such a great amount of opium is really De Quincey's effort to kill him.

Dickinson's use of the foreign Malay underscores her sexual difference from Austin—they do not "converse," being sexually separate. They are separate too in their ways of life. Dickinson's poem makes clear that "the swarthy fellow" is the diffident, aristocratic Earl's enemy. Without speech—much less poetry—he simply *takes* the beloved woman. The Malay has not even had much sexual desire for her. Dickinson's explanation is Shakespearean: "to gain, or be undone – / Alike to Him – One." With magnificent disdain, Dickinson, the Earl, scoffs that her treasure is carried "Home to the Hut!" The Evergreens, her brother's smaller mansion, merges with De Quincey's oriental huts while the twice-repeated (indignant) "Home" may remind us of Dickinson's old longing to give Sue a home, a "nest." Surely the inattentive wooer Austin, who often forgot to write Sue, is the Malay.

The Malay wins the jewel because he "swam," like the diver he is and Dickinson's speaker is not (84). There is no moral at all here; the poem does not "transform material to spiritual gain," nor do I think the poet recommends risk. Rather, the poem is an angry statement of fact: a man with "a Vest of Amber," "a Dusky Breast" has triumphed over the speaker because she "feared the Sea – too much." We have already seen that for Dickinson the sea—a multivalent symbol—is a frequent metaphor for eternity. ("Eternity sweeps round me like a Sea," she writes, "while I do my work" [L 3.750].) In 1865 Dickinson writes a troubled Sue, "You must let me go first, Sue, because I live in the Sea always and know the Road. I would have drowned twice to save you sinking" (L 2.441). Obviously the sea can also, then, mean calamity—the sea of Cole's *Voyage*. But the sea is also one of her metaphors for Sue, hinted at in "You – and Eternity – the Untold Tale." In *Confessions of an English Opium Eater* it is in the sea that the narrator is punished for his unspeakable deed: "I was kissed with cancerous kisses, by crocodiles . . . laid [in] Nilotic mud." The speaker in Dickinson's poem fears the Sea because she fears the deed: taking the pearl and violating eternity's rule whereby pearls go to divers. She fears too, as Pollak hypothesizes, what the sea also signifies: the unknown. Always a complex symbol for Dickinson, the sea is Sue as Unknown in the fullness of her sexuality. It is also Dickinson's own sexuality which she fears here, since taking the pearl must reveal it. Finally, we may recall "blame"—a word the speaker uses in 299 for those who can look at the beloved woman unstintingly "without a blame." Dickinson's speaker *never* really wants to be blameworthy. Indeed, she drops her life into a well in order to become "blameless" as a nun (271). While she is attempting to sacramentalize all the connotations of the sea in poem 452, one might say, the Malay simply claims the speaker's pearl. Yet she never says he steals it. Though she is filled with anger and contempt to think so, the pearl is the Malay's by right. It is his "destiny" as a male to have it.

In Dickinson's writing to or about Sue, the concepts of riches/poverty, intelligence/dullness, and the eastern sea — her complex conceit embracing passion, imagination, and eternal life—often merge. Poem 424 is another exploration of the triangular relationship, in which the poet is akin to the Malay in her failure to perceive her own (more limited but still actual) good fortune. In fascicle 14, this poem precedes the important "Your Riches – taught me – Poverty," and it is an ironic but similar contemplation of her own emotional situation:

> Removed from Accident of Loss
> By Accident of Gain
> Befalling not my simple Days –
> Myself had just to earn –
>
> Of Riches – as unconscious
> As is the Brown Malay

> Of Pearls in Eastern Waters,
> Marked His – What Holiday
>
> Would stir his slow conception –
> Had he the power to dream
> That but the Dower's fraction –
> Awaited even – Him –

Dickinson's language here is at the outset decidedly cryptic, as might be expected when a writer chooses to describe a thorny set of facts and a secret love. She says (using of herself, as she often does, the word "simple") that to be kept from losing (Sue) by gaining her is not a fate that will ever befall her. Her days are too simple; that is, they are insufficiently romantic (masculine) for that to happen. So she has "to earn" what she gets from Sue and sometimes (possibly because she craves more), she is "as unconscious" of her riches "As is the Brown Malay." The Malay, Austin, fails to see the pearls – and the Pearl – "marked His," or that she waits to be taken from "Eastern Waters": the sea of passionate love that ends in marriage. He would be thrilled if he had "the power to dream," to imagine, that anyone even slightly like Sue were awaiting him. But his is a "slow conception." Because some of its diction is drawn from the world usually associated with men—law, mathematics, and economics ("Accident of Loss/Gain," "fraction," "earn")—this emotional poem about rivalry, wherein she chafes at her limitations in love, has a rather hard edge. It implies the restlessness Dickinson's speaker experiences in the Sue cycle as a whole and the pearl sequence in particular because she must confront a painful and enduring reality.

Perhaps of all the pearl lyrics, poem 693 reveals most tellingly and powerfully the awkward yet ineluctable love for Sue. This is an allegory of Dickinson's *own* conventionality and a revelation of what she said love is: witchcraft, a spell. Here she appeals to the (implied) conceit of the sea and the concept of the one true pearl and the many hollow shells that did not contain it:

> Shells from the Coast mistaking –
> I cherished them for All –
> Happening in After Ages
> To entertain a Pearl –
>
> Wherefore so late – I murmured –
> My need of Thee – be done –
> Therefore – the Pearl responded –
> My Period begin

This poem resembles Dickinson's lyrics in which forgotten birdlings (39) are contrasted with the dove (48) who takes up residence in the speaker's heart. In this brief allegory, the shells call to mind her old school chums Jenny, Abiah, and the rest, who were cherished as if they constituted all of the experience of love. Then "in After Ages," Dickinson explains (using the word *entertains*, highly suitable for the social Sue), she happens to play host to the true image of love. This is the Pearl, akin to the "pearl of great price" to which Matthew 13:46 compares the soul.

Surprised because the Pearl appears "so late," the speaker asks her why she has come at all. The time for seeking pearls (soul mates) among shells (girls) is "done." The poem thus implies Dickinson's realization, voiced elsewhere, that her feeling for Sue, which has extended beyond the period of girlish sentimentality, is retrogressive. "My need of thee – be done," furthermore, is both a typical instance of the Dickinsonian continuing subjunctive and, possibly, an expression of determination: "*May* my need of thee be done." Important to the meaning of the poem is the Pearl's answer, which begins with "Therefore." Although and because (replies the Pearl) you no longer require such a love as I can offer, let me show you what it is like. There is delicate ominousness in the last line, which with fine unobtrusiveness suggests the language of a spell.

Into fascicle 10 and following "Come slowly, Eden" (211), Dickinson copied the most ardent of the pearl lyrics, one that fantasizes diving for the dangerous gem whose possession would be deadly. This poem's imagery is quite clear, especially within the sequence:

> *One Life* of so much Consequence!
> Yet I – for it – would pay –
> My soul's *entire income*
> In ceaseless – salary –
>
> *One Pearl* – to me – so signal –
> That I would instant dive –
> Although – I *knew* – to *take* it –
> Would *cost* me – *just a life!*
>
> The Sea is full – I know it!
> That – does not blur *my Gem!*
> It burns – distinct from all the row –
> *Intact – in Diadem!*

> The life is thick – I know it!
> Yet – not so dense a crowd –
> But *Monarchs* – are *perceptible* –
> Far down the dustiest Road! (270)

Sue's life is precious, Dickinson reflects. Like that of a distinguished person, it has consequence. As the emphasis insists, it is only "*One Life,*", yet worth "so much." Still, she herself is bold. Parrying with another emphasis, she promises her soul's "*entire income* / In ceaseless – salary" for the possession of such a person. More plainly, she would sell her soul over and over to possess Sue.

In the second quatrain, "to me" inflects the theme of other pearls, other girls in the sea of life who do not appeal. Sue is "signal," peerless. For her, the speaker would dive even if that meant dying; even if paying for Sue cost her "*just a life.*" (The last phrase has eloquent overtones. If she paid her soul for Sue, it would indeed cost her "just a life" in Christian thinking, where to sell the soul for any gain means damnation. The line conflates heavenly with earthly life if one recalls the burden of the first quatrain.)

Dickinson's exclamations, together with the opening lines of her third and fourth quatrains, convey the drama that is her astonishment at having chosen one pearl from among many: "The Sea is full – I know it!" / "The life is thick – I know it!" Poem 270 is related to many poems like "The Soul selects her own Society" or to 664 in which she declares,

> Of all the Souls that stand create
> I have elected – One –

Here she promises with the regal imagery frequent to this theme of the chosen one:

> When that which is – and that which was –
> Apart – intrinsic – stand –
> And this brief Drama in the flesh –
> Is shifted – like a Sand –
> When Figures show their royal Front –
> And Mists – are carved away,
> Behold the Atom – I preferred –
> To all the lists of Clay! (664)

The sequence about the gathering of the Pearl, then, discloses the many moods in which the poet viewed Sue's importance, and that of her marriage.

7

What about the Pearl herself? What was she feeling? We are never really told in the cluster of pearl poems. Sue sent Emily a cryptic note in autumn 1861, after Ned was born. This she marked *Private*. The summer of 1861 witnessed the crisis of Emily Dickinson's life. Her chief emotional supports were being removed: Bowles was ill and thinking of going abroad, Sue was distracted by her baby. That summer marked Emily's movement away from ordinary social intercourse (however conducted on her own terms) to a life of creative reclusion. Because she loved Sue (and later Bowles), however, she frequently rebuked them for making her choice inevitable, for living beyond her grasp. The Pearl was apparently suffering too. Sue's note shows some sympathy for Emily's sensitive feelings, and implies that she is not happily married:

> *Private* I have intended to write you Emily today but the quiet has not been mine. I send you this, lest I should seem to have turned away from a kiss.
>
> If you have suffered this past Summer I am sorry . . . *I* Emily bear a sorrow that I never uncover. If a nightingale sings with her breast against a thorn, why not *we*? When I can, I shall write.[66]

Longsworth suggests that Sue's continuing love for the Reverend Samuel Bartlett may have been the source of her pain. A festering wound that provokes song could, indeed, describe the memory of love. More probably, the "sorrow" is Sue's realization that she has made the wrong choice, that she should not have married Austin. On the surface, however, she was living with stylish equanimity.

Certain poems in the Sue cycle address the reality of what Dickinson had once feared "when he takes you from me, to live in his new home" (L 1.203)—Sue's altered behavior toward her as Austin's wife:

> She's happy, with a new Content –
> That feels to her – like Sacrament –
> She's busy – with an altered Care –
> As just apprenticed to the Air –
>
> She's tearful – if she weep at all –
> For blissful Causes – Most of all
> That Heaven permit so meek as her –
> To such a Fate – to Minister (535)

"Like Sacrament," "feels to her," "As just apprenticed to the Air": these phrases scrutinize the female subject of the poem, establishing a distance between her euphoric state of mind and the mordantly observant Dickinson's. The picture provided of the subject is of an "altered" being who is suddenly linked with "air," or unreality, and who, having lost the power of deep feeling ("if she weep at all"), has become the typical Victorian sentimentalist, "tearful . . . For blissful Causes." Susan Gilbert, as Mrs. William Austin Dickinson, was becoming a well-known hostess whose oysters at midnight suppers and whose handsome presence in the Dickinson pew at church were much appreciated at first in Amherst. "Happy," "busy," with the "altered Care" of the chatelaine of an important household: this was the Sue who became her "vast, sweet Sister" and the equivalent of Cleopatra. Yet Dickinson was capable of conflating Sue's vastness—her importance to *her* and her social prominence—with Sue's false posturing as a "meek" angel in the house. Other women could have meek and timid faces as in the Victorian formula. Sue, her "queen," could not.

Sue's marriage did not appear unhappy at first. And as late as 1862 Dickinson was recording her guilt for having resented Sue and Austin's apparent content. In poem 538 the word "blame" appears again, this time attached to Sue and Austin, both "beloved," who wound her without intention:

> 'Tis true – They shut me in the Cold –
> But then – Themselves were warm
> And could not know the feeling 'twas –
> Forget it – Lord – of Them –
>
> Let not my Witness hinder Them
> In Heavenly esteem –
> No Paradise could be – Conferred
> Through Their beloved Blame –
>
> The Harm They did – was short – And since
> Myself – who bore it – do –
> Forgive Them – Even as Myself –
> Or else – forgive not me –

Being excluded or abandoned is one of the chief themes of the poems usually associated with Master, yet it appears here (and we have seen it appear earlier) in connection with Sue. One of the striking aspects of this poem is its organization as both argument and prayer to God (a measure of the seriousness of Dickinson's pain). She identifies the harm done her as "short" and employs a frequent conceit, paradise and its relation to earthly loves, as a means of defining the extent of her forgiveness. Just as there can be no paradise for the speaker of "I cannot live with You" (because her beloved has deprived her of the beatific vision of any but himself), so blaming Austin and Sue would provide no paradise for *this* speaker either. Her summary line, however, is lame. She does not make a close rhyme with *do* as she often does to achieve emphasis. Her anger is not quite submerged.

It is possible that the harm done to Dickinson by being forced into the cold was indeed short. But I think that the "early, and painful rejection by Sue,"[67] which Sewall hypothesizes, occurred not only early but steadily and late. "Now I knew I lost Her" was probably written in 1872, and though the worst anguish caused Dickinson by Sue's wedding was confined to a specific period, the sadness of her sense of exclusion persisted until she died.

This was true, quite simply, because of the nature and degree of Dickinson's love for Sue. "The largest Woman's Heart [she] knew," an "unadorned" but munificent Queen, the orphaned adoptee of the Dickinson family had become for Emily, daughter of the Squire himself, the sum of what is desirable, however foolishly so. Love is not always— perhaps rarely—inspired by a suitable object. Her poems prove how clearly Dickinson knew it.

8

I have said that the conceit of "teaching" (certainly an old one in use between lovers) figures in Dickinson's poems about Sue, particularly 299. Ironically, Sue seems to have behaved toward Emily like a teacher—as Sewall says, like "a mentor of some standing"[68]—even when it came to writing poetry. In Sue, Emily had a sophisticated reader: one who liked to preen about entertaining Emerson, one who had the newest books and magazines. Not only notes but poems were sent from the homestead to the Evergreens. One was the first and second versions of "Safe in their Alabaster Chambers." The second version provoked a reserved reply:

> I am not suited dear Emily with the second verse – It is remarkable as the chain lightening that blinds us hot nights in the Southern sky but it does not go with the ghostly shimmer of the first verse as well as the other one . . . You never made a peer for that verse, and I

guess you[r] kingdom doesn't hold one – I always go to the fire and get warm after thinking of it, but I never *can* again –[69]

Although Sue's note ends with a compliment, it is neither complimentary nor encouraging and its tone seems patronizing. "I am not suited": the phrase is itself suited to a queen. Sue's advice had apparently piqued the Dickinson imagination to produce the august stanza "Grand go the Years," replacing the more febrile but witty "Light laughs the breeze." (Sue, though, disliked the replacement.) Dickinson, who identified hearing true poetry with feeling blown apart, must have appreciated Sue's comparison to lightning (especially since they both admired Thomas Cole's exercises in *terribilità* and the sublime). But certainly she may have been affronted by Sue's supposition that she could not equal her poem's first verse. "You[r] kingdom": thus wrote the married woman from her own.

There is no evidence that Dickinson (having tried even a third version to "suit" her) sought Sue's advice again. Each new version was evidently adopted to please a woman who liked grandeur and valued hauteur. So version two presents "Diadems" and "Doges" and version three, "Tents of Marble." Dickinson thanked Sue: "Your praise is good – to me – because I *know* it *knows* – and *suppose* it *means* – Could I make you and Austin – proud – sometime – a great way off – 'twould give me taller feet" (L 2.380). Her image of taller feet suggests those of Egyptian statues, elongated and visualized with high insteps. She was suggesting that she might be able to earn fame, possibly the immortality for which the Egyptians built so grandly. She might then deserve to keep Sue's love. It is a humble and wistful note.

Emily Dickinson always seems to have longed to please and impress Sue as a writer. In October 1882, for instance, she wrote two drafts before sending to the Evergreens a short note bidding goodbye to Sue, who was going to a niece's wedding in Michigan. The note was sent with rose petals. In Tennyson's *Maud,* read by Sue and Emily in the 1850s, the lover is obsessed with rose petals; so they may have been a reminder of their old attachment. Dickinson's note apologizes (wittily) for them, however, and reminds Sue that Emily's love is as unchangeable as the North Star: "Excuse Emily and her Atoms – the 'North Star' is of small fabric, but it denotes much." In order to send Sue this message, Dickinson had drafted two earlier ones. The first has an air of nervousness for which the conscientiousness of an artist does not seem solely responsible:

Sister,

Excuse me for disturbing Susan with fragilities on the eve of her departure – the North Star is but of a small fabric yet it achieves (implies) much

In the second draft, Dickinson brackets the word "denotes" and substitutes "implies." The poem "Cosmopolites without a plea" (1589) appears on the verso of the sheet of paper Dickinson used for her first draft, suggesting that Sue was the cosmopolite who "Alight[s] in every Land." She recognized the worldliness of her "Sister," even the cold heart that Sue might show her. Nevertheless, to win her respect in poetry was an aim she never abandoned.

She evidently knew that Sue's wit, which she often praises, was limited and her imagination curtailed. Sometimes the knowledge shook itself out in brilliant, breathless lines. These were sent across the lawn, signed "Emily":

> I showed her Hights she never saw –
> "Would'st Climb," I said?
> She said – "Not so" –
> "With *me –*" I said – with *me?*
> I showed her Secrets – Morning's Nest –
> The Rope the Nights were put across –
> And *now* – "Would'st have me for a Guest?"
> She could not find her Yes –
> And then, I brake my life – And Lo,
> A Light, for her, did solemn glow,
> The larger, as her face withdrew –
> And *could* she, further, "No"? (446)

This is a dazzling display of psychological insight and a telling revelation of the poet's inner life. Its ordering conceit is the heights of love that the speaker would like to climb with her unwilling beloved. (We remember that Dickinson had used the image of herself climbing hills with Sue in poem 14, "One Sister have I": a tame domestic vision by comparison. In poem 453, "Love – thou art high," she extends "heights" to those of the Ecuadorian mountain Chimborazo, painted by Cole's student Frederic Church.) Climbing, of course, has sexual implications. And Dickinson's speaker, as in "Wild Nights," asks to be embraced: "Would'st have me for a Guest?" The secrets being shown, however, are not only those of the heart but of life itself. Dickinson expresses them as the limits of nature: between morning and night. "We know that the secret of the world is profound," says Emerson in "The Poet," and "the value of genius to us is the veracity of its report" upon it.[70] Dickinson tries to parlay genius for love. She is unsuccessful because the beloved is not convinced: she immediately says "Not so" to the first question; "could not find her Yes" to the more specific second; and withdraws altogether when Dickinson "brake [her] life"—that is, one supposes, when Dickinson abandoned caution to reveal how wholly she depended on her love. The poem's ending is poignant. Dickinson's last question is addressed to herself. Her own revelation of feeling has indeed illuminated the beloved, who does at last understand the grave truth: "A Light, for her, did solemn glow." The light, the speaker's love, only intensifies with the other's withdrawal. But it is that sorry fact of withdrawal, despite understanding, which she cannot credit: "And *could* she, further, 'No'?"

In "There's been a Death, in the Opposite House" (389), Dickinson assumes masculine gender to write the lines "They wonder if it died – on that – / I used to – when a Boy." Marveling at her knowledge of the type of soil needed for growing corn, Samuel Bowles once asked Sue, "How did that girl" acquire it? Sue's reply was a quotation from poem 389, and considering the many occasions on which Dickinson slipped into male gender in poetry, it may have been ironic: "That was Emily 'when a Boy'."[71] The fact is that Sue and Emily as girls seem to have indulged in a sort of light sexual conspiracy, a Rosalind–Celia romance, whereby Emily *was* the boy. The game was both comradely and playful. Cryptic lines from Dickinson to Sue occasionally seem to remind her that the romance was quintessentially a charade: "Sister, We both are Women, and there is a Will of God . . . Thank you for Tenderness" (L 2.445).

Fascicle 16 contains an alternate version of poem 446, in which Dickinson's speaker is a woman being wooed by a man: "He showed me Hights I never saw." It is identical with the version just discussed. Like "Going to Him! Happy letter!" and "Going – to – Her!" / "Happy – Letter!" (494, two versions), 446 demonstrates that she could readily adapt her passionate thoughts across gender. (Indeed, her store of metaphors discloses an economy of means in the expression of love, that challenges a reader in search of distinctions. Since Sue and Bowles were much alike in many ways, the similarity of Dickinson's images may have been inevitable.) In a number of poems, such as "I rose – because He sank" (616), she seems to be relating—in a trope echoing *Jane Eyre*[72]—her victory of virtue over a beloved but libidinous male.

The female speaker in the fascicle version of 446, however, enjoys a similar moral conquest: she says "No," despite the lover's despair. We can see, then, that whether Dickinson's persona is female or male, she imagines the same situation: love and renunciation.

There is a difference, however, in her account of the causes of each renunciation. As the Master materials make clear, Dickinson's female persona in love with Master postpones their communion, expecting to enjoy it in eternity. There is nothing "wrong" in the character of their love; it is wrong only because the "Queen's place" next to him is already taken (L 2.374). In the Sue cycle, however, the passion of the two women, mirror images of each other, is forbidden as a *type*. In some poems ("The Malay – took the pearl") Sue is forbidden because she has been taken by somebody else. (The powerlessness and pathos of Dickinson's speaker are manifest when we recall that as early as poem 14 "he" had already "taken" her.) But by far the majority of the Sue poems report that, unlike Master who regrets being separated from Dickinson's speaker, the female lover rejects Dickinson because—like Sue, as Emily complains in poem 535—she is too conventional, she cannot "climb heights." She is morally afraid to cross the boundary of gender as a lover. Perhaps even more important, something in the headlong extravagance of the other's feeling may deaden her own. This poem at least makes Dickinson the beloved's accomplice in fearing to cross lines. As she says, "I – feared the Sea – too much" (452).

Two well-known poems, 458 and 518, describe this situation and have often either been avoided or, in the case of 518, explained as intended for Elizabeth Barrett Browning.[73] Poem 518, "Her sweet Weight on my Heart a Night," appears in fascicle 29 with others such as " 'Tis Opposites – entice" (355) and "To love thee Year by Year" (434). All describe a relationship like Emily's with Sue. In "Her sweet Weight," the lovers have "scarcely" settled into an embrace (and the speaker sees the partner as her superior: she *deigned* to lie) when the bride slips away. The speaker contrives an intricate shower of verbal/visual camouflage to suggest that this scene may have been a dream, "a Fiction superseding Faith"; but Dickinson's last words in her poems are frequently definitive, and the last one of 518 is "real." When Lavinia first gave her Emily's manuscripts, Sue marked them in pencil according to theme: Love, Nature, Death, and so on. She marked this poem with the initial "S," appearing to acknowledge its relevancy to herself.

Cynthia Griffin Wolff's thesis in her biography of Dickinson concerns the function of eye-to-eye, face-to-face vision.[74] Yet she does not discuss poem 458. "Like Eyes that looked on Wastes" is among the most powerful of Emily Dickinson's poems. It is the crux of the Sue story, as Sue herself seems to have indicated.

In reading "Like Eyes that looked on Wastes" one is put in mind of similar literary materials: Hawthorne's characters, defeated by gazing into mirrors or having their images "stolen" in portraits; the Pre-Raphaelite heroines, enervated by staring into mirrors; Tennyson's Lady of Shalott, of course, with the mirror of shadows and unreality into which she stares until a man's image shatters her. Yet none of these, especially Tennyson's Lady, is precisely relevant to Dickinson's poem. (The Lady falls in love with Lancelot and not her own image.) The mirrors encountered in nineteenth-century art are often measures of the singular powers and dangers of narcissism. Homosexual love has been regarded, widely, as an exercise in narcissism, the worship and service of one's own body in the body of another. But no matter how physically mirroring lesbianism may be, it is still love and there is still an "other," who is like but separate from and so *not* like the "one." The verbal circularity that characterizes "Her breast is fit for pearls" appears once more in this poem, in the circular imagery of two faces. Their reciprocal gaze describes that mirror by which many nineteenth-century painters portrayed Sapphic love:

> Like Eyes that looked on Wastes –
> Incredulous of Ought
> But Blank – and steady Wilderness –
> Diversified by Night
>
> Just Infinites of Nought –
> As far as it could see –
> So looked the face I looked upon –
> So looked itself – on Me –
>
> I offered it no Help –
> Because the Cause was Mine –
> The Misery a Compact
> As hopeless – as divine –
>
> Neither – would be absolved –
> Neither would be a Queen
> Without the Other – Therefore –
> We perish – tho' We reign – (458)

John Donne's image in "The Ecstasy" of "eyebeams twisted" as lovers devour each other in a gaze is matched here by Dickinson's contradictory image of the "wastes" that each lover sees in the other. As the beloved regards her, the speaker encounters "Wilderness" and "Infinites of Nought"—very different from so many poets' usual avowals of beholding in the mistress the sight that forms their world. That "steady" emptiness is, interestingly, uncivilized and related to the wilderness of another poem (604) in which Dickinson renders the experience of an alien and comfortless place. One effect in 458, possibly obtained through familiarity with Hudson River and Luminist paintings, is the sense of a negative extension, an amplitude of large empty spaces that terrify but excite. Cole's *Ox-Bow (View from Mt. Holyoke)*, which was well known in Dickinson's region, is a forerunner of the immense canvases of the Luminists; these could suggest a placid peace, as in George Inness, or, as in Frederic Church's *Twilight in the Wilderness* (1860), a passionate desolation. Although most Luminist canvases are grand and Dickinson's spaces are small, her lines move out on the page in 458 with a rhetorical absence of flourish, and a repetition in stanza two, that conveys a related, unhappy monotony. Furthermore, Luminists like Martin Johnson Heade, also working in the 1860s, often depicted the night sky exacerbated by thunder or hanging heavily above a drowned body on a shore that furnished ingredients of terror, just as poem 458 does.

"Like Eyes that look on Wastes" is distinguishable from other poems of the Sue cycle in which the beloved rejects her while Dickinson's speaker insists, "Precious to Me – She still shall be – / Though She forget the name I bear" (727). In 458 there is no rejection. Instead, there is "a compact in misery," by which neither will be "absolved" from (give up the wrong and thrill of) sexual feeling; nor can become "a Queen Without [marrying] the Other." Dickinson's last line marvelously conveys frustration through paradox: "We perish – tho' We reign," that is, we are killed by the impasse of this love, losing the perfect happiness we should have; yet we are crowned by, and we rule by, our love. This is the single occasion in the poems when the beloved woman and the speaker seem equally impassioned.

An illustration of poem 458 might be furnished by any number of Pre-Raphaelite studies of stricken, brooding women. Since it was painted in 1881, Rossetti's *Mnemosyne* (Memory, the titaness) could not have contributed to Dickinson's poem. But, like other Pre-Raphaelite paintings, *Mnemosyne* displays that hopeless, heavy-lidded stare represented in Dickinson's poem which appears to reflect all sorrows and knowledge. Dickinson could have seen copies of other Pre-Raphaelite portraits or photographs—of Lizzie Siddal, Janie Morris, Fanny

Cornforth—in magazines, each with the woman's wide gaze suggesting infinite evocations of weariness and sin. By the end of the century, women gazing into each other's eyes or kissing in a mirror became symbolic of lesbian love.[75]

9

The titanic power of memory is a theme Dickinson's mature poems often consider and associate with Sue. Her letters frequently show fear that Sue may forget her, especially after the mid-1860s when, for whatever reason, Dickinson ceased visiting her sister-in-law's house. (That the house had been the setting for difficult experiences—the sight of Sue as Austin's wife, her own attraction to Samuel Bowles, and possibly Sue's flirtation with him—may have kept her away.) Though she knew that Sue could be a "pseudo Sister," she addressed her over and over as "sister" in the 1880s, verbally renewing the relationship welcomed in 1856 (L 3.716, 830). Sue, first her muse, had become a kind of Mnemosyne, the source and also the valued secret sharer of remembered moments from which Dickinson made poems.

For Dickinson, memory was occasionally a terrible specter, and she thought "Many would fly" from it had they wings (1242). It could be an old-fashioned garden like her own, yet dangerous; for it was "divine intemperance" to walk there alone, encountering ghosts (1753). More usually, however, she spoke of it in the architectural terms that implied its importance as the foundation of her art. It was a "wily-subterranean Inn" that, once inside, you could not leave (1406). It was a "sacred Closet" (1273). It had "the deepest Cellar / That ever Mason laid" (1182). Like the Dickinson house or Austin's Evergreens, it was full of rooms in which dramas, however private, had taken place and whose accents lingered over time to "silence you" (1273). Like the quiescent volcanoes also associated with Sue, Memory could kill, its roots firm and its effects explosive.

To remember Sue had been the compelling exercise Dickinson set herself in youthful poems. Begging Sue to remember *her* would be the theme of many of her letters. Always associating Sue with the "firmament" and the "Arabian Nights," regarding herself as far less rare, Dickinson would recall her to their early tie (L 2.464, 465). In a witty, newsy, lyrical letter to Sue who was vacationing in Swampscott with her children, Dickinson concluded, "Miss me sometimes, dear – Not on most occasions, but the Seldoms of the Mind" (L 2.509). This gentle request was made in 1873 and may reflect her awareness that Sue did not think of her then with much intensity. For Sue (occupied, after all, with a growing family: an epileptic son, a daughter she was eager to launch socially, and finally another infant), their relationship had become familial. Dickinson's letters of the 1870s and 1880s do not suggest that Sue was always condescending or distant; many notes disclose the intimacy of two householders, exchanging medications, borrowing eggs. Twice Dickinson describes the coffee in the cup Sue leaves after their "annual parting" when Sue took her children to Swampscott (L 2.512). The picture she sketches is of loneliness when a continual conversation is interrupted. Gilbert's death in 1883 brought Emily to Sue's house after almost two decades and brought Sue, apparently, to depend on her sympathy. A semblance of their old romantic friendship quickened and Emily could write Sue: "Your little mental gallantries are sweet as chivalry, which is to me a shining Word." Any show of love from Sue might result in the resumption of courtly imagery: "I sometimes remember we are to die, and hasten toward the Heart which how could I woo in a rendezvous where there is no Face?" (L 3.791–792). As far as Emily was concerned, no passion *ever* died:

> The embers of a Thousand Years
> Uncovered by the Hand
> That fondled them when they were Fire
> Will stir and understand – (1383)

Sue's intensity, however, was chiefly reserved for current ambitions. A number of Dickinson's poems from the late 1850s until the 1870s record the poet's reactions, often her disappointment, as Sue drew away from her. "Precious to Me – She still shall be" was written about seven years after Sue's wedding:

> Precious to Me – She still shall be –
> Though She forget the name I bear –
> The fashion of the Gown I wear –
> The very Color of My Hair –
> So like the Meadows – now –
> I dared to show a Tress of Their's
> If haply – She might not despise
> A Buttercup's Array –
>
> I know the Whole – obscures the Part –
> The fraction – that appeased the Heart
> Till Number's Empery –
> Remembered – as the Milliner's flower

When Summer's Everlasting Dower –
Confronts the dazzled Bee (727)

This poem recognizes that (presumably) Sue is now in possession of "the whole" of love, rather than the mere part represented by Emily's love for her. The poet is reduced to sending her a tress from the meadows – buttercups or other flowers – to serve, like a flower on a hat, as a poor memento of both the milliner and the summer. This is among the few poems that show some knowledge of the sonnet tradition. It begins with a two-line thesis and is logically divided into octave and sestet. Like Dickinson's poems in tercets, 727 indicates that her habitual use of the quatrain derived from choice and not from ignorance. Though she rhymes only fleetingly in the first quatrain, the sestet is exactly rhymed with a nice sense of the ironic connections/identifications rhyme can establish between the "Part" ("flower") and the "Whole" ("Empery," "Dower"). Perhaps because she is writing a love poem (however dissatisfied), perhaps thinking of Elizabeth Barrett Browning's *Sonnets from the Portuguese*, Dickinson composes within the sonnet tradition to make her unique *plainte* of separation. It is possible that her knowledge of Barrett Browning's rhyming techniques, which (as Virginia Woolf remarks in a note to *Flush*) were creatively iconoclastic, helped her to break with tradition in the second quatrain of the octave. The poem itself is about disruption. Sue has forgotten her, both her name and person (note that she mentions her [red] hair and [white?] gown, not too easy to forget). Probably what Dickinson means by saying that "like the Meadows" she "dared to show a Tress" is that she has sent Sue a poem about flowers, hoping she will not "despise" it.

In some poems about Sue's failure to remember, Dickinson meditates that Sue has also forgotten to be herself. Sue's desire, early and late, to get out of Amherst and amuse herself at the shore or at resorts like the Hotel Champlain in Plattsburgh, New York, or at the Brooklyn Opera House and Delmonico's in New York City made her seem to the reclusive Emily a frenetic traveler. A poem like "Cosmopolites without a plea" (1589) contemplates her movements as evidence of pride and superficiality, and there her travels are actual. The more haunting and final "Now I knew I lost her," however, analyzes a beloved who deserts the poet though she is physically present, one who has ceased to *be* who she was:

> Now I knew I lost her –
> Not that she was gone –

But Remoteness travelled
On her Face and Tongue.

Alien, though adjoining
As a Foreign Race –
Traversed she though pausing
Latitudeless Place.

Elements Unaltered –
Universe the same
But Love's transmigration –
Somehow this had come –

Henceforth to remember
Nature took the Day
I had paid so much for –
His is Penury
Not who toils for Freedom
Or for Family
But the Restitution
Of Idolatry. (1219)

In "Like Eyes that looked on Wastes," Dickinson uses spatial imagery to suggest displaced relation and the vivid conviction of emptiness to which the speaker is led by homoerotic love. "Now I knew I lost her" similarly presents a nearly surrealistic portrait of a woman on whose face and in whose voice indifference and pretension are so apparent that they make a void like a receding, empty space. Dickinson's second quatrain is pointed. Sue may live next door but she is alien and foreign; she is no longer the sister of poem 14. Though she pauses in time and space as the resident of the "adjoining" house, her spirit moves endlessly across latitudes with no fixed identity, no firm allegiance, no "place." Dickinson's words "gone," "Remoteness," "Traversed," "transmigration" explain Sue's faithlessness in the language of travel so that what was an occasional pleasure is translated (by a poet who detests leaving home) into the symptom of an altered heart. The poem has a ghostly and, once again, surreal quality; for the speaker watches someone move who is not moving and experiences her close-up looks and words as if they were at a distance.

Dickinson's lines "Henceforth to remember / Nature took the Day / I had paid so much for" are typical of many that belong to the Sue cycle; they are not readily understandable in terms of one poem alone. Poems like 1219 about Sue often have an impulsive cast. The absence of predication in "Elements Unaltered – / Universe the same" suggests rapid calculation. "Henceforth to remember" is a line that seems to be flung at the speaker herself: "Remember this henceforth," or remember what happened, the transmigration of love. The lines "Nature took the Day / I had paid so much for" probably allude, like many lines in other poems, to the fact that Sue's heterosexual nature, whatever it is that moves women toward men, stole the Sue that Dickinson's love paid for.

One may wonder, since it is prominent in the Sue cycle, whether Dickinson's imagery of riches and payment appears so frequently because Sue liked money and things; because of the traditional Elizabethan association of love with wealth that Dickinson met, especially in Shakespeare's sonnets; or both. Many cryptic poems seem addressed in sad censure to someone obsessed with money:

> Surfaces may be invested
> Did the Diamond grow
> General as the Dandelion
> Would you serve it so? (1110)

A brilliant technical touch in 1219 is the rhyming of "Penury," "Family," and "Idolatry" in which penury becomes equated with the idolatry paid Sue, and family serves as a haunting explanatory and ironic reinforcement of the music of absence, disconnection, and want. Poems like "Precious to Me – She still shall be," "Now I knew I lost her," and "Like Eyes that look on Wastes" explore the fear and joy that characterized Dickinson's memorable relationship with her sister-in-law.

A letter from Susan Gilbert to the Bartletts in 1854 (three years before her marriage) is written with breezy charm. She was enjoying the spring and looking ahead to a "tour in the state of New York." The Edward Dickinsons were away. "I forgot to tell you," she adds, "I am keeping house with Emily, while the family are in Washington—We frighten each other to death nearly every night—with that exception, we have very independent times."[76] The large Dickinson house at dark was probably the source of Sue's fright; there were many robberies and break-ins in Amherst. But for the poet, under the same roof alone with the one she loved, the fear may have been more complex.

No record exists of Sue's attendance at her sister-in-law's funeral (though there *is* a report, in Vinnie's angry words, of the loud and lavish party she gave in 1887 on the anniversary of Emily's death). Since Mabel Todd attended the funeral in the company of Austin—and since Sue may have been aware that Emily knew of, and apparently sanctioned, their affair—she may have stayed away. But hers had been the most intimate of all services performed for the dead poet: she dressed the body for burial.

By 1886 Sue was a much-troubled woman. Broken by the death of Gilbert in 1883, daily insulted by Austin's open affair, she preserved some equilibrium in mothering her older children but, by all accounts, grew increasingly despotic and temperamental. Dickinson once painted a tender portrait of her as a new mother in 1862, revealing an appreciation of the sweet intimacy of mother and child that is quite without chagrin at Sue's new occupation:

> Sue – draws her little Boy – pleasant days – in a Cab – and Carlo – walks behind, accompanied by a Cat – from each establishment –
> It looks funny to see so small a man, going out of Austin's House. (L 2.406)

Emily Dickinson was a devoted aunt, remembered with great fondness by her niece and nephew. She liked to join in their games, especially hide-and-seek, becoming like a child with them; and tendered advice with affectionate diplomacy when they were older. When Sue became a mother she was jealous at first. (Her truly bizarre poem for Ned's birth in which she contemplates "tie[ing] him to a pin" [218] makes that obvious.) But through Sue she achieved a near-maternal tenderness: "Kiss little Ned in the seam in the neck, entirely for me" (L 2.434). In another proof of love, not without distinct physicality, she revises her nest image to accommodate Sue as mother: "Here is a crumb – for the 'Ring dove' – and a spray for *his* Nest, a little while ago – *just* – 'Sue' " (L 2.380). The passion for Sue's eyes, face, and kisses was ostensibly funneled now into tender concern. She had written to Sue from Cambridge, "for the Woman whom I prefer, Here is Festival – Where my Hands are cut, Her fingers will be found inside . . . Take the Key to the Lily, now, and I will lock the Rose" (L 2.430).

Rose and Lily, traditionally associated with passionate love and spiritual admiration, respectively, appear in Dickinson's sentence to acknowledge the change in their relationship. Emily's passion for Sue has been locked up. She gives her the key now to another realm: affection. The poetry of Tennyson had been important to Sue and Emily as girls. They read and marked *The Princess* together.[77] *Maud* (1855) was published during Austin's courtship of Sue (and at the height of Emily's own love for her). Despite its open recognition of mental illness, its lush and elegant love lyrics full of floral imagery made it very popular with Victorian couples. Some of her letters and poems show that Dickinson envisioned Sue as Maud. The speaker of Tennyson's poem, a suitor, loves Maud but recognizes deceitful qualities in her. At one point, he cries

> if she were not a cheat,
> If Maud were all that she seemed,
> And her smile were all that I dreamed,
> Then the world were not so bitter
> But a smile could make it sweet. (3.224–228)

Still Maud is his "jewel" (352), and he continually imagines her to be pure:

> Maud is here, here, here
> In among the lilies. (12.422–423)

Like Dickinson with Sue in their early days, Tennyson's hero experiences intense joy at the idea of giving Maud a home:

> I have led her home, my love, my only friend.
> There is none like her, none. (599–600)

She is a "snow-limbed Eve" (626), "a pearl" (640), his "Queen lily and rose in one" (905). The famous lyric "Come into the garden, Maud," set to music so often by the Victorians, imagines Maud's advent to the speaker's heart in images Emily Dickinson was using for Sue:

> She is coming, my dove, my dear;
> She is coming my life, my fate;
> . . . . .
> She is coming, my own, my sweet;
> Were it ever so airy a tread,
> My heart would hear her and beat,
> Were it earth in an earthy bed;
> My dust would hear her and beat,
> Had I lain for a century dead; (10.910–911; 11.916–921)

If Sue remembered "Come into the garden, Maud," she would have taken from Emily's line about roses and lilies not its ostensible meaning, but the opposite: that Dickinson's ardor could never cool. For the last lines of Tennyson's lyric declare, "the rose was awake all night for your sake" and

> The lilies and roses were all awake,
> They sigh'd for the dawn and thee.

The rose, equated by Dickinson with Eden, and with Sue, never dimmed in the "Puritan Garden" of her heart (L 3.687). Years later she would signal it by telling Sue, "I keep your faithful place. Whatever throng the Lock is firm upon your Diamond Door" (L 2.490). Her allusion is to Tennyson's "Did he stand at the diamond door / Of his house" in one of *Maud*'s passages about a woman-pearl (2.64–65). But she developed a new trope with which to explain and to validate her emotion for Sue, one that became ever more suitable and expressive as Sue changed from a high-spirited but gingerly girl into a proud, arrogant woman. This was drawn from the Shakespeare play that had been Emily Dickinson's favorite since youth: *Antony and Cleopatra*.

10

On February 4, 1864, Emily Dickinson consulted an oculist—Henry Williams, M.D.—at 15 Arlington Street, Boston, about some affliction of the eyes. It was probably strabismus, faulty focusing, whereby the sufferer becomes walleyed. (Or perhaps it was what used to be called "hysterical blindness," a hypersensitivity to light induced by psychological causes.) She returned for a full course of treatment from April until November, staying in Cambridge with her Norcross cousins. No reading was permitted her, and her letters to Sue and Vinnie were loud with complaint. Returned home, with the full use of her eyes, she declared that "the only woe [that] ever made [her] tremble"—the forced exile from books—had an ending as spirited as a foxhunt. Her doctor "whistled up the hounds," her "blood bounded," and she raced to her Shakespeare. Joseph Lyman recalled the account she later sent him:

> Shakespeare was the first; Antony and Cleopatra where Enobarbus laments the amorous lapse of his master. Here is the ring of it.
>
>> "heart that in the scuffles of
>> great flights hath burst the
>> buck[l]e of his breast"

She added, appropriately to the play's atmosphere of revelry, "Give me ever to drink of this wine."[78] If she chose to read *Antony* first before "devour[ing] the luscious passages" of other plays, it must have been from old custom, possibly invigorated by her recent experience with

Bowles and her continued feeling for Sue. After 1864, Dickinson used Antony's name to summon up the pain and triumph of that play; on seven separate occasions, it is Antony's fatal and exultant passion that she cites with pity or self-directed irony.[79] Emily Dickinson's open preference for *Antony and Cleopatra* in the age of Thomas Bowdler (when the play was not admitted to honors exams at Cambridge on the grounds of its indecency[80]) verifies the splendid freedom of her imagination. But it also seems incontrovertible that her own situation – being in love with a fiery, fascinating, often duplicitous woman, who never requited her feeling completely – put her in mind of Shakespeare's regal, tortured lovers. Seeing herself as Antony, she often writes to Sue as Cleopatra,[81] using quotations from the tragedy that both knew well. Suitably enough, to regard Sue as a kind of Cleopatra was to continue the imagery set up by the quoting of Tennyson's *Maud.* For the unhappy suitor in Tennyson's poem says of Maud,

> What if with her sunny hair,
> And smile as sunny as cold,
> She meant to weave me a snare
> Of some coquettish deceit,
> Cleopatra-like as of old (6.212–215)

Among the Dickinson books in the Harvard collection, there are six Shakespeares: two sets and two single volumes belonging to Susan Dickinson; an uninscribed single volume; and the *Complete Works* edited by Charles Knight (Boston, 1853) and inscribed "Edward Dickinson: 1854." It seems certain that Emily Dickinson usually read *Antony and Cleopatra* in volume six of her father's Shakespeare. The book bears signs of heavy use. Though it also contains *Troilus and Cressida, Pericles, Cymbeline, Coriolanus,* and *Titus Andronicus,* it opens easily to *Antony and Cleopatra.* The pages of the play are slightly ripped, stained, and even marked with a string at Antony's words in act 4, scene 13, "I am dying, Egypt," perhaps by Emily herself. But she also seems to have borrowed volume six of Sue's *Shakespeare* (Boston, 1856) to pay a fraught tribute.

In that volume, two passages from the play are scored with the light lines in the margin characteristic of Emily Dickinson's markings. (Sue's are quite different, usually in dark ink and broadly applied, like her bold script.) Though one speech is spoken by Enobarbus, both express Antony's perceptions of Cleopatra. The first passage is one to which Dickinson had alluded in 1874, sending Sue a very small piece of paper with the line "Egypt – thou knew'st" (L 2.533). So she was evoking the fierce and pathetic moment in act 3, scene 11 when Antony upbraids Cleopatra for her treachery and explains his "unnoble swerving" from duty by reminding her how much he loves her, which she herself realizes and counts on. The passage is marked to its full extent:

> Egypt, thou knew'st too well
> My heart was to thy rudder tied by th' strings,
> And thou should'st tow me after. O'er my spirit
> Thy full supremacy thou knew'st, and that
> Thy beck might from the bidding of the gods
> Command me. (56–61)

Perhaps Dickinson scored (and also sent) the lines "Egypt – thou knew'st" as a mock-heroic tribute to their old affection, which had been that, the young Emily said, of "a lover" (L 1.215). The quotation may imply the reproach, exasperation, and baffled love of Antony's speech; and it has the courage of self-knowledge. It raises an ultimate question: in view of their history, and of Dickinson's early recourse to the word *blame,* how should we interpret the notion that Sue "commanded" her "from the bidding of the gods"? Of course the quotation also reveals how instinctively Dickinson associated herself with Antony and Sue with Cleopatra. Emily who in her "bleak simplicity . . . knew no tutor but the North" could be overmastered, like Roman Antony, by Sue's Cleopatra of "torrid" depth (L 2.491; 3.791). Sue's presence in the metaphoric East—the Evergreens were to the west—where she might wound as well as charm, sometimes prompted "amorous lapse[s]" from Dickinson's obligation to her own well-being. In 1878 she confesses it playfully: "Susan knows she is a Siren – and that at a word from her, Emily would forget Righteousness" (L 2.612). And the phrase—consider its terrible context in the play—attributes to Sue a power not for good, but for corruption. I have said that Dickinson's poems and letters show her longing to achieve honor; yet it is precisely honor that Antony forfeits in act 3 by being towed from the battle of Actium by Cleopatra. In pointing out these correspondences, I do not mean to suggest anything so primitive and direct on Sue's part as seduction. Sue enjoyed *being* desired, for she was proud and manipulative, but though coldness was her bait she always seems to have avoided hooking her fish. What Dickinson means here is that Sue has revealed to her the same depth of selfishness, the same craze for power, that Antony discovers in the queen. And Cleopatra's epicene self-indulgence, her temper and cruelty, call up in Antony similar behavior that he must struggle to repress. Dickinson obviously sees Sue's power to tempt her to spiritual distemper and disorder.

The second passage scored by Dickinson in Sue's copy of the play is a frank encomium to a fascinator:

> Age cannot wither her, nor custom stale
> Her infinite variety. Other women
> Cloy the appetites they feed; but she makes hungry
> Where most she satisfies. (2.2.236–239)

His courtship letters show that Austin Dickinson never felt he had quite "got" Sue. They accuse her of standoffish pride. (Mabel Todd's swift, ardent return of his idealistic but profoundly physical passion made a distinct contrast to Sue's self-possession.) Emily Dickinson seems to have felt the same. Here is the Sue—like Nature in another version of this poem—who remained "a Stranger yet" since "those who know her know her less / The nearer her they get" (L 2.598). More important, this scored passage isolates the experience that, to the poet Dickinson, epitomized love. It was a hunger that, temporarily appeased, would instantly renew itself and be pacified only by starvation. The imagery of the marked passage, with its allusion to actual and erotic appetite, is emblematic of the world of *Antony and Cleopatra;* yet also of the Dickinson vision. There love is a "Curious Wine," an "ample Bread" that, even as the sensual Antony discovers, satisfies completely only in imagination – or Paradise (579).

Sue's most succinct reputation in Amherst was that of hostess. During his affair with Mabel Todd, Austin rarely attended her parties and referred to their home as "my wife's tavern."[82] In *Antony and Cleopatra* food, drink, and all physical pleasures are associated with the queen while "entangled Antony" is ashamed to recall the Roman virtue of fortitude that once enabled him to starve but win battles. The lines from the play most often quoted by Dickinson in her letters come from the superb account of Cleopatra's welcome to Antony as he enters Egypt. As Enobarbus puts it, a "courteous Antony," vulnerable to women, "goes to the feast"

> And for his ordinary, pays his heart
> For what his eyes eat only. (2.2.226–227)

That is, to get his meal (Shakespeare's "ordinary") he pays by falling in love; but he is only allowed to look at what he loves, not enjoy her.

And so Dickinson's use of the quotation focuses on looking, not having, as in the early poems where she is Sue's prisoner. These Shakespearean lines are first quoted, somewhat altered as was Dickinson's custom, in a note to her sister-in-law written as late as 1883:

> Will my great Sister accept the minutae [sic] of Devotion, with timidity that it is no more? Susan's calls are like Antony's Supper – "And pays his Heart for what his Eyes eat, only –" (L 3.791)

It is difficult not to smile at this allusion to unfulfilled love: an allusion that harks back to the eye imagery of 458 but, like that poem, includes Sue in Antony's deprivation. The note is apologizing for Dickinson's failure to greet her imposing sister-in-law when she visited the homestead at the outset of Emily's last illness.

Shakespeare's Cleopatra, convicted in the play of "wrangling" and unqueenly acts, nevertheless earns the respect even of the conqueror Octavius. Though her suicide is on one hand a selfish strategem that prevents her capture and shame, it is also a brave tribute to her passion for the dead Antony, from whom she refuses to be separated. Dickinson's tributes to Sue—"Susan feeds herself"; "To be Susan is Imagination, / To have been Susan, a Dream"; her "Avalanche of Sun!"—all reflect the kind of astonished, wary attraction that Shakespeare's characters feel for Cleopatra. The play's uncertain acceptance as high tragedy in the nineteenth century was due in part to the ambiguous virtue of Cleopatra. Her vices seemed more vivid than her eventual abrupt show of loyalty and courage. That she finds her own queenship at the play's close and does so on her own terms, however, rescued her for some.

Thus the same Anna Jameson whose study of Marian symbology in art was so popular in the 1860s produced in *Shakespeare's Heroines* (1899) a well-known appreciation of Cleopatra. As an essay it summarizes late Victorian conceptions of the queen (who sounds not unlike Sue, after all):

> Her mental accomplishments, her unequalled grace, her woman's wit and woman's wiles, her irresistible allurements, her starts of irregular grandeur, her bursts of ungovernable temper, her vivacity of imagination, her petulant caprice, her fickleness and her falsehood, her tenderness and her truth, her childish susceptibility to flattery, her magnificent spirit, her royal pride . . . all these contradictory elements has Shakespeare seized . . . and fused.[83]

Victorian stagings of the play were infrequent, but even in the United States Isabella Glyn's glamorous performance as Cleopatra (1867) helped to recuperate the stature of Shakespeare's queen.

In November 1861 the *Atlantic Monthly* published a long essay, written by Julia Ward Howe, in which George Sand is compared to Cleopatra and called "another woman of royal soul." Sand's histrionics, "masculine" ambition, and even her transvestism are excused on the grounds that she was a "passionate loving woman." And—interestingly for Dickinson, the recluse poet—Sand's retirement at Nohant and her destiny as a writer are offered as apologia for the "discords" of her life. Mrs. Howe quotes Horace's encomium to Cleopatra, "Deduci superbo / Non humilis mulier triumpho." The lines, from Horace's ode 37 in book 1, celebrate the majesty of Cleopatra who took her own life rather than let herself be led in a Roman triumph: "scorning chains, she was no craven woman!" Curiously, this admiration for Shakespeare's Cleopatra was also shared by Dickinson's fatherly mentor, Colonel Higginson. Perhaps it merely reflected his ability to be fascinated by brilliant women, such as Emily Dickinson. Perhaps it accorded (like Julia Ward Howe's) with his belief in the possibility of female genius. Certainly Howe's conflation of Sand with Cleopatra, two figures in whom Dickinson was deeply interested, must have struck her. Around 1861, she and Sue began reading *Indiana*.

If she could identify Sue with Cleopatra, Dickinson was willing to see herself as Antony. In the preface to her father's *Antony and Cleopatra*, the editor praises Antony's character, quoting in their entirety the lines that Dickinson admired: "for his ordinary, pays his heart / For what his eyes eat only." What Charles Knight saw in Antony was what Cleopatra acknowledges after his death: his generosity of spirit. "Antony," says the editor "was of the poetical temperament—a man of high genius—an orator . . . a lover, that knew he loved imaginatively . . . even before the touch of grief has somewhat exalted his nature, he takes the poetical view of poetical things." Certainly Dickinson herself knew that she "loved imaginatively," that Susan was, *au fond*, a "pseudo Sister." Certainly she took "the poetical view of poetical things." Herself more experienced as years went on, it was to the experienced yet still entangled Antony that she compared herself. Ashamed of his dishonor, Antony tells his friends to "Let that be left / Which leaves itself" (3.11.19–20). So Emily Dickinson tells Higginson that, before she ever writes poorly, she will give up writing: "leave that

[art] which leaves itself" (L 2.573). In language used earlier to Sue, her nephew Ned Dickinson is thanked in 1885 for too brief a sickbed visit:

What an Embassy –
What an Ambassador!
"And pays his Heart for what his Eyes eat only!"
Excuse the bearded Pronoun – (L 3.894)

Here her use of the quotation is exceptionally revealing, for Ned himself should properly be Antony, his "embassy" being to Emily/Cleopatra. But so customary is Dickinson's association of herself with the vanquished Roman that she reserves to herself "the bearded Pronoun."

Did Sue ever comprehend that (like Antony, a "mine of bounty" [4.6.32]) Emily Dickinson was always loyal to her? Sympathetic to her brother and Mabel Todd in the 1880s, she was also kind to her distressed sister-in-law. Though Sue's cruelties often included her, the poet seems always to have glimpsed the poetry in Sue's ire and pain. "May I do nothing," she writes in 1874, "for my dear Sue?" (L 2.533). The obituary Sue composed suggests that she too understood and valued Emily. But stories to the contrary exist.

In the early 1880s, Mabel Todd first met Sue as Mrs. William Austin Dickinson, the wife of her husband's employer. Long before she fell in love with Austin, she was beguiled by Sue's cordiality and charm. With her Indian shawls, tinkling bracelets, dark eyes, and worldly manner, Sue struck Mabel as wonderfully different from other people in Amherst. Yet one day Sue told Mabel that she hoped she would never visit "the other house" or her sisters-in-law. Still innocent about the Dickinsons, Mabel asked why. "Because," said Sue impressively, "they have not, either of them, any idea of morality. I went in there one day, and in the drawing room I found Emily reclining in the arms of a man. What can you say to that?"[84]

Mabel was frankly amused, and Sue's words give us a glimpse of the chilly, surprisingly prudish wife of whom Austin would later complain. The "man" may have been Otis Lord, whose suit to marry Emily was not favored by Susan. Indeed, Sue's close friend was Lord's niece, Abbie Farley, who was also hostile to the proposed marriage. Judge Lord died while still trying to persuade Emily Dickinson, almost fifty then, to accept him. Lord's money would have been lost to the Farleys in the event of his marriage. Perhaps fiscal alarm motivated Abbie to call Dickinson a "hussy" who was "crazy about men."[85] But where would she have gotten such an idea except from Sue—who knew about Emily's passion for Master in the 1860s[86] and who, in her desire to come first, probably resented it? Sue's remark, "they have not, either of them, any idea of morality," is so sweeping as to suggest deep knowledge. About Lavinia she knew the story of her petting sessions with Joseph Lyman.[87] And about Emily? More than anyone else, Sue was undoubtedly aware of how passion could move Emily. If Mabel's story is true (and there is no real reason to doubt this one), it sheds interesting light on Dickinson's "Only Woman in the World." Ironically, by her phrase "reclining in the arms of a man," Sue makes Emily Dickinson herself a type of Cleopatra; in the nineteenth century, the queen was often pictured reclining.[88] Was Emily's "great Sister" jealous?

Few of Sue's letters to or about Emily remain. Most are cool. Dickinson's letters, however, keep up—early and late—the zeal and the diction of love. It was not to Sue that she sent her last message, "Called back." Perhaps in choosing her Norcross cousins for that poignant experience, Dickinson was rewarding their loyalty, more sturdy than Sue's. But her feelings for Sue never entirely changed. To the imagery of their twenties she could turn at will, writing in 1884: "I never shall see a Rose in the Boat without beholding you, and were you only at the Helm, it would be supreme" (L 3.848). Or she could alter the character of a domestic message with a sudden access to passionate commitment and poetry:

> Be Sue – while I am Emily –
> Be next – what you have ever been – Infinity – (L 3.830)

Indeed, in her letters as in her poems, Emily Dickinson draws a portrait of herself with Sue that is the picture of an established pair. Whatever "master" may have entered her life after Sue's marriage, Sue had mastered her already. For Sue, she said, was her "All."

~ 4 ~

The Narrative of Master

> More brave, more beautiful, than myself must be
> The man whom truly I can call my Friend;
> He must be an Inspirer, who can draw
> To higher heights of Being, and ever stand
> O'er me in unreached beauty, like the moon;
> Soon as he fail in this, the crest and crown
> Of noble friendship, he is nought to me.
>
> —Passage marked by ED in
> Alexander Smith, *A Life-Drama*, scene 8

In 1862 Emily Dickinson sent Samuel Bowles, busy editor of the *Springfield Republican,* the following news, which was preceded by no salutation:

> Title divine – is mine!
> The Wife – without the Sign!
> Acute Degree – conferred on me –
> Empress of Calvary!
> Royal – all but the Crown!
> Betrothed – without the swoon
> God sends us Women –
> When you – hold – Garnet to Garnet –
> Gold – to Gold –
> Born – Bridalled – Shrouded –
> In a Day –
> "My Husband" – women say –
> Stroking the Melody –
> Is *this* – the way?

Communicating (as she often did with Bowles and Sue) by means of a poem, Dickinson added to it these lines of urgent prose:

> Here's – what I had to "tell you" – You will tell no other? Honor –
> is it's own pawn – (L 2.394)

With its bold Christian symbolism, confessional emphasis, and the-atrical exclamation, her message demanded attention. For Dickinson the writer, it was a rare exercise in couplets for the most part, and a synthesis of emblems—Wife, Empress/Queen, Bridal/Calvary—which she had been devising since the early fascicles of 1858. For whatever reason, she never copied this lyric into the packets, another departure from custom. (In 1860 she had sent Bowles a frightening poem, describing herself drowning, "Two swimmers wrestled on the spar," with the explanation, "I can't explain it, Mr. Bowles" [L 2.363]. That poem she *did* enter in fascicle 9, together with "I'm 'wife' " [199].)

She had been in correspondence with Bowles for at least four years. In a note possibly written in August 1858, she thanked him for a "little pamphlet" he may have sent, guarding herself from "mistake" by saying she was "unfamiliar with [his] hand" (L 2.338). By 1862, however, she and Bowles had been together often at the Evergreens, where evenings were spent talking politics, playing shuttlecock, dancing, reciting poetry. Bowles had become Sue and Austin's best friend and Emily, like Sue, was in constant communication with him. (Over fifty letters from Emily Dickinson to Bowles and his wife survive. Her letters to Mary Bowles were usually meant for Bowles himself. After he died, she wrote to Samuel Jr.) Like Sue Dickinson, Sam Bowles was a man who thrived on excitement. Capable of earnest sentiment and even delicacy, he resembled his friend Charles Dickens in liking the hurly-burly and broad theater of public life. Born in 1826, he was four years older than Emily and Sue, though he died in 1878—worn out, by his physician's testimony—eight years before Emily and thirty-five before Sue. He was son of the founder of the *Springfield Republican* and succeeded to the editorship in 1851. A powerhouse of energy, he wrote essays on his wide travels through Europe and the United States, and his editorials became famous.

When he received her mysterious poem in 1862, Bowles was probably accustomed to Emily Dickinson's confidences, as to her probing questions ("Do you think we shall 'see God'?") and to her use of images ("a porcelain life," "a pile of broken crockery"), which would have dazzled a more poetic sensibility than his own. As he could not know, perhaps, these same images Dickinson lavished in letters to him were being set down in the great love poems, such as 640. "Title divine," however, was a distinct, if indistinct, revelation. It might have been expected to provoke a reply, even from the frenetic Bowles whose daily routine as an important journalist left him little time for letter writing.

That Bowles answered Emily Dickinson, and did so with some alarm and with, it seems, questions of his own, may be deduced from another letter Dickinson sent him, apparently soon afterward:

Dear friend
    If you doubted my Snow – for a moment – you never will – again – I know –
    Because I could not say it – I fixed it in the Verse – for you to read –

"Snow" is Dickinson's synonym for integrity. In "Publication – is the Auction / Of the Mind of Man" (709), she urges artists not to invest their snow, or honor, by publishing. In "Doubt Me! My Dim Companion!" (275), a gay but impassioned apology, she tells a man of whom she dreams and who had asked about it—Bowles?—that her snow, her virginity in this case, is intact and, indeed, kept so for him:

> hallow just the snow
> Intact, in Everlasting flake
> Oh, Caviler, for you![1]

In poem 325 she declared, as early as fascicle 13, that "Of Tribulation, these are They, / Denoted by the White," adding that people who "overcame most times – / Wear nothing commoner than Snow."

No matter how inured he was to her metaphors, however, Bowles could only interpret "Title divine" as an announcement of Dickinson's secret "marriage." And though she made it clear, metaphorically, that such a marriage was ideal, unconsummated ("without the Sign," "without the swoon") and that as soon as she felt passion she renounced it ("Born – Bridalled – Shrouded – / In a Day"), he was evidently worried that she was in danger of embarking on a clandestine relationship with someone. Bowles's biographer George Merriam characterized him as a man of "strong, racy, many-sided individuality," the "governing forces" of whose life were attuned to the high Victorian principle of Duty.[2] In answering Emily Dickinson, Bowles exhibited his dutiful side. For evidently he wrote back, asking for more information and counseling prudence.

To his reply, Dickinson's reply not only included the words above from letter 251 but a poem at the end of the letter. This poem she copied into fascicle 36. Once again, the fascicles as worksheets disclose the presence in her mind of various themes and subjects all at once. This packet contains a sad poem about Sue's neglect of her (727) as well as a frustrated one (725) for "Sir," another sort of lover who is always traveling. The poem she sent Bowles seeks to reassure him by saying that she is a martyr, committed to the "polar Air" of renunciation and that passion, or "convulsion," is to her harmless as a meteor.[3] (While, unlike meteorites, a meteor does not inflict damage, it illuminates. So passion, she says, illumines.) This information may have allayed Bowles's anxieties about Dickinson's plans though not, certainly, about her state of mind:

> Through the strait pass of suffering –
> The Martyrs – even – trod.
> Their feet – upon Temptation –
> Their faces – upon God –
>
> A stately – shriven – Company –
> Convulsion – playing round –
> Harmless – as streaks of Meteor –
> Upon a Planet's Bond –
>
> Their faith – the everlasting troth –
> Their Expectation – fair –
> The Needle – to the North Degree –
> Wades – so – thro' polar Air! (L 2.395)

This poem was one of Susan Dickinson's favorites: a proof, she declared, of Emily's godliness. After receiving this strange revelation about resisted "temptation," Bowles became very kind to Dickinson. In subsequent letters Dickinson exclaims, "You are thoughtful so many times, you grieve me *always – now*" (L 2.395). It probably grieved her to trouble one who, she knew, had frequently been made ill by what his biographer would call "the lavish, unstinted drain of [his] nervous power through excessive toil and shortened sleep."[4] It also made her "cheek . . . red with Shame," she told Bowles's wife Mary, "because I write so often" (L 2.358). Shame was the chief ingredient in all strong affections, she found, and ultimately it led to concealment: either to that partial "vail" that was metaphor or to hiding above stairs and behind doors when a beloved person was near. From Bowles himself she was to hide not long after her letter's revelation of a secret love. "Dear Friend," she began a note to be sent down to him as he waited in her father's parlor in late November 1862, "I cannot see you" (L 2.419). When he then sent her a "little Bat" (to remind her of their games of shuttlecock and thus reproach her for not receiving him), she returned, "I did not need [it] – to enforce your memory – for that can stand alone, like the best Brocade . . . Because I did not see you, Vinnie and Austin, upbraided me – They did not know I gave my part that they might have the more . . . had you Exile – or Eclipse – or so huge a Danger, as would dissolve all other friends – 'twould please me to remain" (L 2.419, 420).

In these letters to Bowles, the word *friend* is often repeated. If compared to Dickinson's ardent early letters (in particular) to Sue, the impression they give is of deep affection, not love. Shakespeare's sonnets for his Friend, whose sexuality and grace "beget" his poetry, are tinged with erotic feeling but also with worshipful regard. The Friend, unlike the Dark Lady, has the speaker's respect. Some of Dickinson's letters for Bowles, and all of her letters for Master, declare a love that has its foundation in eros but also in admiration. An American critic (named Robert Bridges, like the English poet) writing as "Droch" was among the first to say that her "love poems are written in the attitude of a worshipper . . . the exaggeration . . . saved from being absurd by its sincerity."[5] Some of the lyrics Droch read in *Poems* (1890), however, in a section entitled "Love," were doubtless for Sue: for example, "Your Riches – taught me Poverty." Some, such as "I cannot live with You," might be thought to describe Dickinson's experience with Sue, but they have consistent imagery patterns which, linked to those of the letters to Bowles, indicate that they are for Master. Most of Dickinson's love poetry, and all that Droch read in 1890, gives the impression that she is in awe of the person loved. In the case of her poems for the beloved woman, however, that awe often comes from dismay: can so false, feline, and distant a beloved exist? In the case of the other lover— judging from her imagery, a man, and judging from the consistency of that imagery in her letters and poems, Samuel Bowles—the awe is fueled by respect, fear, and finally by not a little gratitude. Neither of the lovers will have her. (Nor, of course, could she probably have survived having *them*: "A *Wounded* Deer – leaps highest" [165]; her art is founded on thrilling loss, thrilled sublimation.) The male lover, however, does give to *her* the "jewels"—courtesy, loyalty, physical appreciation— that she gave to the beloved woman, her "Jewel." He thus befriends Dickinson's persona at the highest level of her need, restoring the selfhood damaged during the earlier sexual experience.

The imagistic evidence of her poems and letters, as well as some biographical testimony, indicates that Emily Dickinson not only "made Bowles a confidant in the matter which touched her heart most closely,"[6] a secret love. Even more it suggests that he was the "someone carrying a Light" who had "overtaken [her] in the Dark" where Sue "put [her] down" (631). Dickinson's images for Bowles, as for Master, are those of resurrection. He is associated with Christ as the sun. Telling him that he is "noble" in 1874 she says, "Resurrection can come but once – first – to the same House. Thank you for leading us by it" (L 2.527). To his son, she wrote after Bowles's death, "His look could not be extinguished to any who had seen him, for 'Because I live, ye shall live also,' was his physiognomy" (L 3.667). Even in paradise, his eyes, "those isolated comets," glowed for her (L 3.780).

The fascicles reveal—in keeping with biography (which reminds us of Emily's presence at Sue's evenings for Bowles in the 1850s)—that a man of his description came to capture her thoughts, challenging the beloved woman. A little poem (47) in fascicle 2, probably written in the late 1850s even as Dickinson was writing "One Sister have I in our house," cries

> Heart! We will forget him!
> You and I – tonight!
> You may forget the warmth he gave –
> I will forget the light!

It is the first glimpse the fascicles provide of the figure (at first glancingly sketched) of Master. "He" is Dickinson's light-bearer, even as the beloved woman (though herself crowned with light) is ultimately her consort in darkness, the empty mirror, and "blame." Dickinson's characteristic association of Master with light was natural to a Victorian intellectual, for literature and art in the 1860s linked the heroic male with Apollo. So Ruskin, writing in *Sesame and Lilies* (1865), associated sunrise with the ascent of Apollo in his chariot—or the running of a strong man on his course, thus joining morning and eternal power (familiar Dickinsonian emblems) with masculinity.

It can be no coincidence, I believe, that the "Master" of Dickinson's poems and letters and the "Mr. Bowles" to whom she writes as a redeemer and Christ figure are addressed in identical imagery; or that her concern for Master's health and good opinion so closely parallels the concerns of those letters full of sentiment, timidity, respect, and (at last) ardor that followed Bowles over the sea to England or Europe. To understand and acknowledge this connection permits a more intelligible reading of the Master materials and their imagery.

Margaret Freeman has censured Sewall's biography of Dickinson for its "conservative attitude in retreating to the earlier position of Whicher and Johnson that an actual male lover existed"; for choosing Bowles as that lover; and for thus "ignoring . . . the very real possibilities presented by our increased knowledge of repression in psychological processes and its occurrence in nineteenth-century society."[7] What Freeman means is that Sewall does not regard Dickinson's love for Sue as erotic and that he takes seriously letters to Bowles which begin "Dear Friend" but include such poems as 1398:

> I have no Life but this –
> To lead it here –
> Nor any Death – but lest
> Dispelled from there –
> Nor tie to Earths to come –
> Nor Action new
> Except through this extent
> [The loving you][8]

We live consciously today at what Dickinson called the "Center of the Sea" and acknowledge the power of the unknown where sexuality is concerned. Perhaps only the most naive of persons imagines the boundaries of gender to be inexorably fixed. While analysis of the poems reveals a female figure whom the speaker clearly desires, even as some Dickinson letters show desire for Sue, so too it presents—often in distinctly masculine imagery—the figure of a lovable man. And as in the case of Shakespeare's sonnets, the presence of one does not cancel the power of the other. Rather, the two figures may usefully be compared so as to reveal the larger narrative of Dickinson's experience of love.

The poems of the Sue cycle show that Emily Dickinson wrote to and about her in images taken from literary and graphic works in which both shared an interest. In the same way, the texts underlying letters and lyrics for Master are drawn from works of art and literature that were favorites of Samuel Bowles. The coherence of each demonstrates the presence of what I have called coding. Thus the cryptic lyrics for Master are often Brontean; and we know that Dickinson showed Bowles her affection for *Jane Eyre,* a copy of which he had given to Sue. Bowles's devotion to the Brontë sisters' works was so well known that his biographer, Merriam, remarked upon it, saying that he read and reread *Shirley* continually.[9] The Master letters, written to a voyager while Bowles was voyaging, evoke *Villette* in some instances, although their underlying legend is Cole's *Voyage of Life*. Some of the love poems draw upon South American imagery in the paintings of Frederic Church. Church, Bowles's exact contemporary, often spent his summers where Bowles did, drawing other artists to Eden (now Bar Harbor), Maine. His famous South American trips in the late 1850s and 1860s promoted the interest in nature study that Bowles exhibits in his Yosemite journals. Church's images of Chimborazo, for example, or of the volcanoes— Popocatepetl, Vesuvius, Etna—were also available to Dickinson through scientific and other painterly works of her day.[10] When they are used simply to mean passion in some instances, they have an androgynous character, even as her word *Eden* appears in letters for Sue and in letters about Bowles. Some of the awkwardness encountered in deciphering a poem's possible subject—a female or male lover— may rise from the fact that Sue and Bowles were, in life, very similar in looks and tastes and were joined by association. Both, for example, admired the paintings of the Hudson River School.

Samuel Bowles was Austin Dickinson's closest friend until Bowles died, mourned by all the Dickinsons, in 1878. In letters to Austin, he exhibits a tenderness of tone which was not unusual between Victorian men (Tennyson spoke of himself as his dead friend Hallam's "widow,"[11] though his phrase was considered excessive). So pressed by his life as a journalist that he cannot visit the Evergreens, Bowles writes Austin in 1863: "Can you take less of me in time & word, & feel you have as much as ever, or rather more, in eternity?"[12] An unpublished note to Austin in the Harvard collection addresses him forcefully: "I want to see you. I still love you. But what is faith without works, you say! Aren't you orthodox!"[13] From his vacation place in Eden, Bowles wrote Sue and Austin about his rowing experiences on the wild Maine coast (in a letter dated May 21, 1863); and he writes them constantly from Springfield, from Europe, and even from his hospital bed in New York or Northampton. Bowles's letters to Sue—some signed effusively "Thine"—suggest that they shared an intimacy that was pleasantly flirtatious:

> And so I can't go to Amherst! I am disappointed. I hope you are. I will wear a sentimental ribbon over you—& pray your life may be long in the land—your hair black—your heart gracious—& your friend still a place in it (heart not hair).[14]

So well did Bowles and Sue get on, in fact, that Amherst gossips called their relationship "questionable."[15] Bowles's quiet, dumpy wife Mary—

born a Schermerhorn of Geneva, where Sue spent some of her skimpy childhood—disliked Sue so intensely that she rarely accompanied Sam on his Amherst visits. But Bowles and Sue seem to have enjoyed each other's company because they shared a love of books, paintings, food, and dancing as well as a similarly vivid temperament.

5. Samuel Bowles (ca. 1862). "Hallowed be his name."

It is not difficult to understand how this gregarious, political, democratic father of a large family may have come to be the adored and subtle "Master." In falling in love with Sue Gilbert, Dickinson became absorbed in a person of sensitivity and intelligence who was apparently bolder, more dynamic, and more worldly than she. Bowles (fig. 5) was a masculine and still more powerful type of Sue herself. Like Sue he had dark hair, brown eyes, a bearing that was impressive or, according to Dickinson, "Arabian" (L 3.662), her word for sexually charming. What we know of Dickinson's taste in men suggests that she cared neither for solemn, reticent men nor for the febrile, pedantic sort she met among the lawyers and college professors of Amherst. (Of professors she was particularly contemptuous, calling them "mannekins" whom passion "hurled into Wherefors" or, in another scornful phrase, "pretty as cloth Pinks."[16]) Samuel Bowles was vigorous, earthy, and dashing. That all the Dickinsons admired him would have improved his attractiveness for Emily, to whom family ties meant much. And Sue found him so attractive that she established a salon of sorts in his honor; Sue's interest in him made Bowles doubly appealing to Emily. In the late 1850s when she felt most deprived of Sue's love, she was drawn, as the Master materials show, to a man who fits the description of Bowles.

But Samuel Bowles was also different from Sue. Unlike her, he had a reputation for generosity, pity for the weak, and delicacy toward others' failings. Two orphaned nieces of Edward Dickinson, who lodged many years with Sue and Austin, remembered Sue's petty cruelties toward them as unwanted boarders: just what Sue had been with the Cutlers. The Newman girls had trust funds and thus might have expected cordiality from the young and spendthrift Mrs. Dickinson; but the latter worked them hard as nursemaids and quasi-servants while punishing them publicly for any small fault.[17] By contrast, Samuel Bowles was known for his kindness to people in trouble, what some called his nobility and purity of spirit.[18] For the Newman girls, in fact, his letters to Austin and Sue always included warm messages. Like Higginson, Bowles championed women's rights. (In his favorite *Shirley*, the heroine declares herself masculine in name and position, does business, and demands to become a justice of the peace.) Emily Dickinson, in fact, found herself forced to apologize to Bowles in 1860 for "smil[ing] at women." She had apparently disparaged things feminine in his presence. Perhaps she had thus tried to flirt with Bowles, to win his approval. Instead, Bowles was sufficiently "feminist" to become indignant. Dickinson was then forced to exempt "holy" women, such as Florence Nightingale, who had serious causes and true abilities (L 2.366) from her list of the scorned.

At his funeral, eulogies were made for Bowles as a martyr to justice and the public good. Charles Wadsworth, the Philadelphia minister who is so often a candidate for Master, was not alone among Emily's friends in seeking actively to serve God. Bowles's letters reveal it as his chief end, though he was not dogmatic: "To do right, to be generous, forgiving, kind, charitable, and loving, is not humility," he wrote, "it is only justice and truth to the god in us." "I try to make my life show the result of Christianity and godliness, if I have not the thing in its theoretical form."[19]

Emily Dickinson liked to speak of Bowles's Numidian brilliance (L 2.540). (The mines of Numidia, a source of Roman wealth, were among her erotic metaphors.) But Bowles also appealed to Dickinson because he understood pain and had suffered it in many forms, emotional and physical. Merriam's biography is a catalogue of illnesses and misfortunes. He and his wife Mary lost three children at birth, events that Dickinson sorrowfully commemorates. Furthermore, from 1857 on, Bowles was "in constant battle with physical infirmity." The list of his maladies is long. In 1851, a few years before Dickinson's own eye trouble, Bowles's eyesight was so poor that he feared to lose it entirely. During the period of the Master letters which record anguish for a man who is ill, Bowles had sciatica, dyspepsia, "a weakness of the bowels," and in 1860 a "nervous malady" that "came upon him gradually."[20] Despite an air that could be conspicuously jolly, he harbored a predilection for depression. To fight it, he turned to Nature:

> "What a beautiful world it is," said he, "and why should man murmur at the sometime bitter when the sweet is so royally bestowed? . . . Is there any verbal creed which teaches us so much, or inspires so sure a faith, as the smooth running of that river, the foliage of those woods, the glory of the sky?"[21]

If the prevailing imagery of that cycle of poems intended for the man called Master is compared to the imagery employed in Dickinson's letters and poems for Bowles, they may be seen as identical. These patterns correspond in turn to the imagery of the supposedly inscrutable Master letters. Furthermore, just as the literature she wrote to and for Sue was characterized by literary allusion—to the popular floral verses of the day, to Tennyson's *Maud*, to *Antony and Cleopatra*—so too Dickinson enriched the Master materials by allusion. Both the letters and the poems often refer to Cole's *Voyage* or paintings by Cole's student Church; to the Brontës' *Jane Eyre, Wuthering Heights, The Professor,* and *Villette*. Letters openly addressed to Bowles sometimes alluded to the novels of Dickens, perhaps honoring the two men's friendship. (And her allusions are romantic: thus, " 'Swiveller' may be sure of the 'Marchioness' " [L 2.382]. In *The Old Curiosity Shop* those characters marry.) Even as Dickinson's literary quotations for Sue were drawn from works both liked or read together, the graphic and literary works to which she refers for Master were frequently favorites of Bowles. Since this is the case, and because of the usual address of her speaker as a woman to a man, I think it may be safely held that Emily Dickinson was envisioning a male lover. Once again, as with the beloved woman, Master is unobtainable on earth. There is this difference, however: although always within limits, he returns her love.

Appropriately enough, and perhaps without perceiving it as an irony, Samuel Bowles liked to joke that Emily Dickinson was his "Queen" (L 2.393). She was also to become for him the "Queen Recluse" while, liberal with his compliments, Bowles called Sue, for her conviviality as a hostess, the "Queen of Pelham." Sue of course had been and remained Dickinson's "Queen." In the Bowles-Dickinson circle, the image of the reigning sovereign of England, the country that was Bowles's favorite cultural refuge, seems to have become increasingly prominent. Even the Dickinsons' Irish servant Maggie Maher would write to a woman, as a salutation, "God save the Queen!"[22] While Bowles was jovially calling her "Queen" or "Queen Recluse," however, Emily Dickinson was writing Master privately that she longed for "the Queen's place" next to him at night (L 2.374). And on stationery sometimes embossed with a queen's head, she was copying poems for him into the fascicles.

2

The poem cycle for Master, like the concurrent cycle for Sue, tells a specific story. As I have said earlier, Emily Dickinson's worksheets or fascicles give evidence that she was writing poetry about two different figures in the same interval of time. Taken as a whole, the lyrics on the worksheets and on loose pages describe two bodies of love poetry. Certain elements of the cycles are similar: the speaker's humility before her beautiful and brilliant subject; her fear to displease the subject; her desire to serve and loathing at being parted; her grief at the realization that any permanent or physical union is forbidden on earth; and her determination (often expressed in Elizabethan accents) to "love the Cause that slew Me" (925). These common elements in the related narratives are epitomized by variant poems such as 494, versions 1 and 2, in which Dickinson writes "Going to Him [Her]! Happy Letter!" and describes writing a lover at night and hiding the letter till the following evening in her bodice. This is a coy gesture in which both male and female beloveds are presumed to be interested.

The poems for Master, however, compose a narrative that, while sharing some of the Sue iconography, moves boldly into a different and new design. With a profound concentration on the conceit of Master's face and a vision of him as the source of light and salvation, the Master lyrics[23] are Dickinson's love poems for a man. She presents the female beloved as an exotic Eve (she too is an "Eve" in their mirroring relationship (L 1.24), presiding over an Eden that is forever a synonym for love). She depicts Master as the sun (that old image from her girlhood, when she feared the power of men and husbands to destroy female creativity and freedom).[24] Assertions that Master is "a faceless personage"—that is, his features are not described—are often made to prove that as a "fantasy-husband" he is not derived from a real person.[25] But Dickinson's poems, obsessed with Master's face, regard the latter as dazzling, blinding, a "disc" (474) or sun (so that a description of his features would be inappropriate). The sun as a disc, rising majestically in the sky, was an image popularized in the late 1850s and early 1860s by Church's South American paintings. Cotopaxi (1862), for instance, shows the sun mounting with radiance over mountains and a smoking volcano, its outlines clearly disc-like to suggest "Circumference": here, the endless authority of Nature. Probably Dickinson derived some stimulus for the sun imagery from Tennyson, whose Lancelot is "a bearded meteor, trailing light"; and beards and meteors were key ways to indicate Master's masculinity in the poems, like Bowles's good looks in letters. There are echoes of Tennyson throughout the Master literature and when Dickinson tells Bowles around 1877, "You have the most triumphant Face out of Paradise – probably because you are there constantly, instead of ultimately" (L 2.574), the attentive reader may remember Arthur's angelic aspect and even the lines from "St. Simeon Stylites": "Come, blessed brother, come. / I know thy glittering face."

Unlike the beloved woman, Master is on the whole kind; indeed, he is frequently chivalrous to Dickinson's "freckled Maiden" (275) who admires him. Accustomed as she is to penury and want, his indulgence accords her jewels and riches. Enamored of the beloved woman, she was an Earl; but Master is truly royal—an Emperor—and gives her "the sea," her female identity. Now, poems such as 466 report, the beloved woman is less important to her:

> 'Tis little I – could care for Pearls –
> Who own the ample sea –

Or Brooches – when the Emperor –
With Rubies – pelteth me –

"Pelteth" implies some danger and pain in being so assaulted by love, and it is phallic of course. Like the Virgin Queen Elizabeth, the speaker remains in her pride and courage a "prince," not a princess.[26] She is enlarged by this experience. Dickinson's speaker undergoes with Master a secret ceremony of marriage by which, like Queen Victoria with Albert, she recognizes him as her own "Sovreign" (247) even though she herself is crowned. In many poems, such as "The World – stands – solemner – to me – / Since I was wed – to Him" (493), Dickinson's speaker describes their imaginary union as a dream. Nevertheless, that dream includes lively, vibrant events. "He touched me," she reports, "I groped upon his breast" (506), and "He asked if I was his" (1053). He sends dangerous and thrilling letters and walks with her in the garden. Most important, he engages her gaze with looks of his own, speaking volumes in a "mighty Book" from which—as in the case of Sue—"We learned the Whole of Love" (568). (Emily Dickinson who so loved books would speak to Judge Lord of the imagined consummation of their love as a "chapter in the night."[27])

By comparison with the poems of the Sue cycle, the Master poems include many more sexual fantasies. Some, such as

> I gave myself to Him –
> And took Himself, for Pay,
> The solemn contract of a Life
> Was ratified, this way (580)

imagine the sexual relations of marriage, a "contract." Others focus on the sexual act itself:

> He was my host – he was my guest,
> I never to this day
> If I invited him could tell
> Or he invited me.
>
> So infinite our intercourse
> So intimate, indeed,
> Analysis as capsule seemed
> To keeper of the seed (1721)

Such a poem as this one, with its acute realization of heterosexual experience, makes it improbable that Emily Dickinson's love poetry is devoted only to a woman. The male lover, however, is sometimes regarded—in a use of what might be thought a feminine image—as a "port" to which she comes, seeking her salvation (506, 249, 368). Like the male narrator of *Maud*, Master sometimes receives *her*; not she, him. This is true because she regards him as a redeemer who keeps her from the peril of drowning at sea: her ambiguous sexual identity, wherein she might have been lost. The poem that Dickinson sent Bowles in 1860 may have been a revelation of her earlier relations with Sue. "Two swimmers wrestled on the spar" but "One," Sue, "turned smiling to the land," a safe marriage perhaps; the other, herself, a type of Zenobia in Hawthorne's *Blithedale Romance,* becomes a grotesque face "Upon the waters borne," begging for love as she dies (201). Suggesting such desperate passion to Bowles might have had the effect of transferring her affections to him more easily. He probably never understood her; but, then, "All men say What to me" (L 2.415).

Although the beloved woman reciprocates the speaker's sexual interest only once (458), and with dismay, Master comes to take a decided fancy to her. He notices her figure, for instance, so that in his absence she finds it hard to wear colors, to

> make the Bodice gay –
> When eyes that fondled it are wrenched
> By Decalogues – away – (485)

(Strikingly, "Decalogues," the ten commandments, cause Master's absence.) Unlike the beloved woman, he is willing to single her out for loving attentions; and while the beloved woman subjects her to "glittering" verbal abuse (479), Master is capable of being hurt by the speaker (296). Dickinson's speaker decides finally that God, "the Weaver," has made men far less afraid of passion than women. She is obviously rather exasperated by this reflection. Her lines, written around 1861, may contrast Sue's coldness with Master's warmth. Dickinson's men are often described in "broadcloth," and her women in "organdy" or "muslin." The East is sexual desire:

> The Vane a little to the East –
> Scares Muslin souls – away –
> If Broadcloth Hearts are firmer –
> Than those of Organdy –

Who is to blame? The Weaver?
Ah, the bewildering thread! (278)

For Dickinson, the thread—human sexuality—was bewildering, both in others and in herself. Though she fantasizes that Master enables her to enjoy the status and maturity that wifehood represents, she confides to the reader considerable ambivalence, nevertheless, about being married. Passion and lovemaking, when they appear, she imagines with pleasure (hoping only to be hallowed afterward "much as formerly" [213]). She recognizes how much safer it is to regard herself a woman, and a woman pledged to a man, than it was to be a little girl:

I'm "wife" – I've finished that –
That other state –
I'm Czar – I'm "Woman" now –
It's safer so – (199)

But the same Dickinson who could write, doubtless of Sue, that when a girl "take[s] the honorable Work / Of Woman, and of Wife" she may lose "Amplitude, or Awe" and wear away her gold (732) does not always like the prospect of being "owned" by Master. Her poems for him sometimes provide a glimpse of her distaste for an arrogant Victorian male:

He found my Being – set it up –
Adjusted it to place –
Then carved – his name – upon it –
And bade it to the East

Be faithful – in his absence –
And he would come again –
With Equipage of Amber –
That time – to take it Home – (603)

In the age of Tennyson's *Idylls*, with Prince Albert (to whom they were dedicated) regarded as a type of Arthur returned, stories of the crusading knight and his faithful lady appeared both in poetry and in painting.[28] Emily Dickinson's keenly ironic poem 603 describes the usual Victorian suitor as a crude campaigner. He finds her, a total *person* with a Being, not just a face and a name. But he puts her, like a thing, an "it," in her place as a trophy. Having carved his name on her (a savage image for betrothal), he tells her to be faithful to their love (the East) while he goes about his affairs. She must stay on the shelf until he comes again.

Then he will bring an "Equipage of Amber" to take her home. Rebecca Patterson observes that "amber is associated with the sun-lover."[29] (Samuel Bowles Jr. remembered that yellow was his father's favorite color, worn more frequently than any other.[30]) But Dickinson's use of amber is ambiguous here. Flies were preserved in amber in her time; the woman-trophy that the man takes home will have no more autonomy than such a fly.

Despite her occasional, sharp indictments of Victorian marriage as bondage, however, Dickinson's speaker usually imagines herself fulfilled by loving Master. The word she selects to describe her feelings is "gratitude" (493). "Wear[ing] that perfect – pearl – / The Man – upon the Woman – binds," in one of the marriage poems that reassign the image of Sue as pearl, she says she "had esteemed the Dream – / Too beautiful – for Shape to prove." Jane Eyre experiences the same astonishment when she wins Rochester (whom she calls Sir, as Dickinson does Master). To some extent, Jane's amazement and that of Dickinson's speaker may be attributed to a similar source: the disdain for their looks and accomplishments that another woman has shown them.[31]

3

The early Master poems present Dickinson's speaker as a child, a girl, epitomized by that simple field flower, the daisy (an epithet Dickinson uses of herself in letters to Bowles). Once again, Dickinson's conceit of the daisy shares in a Victorian tradition, for the myth of Apollo and Clytie (the maid changed into a daisy or sunflower out of love for the sun) was prominent in the art of the 1860s.[32]

> The Daisy follows soft the Sun –
> And when his golden walk is done –
> Sits shyly at his feet –
> He – waiting – finds the flower there –
> Wherefore – Marauder – art thou here?
> Because, Sir, love is sweet!
> We are the Flower – thou the Sun!
> Forgive us, if as days decline –
> We nearer steal to Thee!
> Enamored of the parting West –
> The peace – the flight – the Amethyst –
> Night's possibility (106)

Copied into fascicle 7 around 1859, just when Bowles joined the Dickinson circle of intimates, this little lyric describes the days of a timid flower-girl, plucked—she will use the word *plucked* for Master's effect on her (921)—from literary Victorian gardens where the poppy-girls of Frieda Wolfe and Mrs. Hemans' modest lily of the vale represented acceptably Victorian feminine qualities of demure dependency and weakness. The Sun is occupied, self-absorbed, and notices the worshipful flower only at night, when he wakes from the business of illumining the world. Daisy is a Marauder, a plunderer of his power, he implies, seeing (perhaps) in the daisy—the word comes from Old English, *day's eye*—a rival power[33] (The "bearded" redeemer of Master letter 2 [233] will be asked to pity "Daisy's petals," her feminine nature, which, however, is just as nicely articulated in its properties as his own.) Her reply to his question "Wherefore?", which may be rephrased "Why are you interested in me?", is an avowal, simply, of love. Daisies need sun or they die. She steals nearer to him (a continuation of the conceit *marauder*) because he represents not only light but "Night's possibility," the unachieved vision of eros. *Flight*, the conception "as days decline," *peace*, and *west* appear later in the Master letters; but this early poem establishes them as allusions to him.

Her vision of Master as Promethean fire, an alternate image to that of the sun and the effulgent face, is typically expressed by "To my small Hearth His fire came" (638). This is a poem full of verbal power, with characteristic attributes of the male lover as Dickinson recognizes them: abruptness, vehement energy, a forcefulness that invades but sets her in motion, and the permanent faculty to convert a night (associated with the female lover), seen as barren, into noon or day:

> To my small Hearth His fire came –
> And all my House aglow
> Did fan and rock, with sudden light –
> 'Twas Sunrise – 'twas the Sky –
>
> Impanelled from no Summer brief –
> With limit of Decay –
> 'Twas Noon – without the News of Night –
> Nay, Nature, it was Day – (638)

This poem appears in fascicle 33 together with "I cannot live with You" (640), "I am ashamed – I hide / What right have I – to be a Bride" (473), and "They put Us far apart" (474). Each of these poems describes forbidden love while 640 and 474 narrate the final stages of that experience: interdiction, separation, and—brilliant and summary word of 640—"Despair." But 638 recalls or narrates, as if from the immediate past, the male lover's first assumption of sway over the speaker. Therefore fascicle 33 may be said to tell the whole story, while "To my small Hearth" serves as its provisional argument and as a dedicatory poem. Dickinson's image of "hearth," which is allied to that of her small "cottage" (961) and the "little Room" of her heart (405) is appropriately feminine. She uses legal terminology for the man: he is *impanelled,* that is, enrolled on a list (like a jury's) not just for a "Summer brief"— she may be punning on the idea of a lawyer's "brief," a short memorandum—but forever, without "limit of Decay."[34]

The lover, who can be vulnerable and needy despite his glorious appearance of self-sufficiency, has from the first a momentous role in the speaker's life. Even as the sun governs the earth, he exercises godlike dominion over her world. In a feeble but illustrative poem from fascicle 10, he is its primum mobile:

> If He *dissolve* – then – there is *nothing* – more –
> *Eclipse* – at *Midnight* –
> It was *dark – before –*
>
> *Sunset* – at *Easter* –
> *Blindness* – on the *Dawn* –
> *Faint* Star of Bethlehem –
> *Gone down!*
>
> *Would* but some God – *inform* Him –
> Or it be *too late!*
> Say – that the pulse *just lisps* –
> The *Chariots wait* –
>
> Say – that a *little life* – for *His* –
> Is *leaking – red –*
> His *little Spaniel* – tell Him!
> *Will He heed?* (236)

This breathless list of Dickinsonian emblems—Eclipse, Midnight, Dawn, Bethlehem—loosely knitted together by plea and hypothesis, is representative of Dickinson's inferior verse; and one winces at the poem's movement from the grand "Eclipse at Midnight" at the beginning to the image of the bleeding dog at the close. But the poem is useful, in one way, because it shows Dickinson at midpoint between her mature associations of the lover with universal natural rhythms and the juvenile pose that makes her his dog and he, her "master."

Dickinson's choice of the title "Master" was no doubt heavily encoded. "Master" was the title chosen by the disciples for Christ in the New Testament. Dickinson's letters as a girl show her using this epithet. She assures Jenny Humphrey in 1850 that she is garnishing her heart to "make ready for the Master!" (L 1.83). Austin is told in a snappy message that urges him to whip his pupils, "I clothe you with authority and empower you to punish . . . I call you 'Rabbi – Master'" (L 1.125). Matthew's Christ—she most often read Matthew—says "call [no man] master: for [I am] your Master" (23.10). Her epithet, therefore, is audacious. "Master" is the socially correct, if religiously encumbered, title by which Rochester is addressed by Jane Eyre. In the nineteenth century, of course, it was the appropriate address of servant, slave, or pupil for the man in charge. Used of her lover by a woman who is also a genius; used so that it makes of her sometimes his scholar, sometimes his parishioner in their "Sealed Church" (322), but sometimes his dog, it implies depths of psychological and sexual servility that Dickinson's attempts at humor only in part conceal.

As a bridge between unaccomplished and assured poems to Master, "If He *dissolve*" is biographically enticing. We know that after Bowles died, Dickinson awaited the publication of Merriam's biography with excitement. She wrote Sue, "it seems like a Memoir of the Sun, when the Noon is gone" (L 3.828). Sun and Noon, her images for Master in the poems, were thus associated with Bowles in a confidence to Sue, who was fond of him (and had just attended his funeral). "If he *dissolve*" is related imagistically to poem 186 in fascicle 9. "What shall I do – it whimpers so" is another embarrassing portrait of Dickinson as dog, although in this poem, as in Master letter 2 (no. 233), she has included her real dog Carlo (named for St. John Rivers' dog in *Jane Eyre*) and made her more limited topic the "Little Hound within the Heart." Poem 186 appears in the same fascicle as the poem sent to Bowles, "Two swimmers wrestled on the spar," and represents Master as having "a dizzy knee" that the speaker may dare "to climb." This association suggests that she imagines him as providing refuge for the drowning, tortured, probably Sapphic lover of "Two swimmers." She will have to climb his knee—the same sexual symbolism that appears in the Sue cycle. The idea is dizzying and now, instead of being the Earl or "Emily when a boy," she sees herself as a small, timid woman confronting a man. The knee image also appears in Master letter 3 (no. 248), in which Dickinson imagines Daisy kneeling "at the knee that bore her once unto . . . wordless rest." Poem 186 is also reminiscent of letters that Dickinson was sending to the Bowles family at this time.

In December 1858 she writes Mary Bowles to "enclose my heart; a little one, sunburnt, half broken sometimes, yet close as the spaniel to it's friends" (L 2.342). These were days when she was in constant communication with Bowles and his wife (at first a hard-working partner who gave birth to nine children, made his home a refuge, and tried during the illnesses of her childbearing years to be patient with women like Sue and Maria Whitney). "I write you frequently, and am much ashamed," she admits (L 2.352). Her letters employ the images of dogs or children because the pose of innocent dependency might obscure the truth that she was a brilliant and fully developed woman of twenty-eight, whose participation in what Kate Anthon remembered as witty evenings at Sue's certainly had a sexual flavor.[35] (In her own heartbroken letters to Constantin Heger, her French "master" in Brussels, Charlotte Brontë herself adopted the child/pupil pose she would mold into the sterner character of Jane Eyre, consciously or subconsciously to allow Heger as a married man to correspond with her.[36]) So keen seems to have been Dickinson's need for some disguise in writing Bowles that at one point (L 2.398) she masks her feeling for him as Austin's.

The letters to Bowles, however, also employ the great conceits of the Master letters and the major love poems. These images of sea, shore, dawn, dusk, hearts, heaven, boats, petals, suns, death/resurrection, and so on, rise from a sensibility that was developed in part through an acquaintance with various important "texts." These are chiefly Cole's *Voyage,* with its central narrative of boat and voyager achieving heavenly dawn at last, after a perilous journey on life's sea; the drowning scene of Paul Emmanuel in *Villette;* and scenes from *Jane Eyre* in which Jane comforts the blinded Rochester (did Bowles's trouble with his eyes and his terror of blindness also suggest these to her?). Certain of her letters make allusions that cannot, I believe, be properly understood without an appreciation of their coded texture. Thus, when Dickinson writes in Master letter 2 that "God built the heart in me," that is, her propensity for sentiment, she continues: "bye and bye it outgrew me – and like the little mother – with the big child – I got tired holding him" (L 2.373–374). The image is an allusion to Jane Eyre's dream before her impending marriage, where Jane carries a "little child" that she "might not lay . . . down anywhere, however tired were my arms." She has carried the child for many pages; in happy moments, it plays among daisies. The child is Jane herself and represents her past (and the gulf between her and the aristocratic Rochester). So what Dickinson is saying to Master is that she too has outgrown the child's pose; that she now writes to him as an amorous woman. (Without this understanding, some have even interpreted the letter as a message to Master that she is pregnant.[37])

The three Master letters were found among Emily Dickinson's papers after her death. Two are in ink with pencil corrections; one is entirely in pencil. Dickinson usually made drafts of her letters, which she clearly regarded as artistic efforts, like the poems. There is no reason to suppose that the Master letters (or others like them) were not sent off. She often posted letters written in pencil. She often corrected messages written in ink and rewrote them. R. W. Franklin, introducing a facsimile edition of *The Master Letters*, says, "Dickinson did not write letters as a fictional genre, and these were surely part of a much larger correspondence yet unknown to us."[38] No doubt Franklin's close experience in handling Dickinson's manuscripts helps him so firmly to dispense with theories that the letters are fictions. Preserved in the Amherst College Library, the Master letters seem visually to reflect different stages of an actual emotional experience. Imagined events may certainly create excitement in any artist; that in turn fires the life of the art created. Such excitement may appear in the strokes of pen or brush. But there is a peculiar candor about the very appearance of the Master letters which suggests that Emily Dickinson was writing to someone she knew, not to someone she had invented. The two much-corrected drafts reflect turmoil, like that of a person tortured by the problem of what to say to somebody important; that she is an artist by nature and practice has only complicated her problem. Letter 1 (in Johnson's ordering, no. 187), the earliest, possesses a serene assurance in script that accords with the confidence, at that time, of the writer. Like Dickinson's poem-notes folded into small rectangles with "Sue" on the top, the Master letters give every visual indication of being once intended for a real person: one whom the writer wants desperately not to offend or to lose. Her corrections are not made primarily for aesthetic but for, one might say, human purposes: she emends to placate, to please.

Lavinia—finding the letters after Emily's death—must have recognized that the second Master letter, the longest and most revealing, constituted a challenge to her sister's image as saintly spinster. Written in Dickinson's hand of the early 1860s, only six sentences appeared in the Todd edition of the *Letters* (1894), falsely dated 1885. When all three were published at last in the Bingham edition (1955) and in Johnson's edition three years later—their texts set out with Dickinson's alternative words in parentheses—the Master letters provoked a revival of interest in the identity of the addressee. Johnson himself renewed the old debate about whether the addressee was a "he" (Wadsworth, Lieutenant Hunt, George Gould, Bowles) or a "she" (Kate Anthon), declaring, "She may have had the Reverend Charles Wadsworth in mind as 'Master'" (L 2.333). Under this assumption he followed the third Master letter (which exhibits considerable anguish for an offense Daisy had committed) with a pastoral note to "My Dear Miss Dickenson [sic]" from Charles Wadsworth, asking about her "affliction." But Johnson was careful to add that "the letter may have been written at a quite different time" (L 2.393) from Master letter 3. Although Johnson's biography identifies Wadsworth as Master, he may have been acknowledging the similarity in language by surrounding the Master letters with letters addressed to Bowles. Indeed, the letter that Johnson places immediately after Wadsworth's note is Dickinson's apology to Bowles for making some demand of him. It begins, "If I amaze[d] your kindness – My Love is my only apology."

Subsequent to the Johnson ordering, Franklin has proposed a new chronology, based on a study in progress of Dickinson's handwriting. For example, considering her separation of "t" from "he" in the word "the" before 1861 and her linkage of those letters later, Franklin believes that Johnson's third letter ("Oh, did I offend it") ought to be letter 2, and his second letter ("If you saw a bullet"), letter 3. He agrees that letter 1 belongs to 1858, but dates the last two in 1861 because of handwriting patterns established in that year. I shall keep the Johnson ordering known to most readers here for the sake of convenience, although Franklin's reordering is appealing. Placing the longest, most strained letter last, among other things, gives emphasis to Dickinson's plea, "One drop more . . . then would you *believe*?" The letters, which she compares to her own spilled blood, thus form an ever more insistent argument.

The Master letters are love letters that compose a narrative of passion and frustration. The first (187) is imagistically decorated yet decorous, and—concerned with Master's health—remains the message a close friend might send. The second (233), understandably perceived as problematic by her family, is an open confession of passion. Containing much of the imagery of such great poems as "I cannot live with You," it is a message that no one could mistake as anything but a plea for union, even though it hedges and protects itself against rejection with allusions to public censure and morality. Now the earlier, friendly persona declares herself to be a woman first of all, and one so enamored of Master that she will wait to marry him until they are in heaven. The last letter (248), full of grief, hastens to adopt the persona of a child in the effort to displace that of suppliant woman. Somehow the bold woman has gravely displeased Master. This last letter ends by associating Master with God. It maintains the conceit of the love poems: that "Heaven will only disappoint" her by comparison with his affection. Her misery in this unfinished letter suggests itself in the number of deletions and alternate verbal choices.

Dickinson's first Master letter includes the images of violets, the robin, and spring which fill her early love poems. (She puts "Spring" in quotation marks as if conceding the word's special associations, perhaps in her own mind, with love poems like the ones she used to write for Sue.) Then she takes up Thomas Cole's great myth of the spirituality of American landscape, expressed in his words, "We are still in Eden." She borrows his vision (in *Old Age*) of angels that move from heaven's gates to the sea at the river's end. There the voyager waits to be assisted into eternity:

> Indeed it is God's house – and these are gates of Heaven, and to and fro, the angels go, with their sweet postillions – I wish that I were great, like Mr. Michael Angelo, and could paint for you. You ask me what my flowers said – then they were disobedient – I gave them messages. They said what the lips in the West, say, when the sun goes down, and so says the Dawn. (L 2.333)

A letter to Bowles, written probably in late August 1858, summons up a similar vision:

> Good night, Mr Bowles! This is what they say who come back in the morning, also the closing paragraph on repealed lips. Confidence in Daybreak modifies Dusk. (L 2.339)

Clearly she enjoyed confiding in Bowles, as in Master, her thoughts about the living "who come back in the morning" and the dead with their "repealed lips." She also seems to have taken pleasure, often, in saying "Good night" to him, thus intimately including him in the symbolic rhythms of her life.

The next lines of the Master letter remind him that it is "the Sabbath Day":

> Each Sabbath on the Sea, makes me count the Sabbaths, till we meet on shore – and (will the) whether the hills will look as blue as the sailors say.

For Dickinson, the sea was a multivalent symbol that could stand for eternity, or terror, or sexuality, as we have seen. In Master letter 1 it seems primarily to represent Cole's river or sea: quite simply, the sea of life, which also appeared in Victorian hymns and commonplace books. Yet if one remembers her other letters and poems, it is difficult not to assign to this sea overtones of romantic feeling as well: "I am pleasantly located in the deep sea," she tells Kate Anthon, a guest at the Dickinson-Bowles evenings where laughter, music, and food of a European sophistication were the accompaniments of affectionate discourse (L 2.356).

In writing to Master—and to Bowles—the sea, actual or metaphoric, seems to have obsessed her. Seeking a cure for exhaustion and for a depression he could not explain, Bowles arrived in Liverpool in April 1862. In August 1862 Dickinson would write to him, "I tell you, Mr Bowles, it is a suffering, to have a sea – no care how Blue – between your Soul, and you" (L 2.416). In the frightened Master letter 3, Dickinson alludes to an "awful parting," and her letter ends on the vision of the sea. Thus a pathetic relevancy, drawn from her life experience, seems to be conveyed by the image in that letter at least. But it is by no means certain that Master letter 1 was written in 1858. It too could allude to seas that separate Dickinson from Bowles, a frequent traveler. The sea of the Malay/pearl poems, related to the sea of sexuality and death in De Quincey's *Confessions,* is associated with Sue. So too the sea of the Master letters is founded on a painterly/literary heritage, known to Dickinson, Bowles, and their circle.

In the Master letters, both passion and spirituality appear to fuse in this image of the sea. They are similarly associated in chapter 15 of *Jane Eyre* when in dreams Jane is "tossed on a buoyant but unquiet sea, where billows of trouble rolled under surges of joy." Like Dickinson in Master letter 1, Jane sees both the sea—her violent passion for the strange Mr. Rochester—and the shore in one gaze: "I thought sometimes I saw beyond its wild waters a shore, sweet as the hills of Beulah . . . But I could not reach it, even in fancy." Jane cannot reach that shore, a morally sanctioned paradise in which she and Rochester are married, because (as she subconsciously perceives) her "master" is married already. But like Lucy Snowe in *Villette,* Jane *always* envisions herself separated from Rochester and imagines that "brine and foam" will rush between them.[39]

This common use of sea imagery is but one example of the many haunting correspondences between *Jane Eyre* and Dickinson's themes and images in the Master letters and poems. While it has long been acknowledged that her admiration for both Charlotte and Emily Brontë led her to draw upon their works in her own,[40] Dickinson's specific evocation of *Jane Eyre* in the Master literature has never been closely examined. Sandra Gilbert and Susan Gubar have published their observations about the resemblance between Dickinson's Master letters and the ardent, mournful ones that Charlotte Brontë sent her "cher Maître," Heger.[41] They attribute this resemblance to the fact that each was addressing a "larger-than-life male Other who seemed to both these Victorian women to be the Unmoved Mover of women's fates." Their critique is yet another gloss on what they call the "inescapable toils for women in patriarchy,"[42] and does not provide much sense of the sexual charm of both "masters," whose paternal characteristics only thinly veil their romantic appeal. Furthermore, of course, the "toils" for both Brontë and Dickinson were of their own manufacture; for each—if unconsciously—wanted from her married master an intimate relationship that was erotic, not platonic. Neither Heger nor Bowles could safely (or honorably) provide it. Charlotte's pose as Heger's scholar and Dickinson's as Daisy were really, in one style, aggressive acts (though it is painful to envision Heger writing a note for his shoemaker on one of Charlotte's letters, even as Master's anger seems misdirected at such a sensitive being as Emily Dickinson). The fact is, however, that neither Brontë nor Dickinson paid much attention to patriarchy and its codes when they wanted something they considered attainable through language.

The Master materials, however, have not been submitted to comparative analysis with *Jane Eyre*. It is important to remember that *Jane Eyre*, Brontë's fantasy of union with Heger, was lent to Emily Dickinson in 1849 by her father's law clerk, Elbridge Bowdoin, and that she read, reread, and gave it as a gift to friends all through the 1850s. Among the Dickinson books at Harvard is a copy of *Jane Eyre* (1850) inscribed to Susan Dickinson by Bowles. (Another, given to Emily in 1865 by Charlotte Sewall Eastman, is of less significance since by that time she knew *Jane Eyre* well.) In the Bowles-Dickinson circle, the book was a common text. Essentially a parable of virtue and its rewards, the novel was remarkable both for commitment to chastity, honesty, and kindness and for the rapturous celebration of passion. A bestseller in England, it went into three editions in a year and a half, and was equally popular in New England, causing what the *North American Review* (October 1848) called "a distressing epidemic, passing under the name of the 'Jane Eyre' fever."

Currer Bell subtitled it the "autobiography" of a small, plain girl whose intelligence and sensibility enable her to move from the friendless poverty of the novel's beginning to the prosperity, usefulness, comfort, and pleasure to which happy marriage entitles her at the end. In between Brontë provided the feverish excitements of a gothic plot: an intricate, brooding maze of a manor house; the once dissolute but handsome, Byronic master; and the mad wife in the tower. But the focus of interest for the reader—and certainly the focus of Dickinson's interest—was Brontë's theme: the pious consecration of passion through loving service; and the taming of the masterful aristocrat by the meek and little— but clever and good—governess, Jane.

It is not too much to say that the Master materials in part follow this plan, and that Dickinson depicts Master and herself in Brontean imagery. This was an instance in which life and art, art in life, came together. Circumstance made Dickinson Brontë's sister, in suffering as in genius. (Her nephew Ned said, in a rude effort at classification after her death, that Emily "was a left-over of the Brontës."[43]) Confronted by a Brontean life-text, Dickinson sometimes translated it into Brontean words. She could not have known that her own Master letters exhibited the same longing, helplessness, and intensity as those letters sent to the unresponsive Heger by Charlotte Brontë—or, as Brontë called herself with self-contempt, by his "ex-assistant governess."[44] The words Dickinson uses in the Master texts however, are often *Jane Eyre*'s. Thus— as was her custom—she dignified and emphasized the importance of her feeling by associating it with a text that epitomized to her and her friends the ideal bourgeois romance.

In her second, troubled Master letter (233), there occurs almost immediately a reference, as I said earlier, to a crucial passage in *Jane Eyre*. This is the passage in which, on the night before what would have been her bigamous marriage with Rochester, Jane dreams that she is holding a heavy child. The child is certainly Jane herself as an unawakened sensibility, an image from which her desire for Rochester has forever divorced her. Jane cannot now "support" her former self, for she is, and has loved as, a woman. Dickinson's Master letter 2 announces the same fact of alteration and growth:

> God made me – [Sir] Master – I did'nt be myself. I dont know how it was done. He built the heart in me – Bye and bye it outgrew me – and like the little mother – with the big child – I got tired holding him. (L 2.373–374)

The whole of this letter, indeed, is the explanation of a new state in which Dickinson finds herself: one with which she had acquainted

Master and one that he, apparently, still doubts. Her letter opens dramatically:

> Master,
> If you saw a bullet hit a bird – and he told you he was'nt shot –
> you might weep at his courtesy, but would certainly doubt his word.

Poems such as "Not with a Club, the Heart is broken" (1304) tell of "Bird / By Boy descried – / Singing unto the Stone / Of which it died." Birds, in general, in Dickinson's work are often victims and symbols of herself as tried and triumphant woman or artist. A passage like this one in Master letter 2 is not found precisely in Dickinson's poems, however, but rather in words uttered by Samuel Bowles.

Merriam reports that "one of his female friends" had been invited by Bowles to visit his newspaper offices with him on a moonlit evening in 1868. (Bowles acquired so many women friends that his associate editor, Josiah Holland, was moved at his memorial service to declare that "the women whom he loved and who loved him were good women."[45]) They spent time with members of Bowles's staff and then "emerged into the cool moonlight":

> He remarked, "That's done. The women-writers, – I don't like "lady-writers," do you? . . . luckily the women-writers are all at home, as we soon shall be. Women are fascinating creatures; yet it is treading upon eggs all the time to deal with them . . . women, bless their hearts! want to be considered, deferred to; they receive the unvarnished truth as if it were a red-hot bullet."

The phrase makes one wonder whether Bowles's "red-hot bullet" of "unvarnished truth" is the same bullet that hit a bird in Dickinson's letter. The quotation from Merriam's biography restricts "truth" to the value of "the gentle creatures' writing," but Bowles's final comment is mysterious: "I have made [women] shed many tears,—hated myself for it,—and that was not the least of the wrong they did me. A man does not enjoy hating himself."[46]

The "wrong they did me": it is a remark in keeping with what Master seems to have felt about Emily Dickinson. For Master letter 3 (248) begins, "Oh, did I offend it [Did'nt it want me to tell it the truth]." Bowles's outburst to his woman companion apparently fascinated her, for she related the story in minute detail to Merriam. Perhaps she perceived in it a certain misogyny that seemed at odds with Bowles's reputedly pronounced preference for women's company above men's. It is still interesting as a possible revelation of Bowles's complexity and his own imprisonment, doubtless, in what Gilbert and Gubar call the "toils of patriarchy." For those obliged a Victorian gentleman—and Bowles was gentle—to be courteous and delicate in treating with a woman, even about her skills as an employee. But Bowles's vehemence suggests that he was not merely thinking of the difficulties encountered by a frank newspaperman in dealing with women writers. (It should be noted that, as a crusader for women's rights, Bowles would not use the phrase "lady-writer.") Rather, it offers the possibility that Bowles was remembering the embarrassments of dealing with women writers who happened to be in love with him. That group certainly included his wife's relation, Maria Whitney, who was more precisely a scholar but also "wrote"; and by 1868, four years after the momentous sending of so many letters and poems to him, Bowles must have been aware that it included Emily Dickinson.

In analyzing Master letters 2 and 3, it is helpful to acknowledge certain traits in Bowles's personality that enabled Dickinson's association of him with Brontë's Rochester. While Merriam's list of witnesses to his subject's moral excellence is long, he includes much testimony about Bowles's absolute virtue with regard to women. This was probably necessary because Merriam also presented a multitude of anecdotes about the delight women took in Bowles's company and about the *freedom*—the word is a "Mrs. B." 's—that they experienced in their relations with him: "We met but rarely, but when we did meet we were friends, always and at once, understanding and trusting each other more than many who meet daily. Everybody, especially all women, felt his peculiar charm." Mrs. B.'s anecdote, which includes the observation that "it was no easy task for [Sam] to speak the truth when it wounded those he loved," ends with what may be described as a love scene between friends. (There are near-illustrations of such a scene in Victorian paintings like Ford Madox Brown's *An English Autumn Afternoon* [1852], and it was iconographically typical.) "I met him," she says,

> as I was going home after watching all night by Mrs. Farrar's deathbed ... He stopped to inquire about [her], and stood leaning on the fence, his face on his hand, his broad hat shading it and casting a shadow on his eyes, which were full of tender solicitude. I told him of the lesson I had gained by watching the peaceful close of such a beautiful and unselfish life; and he took my hand, looked earnestly in my face, and said ... "will you come and stay with me at the last?" I said, "Do you mean it?" He said, "Certainly I do," – and I promised.[47]

Here are some of the qualities that Jane Eyre finds irresistible in Rochester (and which become more prominent when he has been subdued by suffering at the novel's close): tenderness, instinctive sympathy, and a "feminine"—the word was used often of Bowles—willingness to confess affectionate need, even to women. Here too is that concern for one's last end, and the goal of sharing final moments before death with those one loves, which Emily Dickinson also possessed. Merriam's is the portrait of a Bowles who captured female hearts by *resigning* the male role of master, even like the blinded Rochester, who depends on Jane for his very sight when she comes back to him at the end.

But there is a good deal of evidence as well that the "freedom" women felt in his company sometimes led Bowles to what Victorians called "taking liberties." He sought and relished the society of women, and his manners at a party could be sportive, brusque, flirtatious. Notes from Bowles to Austin show what could be his cruder side: "Come down [to Springfield] and take a course in ale and whiskey with me." In his correspondence with Austin over the years, he made his taste for pretty women very plain: "I would that I might see your wife's beautiful friend [Mrs. Turner] – but *how* can I? Mrs. Bowles is very liberal in her government: would it be fair to take advantage of it to go 40 miles . . . to see beauty & grace & wit in that most enticing of mortal packages?"[48] Ironically, letters such as these would sometimes contain a remembrance for "the sister of the other house"—Emily—"who never forgets my spiritual longings."[49]

The health of Mary Bowles (almost continually pregnant when Dickinson knew them) was the subject of Bowles's daily concern, especially during the depressions she endured after the loss of their children in the late 1850s and early 1860s. Yet Bowles often sought refreshment alone among friends. The evenings in Sue's drawing room did not often include Mary.

There was gossip in Amherst about Bowles and Sue during the 1860s. There was also talk about Bowles's conduct with Maria Whitney. Maria was the daughter of Josiah Whitney, a Northampton banker, and distantly related to Mary Bowles. She became a supervisory companion and housekeeper for the Bowleses during Mary's pregnancies and depressions in the sixties and early seventies. Merriam avoided all evidence that Sam Bowles's interest in Maria (or hers in him) might be more than platonic, but certainly it transcended the ordinary relations between a married man and a younger, pretty, unattached girl. When

Maria left his home briefly to travel to California in 1864, Bowles wrote
to Sue:

> Perhaps Maria's late going had something to do, as you thought, with
> the day's depression; but it would have been a day of torture &
> blueness any way. Her going has been a trial to me; but I should be
> unworthy the rich gift of her friendship did I allow it to blue my life,
> weaken the tide of its flow, or poison the sweetness of its expression.
> Her gifts to me are too great & noble to be spoiled by such unwor-
> thiness.[50]

Bowles speaks of friendship. While traveling in the early sixties, however, he sent six- and seven-page letters to Maria (letters that may be
sharply contrasted with short notes to his wife) which suggest that she
was fast becoming a soul mate. Escorting Maria to San Francisco in
1865, he put her among "preposterous women"[51] in a message to Sue,
but this was in the context of appreciating her high spirits. It shows
how much she attracted him. Mary Bowles resented Maria's presence
in her home, though she was for many years too ill to contest it. Finally,
a letter from Maria to her sister-in-law, written in 1868, reveals that
Maria herself was quite aware of the friction between the Bowleses over
her. With smug complacency, she made it clear that it was she and Sam
who were friends:

> I ought certainly to know if Mrs. Bowles is saying such disloyal,
> unkind things of me . . . Now I want you to tell me who the people
> are who have said to you that "this friendship is a forced one on Mrs.
> B.'s part, only tolerated to avoid further separation from her hus-
> band" . . . The friendship is as precious to me as to him, and he has
> not attempted at any time to persuade me to any thing that my
> judgment and inclinations did not sanction.[52]

By the time of his death, Maria had left Bowles's house to become a
language professor at Smith College. But Bowles's associate, Dr. Holland, pointedly remarked at his funeral that "Sam's unswerving and
undiminished loyalty to the wife of his youth was known to . . . those
noble women who became the . . . cherished friends of his later years."[53]
The "common sentiment," Merriam said, of all who loved him was
expressed "by one who wrote, 'Not to see you sometimes, not to hear
from you, is a kind of eclipse.'"[54] This woman was perhaps Emily
Dickinson, for whom "eclipse" always signified trauma. And to Maria

1. Charles Allston Collins, *Convent Thoughts* (1850). Conveys the Pre-Raphaelite interest in the Christian symbolism of lilies.

2. Thomas Cole, *The Voyage of Life* (1840): *Childhood*. Child issuing from eternity's cave reflects Wordsworth.

3. *The Voyage of Life: Youth.* The most popular panel in Dickinson's time.

4. *The Voyage of Life: Manhood.* For mid-Victorians, an expression of the Burkean sublime.

5. *The Voyage of Life: Old Age.* "[Jacob] dreamed . . . and behold the angels of God ascending and descending" (Genesis 28:12).

6. Elihu Vedder, *The Cup of Death* (1886). Vedder produced orientalist
fantasies for popular consumption during and after Dickinson's lifetime.

7. William Holman Hunt, *The Light of the World* (1853–1856). Famous English religious painting; probable subtext of "Just so – Jesus – raps."

8. Thomas Cole, *Expulsion from the Garden of Eden* (ca. 1827–28). Burke's double-edged aesthetic: pleasure and pain.

Whitney, Dickinson would write for many years mourning the dead Bowles. Her generous letters associate her with Maria in a widowed sisterhood. One calls Mary Bowles "ungenerous" (2.623).

Like his friend Charles Dickens, whose love for his wife's sister Georgina Hogarth had a cruelly selfish side, Bowles indulged himself in befriending Maria Whitney. Nonetheless, Dickinson's comparisons of Bowles to the sun were descriptions of a glowing personality that effortlessly brightened others' lives. Women—daisies—could not resist turning their faces up to him. Edward Rochester has a similar effect on Jane Eyre. Yet, like Bowles with Dickinson, Jane's Master likes to tease and to toy with her. Rochester's wooing of Jane is secretive and even sadistic; although he keeps from her the fact of his real marriage, he puts continually before her the prospect of his marriage with Jane's foil, the buxom, snobbish, ignorant Blanche Ingram. The masochism that partly characterized Brontë's love for Heger discloses itself in Jane's attraction to Rochester; for she flagellates (yet also congratulates) herself about her small size, her homeliness, poverty, and insignificant past beside his well-grown stature, his fine eyes and head, his wealth and sophistication (p. 227).

Dickinson adapts most of Brontë's formulaic antitheses in describing herself in contrast with Master. Indeed, the following terms for Jane— "a little small thing," a "sparrow," "low born," "a little girl," "a nun"—are adopted for her own persona as a deprived lover or as Daisy (pp. 375, 247, 119, 108). If Dickinson made the identification of Bowles with Rochester, it is not difficult to see why. Though he lacked Rochester's riches and luxurious past, Bowles was a glamorous man, clever and successful. He was the friend of Emerson, a world traveler, a connoisseur of ideas and people. And he too, like Rochester, could be sardonic, moody, and, though a humanist, a scoffer at orthodoxy and certainly an unwitting trifler with female "hearts" (p. 398).

In Master letter 2, the conceit of the heart is important and joins the Master letters as a whole with letters openly addressed to Bowles. Those, in turn, are associated with poems like the early "Heart! We will forget him" and all, with *Jane Eyre*. Using another of her South American conceits for love as wealth—Potosi, related for her with Peru—Dickinson wrote the absent Bowles in April 1859:

Will you not come again? Friends are gems – infrequent. Potosi is a care, Sir. I guard it reverently, for I could not afford to be poor now, after affluence. I hope the hearts in Springfield are not so heavy as they were – God bless the hearts in Springfield! (L 2.352)

Now, in Master letter 2, she tells Master about her own stricken and bleeding heart and of "the gash that stains your Daisy's bosom." Her letter has great power and is an anthology of the conceits in the love poems of the Master cycle. Dickinson would one day remind Bowles that he had once led her by Resurrection. In Master letter 2, from her position, she told Sue, "at Center of the Sea" or as she said to Bowles himself, "far from Land" (L 2.390), she tells him a different story. This letter should be cited at length:

> I heard of a thing called "Redemption" – which rested men and women. You remember I asked you for it – you gave me something else. I forgot the Redemption [in the Redeemed – I didn't tell you for a long time, but knew you had altered me – I] and was tired – no more – [so dear did this stranger become that were it, or my breath – the Alternative – I had tossed the fellow away with a smile.] I am older – tonight, Master – but the love is the same – so are the moon and the crescent. If it had been God's will that I might breathe where you breathed – and find the place – myself – at night – if I (can) never forget that I am not with you – and that sorrow and frost are nearer than I – if I wish with a might I cannot repress – that mine were the Queen's place – the love of the Plantagenet is my only apology – To come nearer than presbyteries – and nearer than the new Coat – that the Tailor made – the prank of the Heart at play on the Heart – in holy Holiday – is forbidden me –

Master letter 2 contrasts that Redemption which Christians hope to rest in, one made available to them by their Master, Christ, with the private transformation of her sensibility accomplished by her Master. It is a momentous transformation; her bracketed deletions, still often implicit in the text, demonstrate complex efforts to express it. Master is himself redeemed, that is, saintly. His association with sorrow and frost makes him heroic. But he does not offer *her* redemption. Rather, his gift is "something else": the phrase, rather coy perhaps, suggests that it is passion and the ability to express it. He therefore saves her from the ennui of her former life; she is alive and no longer tired. But he destroys her ambition to be saved. (This was not hard to do of course in the case of Emily Dickinson, who longed for a nonsectarian "heaven" and whose respect for theological ideas like being "saved" was always displaced by independent perception of the divine). Hers is essentially a confession that she has assigned Christ's proper role to Master. It is made again and again in Master poems such as ("Your Face / Would put out Jesus'") or 464, which asks

> The power to be true to You
> Until upon my face
> The Judgment push His Picture –
> Presumptuous of Your Place –

And it has its counterpart in Jane Eyre's acknowledgment that "him who . . . loved me I absolutely worshipped" and that Rochester is to her like God, "dread but adored" (pp. 241, 252).

Dickinson's letter declares that she has grown in, and by, loving Master. Her sentence, "I am older – tonight, Master – but the love is the same – so are the moon and the crescent," has a Brontean analogue. *Villette*'s Lucy Snowe is told "the orb of your life is not to be so rounded [with love]; for you the crescent-phase must suffice." But Dickinson's speaker tells Master that her love is unvarying; the beginning of love (crescent) and its maturity are the same. This sentence finds a referent in several love poems, especially "I make His Crescent fill or lack" (909). As Jane does with the humbled Rochester, the speaker in 909 enjoys mastery over the man who mastered her; to express it, she identifies him with the moon. A traditionally feminine symbol, the moon image thus insists upon the male lover's tenderness and vulnerability. Meanwhile Dickinson herself, like the sighted Jane, becomes the sun:

> I make His Crescent fill or lack –
> His Nature is at Full
> Or Quarter – as I signify –
> His Tides – do I control –

Dickinson's yearning in her sentence, "If it had been God's will that I might breathe where you breathed," summons a recollection of her ardent girlhood letters to Sue. Yet its accents are essentially different. "God's will," the concept of the appointed place, the "Queen's place" next to the Plantagenet king: these phrases connote *marriage*, not merely love. Marriage, as Jane understands it in Brontë's novel (and as she teaches Rochester) is not only the institutionalized expression of sexual feeling but a sacred covenant. Dickinson's phrases imply the sacredness as well as the character of marriage as a union of *different* persons, male and female. Just as her poem "Like Eyes that looked on Wastes" expressed the sexual equation made by Sue and Emily as lovers, so

Master letter 2, and many Master lyrics, emphasize sexual difference. The ritual of marriage and lovemaking—"the prank of the Heart at play on the Heart"—obscures those differences in communion; yet they remain, older than queens and dynasties.

Dickinson's phrase, "To come nearer than presbyteries," is emblematically related to the sacerdotal imagery of such poems as 640 (Sexton, Cups), 322, and 506. It has long been used to support the hypothesis that Master was the Philadelphia minister, Charles Wadsworth. Dickinson is thus supposed to be saying that she would like to be closer to Wadsworth than his staff, the elders (and other ministers) of his church. She wants, then, to be at once Wadsworth's wife, his professional or at least intimate associate, and "nearer than the new Coat – that the Tailor made," that is, close to his skin!

I think, however, that presbytery has a different meaning in Master letter 2, as the place set apart for the clergyman in a church; and that it alludes to chapter 26 of *Jane Eyre* where Jane's marriage to Rochester is prevented by Bertha Mason's brother. In that chapter, the "master" comes to the church with Jane, whose wedding veil and jewels are emblems of a joy with which she is unfamiliar, like the adorned speaker ("late a Dowerless Girl") of Dickinson's marriage poem, "I am ashamed – I hide – / What right have I – to be a Bride" (472). The minister has emerged from the presbytery and awaits them at the altar. The presbytery or vesting room is thus associated with preparation for an expected marriage, one that is not formalized before the altar for Jane and Rochester. Dickinson's word *presbyteries* may indicate that she is thinking about expectation and actuality and, like the new coat Rochester wears on his wedding day, wishes to become one with his figure, his aspect, himself. She would, in short, like to marry Master and so she informs him.

Lines that follow these make such a supposition even more likely. Dickinson alludes to Byron's poem "The Prisoner of Chillon," saying she is in Chillon, which she also tells Bowles in a note written in 1862 (L 2.393). She objects that to be thus imprisoned by futile love "is not funny." Then she asks:

> Have you the Heart in your breast – Sir – is it set like mine – a little to the left – has it the misgiving – if it wake in the night – perchance – itself to it – a timbrel is it – itself to it a tune?

Her words propose to Master a parity of feeling between them as lovers which is reminiscent of *Jane Eyre*. Before proposing marriage, Rochester asks Jane:

Are you anything akin to me . . . Jane? . . . Because I sometimes have
a queer feeling with regard to you . . . as if I had a string somewhere
under my left ribs, tightly and inextricably knotted to a similar string
. . . in your little frame. (p. 221)

Jane Eyre is of course ashamed of the degree of her love for Rochester,
and they challenge each other to duels of self-repression or avowal.
Dickinson's symbols for love in Master letter 2 epitomize the attraction
that Jane and Rochester experience, one that Jane calls "not like an
electric shock: but . . . quite as sharp" (369). (The phrase may have
prompted Dickinson's description in 1883 of a biography of Emily
Brontë that she called "more electric far than anything since 'Jane
Eyre'" [L 3.775].)

Dickinson admits in Master letter 2 that she has "confessed – and
denied not" the hallowed feeling for Master that he seems to accuse
her of concealing. Writing now of her disclosed passion, she seeks
metaphors that are explosive, not merely electric. They were thought
indecorous by Lavinia and Austin. Although "Vesuvius" and "Etna"
were kept, most of the letter was deleted in the first edition of the
Letters (1894):

Vesuvius dont talk – Etna – dont – [Thy] one of them – a syllable –
A thousand years ago, and Pompeii heard it, and hid forever – She
couldn't look the world in the face, afterward – I suppose – "Tell you
of the want" – you know what a leech is, dont you – [remember that]
Daisy's arm is small – and you have felt the horizon hav'nt you – and
did the sea – never come so close as to make you dance?

Love as an explosion, felt in the soul and echoed by the body, is recorded
many times in Dickinson's poetry. The volcano is her symbol for passion
suppressed, not only love but rage. Her choice of it was apt (particularly
in the case of Chimborazo, an active volcano ringed by ice); it also
demonstrates her awareness of the great themes and events of her time.
(Recall Church's *The Heart of the Andes* [1859], the grand painting
displayed in New York and touted in the Springfield and Boston newspapers, which romanticized Chimborazo.) Volcanoes like Vesuvius or
Etna resembled herself; they didn't "talk." When the volcano talks, she
tells Master, it has the power to destroy:

I have never seen 'Volcanoes' –
But, when Travellers tell
How those old – phlegmatic mountains
Usually so still –

> Bear within – appalling Ordnance,
> Fire, and smoke, and gun,
> Taking Villages for breakfast,
> And appalling Men – (175)

In this poem of five quatrains, the predication "I think that . . ." is omitted after the second quatrain in an eloquent example of Dickinson's occasional elision of central constructions. It should be mentally introduced before the last three quatrains:

> If the stillness is Volcanic
> In the human face
> When upon a pain Titanic
> Features keep their place –
>
> If at length the smouldering anguish
> Will not overcome –
> And the palpitating Vineyard
> In the dust, be thrown?
>
> If some loving Antiquary,
> On Resumption Morn,
> Will not cry with joy "Pompeii"!
> To the Hills return!

Emily Dickinson could recognize "Vesuvius at Home" in Sue, about whom poem 1705 ("Volcanoes be in Sicily") was probably written. But she herself was a volcano that concealed fiery depths beneath her quiet demeanor. In everyone, the "palpitating Vineyard"—the living rage and/ or love—may one day be buried in death. But at Resurrection, she decides, it may return, like Pompeii—the city of humanity. It is human to suffer anguish and New Englandly to suppress it. Still the erupting peaks Bowles was describing in the *Springfield Republican,* volcanoes that Church and Heade traveled to Italy and South America to paint, had analogues in Dickinson's everyday life and in her own nature:

> On my volcano grows the Grass
> A meditative spot –
> An acre for a Bird to choose
> Would be the General thought –
>
> How red the Fire rocks below –
> How insecure the sod
> Did I disclose
> Would populate with awe my solitude (1677)

Samuel Bowles, her niece reports, called Emily Dickinson "half angel, half demon."[55] In her poetry about volcanoes, she fears that the fire "below," her suppressed passions, will come to the surface, shocking "the General thought." In Master letter 2 she declares that Vesuvius has finally erupted. The result, she fears, may be (as in the case of Pompeii in poem 175) the burial or "appalling" disappearance of the beloved. (Curiously, of course, it was Dickinson herself who ceased to "look the world in the face" shortly after the Master letters were written. Having spent several months in 1862 mourning Bowles's absence in Europe, she could not summon the nerve to greet him upon his return.) This conceit of burial and destruction after love's explosion surely has some relation to her own life. Certainly it is apposite to the considerable number of her poems which imagine both beloveds— female and male—as entombed with her: "I see thee clearer for the grave," (1666), for example, or "I see thee better – in the Dark" (611).

Master has asked her to "tell [him] of the want." (One imagines Bowles saying, "What is the matter?") Her question, "you know what a leech is, dont you," is significant; in the nineteenth century, leeches were still applied to bleed away sickness and were thus literally bloodsuckers. The terrible love she feels for him is draining: promising to be a cure for ennui, it is using up her life. And he should remember that "Daisy's arm is small," so that her energies were not great to begin with. *Horizon, sea, dance,* all allude to the great design of Nature of which passion is a part. Both Master and herself have perceived this design in the fluctuating seasons of the Massachusetts landscape as in the landscapes of the American painters. She admits that the sea of love has come too close to her. (This theme Dickinson engages in many poems. In "Three times – we parted – Breath – and I" [598], for example, the sea of desire nearly drowns her, while in 284 she rescues herself by losing herself in its waters, equated with the lover. The ways in which she treats the sea are different versions of her scenarios about love or eternity.)

Master has "the Beard on [the] cheek," a description Dickinson frequently chooses to identify men. She who could easily imagine herself a man, however, asks him what he would do if their sexual roles were reversed, if he "had Daisy's petals" and "cared so for me – what would become of you?" Her letters to Master, for all their syntactical quixotry and irresolution, reveal a woman employing her resources as a writer in order to affect an urbane man. The letters are both appeal and performance, Dickinson's equivalents of the salons Sue held for Bowles:

Could you forget me in fight, or flight – or the foreign land? Could'nt
Carlo, and you and I walk in the meadows an hour – and nobody
care but the Bobolink – and *his* – a *silver* scruple? I used to think
when I died – I could see you – so I died as fast as I could – but the
"Corporation" are going Heaven too so [Eternity] wont be sequestered – now [at all] – Say I may wait for you – say I need go with no
stranger to the to me – untried [country] fold – I waited a long time –
Master – but I can wait more – wait till my hazel hair is dappled –
and you carry the cane – then I can look at my watch – and if the
Day is too far declined – we can take the chances [of] for Heaven –
What would you do with me if I came "in white"? Have you the
little chest to put the Alive – in?

Dickinson's question, "Could you forget me in fight, or flight – or
the foreign land?" slips into trimeter as the poet's feeling intensifies.
These are the most Brontean of her lines, written for a man far away.
Had Dickinson composed the letter in 1862, the phrase "fight, or
flight – or the foreign land" could easily refer to Bowles. His journey
in early April 1862 to England, Switzerland, and Germany was, in fact,
a flight from cares and exhaustion brought on by a journalistic fight
over Lincoln's election. Dickinson remembered in later life that April
was the month that had "robbed" her the most (L 3.744). And indeed,
on April 25, 1862, three days after Bowles landed in Liverpool, the
Philadelphia Daily News reported that the Reverend Charles Wadsworth, her "Dusk Gem, born of troubled Waters" (L 3.745), would
accept a pastorate in San Francisco. She may have known that he
intended to. Certainly she had been prepared for Bowles's journey to
recruit his spent strength; but she was not resigned. "When the best is
gone," she informed Mary Bowles, "other things are not of consequence – The Heart wants what it wants" (L 2.405).

Bowles had decided in September 1861 that it was necessary for his
health that he go abroad. Immediately after he left, an intense Emily
Dickinson dispatched her letter (received on April 16) to Thomas Wentworth Higginson, enclosing four poems and asking if they were alive.
Then she told Higginson in the second letter of April 25, "I had a
terror – since September – which I could tell to none – and so I sing, as
the boy does by the Burying Ground – because I am afraid" (L 2.404).
It is never necessary, I think, to confine to just one the causes of Emily
Dickinson's complex responses. But as an (increasingly distant) member
of the Susan and Austin Dickinson circle that included Bowles, she
would have known immediately of his September plan to visit Europe.

Her "terror" would come from fearing his death by drowning; from fearing that he would forget her, as she tells Master; from the fear that, having lost one great love in Sue, she was about to lose the company, at least, of another; from fears that she could not, being so dependent, avoid psychological imbalance, were he to go; finally, from the consideration that her "song" or art, four years in preparation by 1862, might not be enough to keep her alive.

Franklin's study of Dickinson's handwriting, however, indicates that this letter should be dated in 1861. Even so, its heightened metaphoric style is appropriate. Bowles was a sufficient traveler, Dickinson so pronounced a stay-at-home, that his trips to New York City in late 1861 seemed to put him "far from Land," from herself (L 2.390). So painful was Dickinson's awareness of the price paid for what she had once called the untasted "feast" of human love, that she told Mary Bowles it left no resources for loving God: "I often wonder how the love of Christ, is done — when that — below — holds — so" (L 2.406). It is precisely Jane Eyre's reflection when Rochester's face begins to eclipse God's. Like Dickinson's Master, Rochester is associated with foreign places for Jane (and even with fight and flight, for he rehearses to her the history of his scarred affair with a Parisienne that resulted in a duel and his escape to England). And Jane, that excellent Protestant girl, imagines what life might be if she falls prey to the dream of living as his mistress in the Catholic places he prefers: "to wake . . . in a southern clime . . . delirious with love" (p. 316); or, as Dickinson sees it, in Eden, say, or Domingo, Zanzibar, and Cashmere.

Dickinson's language to Master becomes increasingly suasive, piteous, and allusive when she envisions going with him to the "untried fold" of paradise. "I waited a long time — Master," she declares,

> but I can wait more — wait till my hazel hair is dappled and you carry the cane — then I can look at my watch — and if the Day is too far declined — we can take the chances [of] for Heaven —

Here is the central theme of the Master literature, a loving union that takes place only in heaven. It also finds its counterpart in *Jane Eyre*. When Jane is at last reunited with Rochester (whom she still calls "Sir"), the two walk with their dog on to "cheerful fields." For Dickinson, it is the bobolink that sings; for Brontë, the skylark. They review the history of their cruel separation, regretting their increased age. Because Rochester's strength is much diminished, he must walk with a cane. The lovers are so absorbed in each other that they scarcely notice the

hour, but Jane says suddenly, "The day is far declined from its meridian
. . . Let me look at your watch" (p. 392). These are Dickinson's words
to Master: "I can look at my watch – and if the Day is too far declined –
we can take the chances [of] for Heaven."

Subsequent lines of Master letter 2, like the rest, have provoked
much conjecture, particularly these:

> Could you come to New England – [this summer – could] would you
> come to Amherst – Would you like to come – Master?

Vivian Pollak regards them as more appropriate to Charles Wadsworth,
a Philadelphian in San Francisco, than to Bowles who, as she says "had
lived in New England all his life." She concludes,

> Samuel Bowles is not the person to whom the "Master" letters were
> addressed. This point is further clarified if one compares the letters
> Dickinson wrote to Bowles while he was in Europe, which refer to
> other people in Amherst who are missing him, to places he has known
> and loved, and which treat his absence, rather than his presence, as
> exceptional.[56]

Dickinson sent Bowles an earnest note when he left Northampton
for New York in 1861; it complains that the hills seem foreign in his
absence and alludes to New York as his "Cage" (L 2.383). Like other
letters, it establishes herself as the fixed New England presence and
Bowles as the wanderer, not necessarily associated with Springfield. If
Master letter 2 was written in 1862, Dickinson's invitation is to a man
far away in Europe. Her letters to Bowles before his departure show
that she was deeply concerned about what his journey would do to her
in summer. "*Please* do not take our *spring* – away," she writes, object-
ing to his failure to visit her in that crucial April, "since you blot
Summer – out!" "I have the errand from my heart," she writes to him
in early summer. "Would you please to come Home?" (L 2.410). In
specifying New England and Amherst she was probably putting before
him the seductive names and the beloved landscape—"the Roses hang
on the same stems – as before you went"—on which she counted to
draw him back as soon as possible (L 2.409). As for others who were
missing him, to mention Vinnie and Austin and the rest as loving and
needing him was her stratagem always: "The Hearts in Amherst –
ache – tonight," she might write in one letter. Yet *her* need would
prevail: "I tell you, Mr. Bowles, it is a Suffering, to have a sea – no
care how Blue – between your Soul, and you" (L 2.410, 416). But if

this letter was written while Bowles was in New York during the winter of 1861–62, the metaphoric system whereby Dickinson sees herself as "Amherst" and Bowles as far away still applies.

The last lines of the letter express the themes of Master's godlike superiority, her childlike joy in gazing at his face, and her yearning to live with him in a time that is out of time:

> [Would it do harm — yet we both fear God —] Would Daisy disappoint you — no — she would'nt — Sir — it were comfort forever — just to look in your face, while you looked in mine — then I could play in the woods till Dark — till you take me where Sundown cannot find us — and the true keep coming — till the town is full. [Will you tell me if you will?]

I have said earlier that Dickinson's assumption of white clothes may indicate her vision of herself as one with those who overcome tribulation (as cited in such scriptural passages as Revelation 3:5): "But the ones who overcame most times — / Wear nothing commoner than Snow" (325). Her white clothing is the proper apparel for a wedding feast in heaven (as it is for a nun). She carries Master's face as a card of entry:

> The face I carry with me — last —
> When I go out of Time —
> To take my Rank — by — in the West —
> That face — will just be thine —
> . . . . .
> I'll hand it to the Angel —
> . . . . .
> He'll take it — scan it — step aside —
> Return — with such a crown
>
> As Gabriel — never capered at —
> And beg me put it on —
> . . . . .
> And then — he'll turn me round and round —
> To an admiring sky —
> As one that bore her master's name —
> Sufficient Royalty! (336)

In this way, Master's face, which she loves to look into, becomes a passport to paradise. She hands it to the angel who guards the entrance to her new Eden; it is thus a kind of coin of the realm, related to the "disc" that is both setting sun and Master's face in poems such as 474. As the supreme expression of his authority and personality, Master's image verifies Dickinson's right to be counted among the elect. Her white raiment, the sign of her integrity as of her triumph over suffering and secular love, is also that of a soul "at the White Heat": one who has earned heaven by the full exercise of God-given artistic powers (365).

Dickinson's letter continues by remarking to Master,

> I did'nt think to tell you, you did'nt come to me "in white," nor ever told me why . . .

Her remark is probably an observation that—unlike herself, the "Sufferer polite" of poem 388 who meets Master dressed in white—he has not "come to her in white"; or that he has not fallen in love with her and therefore has nothing to "overcome." This sentence is related to her earlier questions, "What would you do if I came 'in white'? Have you the little chest to put the Alive in?" They may be interpreted, probably, as "Suppose I declared myself openly and intruded upon your life?"; and, "Do you have a coffin for my corpse?" They present the macabre picture of a declaration which may only be made by a ghost. Certainly they are manipulative and show her evident power in what appear to be weakness and passivity.

Such ghostly visitations Dickinson frequently imagined. (Indeed, so did her friends.[57]) Her letter ends in an unrhymed tetrameter couplet, whose final foot is catalectic, witness to the unfulfilled aspect of her love. The images are the old ones for Sue and the springtime of sentiment, but Dickinson herself is now the beloved woman:

> No Rose, yet felt myself a'bloom,
> No Bird – yet rode in Ether. (L 2.391–392)

4

Dickinson's last Master letter, written in pencil with much indecision as reflected in its many parenthetical and bracketed words, is a response to the indignation of "recipient unknown." She begins, "Oh, did I offend it – [Did'nt it want me to tell it the truth]." This letter lends support to the supposition that, by some gesture or sentence or in a note that has not survived, she told Bowles of her love. Attributed by Johnson to "early 1862?", it offers as self-defense against an unstated accusation her stoical acceptance of Master's departure:

Daisy – who never flinched thro' that awful parting, but held her life so tight he should not see the wound –

In its assurance that her posture toward him is merely affectionate, servile, sisterly, the letter is related to many poems for Master in which Dickinson associates herself with the Jane Eyre who envisions herself as Rochester's servant, or with the Jane who cares for the blinded Rochester in his cottage at Ferndean. (So Dickinson imagines Master as "Tenant of the Narrow Cottage" and herself, his "Housewife" [961], whose chief function is to "lay the marble tea." As poem 1743 makes clear, *their* Ferndean will be the grave.) Her letter's assertion that she "bends her smaller life to his meeker [lower] every day" and that she "only asks – a task . . . something to do for love of it" reminds the reader of what Mark Spilka points out in an essay on Henry James: that Victorians, "for whom sexual feeling was severely repressed and talk about sex forbidden," sought to disguise erotic feeling in the sacred covenant of friendship or marriage.[58] To insist that she was only being sisterly would be especially disguising, if Bowles were Master. Austin looked on him as a brother.

Master letter 3 is a subterfuge that combats Master's apparently "appalled" realization of her romantic attachment to him by the resumption of a childish pose. It is a regression to the images and tone of such Master poems as this one, where the propriety of concealment is worn like a royal costume:

> Mute thy Coronation –
> Meek my Vive le roi,
> Fold a tiny courtier
> In thine Ermine, Sir,
> There to rest revering
> Till the pageant by,
> I can murmur broken,
> Master, It was I – (151)

Here Dickinson's persona masquerades as a courtier. Yet to recall the other Master poems is to recognize her as in reality that dynamic Queen, whose tiny stature, like Victoria's, is the inverse measure of an inherited power; and whose temperament, for all the reverence she does Master, is so volatile as to make continual claim upon him. Here is Daisy again, with her smaller, meeker, life and her "small heart," the very archetype of Dickens' child-bride in *David Copperfield* and other fictions, and still the sister of Jane Eyre. Dickinson's suite of infantalizing images ends in

the reassurance that her bosom is not "big eno' for a Guest so large."
She is a little girl, not physically ready for sexual experience with a man
(Dickinson is thirty-two years old as she writes).

The old tie with Brontë's novel helps to explain one of its passages,
often considered puzzling. Just once, and it is here, does Dickinson
record that Master initiates an embrace. Having disavowed her own
breeding, taste, intelligence, and knowledge before him (a "patrician,"
while she is a mere "Backwoodsman"), Dickinson writes:

> Low at the knee that bore her once unto [royal] wordless rest [now]
> Daisy [stoops a] kneels a culprit –

Dickinson's biographers debate whose knee it was—and was there a
knee?—upon which she sat to be borne to that "rest" always associated
with redemption.[59] Perhaps there was a real knee. It is possible that
Sam Bowles, whose treatment of Emily Dickinson seems to have been
half-protective, half-playful, may have taken her on his knee one evening
in affectionate sport or even in serious concern.

But Victorian novels and pictures frequently feature a woman enthroned on a gentleman's knee as a visual euphemism for sexual encounter. Although William Holman Hunt's famous picture *The Awakening Conscience* (1854) indicated that the fallen woman regained her
moral conviction by showing her in the act of rising from her lover's
knee, many pictures and stories celebrated the happy wife, held by her
husband on his knee as both sweetheart and child. As *Jane Eyre* ends,
Rochester places Jane on his knee to emphasize their joyful, now sanctified union. At the same time, Dickinson's allusion to Daisy kneeling
before Master has its counterpart in Brontë's poem "Master and Pupil,"
which Dickinson would have met in her copy of *The Professor*. There
the pupil, also "Jane," remembers her fête day in words central to the
Dickinson experience:

> Low at my master's knee I bent,
> The offered crown to meet.[60]

Here are important elements of Dickinson's romance with Master: the
bright and submissive girl student (a safe role for a Victorian spinster
to assume toward an attractive man); the charismatic master-teacher;
the crown of intellectual and spiritual virtue, transmuted by fantasy
into the royal crown worn by queenly wives; and the bending and
climbing of knees. Whether Bowles (or another) took Dickinson on his

knee, such a modest consummation of feeling was what she dreamed of, and she may have taken it from Victorian iconography.

Master letter 3 seeks to placate her "Lord" by saying that she is ill and that her illness is exacerbated by his disapproval:

> I've got a cough as big as a thimble – but I dont care for that – I've got a Tomahawk in my side but that dont hurt me much. [If you] Her master stabs her more –

The letter ends on a scene that replaces the old one of drowning (related to the conclusion of *Villette* where Brontë suggests that Paul Emmanuel drowns before he can marry Lucy Snowe), probably drawn from Cole's painting *Old Age*. In it, Master becomes the Lord indeed; and like God, whose face may be imagined in the opening clouds above Cole's voyager and the guardian angel, he takes Dickinson to his bosom. As she dreams it:

> Oh how the sailor strains, when his boat is filling – Oh how the dying tug, till the angel comes. Master – open your life wide, and take me in forever, I will never be tired – I will never be noisy when you want to be still. I will be [glad] [as the] your best little girl – nobody else will see me, but you – but that is enough – I shall not want any more – and all that Heaven only will disappoint me – will be because it's not so dear

Cole's beautifully serene *Old Age*, its angels descending in dazzling light to receive the weary voyager, is of course preceded by the panel *Manhood* where the "sailor strains" indeed as his boat dashes along the violent stream of life. Dickinson imagines the "wide" divine embrace that Cole depicts, but she returns at last to her own well-established conceit of Master's superiority to God. To be taken in to *his* life would be better than entering paradise.

Even thus she says to the nameless beloved of "Wild Nights,"

> Might I but moor – Tonight –
> In Thee (249)

Because Sue is closely associated with Eden, and because poem 249 envisions "Rowing in Eden," I have heard critics list "Wild Nights" as one of Dickinson's homoerotic poems.[61] But the curious little fact of Bowles's letter to Sue about rowing in Eden, Maine, together with Emily Dickinson's avowal that Bowles "was himself Eden," inhibits easy assignment of this poem to the Sue cycle. Furthermore, there were Victorian lyrics in which beloved men were imagined as providing safe harbor for a woman or in which the sexual embrace was regarded as a fusion of two sexes into one, neither the man nor the woman being regarded as host, simply, or guest (see poem 1721).

Thus in Tennyson's *Princess* Ida recites a poem for the male narrator. It comes from "A volume of the Poets of her land" and is written by a man. Yet it is her woman's voice that says the words. The effect, like that of "Wild Nights," is thus seductively androgynous:

> Now folds the lily all her sweetness up,
> And slips into the bosom of the lake.
> So fold thyself, my dearest, thou, and slip
> Into my bosom and be lost in me. (7.171–174)

Emily Dickinson once told Judge Lord that she had been thinking of him by writing, "I have been in your Bosom" (L 3.727). Similarly, Dickinson in Master letter 3 yearns to be taken in to him forever, like his bride or his child or, perhaps, like Abraham in Jahweh's bosom: a saved soul in heaven.

5

Closely related to the Master letters are those wistful lyrics written about or by Daisy; others in which Dickinson seems to dramatize the perilous experiences of Jane Eyre; and, finally, the great poems of passion, renunciation, and heavenly consummation, such as "There came a Day at Summer's full" (322), "They put Us far apart" (474), and "If I may have it, when it's dead" (577). In her poems of the last category, Dickinson presents a speaker who discards the childish mask worn in the Daisy-Jane lyrics and voices the satisfaction of a woman "sumptuous" (Richard Wilbur reminds us[62]) in her "destitution," and so able to fuse imagery of sexual passion and denial, psychic communion and loss, spiritual emptiness and expectation. For this speaker, the metaphorical garden, the grave, Calvary, paradise, bliss, and want join to become one "Province – in the Being's Center" (553). To her, deprivation has become possession. As she told Otis Lord in refusing to marry him, " 'No' is the wildest word we consign to Language" (L 2.617).

What I shall hypothesize as a fourth group of lyrics—all are, of course, cross-referential—is made up of poems that chiefly explore erotic feeling in association with one of Dickinson's favorite emblems,

Eden. The poems "Come slowly – Eden" (211), "He touched me" (506), "Love – thou art high" (453), and "Wild Nights" itself compose a representative group of love lyrics, each of which contemplates erotic consummation as, and in, an Eden. They show us the virtuosity that enabled Dickinson to treat one theme in the same images but in a different manner. By their close association in the fascicles (as by their interplay with related themes), they illustrate her powers of concentration as a poet. And wonderfully, considering their subject—physical desire—they are also related to a variety of Victorian graphic, painterly, literary and scientific texts from which they may, in part, have sprung. Emily Dickinson was a learned poet, and her learning becomes poignantly persuasive in these love poems.

"Come slowly – Eden" appears in fascicle 10, preceding "Least Rivers – docile to some sea" (212). The latter is a couplet on Dickinson's frequent theme of losing the self in the beloved as a river flows into the sea. In Cole's *Manhood* the desperate voyager's craft heads for open sea with the careening violence of Dickinson's words:

> What Twigs We held by
> Oh the View
> When Life's swift River striven through
> We pause before a further plunge (1086)

But "Least Rivers" envisions her preferred image of lesser waters disappearing in tranquil and hospitable oceans. And that is the sense given by Cole's *Old Age,* where the "Ether Sea" of heaven fuses before the voyager's eyes with the rivers of life. "Come slowly – Eden" depicts the moment of sexual communion as a land- rather than a seascape, one based on that Mediterranean garden described in Genesis, in Milton's *Paradise Lost,* and by the American painters. Like the landscape Cole envisions in *Childhood* and *Youth,* where palms and maples grow together, Dickinson's Eden contains flowers that are exotic (the jasmine is Persian), placed in the usual country context one associates with Amherst.

Dickinson's family liked to point out that it was Bowles who gave Emily what she called a jasmine tree. (To nineteenth-century gardeners, its fragrant white flowers were known as "Poet's jessamine.") In July 1882 she sent one of its "priceless" flowers to his son, Samuel Jr. The dead man's "Immortality," she said, was "Secreted in [the] Star" that was each blossom (L 3.839). For her, "Jessamines"—she adopts the horticultural and Tennysonian spelling—connoted passion. In "Come slowly – Eden" the perfume of the jasmine is an exotic liquor that may be drunk. Like Tennyson's lily in the lake, the ubiquitous Dickinson bee is lost in balms, her word for healing pleasures:

> Come slowly – Eden!
> Lips unused to Thee –
> Bashful – sip thy Jessamines –
> As the fainting Bee –
>
> Reaching late his flower,
> Round her chamber hums –
> Counts his nectars –
> Enters – and is lost in Balms (211)

Including this lyric in the 1890 *Poems,* Colonel Higginson may be supposed to have provided the inappropriate title "Apotheosis," which clouds the poem's basic sexuality. Mrs. Todd altered "Jessamines" to "jasmines," marring as well the sensual, playful trochaic rhythm of the third line. But neither was evidently troubled by the poem's sensuality, though they did place it on the page opposite what they called "The Wife"—"She rose to His Requirement" (732)—thus borrowing from the latter a measure of sobriety.

Bees as prototypes of God the Father or as types of the eager lover appear throughout Dickinson's poetry, and in the same fascicle as "Come slowly – Eden" she humorously identifies bees with herself:

> We – Bee and I – live by the quaffing –
> 'Tisn't *all Hock* – with us –
> Life has its *Ale* – (230)

Yet the bee of poem 211, fainting, late, lost in love for the balms of his beloved's body, is but the means of exploring the experience of Eden, a nectar pressed from flowers.

The appearance of the word *Eden* in so many of Emily Dickinson's poems and letters reflects the connection of her art to its time. In the 1830s, scientific exploration in Mexico and South America gave rise to an extraordinary interest on the part of writers and painters in the tropics as a new Eden. Charles Darwin, himself a South American explorer, traced this interest to the vivid descriptions of Alexander von Humboldt in *Cosmos* (1850), a mixture of scientific fact and romantic thoughts inspired by Latin America. In search of answers about the source of life, geologists and paleontologists flocked to the fertile and virgin American tropics. Eager for fresh and (to all accounts) lush scenes, painters like Catlin, Church, and Heade followed in their wake. As early as 1820, however, Thomas Cole had journeyed to the island of St. Eustatius in the West Indies. He wrote (in a short story) that it reminded him of what Eden must have been: "Fields of flowery luxuriance, groves of dark and glistening green made the spaces between the sea-shore and the distant slopes look to his enamored eyes like Paradise."[63] Cole created the vision of a lost paradise, founded on Latin American scenery, in *The Garden of Eden* (1828) and in *Expulsion from the Garden of Eden* (1827–28).

The former painting, unseen in public since 1831, was acquired in 1990 by the Amon Carter Museum in Fort Worth, Texas. *Expulsion*—in the Museum of Fine Arts, Boston—may have been known to Emily Dickinson. In a letter of 1878 she may be quoting Cole's title in acknowledging a gift of flowers: "Expulsion from Eden grows indistinct in the presence of flowers so blissful, and with no disrespect to Genesis, Paradise remains" (L. 2.610). This had been Cole's thought in saying, "We are still in Eden." It was Ruskin's when he claimed in part 6 of *Modern Painters,* "For what can we conceive of that first Eden which we might not yet win back, if we chose?"[64] By thus envisioning Eden as recoverable through the experience of love or beauty, Cole manifested the nineteenth-century passion for Nature at its height. Cole's *Expulsion* (plate 8), its canvas bisected by a cave door separating a serene but tropical Eden on the right from the dark and ravaged precipices on the left, dramatically describes Dickinson's distinction between loss and gain. The loss of Eden is the first and fundamental loss. For Dickinson it is always the underlying premise of which all other losses are metaphors:

> Of so divine a Loss
> We enter but the Gain,
> Indemnity for Loneliness
> That such a Bliss has been. (1179)

In love poems like "Come slowly – Eden" she depicts tropical flowers, such as the jasmine kept in her conservatory, thus implying a paradise regained through passion.

"Come slowly – Eden" meditates not on marriage but on a physical union that is unaccustomed and long deferred and that the bashful speaker wishes to savor slowly. Is the poem about Master? Is the poem for Sue, with whom she so often associated Eden? Copied into fascicle 10, after the couplet about "Least Rivers," is poem 270, which is transcribed with great emphasis (exhibited in its excited, multiple uses of italics):

> *One Life* of so much Consequence!
> Yet I – for it – would pay –
> My soul's *entire income* –
> In ceaseless – salary –
>
> *One Pearl* – to me – so signal –
> That I would instant dive –
> Although – I *knew* – to *take* it –
> Would *cost* me – *just a life!* (270)

Declaring that "The Sea is full – I know it! / That – does not blur *my Gem!*" the speaker prefers her pearl—Sue, certainly—above all other possible lovers. The appearance of this poem from the pearl cluster directly after "Come slowly – Eden" might suggest, then, that the latter is also for Sue. That she continued to write love poems for Sue throughout the Master period may be gathered from poem 869, written in 1864–65, not copied into a fascicle and now numbered in Franklin's set 5. In this poem the word *blameless,* with its old vibrations of doomed lovers and blame, recalls other poems of the Sue cycle. Delicately designed in triplets, with precise rhymes, it also presents a bee, viewed more intimately than the one of "Come slowly – Eden":

> Because the Bee may blameless hum
> For Thee a Bee do I become
> List even unto Me.
>
> Because the Flowers unafraid
> May lift a look on thine, a Maid
> Alway a Flower would be. (869)

This poem translates the maid, Dickinson, into both bee and flower and, in the last six lines, into a robin, thus perpetuating the imagery of girlhood romance, just so (she says) "I that way worship Thee." But "Come slowly – Eden" seems, by comparison, a pictorial meditation on sensuous fulfillment, delicately and wittily struck off in the manner of the landscape painters. As a fanciful but lush meditation, it is genuinely indifferent to gender, the "I" is ceremonial if vocal, and the focus is on the pastoral scene itself.

Following these poems from fascicle 10, however, fascicle 11 presents the calmly transcribed but incandescent "Wild Nights," another portrait—although disguised—of people:

Wild Nights – Wild Nights!
Were I with thee
Wild Nights would be
Our luxury!

Futile – the Winds –
To a Heart in port –
Done with the Compass –
Done with the Chart!

Rowing in Eden –
Ah, the Sea!
Might I but moor – Tonight –
In Thee! (249)

"Wild Nights," its theatrical opening spondees worthy of turbulence and storm, justifies Dickinson's heritage as an admirer of Emily Brontë and *Wuthering Heights.* The seas that separate or unite Charlotte Brontë's heroines and their "masters" also come to mind. Here is a scene reminiscent not only of the intensity of the Brontës' world but also of hundreds of dark canvases by the Hudson River and Luminist painters. Cole's *Tornado in an American Forest* (1835), like his *Expulsion from Eden,* had made the frenzy of storm synonymous with *passio*—distress or love—while seascapes like Fitz Hugh Lane's *Ships and an Approaching Storm off Owl's Head, Maine* (1860) or Heade's *Approaching Storm: Beach Near Newport* (1860) made angry seas expressive of the sea of feeling. Furthermore, Dickinson's image of the rowboat was conceived during the 1860s, when the idea of the lone boat in contest with high seas was particularly popular.[65] There were many studies like Church's *An Old Boat* (1850), in which failure and loss were described by an abandoned rowboat at the edge of brimming, light-filled waters. Whistler expressed *The Sea* (1865) of defeat by picturing a rowboat stranded at the edge of sullen tides. Dickinson's lyrics about the "Edifice of Ocean" with its "tumultuous Rooms" (1217) would find analogues in the vehement seascapes of Winslow Homer, for whom the ocean could also be a metaphor of grandeur and grief. As a favorite nineteenth-century sport, however, rowing on smooth water was described by Thomas Eakins' Luminist paintings: for example, the famous *Max Schmitt in a Single Scull* (1871), which has a serene if rather triste formality.

Having said all this, it is equally important to say that "Wild Nights" is among the most Dickinsonian of the lyrics: ironic, paradoxical, voluptuous, and terse all at once. At first it projects a tumultuous nocturnal seascape, the wildness Nature's. But the next three lines of the first quatrain propose this as a luxury: that is, a rare experience to be enjoyed. Thus the imagined wildness is also human, internal, joyous. The next quatrain, spoken from the vantage point of one who has felt winds, declares how futile they would be in port, at rest, where neither they nor a compass or chart—the scientific instruments of explorers— are needed. By the closing quatrain, the speaker is "Rowing in Eden," her visionary desire having triumphed over the course of a life's voyage. Dickinson may have been remembering Bowles's rowing in Eden and all those betrothed nineteenth-century lovers so often depicted rowing together as one stroke in the same boat. (Thus in chapter 41 of *Little Women,* to give a popular example, Amy and Laurie row their boat "smoothly through the water" opposite Chillon, then decide to marry.) In Eden Dickinson finds a sea of love that is pleasurable, not frightening, and a Thee in which she might safely moor or harbor. Dickinson's inclusion of a sea in Eden, a garden, reminds us that the book of Genesis provides a river in Eden that waters the garden (2:10). (Other poems, such as "My River runs to thee" [162], may be related to her imagery of primal—sexual—waters. That poem was sent in a letter to Mary Bowles in August 1861; but like most of her words to Mary, it was probably intended for her husband.) In *Expulsion from Eden* Cole included a placid lake and a gentle waterfall in his Eden. When Dickinson's first quatrain is taken together with the last in poem 249, however, the reader realizes that she means to "moor" in passion, to luxuriate in wildness. For though hers is a boat that rows rather than rides the waters, her satisfaction in "Wild Nights" comes from strong delight. Even in Eden, she hears the sea. To moor is still to be wild for this prohibited voice that prays "Might I . . .".

It has been truly said that this lyric has a "prelapsarian quality."[66] The word *Eden,* of course, conjures the lost, surrendered paradise, the holy place of perfect harmony where sexuality, like nature itself, may be explored without shame. Cole's *Expulsion,* like John Martin's mezzotints of *Paradise Lost*—both well known in Dickinson's day and in New England—provided a ground style and a subject for other painters like Church who saw in the United States and South America new Edens. Darwin's voyage in the *Beagle* and his subsequent publication of his *Diary* (1839) and *Origin of Species* (1859) awakened interest in Genesis as a fiction as well as further cultural absorption in the South

American tropics as Eden metaphors. Dickinson's Eden poems, like her mention of Popocateptl, Potosi, and Peru, show the same fascination with Latin America exotica that took Frederic Church to the Cordilleras, Bogota, Cotopaxi, Chimborazo, and what his most famous painting called the "heart of the Andes."

She makes no poetic allusions to Bogota, the Andes, or Cotopaxi. But mountains figure in Dickinson's poems as emblems of permanence (even as they do in the work of Cole, Church, and the landscape painters). The Andes were much in the American news in the 1860s. Dickinson uses Chimborazo as an important symbol in poem 452 and on three occasions speaks of the Cordilleras. Church's *The Cordilleras: Sunrise* (1854) was an important pastoral that helped to establish his reputation as a painter of the South American Edens that Humboldt had included in his book. The Cordilleras became associated in the 1860s with Church. In poem 268 (ca. 1861) Dickinson writes a modest lyric using his imagery:

> Me, change! Me, alter!
> Then I will, when on the Everlasting Hill
> A Smaller Purple grows –
> At sunset, or a lesser glow
> Flickers upon Cordillera
> At Day's superior close!

While this poem is about sunset and Church's painting depicts sunrise, his colors are hers. In poem 534 (ca. 1863), however, Cordillera is linked with morning:

> We see – Comparatively –
> The Thing so towering high
> We could not grasp its segment
> Unaided – Yesterday –
>
> This Morning's finer Verdict –
> Makes scarcely worth the toil –
> A furrow – our Cordillera –
> Our Apennine – a Knoll –

Dickinson's poem declares that a new day can revise one's estimate of a thing's importance. In this morning's light, yesterday's towering reality becomes a furrow. In poem 1029 (ca. 1865) she writes simply,

> Nor Mountain hinder Me
> Nor Sea –
> Who's Baltic –
> Who's Cordillera?

These allusions argue Emily Dickinson's familiarity with the art of Frederic Church, whose massive *Heart of the Andes* "gave visual form to [the public] idea of tropical America: it represented the long-lost Garden of Eden, a nascent world left untouched since the creation."[67] Yet a seventeenth-century poetic fiction about Eden had been at hand for years. In that Eden created by John Milton—to whom Dickinson refers a month before her death as "the great florist" (L 3.900)—the flowers are exceeded in beauty only by Eve herself, another flower; and Adam sins in book 9 not from pride but for love of Eve and from a determination to die with her rather than live alone in the garden. The comforts of shared love in a place of pure natural joy were emphasized by Milton, and were associated with a fortunate time before ambition, followed by greed and lust, caused the prohibition of edenic freedoms to humanity. (Dickinson liked to quote the account in Genesis 3:24 where God drives out "the man; and . . . placed at the east of the garden of Eden Cherubims, and a flaming sword which turned every-way, to keep the way of the tree of life.") Pleasure and its interdiction, happiness forbidden: Eden emblematized just that for her. Thus "Wild Nights" earns its allusion to Eden, in one way, simply by positing the prevented aspect of the speaker's love.

This book proposes that Dickinson had two experiences of love, with "just two Hearts"—Master and Sue—in the middle years that shaped her as an artist. Is it possible to decide for which (if for either or anyone) "Wild Nights" was intended? Its appearance in fascicle 11 with poems 245, 248, 251, 246, 317, 1737, and 284 makes it the perfect example, I think, of the way in which both figures provided inspiration for her.

Does the fascicle into which it was copied tell us anything? In fascicle 11 (around 1861) Dickinson meditates for the most part on two themes: her exclusion from a love once valued and her commitment to a new, "married" love that she intends to enjoy "forever" (246). Thus, in "I held a Jewel in my fingers" and "Why – do they shut Me out of Heaven?" and "Just so – Jesus – raps," the speaker sees herself (quite in the iconographic style of Hunt's *Light of the World*[68]) as "the Gentleman / In the 'White Robe' " with "the little Hand – that knocked" (248) while "they"—frequently understood to be Sue and Austin—keep her from paradise. The beloved woman is the jewel, for whose exclusive, remembered possession she grieves. In 251, she imagines herself a boy going over the fence to where strawberries grow, an allusion, it seems, to forbidden female fruit in a poem that has little reason to exist, except as a mischievous observation that "Berries are nice!"

At the same time, however, fascicle 11 presents "Rearrange a 'Wife's' affection!" and "Forever at His side to walk" and "The Drop, that wrestles in the Sea." These are poems that, in the images and accents of *Jane Eyre*, seem clearly addressed to Master. Indeed, "Rearrange a 'Wife's' Affection" (which the Dickinson family refused to publish and tried to destroy altogether) tells the terrible, regal story of Dickinson's secret love and eternal marriage: "None suspect me of the crown, / For I wear the 'Thorns' till *Sunset*." And it is written from the perspective of a woman, not a boy: "Amputate my freckled Bosom! / Make me bearded like a man!"

Fascicle 11, then, seems to describe a situation in time just before that of the speaker in poem 466 who no longer regrets the loss of the beloved woman, the pearl or jewel, since she is now in full possession of her own womanhood and, crowned by her Emperor, is herself jewel and bejeweled:

> 'Tis little I – could care for Pearls –
> Who own the ample sea –
> Or Brooches – when the Emperor –
> With Rubies – pelteth me –
>
> Or Gold – who am the Prince of Mines –
> Or Diamonds – when have I
> A Diadem to fit a Dome –
> Continual upon me –

Whereas in "Your Riches – taught me – Poverty," Dickinson tells a beloved woman, as we have seen, that she is unacquainted with *mines,* wealth is hers in poem 466, a fact she shyly admits in 1859 by telling Bowles, for instance, to care for his health: "I could not afford to be poor, now, after affluence" (L 2.352). To own mines and the sea is to row in Eden, to meet eros without fear. And it is Master, not the beloved woman, who makes that possible.

Therefore I think that "Wild Nights" is written, if for anyone, for Master. In poem 453, as well, she depicts a painterly scene in which climbing mountains (a feat she always associates with the dangerous feat of love) and rowing with another in a boat are envisioned in summer and linked with her Master symbol, the sun. This lush poem, even like "Wild Nights," has for a central premise the speaker's understanding of what love is and her yearning to possess the lover she desires:

> Love – thou art high –
> I cannot climb thee –
> But, were it Two –
> Who knows but we –
> Taking turns – at the Chimborazo –
> Ducal – at last – stand up by thee –
>
> Love – thou art deep –
> I cannot cross thee –
> But, were there Two –
> Instead of One –
> Rower, and Yacht – some sovreign Summer –
> Who knows – but we'd reach the Sun?
>
> Love – thou art Vailed –
> A few – behold thee –
> Smile – and alter – and prattle – and die –
> Bliss – were an Oddity – without thee –
> Nicknamed by God –
> Eternity – (453)

"Were there Two / Instead of One": it is the wish and supposition on which are founded many of the Master (*and* Sue) poems; it is an appeal to nineteenth-century iconography in which two row in the boat; and the word *veiled* may imply the truth of Emily Dickinson's life as a woman—that there were never really "two." Yet eternity, she said, swept round her like a sea, and she declared herself to Master in the 1860s as "altered" (L. 2.374). She could "behold," entertain, the complete experience of love without needing to have it.

Her allusion to Chimborazo in "Love – thou art high" may show Dickinson's intimacy with Elizabeth Barrett Browning's *Aurora Leigh* in which the heroine wonders "by how many feet / Mount Chimborazo outsoars Himmeleh" (1.14). Dickinson herself alludes to Himmeleh in four poems, implying knowledge of those lines. Emerson associates "a Chimborazo" with a high mountain in "The Poet."[69] Dickinson's allusion may also have stemmed from her knowledge of that essay, which she was reading in December 1861. But, more important, like her imagery of water and eternity, it may once again indicate a knowledge of Church's treatment of Chimborazo in *The Heart of the Andes.*

His well-known *Chimborazo,* in fact, depicts a scene that resembles Dickinson's in poem 453: the mountain peak towering nearly into invisibility and a single rower, trying to cross water toward it, as someone watches him in the summer sunlight. *Chimborazo* was finished in 1864, while Dickinson's poem was probably written in 1862. But there were many sketches of Chimborazo, done in Eden, Maine, which Bowles might have heard of, or seen, and described to the Dickinsons. Austin and Sue's collection of Luminist paintings contained no work by Church—it may have been too costly for them in the early 1860s. The painter nearest him in technique, whose landscape *Autumn Evening* they acquired, was the less-renowned Sanford Gifford. But whether from Bowles or in New York art circles, Austin must have heard of Church. As Cole's only protegé, Church continued the work of recording the moral beauty of the American continent, popularizing Hudson River art through his celebrated exhibitions in New York, Philadelphia, and Boston.

The Heart of the Andes (fig. 6), like his earlier *Niagara,* was not a mere painting but a national event in 1859. The picture was inspired by the landscape of Ecuador, composed of many scenes Church had viewed there. Ten feet long and epic in scope, the painting attempts a detailed depiction of flora and fauna, geography, color, and atmosphere. The icy volcanic peak of Chimborazo gleams in the distance of the canvas at the left. A blasted tree, suggesting violent weather, stands to the left of the mountainous plains. Slightly to the right of center, a quotation from *The Voyage of Life*—the river and falls—catches the viewer's eye. At the far right there are lush blue flowers, ferns (often used by the painters to suggest primitive foliage), and trees that might be North American birches together with tropical eucalyptus. The sky overhead is aquamarine. A small wayside shrine allows Church once again to quote Cole by including a cross near the left center of the canvas.

It is difficult now to convey the sense of the excitement created by this painting when it was shown to a broad spectrum of the public on April 27, 1859, in New York City. Benches were ranged before it so that visitors could study the painting during the three weeks it was on display. Thousands passed by, hot, jostled, but reverential. The sickly Washington Irving traveled from Sunnyside, his New York estate, to see it on the last day, when the viewing was found to have taken in the extraordinary sum of $3000 in receipts and $6000 for subscriptions to the engraving. Just as she probably saw engravings of Cole's *Voyage,* it is likely that Emily Dickinson saw a copy of *Heart of the Andes.*

The painting prompted a pamphlet by Theodore Winthrop, on whom the *Atlantic Monthly* published an article that Dickinson would have seen in August 1861. Winthrop is moved to exclamation by "Chimborazo then!—clarum et venerabile nomen":

> this miracle of vastness, and peace, and beauty, not merely white snow against blue sky, but light against heaven. No poetry of words can fitly paint its symmetry, its stateliness, the power of its crown, up into the empyrean. The poetry is before our eyes . . . It gives a vision of glory, and every one who beholds it is a poet.[70]

When Dickinson speaks of the majesty of love in poem 452, she speaks of "the Chimborazo." Her use of the article forces the proper name into a synonym for the experience of passion. Her choice of Chimborazo may merely reflect an intelligent predilection for a name whose ring was foreign—the poem concedes love's foreignness—exotic, and sanctified by Browningesque association. She may have set it down instinctively as the most prominent South American peak when she was writing. And perhaps Bowles, on one of his frequent trips to New York "for a little recreation,"[71] as he writes in November 1859, saw some of Church's paintings at the Tenth Street Studio, a mecca for lively connoisseurs of painting. Certainly, as in the case of her allusions to *Jane Eyre*, the word "Chimborazo" seems to be encoded.

Writing in poem 368 that "*One port – suffices – for a Brig – like mine*":

> Our's be the tossing – wild though the sea –
> Rather than a Mooring – unshared by thee,

Dickinson retains the metaphor of the port in "He touched me, so I live to know." Her usage shows that the male lover may indeed be the port of "Wild Nights" and that in employing the image she may be writing with "gratitude" (493) to Master as a deliverer. Here we see the several themes of the Master literature: the superb "awful" master; the sea of passion; the small gipsy figure who has wandered like Jane after leaving Rochester; the crowning by love. Her last stanza (deleted in her niece's edition of the *Poems*) concludes on the emblem of eternal marriage ("Crucifixal sign") and on her sun metaphor for Master:

> He touched me, so I live to know
> That such a day, permitted so,
> I groped upon his breast –
> It was a boundless place to me

6. Frederic Edwin Church, *The Heart of the Andes* (1859). The peak of Chimborazo is at left.

And silenced, as the awful sea
Puts minor streams to rest.

And now, I'm different from before,
As if I breathed superior air –
Or brushed a Royal Gown –
My feet, too, that had wandered so –
My Gipsy face – transfigured now –
To tenderer Renown –

Into this Port, if I might come,
Rebecca, to Jerusalem,
Would not so ravished turn –
Nor Persian, baffled at her shrine
Lift such a Crucifixal sign
To her imperial Sun. (506)

Here the intimate simplicity of the phrase "He touched me" initiates an extended group of actions that concludes in the speaker's comparison of herself to Rebecca, traveling toward Jerusalem for her marriage with Isaac, and to herself also as a baffled Persian. The yoking of these comparisons is unexpected (and probably prompted their deletion by Mrs. Bianchi). Once again, however, Dickinson's awed vision of Master and the outlines of her Master narrative are supported by her words. Genesis 24 relates the story of God's command to Isaac that he send to another country for a bride; and of Rebecca, whose service to Isaac's servant marks her as that bride; and who, when she sees her "master," "took a veil, and covered herself" with modesty and joy (24:65). Entering Jerusalem, her earthly paradise, Rebecca hides her face. (The thought of the poet herself, behind her door during Bowles's visits, comes to mind.) A Persian, frustrated and "baffled"—a lover of jasmines, like the speaker in "Come slowly, Eden" but one who may not have them—she must take up her crucifix, lifting it to the "Sun" to whom it pays homage.

6

Samuel Bowles published a few of Emily Dickinson's poems in the *Republican*.[72] But he never perceived the real merit of her poetry. From Vevey, during what was for Dickinson the terrible summer of 1862, he wrote Sue, "tell Emily to give me one of her little gems!"[73] Dickinson endured a form of triangulation even with respect to her art, moreover. For Bowles used to urge Sue as well to send him something—an essay or story—for the paper. After he died, Dickinson associated him, like Master, with that deathless sun, the Son of God. Despite (or because of) her feeling for him, however, their relationship did have its angry episodes. The best known is also comical: Dickinson refuses to see him in 1877, whereupon Bowles shouts up the stairway, "Emily, you damned rascal! No more of this nonsense! I've traveled all the way from Springfield to see you. Come down at once." And having achieved her aim—to nettle Bowles so thoroughly that he becomes truly "Masterly," one supposes—Dickinson descends the stair and is "charming and sociable."[74]

Two especially provocative poems describe experiences with Master in riddling words. One is "Struck, was I, nor yet by Lightning – " (ca. 1864); the other, the much-debated "My Life had stood – a Loaded Gun" (ca. 1863). Such poems seem to many readers the quintessence of Emily Dickinson's art, one of verbal puzzles and complex ellipses that invite ever more daring and perilous analyses. The Loaded Gun poem, in particular, has assumed in her oeuvre the position of the Prelude in C-sharp Minor for a student of Chopin: it is expected that anyone exploring her poetry will treat it. Yet if Emily Dickinson created these poems as riddles, she probably intended them to "vail" their full meaning—perhaps as a strategem for acquiring and retaining her own poetic power. Furthermore, both poems are certainly *about* power and its relation to art and to sexual love.

In both poems the scenes presented are largely mythic; the landscapes are part of that "Province – in the Being's Centre" (553), the heart. Superficially, though, each landscape has graphic analogues in the painting traditions of Dickinson's day. Here we have a number of apparently unrelated emblems or signs (in the fashion of a primitive landscape or tapestry) to explain the shock of love:

> Struck, was I, nor yet by Lightning –
> Lightning – lets away
> Power to perceive His Process
> With Vitality.
>
> Maimed – was I – not yet by Venture –
> Stone of stolid Boy –
> Nor a Sportsman's Peradventure –
> Who mine Enemy?

Robbed – was I – intact to Bandit –
All my Mansion torn –
Sun – withdrawn to Recognition –
Furthest shining – done –

Yet was not the foe – of any –
Not the smallest Bird
In the nearest Orchard dwelling
Be of Me – afraid.

Most – I love the Cause that slew Me.
Often as I die
It's beloved Recognition
Holds a Sun on Me –

Best – at Setting – as is Nature's –
Neither witnessed Rise
Till the infinite Aurora
In the other's eyes (925)

This poem has an Elizabethan quality, generated by the conceit of orgasm as death ("Often as I die"); and by the supple paradox, "I love the Cause that slew Me," the abstraction *cause* juxtaposed with *slew* in a typically Elizabethan suggestion of argument and legalism. The poem seeks to describe love's *coup de foudre,* or lightning bolt. Indeed, she has been struck, maimed, and robbed by what appears to be an assailant/rapist of whom she is extremely fond. No stolid boy, no sportsman (like the hunter of 754), and no bandit have done this; she is nobody's foe. The lightning bolt, the boy with slingshot, the ruined mansion and setting sun, are all biblical images used elsewhere in her poems and frequently to be found in samplers and needlework. Her last stanzas gather force to give her riddle the full extent of its power. She loves what kills her; and the penultimate quatrain envisions Master's face, a sun, watching her as she dies. Since the speaker is the same person who dreams always of eternity, she imagines the man and herself dead (love, like the sun, is "Best – at Setting"); then risen together to the new dawn in each "other's eyes." All imagistic and thematic signs indicate that this poem is for Master; and it is typical of Dickinson that her attitudes toward passion are complex and her vision of lovemaking, specific. Thus being loved, for a virgin, means being "maimed," having one's "Mansion torn." But this poem welcomes such power in the lover. Higginson's observation in an *Atlantic Monthly* essay of 1870 that "the

American poet of passion is yet to come"[75] now seems ironic in view
of poems like this one, or "Wild Nights."

In "My Life had stood – a Loaded Gun," however, the speaker's
attitude toward killing is differently ordered, and she is not able to die:

> My Life had stood – a Loaded Gun –
> In Corners – till a Day
> The Owner passed – identified –
> And carried Me away –
>
> And now We roam in Sovreign Woods –
> And now We hunt the Doe –
> And every time I speak for Him –
> The Mountains straight reply –
>
> And do I smile, such cordial light
> Upon the Valley glow –
> It is as a Vesuvian face
> Had let it's pleasure through –
>
> And when at Night – Our good Day done –
> I guard My Master's Head –
> 'Tis better than the Eider-Duck's
> Deep Pillow – to have shared –
>
> To foe of His – I'm deadly foe –
> None stir the second time –
> On whom I lay a Yellow Eye
> Or an emphatic Thumb –
>
> Though I than He – may longer live
> He longer must – than I –
> For I have but the power to kill,
> Without – the power to die – (754)

There are a great many interpretations of this poem. Not the best,
not even the most characteristic, poem in the Dickinson canon, it has
become—especially after the feminist interpretations of Adrienne Rich
and Albert Gelpi[76]—a touchstone in Dickinson criticism. (One famous
Americanist told me, "I test all writers on Dickinson by just one thing,
their performance on 'My Life had stood – a Loaded Gun.'") But must
the poem bear all this weight? In some ways it is sui generis as a
Dickinson poem, moreover, so that one has three alternatives as a
reader: to regard it in itself alone; to explore the poem's language for
its significance within her canon, where its words appear elsewhere; or

to attempt both with some balancing. Important to remember, in any case, is the poem's extraordinarily bright and capable self-possession. To treat it as a riddle or as a strict allegory is less rewarding than to see it primarily as an accomplished and mysterious ballad with suggestions of Elizabethan obliquity and physicality.[77]

One of the notable qualities of this poem is its formidable directness of statement. Both the substance and the shape of the rhetoric seem straightforward. The ideas of guns and killing are not, superficially, invested by the speaker with negative properties. Far from it. The speaker recounts life with her master in tones of heady confidence and pleasure. If we did not know that this poem had been written by a woman—perhaps especially by "Miss Emily"—some of its presumed complexity and ominousness would be reduced. Let us say that Emily "when a Boy" is speaking; then it may be easier to credit the open delight of the speaker. Liberated from corners in the poem, he/she is freed into a grown-up gunman's life of authority and power, and she likes the idea exceedingly. All the piled-up, dynamic "And"s tell us so.

Or, if we cast her as a woman, she is what has been called "a man's woman"; everything he likes, *she* likes. She likes hunting, and her instincts are not pacifist or nurturing—no ducks and does for her. She smiles at her work of killing; Nature smiles with her (the firing of the gun makes a glow like Vesuvius); and at night she can pronounce the day good. (Hunting is, after all, not always a selfish sport; often it is a protective measure. "Sovereign Woods," of course, suggests a royal preserve, an unfair advantage for the hunter.) Because of her identification with the man, she is nearly human, but with a "Yellow Eye"— the color of explosion in an oval gunbarrel—and "emphatic Thumb." The American hunting pictures of Dickinson's day, like the landscapes of Bowles's favorite painter, Sanford Gifford, present hunting scenes like Dickinson's. Her bouyancy of tone accords with them, depicting easy days roaming in the open air, taking from an apparently complaisant nature all that the Master wants. If we imagine the speaker as a boy with his designated sponsor or master, then she is—up to the last quatrain—learning how to be a man in the rustic world dreamed up by Fenimore Cooper.

"Owner," however, suggests sexual love, and to anyone versed in the language of Emily Dickinson, it inflects one of her central themes:

'Twas my one glory —
Let it be

Remembered
I was owned of thee – (1028)

For that reason, and because there is such heroic intimacy between the gun and Master, one can see this as a poem of sexual love that emphasizes comradery, robust equality. It may be considered part of the Master cycle and related to "He touched me," where the speaker begins to "live" when Master touches her or carries her away. Although she is a woman, because the two are one in love she imagines herself like him; like him, empowered. (In *Antony and Cleopatra* the rowdy lovers dress in each other's clothes, and Antony becomes a woman to amuse the queen who wears his sword. Similarly, here the speaker appropriates Master's masculinity; she is a loaded gun.) Together they become one person, one royal We in a happy life of power. The speaker has always wanted to exercise her stored-up bullets or faculties; now she can. In a letter to her cousin Louise Norcross in 1880, Dickinson used these same images: "what is each instant but a gun, harmless because 'unloaded,' but that touched 'goes off'?" (L 3.670). Although she omits one step, loading the gun, she is describing in her letter what she may be describing in her poem: love, "touching," as a means of being empowered.

There remains the final quatrain. It reads as a tightly wrought riddle, inviting explication. In one way, the stanza points up the incontrovertible difference between the mechanical gun and the human owner. He is the complete being, having both the power to die and the power to kill (even without her help). For all her fusion with him in their acts of love and death, she must still depend on him; she must be "carried." Thus this poem is often read—and read brilliantly—as a revelation of the limitations experienced by women under patriarchy, or even of the dependency of the female artist who needs male masters like Higginson to help her exercise her powers.

In reading this poem, however, I think that emphasis should always be placed on the pleasure the speaker experiences. The Master may be carrying her, but she is also speaking for him. He cannot do without her. That the gun's firing is compared to the pleasure of "a Vesuvian face" accents destruction, certainly; and it is hard to exempt this use of Vesuvius from all the others, always destructive, in the Dickinson canon. But the speaker seems to welcome her own destructiveness. She has been waiting a long time in many "corners" until the right lover lets her speak. For Dickinson, love is always the muse. Her variant for "the *power* to kill" in the penultimate line is *art*—which could make others die, from love or from aesthetic rapture. She herself—the gun, the artist—can never "die" like a real woman, however. She is but the arresting voice that speaks to and for the Master.

In "My Life had stood – a Loaded Gun," as in the larger canon, Master is Dickinson's redeemer. Over and over she returns to the vision of his face, shining for her in paradise. As late as 1882, Susan Dickinson remained her "Avalanche of Sun," her fatal Cleopatra. In that way both Master and Sue share to some extent in Dickinson's Phoeban imagery. But the gratitude that the speaker of the poems reserves for master underlies Dickinson's remembrances of Bowles. To his widow she wrote that he had "led" her; that "he was himself Eden" (L 2.602, 620). To Samuel Bowles Jr. she said simply, "hallowed be his name" (L. 2.634). His "deep face" she urged the Norcross cousins to remember (L 3.856). To Maria Whitney, who was still mourning Bowles in 1885, she confided, "I fear we shall care very little for the technical resurrection, when to behold the one face that to us comprised it is too much for us" (L 3.862). Finally, to Sue, returning from Bowles's funeral, Emily Dickinson wrote of him in her customary imagery of light, quoting 2 Samuel 12.23 (L 2.600):

> The beginning of "Always" is more dreadful than the close–for that is sustained by flickering identity –
>
> > His Nature was Future –
> > He had not yet lived –
> > David's route was simple – "I shall go to him"

～ 5 ～

A Vision of Forms

Without Minute Neatness of Execution, The Sublime cannot
Exist! Grandeur of Ideas is founded on Precision of Ideas . . .
The Man who never in his Mind & Thoughts traveled to
Heaven Is No Artist.

—William Blake, *Marginalia to Reynolds' "Discourses"*
(ca. 1808)

For Emily Dickinson, as for Emerson and the Luminists, the vision of
light—first mystery of Genesis—was primary to all conceptions and first
among artistic metaphors. In the tradition of Thomas Cole's writings
and paintings in which divine light, or love, invades even the most
terrible wilderness,[1] Dickinson numbly complained about her grief at
her mother's death: "As we bore her dear form through the Wilderness,
Light seemed to have stopped" (L 3.752). The light emanating from
eternity to illumine Amherst, the garden, her room, a circus going by
to the train at dawn, her mother's corpse, a bird, sometimes failed; the
connection failed her. When it did, she disclosed her understanding that
"seeing" below, on earth, was associated with beloved forms that inspired her. Losing Samuel Bowles, she turned him once again into a
type of Apollonian Christ: "His look could not be extinguished"
(L 3.667). And her "ranks," as she numbered her friends by the 1880s,
were so "shattered" that her pain could only be described by Emily
Dickinson, finally, as a cessation of light (L 3.820).

There were but two comprehensive subjects, Dickinson thought,
"Love and Death" (L 3.803). She best and usually expressed them as
seasons, qualities, or appearances of light. Thus, around 1862, she tells
the woman she has loved that

> overtaken in the Dark –
> Where You had put me down –

245

> By Some one carrying a Light –
> I – too – received the Sign (631)

Then, confessing her love for Master, she imagines herself answering his redeeming gesture of extending the "sign of light" with a faithful one of her own. She is like a miner with a lamp, standing in the mine or grave—here love and death revealingly fuse. And she gives *him* a sign: "the Light / I held so high, for Thee." She exclaims (conflating those perilous opposites, being and nothingness, contemplated by her poems):

> What need of Day –
> To Those whose Dark – hath so – surpassing Sun – (611)

Poems 631 and 611, read together, make light and dark antithetical, complementary versions of experience. In life, they are antipodes; Dickinson's images make them so in art. This painterly address to the problem of writing poetry as a problem of rendering light helps to reveal the nature of her aesthetic: her conception of what art is and ought to be.

It has been said that Emily Dickinson *has* no aesthetic; that she is "the only major American poet without a project"; that hers is a "canon of odds and ends," full of "hyperconsciousness without system or order"; that her poetic aimlessness is exemplified by her failure to furnish titles for most of her poems.[2] Judged by such rules requiring that poets also function as critical exegetes of their work, the author of Shakespeare's (untitled) sonnets and plays, holding mere verbal mirrors up to nature, is a failure. Emily Dickinson—writing for honor and herself, not for fame and publication, and not for the academic or editorial or even general community— did not know (however she may have hoped) that she would one day become "Emily Dickinson." As a private poet, her task was nevertheless the universal one of poets: to realize her vision in single poems as completely as she could. Her revisions and alternate wordings show that she regarded that task with great seriousness. (It is interesting that, when she *does* provide titles for her work, they are afterthoughts, and primitive: "The Bird" for 1561, "A Thunderstorm" for 824, "A Humming Bird" for 1463, "A Country Burial" for 829. These were titles she assigned for the publisher Thomas Niles when she sent him what he called, without appreciation, "specimens of [her] poetry" [L 3.769–770]. They were obviously selected because she knew titles were customary, not because she conceived of them as improving the coherence of her work.) Though she had a great deal to say about what she thought poetry is, speaking of it frequently in terms of painting, she left no major apologetic gloss upon her art. But she did have a poetic "project," and throughout her oeuvre it is perceptible. This was to depict "Eternity in Time" (L 3.689). To carry out this design she became herself a kind of painter, according to the Ruskinian traditions of her day. She dramatized the beautiful, the sublime, and sometimes the picturesque, eternizing the "waylaying Light" of immortality as it surrounded and clarified the forms she saw (L 2.840).

Love, as in the case of the great romantics, allowed her to glimpse and record the relation between this world and the next. Passionately fond of Susan Gilbert when both were twenty-one, she announces that they two are artists. (Indeed, they "are the only poets" [L 1.144].) At twenty-four, she writes to her in a pattern demonstrable throughout her love letters. First she tells Sue that the "world stands still," lifeless, without her; next she apologizes for her ardor; then she imagines Sue "kiss[ing] my cheek, and [telling] me you would love me," and finally, warmed by her imaginings—the secular equivalents of monastic meditations on this world's inadequacies and God's love—she tells Sue that their romance has brought her an understanding of the infinite. Love has given her, she admits, her great subject, which is not death or even love but eternal life:

> Dear Susie, I dont forget you a moment of the hour, and when my work is finished, and I have got the tea, I slip thro' the little entry, and out at the front door, and stand and watch the West, and remember all of mine – yes, Susie – the golden West, and the great, silent Eternity, for ever folded there, and bye and bye it will open it's everlasting, arms, and gather us all – all . . . (L 1.223–224)

"All of mine," everyone she loves, including Austin, are more entitled to love Sue; though Emily liked to think of herself as "the Youth, the Lone Youth" in Sue's life, Austin's courtship was then at its height (L 1.222). To imagine them all folded into Eternity is to spiritualize her real desire, to "have you in my arms," and to be herself enfolded by Sue's love (L 1.169).

Nevertheless, her feelings result in a radiant conception of immortal life equivalent to the one Cole presents in the *Old Age* panel of his *Voyage of Life*: the golden West, the wide, opalescent sky, the gathering, descending angels. There is nothing morbid about this dream vision. On the contrary, it is full of elation, rapture, and self-forgiveness. But it is love, and the painful longing issuing from it, that give Dickinson her vision of eternity. Love also provides what she called "the peculiar form – the Mold of the Bird" (Sue had been her "bird"), which captures eternity's partial reflections (L 3.679). If Dickinson's poetic productivity largely ceased after 1868, the reason had to do with the assimilation of her two great passions for Sue and for Master. She composed with less personal urgency even though her subject matter does not markedly change.

In order to carry her thoughts to the heaven that William Blake judged a subject for painters, however, Emily Dickinson used methods he described as showing a "Minute Neatness of Execution." Her poetry is great in one way because it attempts to envision the most inchoate, unspeakable, structureless conceptions, such as immortality, in the practical, specific details of every day. Such a "convex–concave witness" (906) to the miracle of poetic consciousness can be seen as evidence of her knowledge of and kinship to the metaphysical poets. But there were other sources of "compound vision" closer to hand. The painters of her own day—not only Cole but Church, Heade, and the group called the American Pre-Raphaelites—were legislating and attempting modes of observation devised to capture and redact the infinite in the earthly. Austin and Sue's profound interest in the landscapes of Church's followers was shared with Emily in the late 1850s, and we know that Emily herself showed an interest in art from her earliest years. Thus the artistic pseudonym she chose as a girl was not a poet's name but a painter's: "Cole" (L 2.359–360). MacGregor Jenkins, Dickinson's neighbor, recalled Miss Emily's habit of sending sketches as companions to poems, and Sue herself saved a few of Emily's drawings.[3] And when Dickinson explained how she was working as a writer, or what she thought poetry was, she frequently alluded to landscape painting and to its treatment of light. If one understands her particular conception of poetry as painting—that old Horatian theory of *ut pictura poesis* honored especially in the nineteenth century—Emily Dickinson's aesthetic design becomes manifest.

2

Writing a letter to Samuel Bowles just before his departure for Europe in April 1862, Emily Dickinson's words (punctuated with an unusually great number of dashes, like sighs or outcries) make her love for him perfectly plain. She describes herself as like flowers in a vase waiting to say goodbye. When he does not come, "My Hope put out a petal"; but it is crushed. So clearly were such letters love letters that Bowles's quiet acknowledgment of them in an unpublished note to Austin as "Emily's beautiful thought" may reflect a decision to be mute on the subject. Despite her letter's color and imagery, though, Dickinson was not satisfied with its descriptive powers. So she says she will add a sketch at the end: "I must do my Goodnight, in *crayon* – I *meant* to – in Red" (L 2.402). Drawing seems to have been for her a natural form to make emotion clear. Red was the color of passion, associated with the blood and bleeding hearts that appear in the Master and Bowles literature. She tries, she says, to "tell [him] about the picture" she herself constitutes when thinking about him (L 2.395). But words are not adequate, and she is no draftsman. So superb a vision is Bowles's imagined face upon his return from Europe that Dickinson becomes neither writer nor painter as she considers it. Now she is the mere material of which art is made. Bowles is himself both subject and artist:

> I said I was glad that you were alive – Might it bear repeating? Some phrases are too fine to fade – and Light but just confirms them – Few absences could seem so wide as your's has done, to us – If 'twas a larger face – or we a smaller Canvas – we need not know – now you have come – (L 2.419–420)

Here Dickinson's rather tortuous syntax suggests her aggravated emotions: she says she does not know whether the theme of her subject was larger than it is usual to encounter; or whether she is too small a canvas or receptor upon whom he might imprint himself. (Her image of herself, the artist, as mere material for Bowles's "designs" is of course painfully indicative of a willingness to be submissive to a lover, and it certainly rises in part from Dickinson's education as a Victorian woman.) What I wish to point out in these examples of her imagery, however, is that she customarily appeals to the idea of painting or graphic design as a means of recording her love. She associates art with language: "Some phrases are too fine to fade." But both must endure the test of "light": being *seen* and being judged as means of immortalizing what is valued.

Shortly after Bowles sailed for Europe, Dickinson addressed her famous letter to Wentworth Higginson, asking him to tell her whether her "verse is alive." She enclosed for his perusal the poem she had worked and reworked to please Sue—"Safe in their Alabaster Chambers," a poem probably about Sue herself (320), a poem about eternity (319), and "I'll tell you how the Sun rose." Thus she gave him an idea of her major subjects: love, death, art, life everlasting, and what the Dickinsons called "landscape,"⁴ or the relation of those themes to nature. The most accessible of these poems for a transcendental essayist-poet like Higginson was probably "I'll tell you how the Sun rose." In his reply he seems to have complimented her particularly on her vision of nature. (Since he always had reservations about the Dickinson style, his praise seems to have been given to her subject matter, which in most cases she shared with even the worst poets of her time.)

Her answer told him that she wrote out of a terror dating from September (she had, of course, been writing since she was thirteen at least and prolifically since 1858) and focused on the aspect of her production that he might best appreciate. She presented herself as the heir of romantic tradition, composing in order to cope with emotional pain and inspired by the benign and tutelary powers of nature. The hills, sundown, and a dog (she considered her dog Carlo immortal) were, she said, her sublime companions; and she adhered to the romantic prejudice against artifice by declaring that "the noise in the Pool, at Noon – excels my Piano." Altogether she gave Higginson a picture of herself that was, on one hand, not quite accurate; but on the other, strikingly exact: that she "sang off charnel steps" she had already told her Norcross cousins (L 2.436); she was indeed not, as she confessed to Higginson, conventionally religious; and in recording that she liked the prose of Ruskin, she provided him with a helpful hint about her conception of art—that it was well-represented by the works of Turner and the Pre-Raphaelites, recommended in *Modern Painters.*⁵

Her letter to Higginson of June 7, 1862, continues in this vein. But now Dickinson is more frank in disclosing that her ambition to be a poet is not recent in origin, and she associates it with love, loss, and the concept of light—always her stimuli in achieving artistic form:

> My dying Tutor told me that he would like to live till I had been a poet, but Death was much of Mob as I could master – then – And when far afterward – a sudden light in Orchards, or a new fashion in the wind troubled my attention – I felt a palsy, here – the Verses just relieve – (L 2.408)

Her word *palsy* makes an attribution of poetry's source to pain in the poet. Like the romantics, Dickinson conceives that pain to be the deep-seated response to an emotional situation: the death of her tutor. ("Far afterward," coupled with her earlier remark about a "terror – since September," makes it more likely that experiences with Sue and Bowles were her poetic catalysts. The charnel steps from which she sang belonged to the tomb of her illusions about Sue [and even Bowles] more than to any other. Like Wordsworth or Whitman, however, she goes faithfully back to childhood, tracing the river to its source.)

Dickinson's tutor was her father's young law clerk, Benjamin Franklin Newton. He studied law with Edward Dickinson from 1847 to 1849, was admitted to the bar at Worcester in 1850, and died of tuberculosis in 1853. While Newton was under Dickinson's tutelage in the law, the teenage Emily accepted guidance from him in reading literature. It was he who made her the important present of Emerson's *Poems* in 1850. A letter from Emily to a schoolmate in January of that year hints that she has a crush on him, and when she tells Austin of Newton's marriage in 1851, it is in surprised italics: "*B F N is married*" (L 1.116). Dickinson wrote to Newton after he moved to Worcester and until his death, which caused her great pain: "Oh Austin, Newton is dead," she writes three days after the event, "the first of my own friends. Pace" (L 1.236). As she would do in the case of others, she wrote to Newton's friends—even to his pastor, Edward Everett Hale—to see "if his last hours were cheerful" (L 1.282). (This she did not in curiosity, I think, but in worried concern. How one met death was an indication of one's spiritual state. Then too Dickinson always sought exemplars for that journey.) She never forgot Newton, told Higginson that he had taught her immortality, and recalled, long after his death, his promise to visit her in spirit if he died. He was the first person to encourage Emily Dickinson as a writer.

Dickinson's line, "Death was [as] much of Mob as I could master – then," suggests that the loss of one who so believed in her delayed her growth as a poet. She had to grieve before she could continue to develop (and the grief was itself a means of developing). But she connects her anguish over Newton with the palsy she feels in seeing a "sudden light in Orchards" or "a new fashion in the wind." His passing, like the experience of seeing light or feeling wind, was apocalyptic. Poems were made to relieve the palsy inflicted by such momentousness, and also to memorialize the moment itself. It is characteristic, at last, that it is not the orchard but the "sudden light" upon it that moves Dickinson. The Master and Sue cycles explain moments of revelation—joy, despair, desolation—by lightning, sunshine, moonlight, or their absence. In grand poems or in *jeux d'esprit,* the various modes of light are made to describe events or to qualify themes. Dickinson typically behaves like the painter she imagined herself—"Do I paint it *natural?*"—establishing various perspectives on a subject, shedding light on it (L 1.193). It must be freshly designed by the "bolts of melody," thunderbolts or sun's rays, which she called her lines. Even her dashes may be subsidiary, conscious or subconscious, means of achieving a design; all painting begins with the making of marks, after all, the attempt to record the process of thought by covering a white space with a sign.[6] The young Emily Dickinson called her letters to friends "symbols traced upon paper" [L 1.46]. She was, then, highly conscious of the physical process of recording, of her lines as designs, verbal arrangements.

Deprived of the company of Susan Gilbert in early winter 1854, Dickinson wrote to her in the painting metaphors she often used when she wanted to make her feeling clear and as indelible as words might render it. So lonely is she for Sue that she wishes she were a painter (not a writer):

> I would paint a portrait which would bring the tears, had I canvass for it, and the scene should be – *solitude,* and the figures – solitude – and the lights and shades, each a solitude. I could fill a chamber with landscapes so lone, men should pause and weep there; then haste grateful home, for a loved one left. (L 1.310)

This was the sort of portrait or landscape that Thomas Cole described in a journal entry written in the Catskills in 1838. He was finishing *The Tower*:

> I am now engaged in painting a picture representing a ruined and solitary tower, standing on a craggy promontory, laved by the unruffled ocean. Rocky islets rise from the sea at various distances: the line of the horizon is unbroken but by the tower. The spectator is supposed to be looking east just after sunset: the moon is ascending from the ocean like a silvery vapor; around her are lofty clouds still lighted by the sun; and all are reflected in the tranquil waters. On the summit of the cliff round the ruin . . . is a lonely shepherd. He appears to be gazing intently at a distant vessel, that lies becalmed on the deep. . . . I think [this picture] will be poetic . . . [and will produce] in a mind capable of feeling, a pleasing, poetic effect, a sentiment of tranquillity and solitude.[7]

Cole's imagery—the ruin, the promontory, the serene sea, sunset, the climbing moon, the distant ship, a cliff, and certainly the solitary dreamer—may be found in the love poems, in particular, of Emily Dickinson. But her letter to Sue shows that she does not resemble Cole in wanting to create a "sentiment of tranquillity." She wants the viewer—of her words as paint—to be harrowed, to "pause and weep," and to be grateful for the loves that are still left to him. This is the stormy romanticism of Delacroix, not Cole; or, more properly, it is the sort of romantic feeling Cole experienced and inspires with such exercises in the sublime as *The Voyage of Life* or *Expulsion from Eden.*

Contemplating the death of his brother John—in a shipwreck, for Ruskin a powerful emblem of the sublime—Wordsworth describes himself alone by a ruin and still water, longing to be a painter like Beaumont:

> Ah! THEN, if mine had been the Painter's hand,
> To express what then I saw; and add the gleam,
> The light that never was, on sea or land,
> The consecration, and the Poet's dream. ("Elegaic Stanzas,
>   Suggested by a Picture of Peele Castle, in a Storm,
>   Painted by Sir George Beaumont")

Wordsworth gives to the poet an advantage, however, for it is the poet who paints "the light that never was." The young Emily Dickinson, thinking of the departed Sue, regards the painter as the more eloquent illustrator of anguish. Only in the 1860s, in her poems about the poet as a lighter of lamps, will she too see poetry as the primary form of art as light. In her final sayings about art, painting dims by contrast with poetry, even as the daguerreotype was much less effectual than paint.

In poem 505, written almost ten years after her letter to Sue, Dickinson is still (respectfully) aware of painting's power to evoke feelings of pain by what has been called "the affective intensity of art."[8]

> I would not paint – a picture –
> I'd rather be the One
> Its bright impossibility
> To dwell – delicious – on –
> And wonder how the fingers feel
> Whose rare – celestial – stir –
> Evokes so sweet a Torment –
> Such sumptuous – Despair –

Such despair and torment were sweet and sumptuous, but not because Dickinson was sadomasochistic, a "self-oppressed heart" for whom "beauty and pain sensually mix" or cannot exist. Her phrases evince not decadence and sadism[9] but her consistent effort to explain the enormity of the aesthetic experience as it was known by the artist. No beauty could be truly exquisite unless it was doomed to fade. Nothing created could be awesome ("sublime") unless its lofty grandeur inspired feelings of imperfect comprehension or terror. Burke's *Philosophical Inquiry into the Origin of Our Ideas of the Sublime and Beautiful* (1757) was, as I have said, fully established as an influential critical text when Cole and Church painted and Emily Dickinson wrote. It had passed into the culture of her time, associating artist with viewer/reader/listener in one mutual interpretive venture. If Dickinson sometimes presents herself as acted upon in the enterprise rather than as the actor, it is surely not because she lacked a poetic project but that for whatever reason—modesty?—she preferred to focus on one element in the artist's undertaking. Burke had claimed that "the psychology of the percipient" enabled him to detect the sublime and the beautiful. Or, as Dickinson writes, in a rare use of music as her subject, some people cannot perceive what the artist has done. For her, as for Shelley, the bird is often an archetype of the poet.

> To hear an Oriole sing
> May be a common thing –
> Or only a divine.
> . . . . .
>
> The Fashion of the Ear
> Attireth that it hear
> In Dun, or fair –
>
> So whether it be Rune,
> Or whether it be none
> Is of within.
>
> The "Tune is in the Tree – "
> The Skeptic – showeth me –
> "No Sir! In Thee!" (526)

Unless one hears a birdsong as the otherworldly magic that it is, she says, the "tune" has not been translated into art, at least for that listener. Such conceptions as this one may have lent her "balm" when she was wounded by the condescension of her own readers, such as Bowles.

"I would not paint – a picture," therefore, emphasizes the pleasure of feeling the poignancy of life, captured in art. And, characteristic of Dickinson, it makes its point by addressing the phenomenon of light. A picture is delicious because of its "bright impossibility": that is, because it imitates the celestial miracle Genesis narrates, by doing the impossible—creating shapes out of the dark.

3

Emily Dickinson's poems about painting reveal her desire to immortalize the beautiful, sublime, and picturesque in a fashion that was "surprising," as she liked to put it: a manner and style that were unconventional enough to teach and convince. In a moving passage from her late letters—often moving when sent to her Norcross cousins, who were vigorous, well read, sympathetic, and undemanding—she uses the word *surprise*. This passage is a qualified *credo in aeternam* and it unites her primary themes. "I believe," she told Fanny and Louisa in 1882,

> we shall in some manner be cherished by our Maker – that the one who gave us this remarkable earth has the power still further to surprise . . . Mother was very beautiful when she had died. Seraphs are solemn artists. The illumination that comes but once paused upon her features, and it seemed like hiding a picture to lay her in the grave; but the grass that received my Father will suffice his guest, the one he asked at the altar to visit him all his life.
>
> I cannot tell how Eternity seems. It sweeps around me like a sea [while I do my work]. (L 3.750)

God, then, is the sublime artist, able to surprise his creatures with whatever pictures they will see beyond the grave. The angels too are sculptor-painters, fixing the "illumination," the *éclaircissement*, that comes with the transitus. Dickinson's mother becomes an artistic image—a "face"—to be hidden like her daughter's. Edward Dickinson's marriage vow is an emblem of fidelity, memory, and the fleeting made permanent: like God, he has asked Emily's mother to be his lasting guest. Her prevailing conception of love inspiring art enables Dickinson to write her final sentences. There eternity is felt in time, and its sea is linked to her work. This eloquent line is abbreviated in the Johnson text of the *Letters* to read "[Eternity] sweeps around me like a sea." But its concluding adverbial clause, set out by Jay Leyda, is of distinct importance.[10] Writing poetry was necessary to Emily Dickinson because it fixed the "Forever" in the "Now" (624). Her vision was of the next world *next* to her as she did her housework, all that baking, canning, cleaning, and sewing so balefully recorded in her letters. The eternal Sea and its unsounded depths were in her very house and consciousness.

Art was essential as the means of showing ("forever") this uncanny and surreal experience.

Dickinson's recourse to the language of painting in such letters as this one may be explained not only by the prestige and influence of the landscape tradition in the nineteenth century but by the importance of painting to those she loved. Her ambition to be a poet had been first shared with Sue and, less openly, with Austin. In Dickinson's most creative years, that couple's imagination was fired by the Hudson River painters. Sue remained a voracious reader, but the (unpublished) letters of Samuel Bowles in the Harvard collection register his respect for Sue's interest in paintings and in Austin's acquisitions.

One of Bowles's letters (ca. 1863) begs Austin to lend his landscapes to a Northampton exhibit for charity. In a message written on Christmas night, 1861, to Bowles (she addresses her greetings to him, not including his wife), Susan Dickinson confides,

> Austin came home [from New York] in a feverish excitement over pictures—utterly worn out with his passion—The real fact of the matter is his desire and half plan for three of the Düsseldorf collection—He is fascinated with the longing, and I advise him to get them. I have not seen him so convulsed with excitement "since the days when he went gypsying"[11]

According to Martha Dickinson Bianchi, the installation of a painting at the Evergreens was not merely supervised by Sue and Austin. In the late 1850s and early 1860s, Emily was invited, "revelling in a new emotion of color as she gazed."[12] Barton Levi St. Armand includes a list of the Dickinsons' paintings in *Emily Dickinson and Her Culture*. He assumes that Kensett's *Sunset with Cows* with its iridescent shimmer may have inspired Dickinson's imagery of "Opal Cattle" in her sunset poem, 628.[13] Kensett's painting was Sue's favorite. It quotes Cole's theme of the river of life, merging with the light of eternity, a theme and a visual motif that may have had an effect on Emily Dickinson's poetic style.

In poem after poem, Dickinson connects poetry with painting. As late as 1883, she drafts a letter to accompany the poem "Forever honored be the Tree" (1570), explaining

> I cannot tint in Carbon nor embroider in Brass, but send you a homespun rustic picture I certainly saw Saturday in the awful storm Please excuse my needlework – [14]

She evidently still saw herself as a nature painter, her mode the sublime: an "awful storm." Her assembled allusions here are revealing. "Home-spun rustic picture" implies provinciality, gaucherie, but fidelity to the truth. And she calls her poetry "needlework," as if she were including herself among gentlewomen who did crewel or embroidery. The North-ampton Needlework Academy for young ladies had flourished in Emily Dickinson's childhood and was still well known. In my possession is a sampler, completed there by "Mary Short, Nov 18, 1828," that reveals the fashionably high-minded quality of the texts assigned the girls to embroider. Mary has stitched Thomas Moore's "Earth and Heaven":

> This world is all a fleeting shew,
> For man's illusion given,
> The smiles of joy, the tears of woe,
> Deceitful shine, deceitful shew,
> There's nothing true but Heaven.
>
> And false the light on glory's plume
> As fading hues of even,
> And love, and hope, and beauty's bloom
> Are blossoms gathered for the tomb
> There's nothing bright but Heaven.
>
> Poor wanderers of a stormy day,
> From wave to wave were driven,
> And fancy's flash, and reason's ray
> Serve but to light the troubled way
> There's nothing calm but Heaven.

Such sentiments as these (frequently illustrated by tombstones and waves) were conceived to be linguistically improving and formative of piety and fortitude as well as skills at needlework. Like tinting or painting on china, canvas, or silk, working with one's needle could be a high accomplishment in Dickinson's day. As soon as women were given a more formal education, however—a custom that began in the American upper middle class around the 1840s—the needlework aca-demies declined.[15] Emily Dickinson's father was willing to purchase for her a more "masculine" education in history, philosophy, science, and letters at Mary Lyon's than any needlework academy could provide. But she had worked one elementary sampler as a child and always sewed.[16] Indeed, she sewed the seven hundred fascicle poems together with binding thread. By saying "needlework" in the letter accompanying "Forever honored be the Tree," she may have been striking a note of apology to consort with "Please excuse." Needlework, however, still considered an art form in New England in 1883, ranked just below pictures. Her reference to embroidering "in Brass"—an impossibility—implies that she did not regard needlework as an inferior art. It lasted, after all. As I shall suggest later, her comparison of poetry to needlework has meaning for the form and appearance of the poems.

Her many poems about painting or about poetry as painting concede that the artist's task of surprising by showing the infinite in the nows is a hard one. Emerson had associated art with the nature that, to him, generated it. Sonnets are seashells; summer is an epic poem.[17] In "Art," his observations on the literary task of imitation make it sound easy for a clean-living artist. Dickinson said, however, that on a great many occasions nature's effects were almost too picturesque, too beautiful, or too sublime for any artist to record. In one of her boldest and yet most specific poems (606) about a summer day, she vies with painters in the act of description. Her poem has a superb music, accomplished by skillfully interwoven alliterative patterns and the manipulation of the common meter of the hymn stanza so that it seems ample enough to contain her thought. Camille Paglia asserts that Dickinson's poetic "structure cramps and pinches [her] words like a vise" while her "poems shudder with a huge tremor of contraction."[18] As scores of Emily Dickinson's poems demonstrate, extreme contraction appears when the subject requires it. So too does a more sumptuous line. Although her usual tetrameters create small spaces on the page, her high accomplishment in using consonance, assonance, and other forms of internal rhyme allows Dickinson to expand and amplify the effect of her linear units.

Poem 606 with its dexterous rhythms and sonorities accommodates the tetrameter line to its theme—lazy latitudes of summer air, which, like love, create yearning and include "all creatures great and small" in their embrace. (I use that famous phrase from C. R. Alexander's hymn "All things bright and beautiful" [1848] because Emily Dickinson undoubtedly knew it, so popular was it in New England. Its subject matter is the little world of creation, treated in her poem.)

> The Trees like Tassels – hit – and swung –
> There seemed to rise a Tune
> From Miniature Creatures
> Accompanying the Sun –

Far Psalteries of Summer –
Enamoring the Ear
They never yet did satisfy –
Remotest – when most fair

The Sun shone whole at intervals –
Then Half – then utter hid –
As if Himself were optional
And had Estates of Cloud

Sufficient to enfold Him
Eternally from view –
Except it were a whim of His
To let the Orchards grow –

A Bird sat careless on the fence –
One gossiped in the Lane
On silver matters charmed a Snake
Just winding round a Stone –

Bright Flowers slit a Calyx
And soared upon a Stem
Like Hindered Flags – Sweet hoisted –
With Spices – in the Hem –

'Twas more – I cannot mention –
How mean – to those that see –
Vandyke's Delineation
Of Nature's – Summer Day! (606)

Anthony Van Dyke (1599–1641), a student of Rubens, is not known for landscape painting but for portraiture. His superbly insouciant and graceful portrait of *Charles I, King of England, Hunting* in the Louvre typifies the charm and dignity he could impart to his subjects. Though he was not much interested in landscape, he was an accomplished and famous painter; thus Dickinson cites his name as a synonym, simply, for all painters. (Possibly too she requires the alliterative *d*.) And she says that nature makes a better summer day than Van Dyke's, which would be mean by comparison. Since she values art so highly, her statement is an hyperbole by which to celebrate nature.

Nevertheless, on most occasions Dickinson's painter (or painter-poet) is more than equal to the challenge of replicating, and thus honoring, creation. She mentions Guido Reni, Domenichino, Titian, Leonardo, and Michelangelo as well as Van Dyke and Cole. In 291, some of nature's visions paralyze their pencils. But usually her artists may lay claim to immortality because, like God, they can make another day. Thus they are superior to Nature, for all her chthonic powers:

> The One who could repeat the Summer day –
> Were greater than itself – though He
> Minutest of Mankind should be –
>
> And He – could reproduce the Sun –
> At period of going down –
> The Lingering – and the Stain – I mean –
>
> When Orient have been outgrown –
> And Occident – become Unknown –
> His Name – remain – (307)

Written in triplets, this poem shows a clear effort to achieve the connective melody of rhyme, though the rhymes—day/be, sun/down/mean, outgrown/remain—are the slant ones Dickinson prefers. The poem is aphoristic. Its effort to assert the importance of the artist is moderated by the second triplet with its eccentric use of *And*. Here Dickinson really means the weak form *an,* an archaic synonym for "if" (as in Tennyson's *Gareth and Lynette,* line 251, "But an it please thee not"). If the artist can replicate a sunset, as she tried to do in a score of poems, his or her name will remain. The sunset (painted over and over by Cole, Church, Gifford, Inness, and the other landscape artists) was the emblem of the sublime, of passion and terror joined in one awful moment.

God is the Artist who "drew" Emily Dickinson (155). She herself, in turn, needed and strived to be an artist. This was a form of competition with God, perhaps; on the other hand, it was also a cooperation, the use of her gifts. Sometimes she could be humorous about this deep desire, but her humor had steel in it:

> I send Two Sunsets –
> Day and I – in competition ran –
> I finished Two – and several Stars –
> While he – was making One –
>
> His own was ampler – but as I
> Was saying to a friend –
> Mine – is the more convenient
> To Carry in the Hand – (308)

William Carlos Williams is said to have joked that he gave up painting for poetry because he couldn't carry a canvas on the subway. Dickinson jests here that her poems about a sunset, unlike the experience itself, can be carried. By this she means that they can be kept even while the natural miracle of sunset passes away. Despite its playful overtones, hers is a serious claim. The poet was, first of all, "Of Pictures – the Discloser" (448). But one's methods had to be concrete enough to secure immortality for these disclosures.

4

About four years before Emily Dickinson's death—which she often imagined as the leap of the soul into light above—she composed a hymn to light:

> Image of Light, Adieu –
> Thanks for the interview –
> So long – so short –
> Preceptor of the whole –
> Coeval Cardinal –
> Impart – Depart – (1556)

A six-line lyric, suggesting the brevity of her experience, Dickinson's poem addresses a ray of light with which she has had a swift meeting or interview. It was the "Image of Light," that is, as in Plato's thinking, the temporal reflection of the eternal *imago* of light. In her third line she describes its quality and its effect. It is both long and short, illuminating objects in the near as well as the far distance; it has made her see, or understand, a great deal although its duration has been brief. Like the first lines of the gospel of John, which compare Christ to light and light to learning, Dickinson's poem makes light "Preceptor of the whole." It teaches her what meets her earthly eyes and is the harbinger of what will greet her in paradise. So she calls it "Coeval Cardinal." Her gnomic phrase connects those two adjectives as one substantive: the image of light is "coeval," of or belonging to the same age, time, or duration as the "cardinal": the theme of prime importance. That is, the ray of light is God, because made in his image. In her last (as in her third) line, Dickinson playfully imitates its action: "Impart – Depart – ." It comes to teach, illuminate, impart, and then, like all intimations of immortality, it vanishes. Dickinson knew the etymology of her words. Her favorite companion, Webster's dictionary (probably 1847), told a reader that "interview" comes from the French "entrevue," a glimpse. Her poem sustains that meaning, for, like the nineteenth-century landscape painters, she makes this world's lesser light an inference of the light of heaven.

The presence in her work of so many poems anatomizing the nature of light caused Mabel Todd to compare Dickinson to an impressionist painter. Writing an introduction for *Poems, Second Series* in 1891, she spoke of a Dickinson who "scrutinized every thing with clear-eyed frankness" and yet eschewed "conventional form." Instead, Todd thought, she responded to the clarification of outlines by light in bold, "rough"[19] strokes, or "bolts of melody."

Todd's comparison was, like many of her notions, intelligent. She was trying not only to categorize Dickinson's preoccupation with light but the boldness of her technique. So she related it to that of the new, iconoclastic school of French painting for which, in 1874, the term "impressionist" had been coined. The underlying aim of the impressionists was to capture the transient luminosity of forms. Todd's choice of the word "rough" for Dickinson's prosody was equally appropriate for the scumbling and impasto techniques of Monet, say, or Renoir; and she was doubtless using it to justify Dickinson's unconventional fondness for ellipsis, catalectic meters, and off-rhyme. To say that Dickinson was like an impressionist was to make her modern, to compare her to the painters just being noticed in the United States as her *Poems* (1890) appeared. Todd proposed that the strange staccato brightness of the impressionists' canvases—despised by George Inness, praised by Mary Cassatt—might be compared to the dazzling celerity of a Dickinson poem. But the more appropriate, if less fashionable, comparison would have been to the Hudson River or Luminist painters. For as Cole or Church had done in the 1840s, Dickinson essentially sought to reveal the spiritual landscape. The study of this world was also a means of suggesting the next:

> Sunset that screens, reveals –
> Enhancing what we see
> By menaces of Amethyst
> And Moats of Mystery (1609)

In an analysis of American Luminism, Barbara Novak observes, "If we say that [French] Impressionism is the *objective* response to the *visual* sensation of light, then perhaps we can say that [American] luminism is the *poetic* response to the *felt* sensation." There was, Novak contends, no real American impressionism, for "the American necessity for the ideal . . . which needs but a touch of profundity to become 'lyricism,' militated against an objective, analytic dissection of God's world."[20] While Emily Dickinson, like the Luminists, is given to recording the measured and the specific, her vision of light leads to emotional or spiritual feeling— one of the meanings of her word "circumference." She does not regard objects as mere masses or volumes, as did impressionists like Monet, but considered them proofs of the "great . . . Firmament," eternity, which "Accompanies [each] Star" (1541).

Dickinson's most frequently anthologized landscape poem is probably "There's a certain Slant of light" (258). Harmed by emendation, it was brought out by Mrs. Todd in the first *Poems* possibly because she considered it both "impressionist" and an uncomplicated response to seasonal experience in the manner of fashionable Victorian nature poetry. But Dickinson's quatrains in 258 disclose not only a personal reaction to bleak winter light; they are in harmony with the painterly aesthetic of Ruskin, who advocated the creation of the "mystery of distance" in landscapes and praised the "unfatigued veracity of eternal light,"[21] captured in Turner's canvases. The poem is a subtle word painting that adheres to the American landscape tradition by linking sky (and its metaphor, heaven) with earth:

> There's a certain Slant of light,
> Winter Afternoons –
> That oppresses, like the Heft
> Of Cathedral Tunes –
>
> Heavenly Hurt, it gives us –
> We can find no scar,
> But internal difference,
> Where the Meanings, are –
>
> None may teach it – Any –
> 'Tis the Seal Despair –
> An imperial affliction
> Sent us of the Air –
>
> When it comes, the Landscape listens –
> Shadows – hold their breath –
> When it goes, 'tis like the Distance
> On the look of Death – (258)

St. Armand's discussion of this poem declares it "the most lone of Dickinson's lone landscapes" and categorizes it also as her "negative crisis conversion to unbelief." He finds Dickinson herself appearing in it "as passive as the fly sealed in amber."[22] True, there is a kind of passivity recorded by the speaker, who recognizes that this peculiar winter light is "sent us" and who includes herself in "us." But her speaker, like an artist, has had to look at, calculate, and describe the quality, direction, and placement of this light in the sky in order to react to it. Her reaction is decided, immediate, and occurs in the second quatrain. As a function of intellection, not passivity, she determines about this light that it cannot be taught anything by anyone. (Indeed, it is itself a teacher that makes the landscape listen and the shadows suspend their breath or influence.) As a "seal," the light is uncommunicative yet signals the end of communication. There is probably a characteristic Dickinsonian play on words in her "Any," which suggests "None may teach it – Any[thing]" as well as "None [not any one] may teach it." (Todd reduced that complication by rendering the line, "None may teach it anything.")

Although the speaker, like the landscape, experiences affliction, the last quatrain dissociates her from passivity by making her the active artist-observer of time: "When it comes," "When it goes"; and place: "the landscape," "the distance." As the first line indicates, this poem, recalling "Image of Light, Adieu," presents the poet studying what Ruskin thought the spirituality of atmospheric phenomena. The nineteenth-century painter, or poet-painter, was expected to practice John Constable's discipline of "skying," or studying the sky as the source of light in nature, governing everything.[23] Constable's cloud studies were well known to Thomas Cole, Frederic Church, Albert Bierstadt, and Jasper Cropsey, all of whom drew works called simply *Cloud Study* in the 1840s, '50s, and '60s. To note, even to diagram, *The Formation of a Rainbow* (ca. 1833) was, for Constable, to use the prismatic gradations of light in order to indicate the intensity of nature as a reflection of the divine.

It is probable that Emily Dickinson never heard "Cathedral Tunes," only churchbells. Yet the hymns she compares to winter light are weighty, solemn, befitting a cathedral's grandeur, and they oppress (like the gray, searching rays). Behind them—as behind the light—is that ponderous hypothesis, God. Dickinson's onomatopoeic provincialism "heft," for which Mrs. Todd substituted the neutral "weight," conveys the difficulty of lifting up the heart, of believing in what cathedrals stand for, especially at the death of the year, near the end of the day. The synaesthetic connection between the stroke of light and the chords of music operates to attribute the "imperial affliction" of despair to the will of the Creator. "Changes of light . . . placed at the service of a devotional idea" may have appeared in American artwork.[24] Dickinson's poem bespeaks no devotion.

The landscapes and theories of John Constable were well known in Dickinson's region. Cole, Church, and especially Asher Durand numbered Constable (with Turner, Claude Lorrain, and Salvator Rosa) among their chief foreign models. Constable's many studies in oil and pencil of Salisbury Cathedral, of which *A View of Salisbury Cathedral* (1820–1822?), now in the National Gallery in Washington, was most radiant, were considered exemplums of Constable's pronouncement that painting was both poetry and prayer. *Salisbury Cathedral* is not a winter but a summer scene; the aspirational white steeple of the thirteenth-century relates shimmering clouds to the weighty edifice and then to the ground with a confidence meant to inspire devout serenity. As was also true of his other influential paintings of the scene, such as *Salisbury Cathedral from the Bishop's Grounds* (1823), Constable's view composes the created (cows graze beneath the steeple) and the creator (a cross on the steeple points to the heavens) in a sympathetic relationship. Light and dark, sky and cathedral, imply the easy union of the actual with the infinite.

George Inness, in defining American impressionism, would trace it to the Americans' study of Constable's fusion of solid objects and transparent shadows in a breathable atmosphere through which one is conscious of space and distance. In Constable's landscape, different from Dickinson's landscape poem, the sky predicates faith, not despair. The *Salisbury Cathedral* studies, icons of peaceful belief, copied in steel engravings, were probably known to Emily Dickinson. Her poem expresses the precise opposite of Constable's works, and her oppressive cathedral tunes provide ironic antitheses to his cathedrals bathed in light. "There's a certain Slant of light" was among several Dickinson poems that prompted Todd, however, to call her work "Impressionist."

5

Mabel Todd might also have compared certain qualities in Dickinson's work with those of another group of painters, the American Pre-Raphaelites, active in the 1850s, '60s, and '70s. William Stillman—who, as Church's only pupil, would ultimately seek to destroy his reputation—was the prime mover of this group. The Pre-Raphaelites were unsympathetic to the grand, inspirational canvases of the Hudson River School. In doing landscapes or still lifes, they imitated the British Pre-Raphaelites, paying strict, scientific attention to the appearance of objects. Cole, Church, and what they stood for—seeing nature as the measure of a spiritual reality—seemed to artists such as Thomas Farrer, John Henry Hill, and William Trost Richards to betray the material universe. The Hudson River painter Asher B. Durand was humiliated at being denounced by this crusading group, even though his son John was one of their chief spokesmen. Asher Durand himself had urged careful observation of nature in his "Letters on Landscape Painting" (1855), which appeared in the art journal *The Crayon,* edited by John Durand and Stillman. (It was in *The Crayon,* as we have seen, that Rossetti's "Blessed Damozel" was recommended to the American public.) But Durand's advice was insufficiently revolutionary for the American Pre-Raphaelite movement. Inspired by Ruskin's *Modern Painters,* Farrer, Hill, and Stillman sought to render portraits of nature that were scientifically exact. Leaves had to have a precise botanical identity and accuracy. (Church, who was not a member of the group but would sometimes paint in this mode, was said to have turned to doing icebergs in the 1860s because his wrist ached from outlining the details of leaves in his early landscapes.) Brilliant color, plain and faithful rendering, an intensity of conception: by these qualities the American Pre-Raphaelites hoped to achieve the naturalness and sincerity they attributed to Millais or Holman Hunt and, originally, to Giotto.

I think there can be no doubt that, like Hawthorne before her,[25] Emily Dickinson had direct knowledge of the American Pre-Raphaelites. In addition, she seems to have known some works by their British counterparts. There had been an exhibit of British Pre-Raphaelite art held in New York and Boston in 1857, planned by Rossetti and sponsored by the National Academy of Design. In Boston the exhibition was enthusiastically reviewed by the *Daily Courier* and *Daily Advertiser,* though the *Boston Post* compared the English paintings unfavorably with "Mr. Church's magnificent picture,"[26] *Heart of the Andes.* Of all the paintings that the show included, William Holman Hunt's *Light of the World* (plate 7) caused the most violent and contradictory reactions. The *New York Times* was full of praise for its Christian sentiment and luminous tones; the *Philadelphia Sunday Dispatch* described it as blasphemous; the Boston newspapers praised it wholeheartedly. So moving was the painting that some of the young men hired to hang it in New York were said to have wept openly as they did so. The painting is a portrait of the crowned Christ in kingly robes, carrying a lantern, and knocking on the door of a cottage whose entrance is blocked by weeds. The elaborate gilded frame that Hunt provided for the painting bore above it the inscription "The Light of the World," an allusion to John 8:12. Beneath the painting were the (unpunctuated) words "Behold, I stand at the door, and knock: If any man hear my voice and open the door, I will come in to him, and will sup with him, and he with me" (Revelation 3:20). Hunt's vision of the rather androgynous, red-haired Christ (women had posed for him) glows with a refined grace that is in marked contrast to the setting—the decayed cottage and the sinuously interlaced trees in the distance that suggest evil and, in particular, deceit.

Ruskin had written about the painting in 1854:

> On the left-hand side of the picture is seen the door of the human soul. It is fast barred; its bars and nails are rusty; it is knitted and bound to its stanchions by creeping tendrils of ivy, showing that it has never been opened. Christ approaches it in the night-time, in His everlasting offices of Prophet, Priest, and King. He wears the white robe, representing the power of the Spirit upon Him; the jewelled robe and breastplate representing the sacerdotal investiture; the rayed crown of gold, interwoven with the crown of thorns, but bearing soft leaves for the healing of the nations. He bears with him a two fold light: first, the light of conscience, which displays past sin, and afterwards the light of peace, the hope of salvation.[27]

Not everyone who viewed this painting could be expected to see the complex iconographic symbolism that Ruskin did. Those who wrote about it, however, did not fail to respond to its prevailing mood of sadness, delicately evoked by contrasts between the surly darkness and the muted loveliness of the light of Christ's lantern. His expression of resignation, disappointment, and yet persistence, the discrepancy between the riches of his robes and the wretchedness of the obdurate soul in its hovel, aroused admiration. The painting was also thought by the American Pre-Raphaelites to possess that clarity of purpose, the simplicity and precision of line, they were adopting in landscapes, portraits, and still lifes.

Emily Dickinson shows her familiarity with Holman Hunt's famous painting. This poem was probably written for Sue, to whom it was addressed and sent, about 1862:

> Just so — Jesus — raps —
> He — doesn't weary —
> Last — at the Knocker —

And first – at the Bell.
Then – on divinest tiptoe – standing –
Might He but spy the lady's soul –
When He – retires –
Chilled – or weary –
It will be ample time for – me –
Patient – upon the steps – *until* then –
Heart! I am knocking – low at thee. (317)

Hunt's painting alludes to a scriptural passage from Dickinson's cherished Revelation. She surely knew it and also the passage that immediately precedes it: "I counsel thee to buy of me gold tried in the fire, that thou mayest be rich; and white raiment, that thou mayest be clothed" (4:18). Her jaunty but earnest poem, however, with its picture of the act of rapping and its understanding of Christ as chilled and weary, describes the content of the painting more closely than that of the biblical passage. As a "painting," Dickinson's poem condenses Holman Hunt's focal image: the knocking, patient, weary Jesus. She herself becomes a type of Jesus at the last, knocking at the door of Sue's heart. Characteristically, though, Dickinson reveals her skittishness about religious doctrine with humanizing touches; thus Jesus is "on divinest tiptoe." The poem ends with another Dickinsonian stratagem. She informs the beloved woman that she—ever persistent—loves her more than Christ does and tells her, therefore, to open the door.

Ruskin's observation that this cottage door has *never* been opened is of course apposite to her relationship with Sue. Sue's heart has never been opened to her as a lover. It is continually revealing that Emily Dickinson configured so much of her life and her art in this way, with images of doors open or half-open, shut or half-shut. Revelation's passage "If any man hear my voice and open the door, I will come in to him, and will sup with him" finds echoes, for instance, in many Dickinson poems. The speaker's knock in a "dumb – and dark" night (207) may admit her to human society and nourishment. In her own living, Dickinson often shut her door on others: "The Soul selects her own Society – /Then – shuts the Door" (303). Near the end of her life, Dickinson became sufficiently disenchanted with Sue to keep *her* outside. Shortly after Ned's birth in 1861, however, she feared the reverse, sending Sue a pleading note, using the favorite theme: "Could *I* – then – shut the door – / Lest *my* beseeching face – at last / Rejected – be – of *Her*?" (L 2.381).

Some of the smart consequence of this poem derives from Dickinson's comparison of herself to Christ. He may get tired but *she* doesn't. When he leaves, the urgent, rather insinuating speaker will put her own case: "Heart! I am knocking – low at thee." It was just this sort of boldness that would make the devout Anglican poet Christina Rossetti recoil. Like Dickinson, Hunt's Christ has red hair and is wearing the crown and jeweled robes, even the halo or "disc" about his head, with which her speakers often imagine themselves adorned. "The supper of the heart" as one of her letters puts it, is what this Christ desires (L 2.452). The imagery of Hunt's painting and the words on its frame are of light and darkness, hunger and nourishment. It is a sacred exploration of the imagery of light and dark, food and feasting, that appears with such secular magnificence in *Antony and Cleopatra*. Dickinson's wistful Christ does not have a lantern like Hunt's (although in several poems it is by holding up a lantern that her amorous speaker sees Master). Her poem, which builds to the exclamation "Heart," is passionate for all its whimsy. Dickinson's first version of 317 in fascicle 11 put Christ in place of Jesus in the first line. Instead of "the lady's soul," it read "the hiding soul," emphasizing the reluctance of the beloved. Both versions, however, show her using Revelation's passage about the savior as outsider, suitor, and exiled king. Both put her in Christ's place, as one left outside but still seeking entry. And both suggest that (as a Dickinson, who liked art and read the art news), Emily had seen a copy of Holman Hunt's painting.

The radiant particularity of *The Light of the World* was what the American Pre-Raphaelites tried to achieve in their own painting. While they excelled at still life, they also did outdoor scenes whose sharp outlines and vivid colors were implicitly dramatic. Many seemed related to the somewhat earlier tradition that had produced Church's fiery paintings of Ecuador. As in Martin Johnson Heade's studies of birds— for example, *Passion Flowers and Hummingbirds* (ca. 1865)—the desired effect was one of mystery yet recognizable contour. Heade's hummingbirds have beaks resembling the stamens of the flowers (and echo their placement on the canvas). No one could mistake the species of bird or flower. Yet behind the precise subjects of Heade's painting, mists recede and light is clouded over. Dickinson's poems about hummingbirds (500, 1463) also present a fusion of realistic detail and vaporous suggestion. Her bird rides on a wheel before her eyes. But his spokes make "a dizzy Music" among "vibrating Blossoms" as he returns to "remoter atmospheres" (500). Like Heade's many paintings of hummingbirds, Dickinson's suggest that "this World is not Conclusion."

A letter of Dickinson's that is as masterly as anything she wrote shows the same recourse to precision of detail, shape, and hue sought by the American Pre-Raphaelites. At the same time, it is a meditation on the mystery of earthly mutability and so presents a world of destruction, shadows, and vagary. The letter is written to the Norcrosses, about a fire that destroyed the business center of downtown Amherst on July 4, 1879:

Dear Cousins,

Did you know there had been a fire here, and that but for a whim of the wind Austin and Vinnie and Emily would all have been homeless? But perhaps you saw *The Republican*.

We were waked by the ticking of the bells, – the bells tick in Amherst for a fire, to tell the firemen.

I sprang to the window, and each side of the curtain saw that awful sun. The moon was shining high at the time, and the birds singing like trumpets.

Vinnie came soft as a moccasin, "Don't be afraid, Emily, it is only the fourth of July."

I did not tell that I saw it, for I thought if she felt it best to deceive, it must be that it was.

She took hold of my hand and led me into mother's room. Mother had not waked, and Maggie was sitting by her. Vinnie left us a moment, and I whispered to Maggie, and asked her what it was.

"Only Stebbins's barn, Emily;" but I knew that the right and left of the village was on the arm of Stebbins's barn. I could hear buildings falling, and oil exploding, and people walking and talking gayly, and cannon soft as velvet from parishes that did not know that we were burning up.

And so much lighter than day was it, that I saw a caterpillar measure a leaf far down in the orchard; and Vinnie kept saying bravely, "It's only the fourth of July." (L 2.643–644)

Dickinson's narrative continues, "It seemed like a theatre, or a night in London, or perhaps like chaos"; but its best effects are achieved by the initial description of the scene in which sound and light conspire to create terror and awe. (It was said of Church's landscapes that they could be "heard," especially *Niagara*.) Present in Dickinson's "painting" are several elements one often meets in the nineteenth-century Pre-Raphaelite landscape: the high shining moon, the "awful sun" that is the fire, the excited birds making a din, even the woman at the window as in Farrer's *Gone! Gone!* (1860). But it is a unique scene, full of life—all the participles of the seventh paragraph especially help to suggest that; the child-woman, led by her sister to her mother's side and informed of danger by her maid, sees it all with an absolute clarity, yet finds it tactful and considerate to keep silent.

Whatever Dickinson's youthful disorder of the eyes may have been, it never kept her from carefully noticing the world around her. Since her garden began at some distance from her parents' room, however, it is hard to believe that she really "saw a caterpillar measure a leaf far down" its extent. What she was doing was painting a scene of what art historians call nocturnal luminism. And she was rendering a vision of *terribilità*, however restrained by the homely conventionalities of genre painting. (The test of *terribilità* is often the reordering of time, as in so many Master poems.) Her letter's concern is with the immediate and with sight and sound. Yet by contrasting the mystery of darkness and all it conceals with the light of the conflagration, it also establishes a world in which experience is terrible. Nature's vulnerability is suggested by the tiny body of the caterpillar, lit up by the glare of the flames. The picture she presents is still handsome, even as fire can be beautiful while it destroys. The caterpillar goes on measuring a leaf—the phrase is lyrical, suggesting the proportions of design; it crawls along in search of food amid reflections of the blaze. Emily herself is soothed by Vinnie's love, and the letter is moving in its recognition of how solicitously she is cared for, as in its symbolic picture of a recluse who sees and hears events from which she is apparently remote.

Emily Dickinson's passion for exactitude in language was matched by the joyful delight with which she drew pictures of objects or scenes. She evidently sought to reveal the secret inner nature of the thing observed. This was the special mission of the still life painter. It is in her careful creation of a world of birds, beasts, flowers, and hills that her technique most resembles that of the American Pre-Raphaelites. If one studies William Trost Richards' *Ferns in a Glade* (1859), John Henry Hill's *Fringed Gentians* (1867), or the well-known painting of *Mount Tom* (1865) by Thomas Farrer, the same "distillation" of subject that distinguishes a Dickinson poem may be observed.[28] Farrer's painting of Mount Tom—a mountain peak Dickinson could see every day— was exhibited in Northampton in 1865 and, like his *View of Northampton* (1865), seemed a redaction of the inner truth of landscape, a refined and heightened vision of its integrity. It was in their small paintings of flowers, trees, nests, and birds that these painters achieved a specificity of detail by which, as Ruskin enjoined, scientific fact was pressed into the service of beauty.

Except for her studies of the dead, Emily Dickinson does not often paint *nature morte;* for her, it was "the Alive" that mattered first. When she studies nature, it is usually at a point of transition or motion. Her birds and bees are most often in flight; her trees withstand tempest or seasonal change, and her skies shift their hues from one of her lines to the next. In some poems, however, she attempts what the still life painters did: to show the poignancy of an object by observing it motionless, a theme for memory. Her stern poem 1102, written around 1866, calls up the *Dead Blue Jay* (1865) of John William Hill, Robert Brandegee's *Dead Bird* (1867), and the many other studies of dead birds done by the American Pre-Raphaelites:

> His Bill is clasped – his Eye forsook –
> His Feathers wilted low –
> The Claws that clung, like lifeless Gloves
> Indifferent hanging now –
> The Joy that in his happy Throat
> Was waiting to be poured
> Gored through and through with Death, to be
> Assassin of a Bird
> Resembles to my outraged mind
> The firing in Heaven,
> On Angels – squandering for you
> Their Miracles of Tune – (1102)

Remembering the usual vitality of a Dickinson landscape in which

> The Bird did prance – the Bee did play –
> The Sun ran miles away
>
> . . . . .
>
> The morn was up – the meadows out
> The Fences all but ran, (1107)

a reader may find the stolidity of this scene remarkable. The alliteration of "clasped," "claws," and "clung," the *l*'s of "low," "lifeless," and "gloves," the use of the word "gored," slow the poem, as do the participles "hanging" and "waiting." The eye of the poet regards a bird that used to cling to a bough but now hangs from the hand while his claws also hang, or dangle. Her image of gloves adroitly depicts the pathetic nullity of the lifeless body. Once full of joy, which—like all Dickinson's birds—he was eager to lavish on a listener in song, now he is indifferent. Even his joy has been gored. So indignant is the poet that she drives home the point of her picture with some asperity. (There is even a certain impatience to do so, suggested by the lack of punctuation after "Death.") For Dickinson, this bird was like a human being; he has not been merely killed but murdered by an assassin. In a final image, which is not entirely earned, she says the deed is like shooting angels in heaven, "squandering for you / Their Miracles of Tune." Her allusion is probably to angelic choirs, but those sing for God, not for human beings. What underlies her conception here is characteristic, though: songbirds generously serve humanity, "Split the Lark – and you'll find the Music," "Gush after Gush, reserved for you" (861).

John Henry Hill's *Sketches from Nature* (1867), popular etchings whose minute observations in drypoint on white paper were likened to Albrecht Dürer's, contains the drawing of a *Black-Capped Titmouse*. Its dangling claws and shut beak focus the viewer's attention. What Dickinson in poem 1102 calls the clasped bill and gloves are similarly John William Hill's chief themes in his affecting watercolor, *Dead Blue Jay*. Even as Dickinson remarks the bird's "Feathers wilted low," Hill gives meticulous attention to the jay's plumage, still bright blue in death, while its beak (shut as if to song itself) and its feet are rigid. Writing of this watercolor, May Brawley Hill observes that the bird's "lifeless-ness is emphasized by the open window that frames a tree, the bird's natural habitat, just above its head. The cumulative, patient, and loving labor given this drawing adds weight to the moral implications of the subject."[29] As in the case of Dickinson's poem, there *are* moral impli-cations suggested by the still lifes of birds done by the Pre-Raphaelites; but not every painter made so much of them as Hill. A particularly ugly allusion to mankind's spoliation of nature was made by the painters who did still lifes of dead game. John William Hill's *Hanging Game— Ducks* (1867) and *Hanging Trophies—Snipe and Woodcock in a Land-scape* (1867) were praised for their clarity and precision; but, as in the case of the paintings of dead animals done by William Michael Harnett in the 1880s, what made Hill's scene effective was their suggestion that a more innocent life than man's had been sacrificed to his greed.

The assassin in "His Bill is clasped – his Eye forsook," of course, was probably one of Lavinia's many cats, for which Dickinson's letters show scant sympathy. In the little world her poems make, the cat of 507 stalks a bird who is equated with bliss and therefore—as bliss always does in Dickinson's thinking—flies away. Like most of the ani-mals in her poetic bestiary, the cat is described with vigilance. The same poet who pictured what remorse or doubt or hope is, how a snake crawls or what a cassia carnation looks like when it splits, catches the cat in a typical act, hunting. The cat may be a predator but she is considered with high humor. For she is fulfilling her own nature, which Dickinson regards as comically avid:

> She sights a bird – she chuckles –
> She flattens – then she crawls –
> She runs without the look of feet –
> Her eyes increase to Balls –
>
> Her Jaws stir – twitching – hungry –
> Her Teeth can hardly stand –
> She leaps, but Robin leaped the first –
> Ah, Pussy, of the Sand,
>
> The Hopes so juicy ripening –
> You almost bathed your Tongue –
> When Bliss disclosed a hundred Toes –
> And fled with every one – (507)

Dickinson's short meter, bristling with verbs, imitates the energy of the cat. She uses the word "sand" in its standard meaning as well as its slang context (Pussy of Earth, not sky, as well as Pussy of Courage or Grit). Her apostrophe reveals the pleasure she takes—since the robin got away—in the cat's gusto and rippling speed. Salivating with open jaws at the prospect of a good meal, the cat is disappointed. For bliss has fled: on its toes in this version, as on its wings in an earlier one. (Her final choice wittily relates cat to bird in their efforts to survive.) Like the poet herself, she must dine on air. This sort of nature study through characteristic movement is Dickinson's preferred mode.

Nevertheless, like "His Bill is clasped – his Eye forsook," some of her poems about trees and flowers disclose an interest in formal arrangement and in objects observed for the harmony of their parts that characterizes the Pre-Raphaelite still life. When Mabel Todd sent Emily Dickinson her drawing of Indian pipes in 1882, she offered her a gift painted in a style favored by the Pre-Raphaelites; the flowers are standing alone against a self-effacing background, specimens that thus attest to an "understanding of order in the natural universe."[30] (John Ruskin's watercolor and gouache *Twig of Peach Bloom* [ca. 1874], now in the Fogg Art Museum at Harvard, is remarkably like Todd's *Indian Pipes* in its diaphanous yet concrete shape.) Church himself adopted the detail and formula of the Pre-Raphaelite still life when he returned from Jamaica in 1865 with an enthusiasm for tropical flowers. Inspired by Humboldt's interest in plant life as an index of the original Eden, and respectful of Ruskin's injunctions to draw with insight and fidelity, Church produced still lifes of Jamaican flowers, such as his 1865 *Cardamum* (fig. 7). If one contrasts them, however, with other Pre-Raphaelite still lifes—Fidelia Bridges' *Calla Lily* (1875), for example, or Robert Brandegee's *Anemones* (1867)—Church's pictures are seen to be far more impressionistic. While his draftsmanship is sufficiently meticulous to provide the reader with botanical information, Church's conception of the aromatic flower hints at the fleeting tremulousness of its scent; the overall effect of his painting is vaporous. He is interested in rendering the characteristics of the species observed, but he remains the painter of morning, twilight, and the evanescent moment. Like Dickinson's, his attitude toward all nature is essentially post-romantic. His *Cardamum* is not stiffly presented but has a shimmer that suggests it might move at any moment in the Jamaican breeze.

Just so, Dickinson's "still lifes" of her many flowers—rose, dandelion, crocus, gentian, daffodil, anemone, clematis, tulip, pink—list their attributes but are more interested in what they symbolize: usually the transient moment of bloom as a "Bright Affair" of light or hope (1058). Her still lifes have the evident objective of classifying and describing the genus (though she does it often as a game).[31] Yet they lack the sciential coldness of Pre-Raphaelite floral studies. Different from most still-life painters, Church, one feels, is deeply moved by his white cardamum blossoms. Dickinson's feelings for flowers are intense, anthropomorphized, and personal. So her flowers are rarely seen purely as designs.

In painting the lily, for example, that favorite emblematic flower of all Pre-Raphaelites (and the flower she carried in her hand as a greeting), Dickinson ascribes to it a process of spiritual and emotional development. It is seen in motion from the first word in her poem: "through." She makes it a human prototype, not a botanical fact. Her lily is analyzed to some extent: as a bulbous rootstock with bell or funnel-shaped blooms, it likes rich ("dark") soil. But for Dickinson, who said she carried a flower to her lover "My face to *justify*" (663), it symbolizes beauty fulfilled and the sensuous completion of nature:

> Through the Dark Sod – as Education –
> The Lily passes sure –
> Feels her white foot – no trepidation –
> Her faith – no fear –
>
> Afterward – in the Meadow –
> Swinging her Beryl Bell –

> The Mold-life – all forgotten – now –
> In Ecstasy – and Dell – (392)

A letter written by Dickinson in 1874 told Adelaide Hills that

> Flowers are not quite earthly. They are like the Saints. We should
> doubtless feel more at Home with them than with the Saints of God.
> Were the "Great Crowds of Witnesses" chiefly Roses and Pansies,
> they would be less to apprehend, though let me not presume upon
> Jehovah's Program. (L 2.527–528)

In conceiving the lily, she makes it the emblem of a soul's spiritual
"program." With its white foot in the dark sod as a bulb, it is akin to
the hidden nun or devotee learning through sequestration and faith about
God. Afterward, however, the flower enjoys ecstasy; that is, the joy of
the soul released from the "Mold-life" and fully itself. (The dell is not
this life only but heaven as well.) Her picture of the light green, transparent bell of the lily swinging in the meadow poses against the cloistral
sod a synaesthetic imagery of air, music, and motion. Its ecstasy in the
dell (the word "Dell" rings to rhyme with "Bell," thus making land
itself like melody) represents the mystic pleasure of the soul moved by
God. Somehow the lily "Swinging her . . . Bell" is, for all these conventual connotations, richly sensual, even mischievous.

The first line of poem 392 has the same cadence as 792:

> Through the strait pass of suffering –
> The Martyrs – even – trod.
> Their feet – upon Temptation –
> Their faces – upon God –

Thus (as her letter to Mrs. Hills makes clear) the flower puts her in
mind of the saints and the progress of those who suffer for Christ in
Revelation—a group with which she associated herself by wearing white
and pointedly, even ironically, alluding to it. She uses the same hymnlike
cadence to characterize the lily as to identify the martyrs; and since she
envisions the foot or feet of both passing through educative travail, it
is not an actual still life that she is painting in 392. Her conception of
the jasmine as associated with passion and the lily as a metaphor of
sensuous spirituality led to a vision of both in animation or in stages
of growth. ("Susan" or "Susa" means *lily* in Persian. Whether or not
her preference for lilies came in part from this connection with Sue,
Dickinson does not reveal.)

Few American Pre-Raphaelite painters did pictures of roots or bulbs,

7. Frederic Edwin Church, *Cardamum* (1865). Church's floral
impressions reflect his interest in Darwinian evolution and the eternal Eden.

though it was commonplace to draw eggs in nests, water lilies in mid-flower, and buds. Truth and earnestness were supposed to move artists profoundly in their depictions.[32] Of all floral subjects in the 1860s, the lily was the most popular in art. Dickinson augmented the variety of lilies—full blown or just opening—depicted in the oils, watercolors, and numerous lithographs of the decade. She was willing to do lilies as bulbs. As might be expected of the poet of the hidden face, she was fascinated by their burial in the earth and the idea of the bloom that would come from it. In an early poem she views lilies as types of the resurrected soul or the secret, and then discovered, artist:

> Many a Bulb will rise –
> Hidden away, cunningly,
> From sagacious eyes. (66)

In a late poem she is still thinking of the powers of endurance a bulb must have before it may be recognized:

> What Constancy must be achieved
> Before it see the Sun! (1255)

She wrote to Cornelia Sweetser, "I have long been a Lunatic on Bulbs, though screened by my friends, as Lunacy on any theme is better undivulged" (L 3.775). She sent bulbs to friends—often hyacinth to Sue—because they had a "divine prospective" (L 3.776). Just as the form of her poems discovers music in compression, so a bulb seemed to her to contain a wealth of bloom in its best form: the ideal. She wrote to Maria Whitney (during their long correspondence after Bowles's death), "is not an absent friend as mysterious as a bulb in the ground, and is not a bulb the most captivating floral form?" (L 3.776). (To Maria, who had also loved Bowles, the allusion to the buried bulb as "captivating" may have seemed less Dickinsonian and original than weirdly necrophilic.) Her niece Martha remembered her in the winters,

> up in her own room, forever associated for me with the odor of hyacinths, for the way of a bulb in the sunshine had an uncanny fascination for her, their little pots crowding all four window-sills to bring a reluctant spring upon the air. From the first prick of the green above the earth she detected every minute sign of growth.[33]

Poem 392 begins by contemplating the bulb of the lily. From the bulb would come the bloom; from the darkness, light. Dickinson depicted the same noble development in plants, calling it in trees and acorns "A homelier maturing – / A process in the Bur" (332). It was the equivalent in nature of the seedtime and blossoming of the human soul. To long for something (honor or love) was to be like the seed

> That wrestles in the Ground,
> Believing if it intercede
> It shall at length be found. (1255)

To "be found at length" was what Emerson had promised his ideal, reclusive poet.

For Dickinson, that poet was the distiller of rare perfumes from familiar flowers; and the poet herself, one whose vision grew steadily in secret. Dickinson and her flowers could be one person. In fact, her flowers *were* the poet and she sent them, or poetic drawings of them, in her place:

> Where I am not afraid to go
> I may confide my Flower –
> Who was not Enemy of Me
> Will gentle be, to Her.
>
> Nor separate, Herself and Me
> By Distances become –
> A single Bloom we constitute
> Departed, or at Home – (1037).

In one of the more prosaic passages of her talkative *Aurora Leigh*, Elizabeth Barrett Browning compares the woman artist to a flower that is created, to create in turn:

> No perfect artist is developed here
> From any imperfect woman. Flower from root,
> And spiritual from natural, grade by grade
> In all our life. A handful of the earth
> To make God's image! (9.648–652)

Like the speaker in *Aurora Leigh* (a poem she extravagantly admired), Dickinson also regarded flowers as types of the developing artist. And because the lily had specific scriptural significance, its growth and aspect had added metaphoric import. When her Aunt Katie Sweetser sent her lilies in November 1884, she wrote, "The beloved lilies have come, and my heart is so high it overflows, as this was Mother's week [of burial], Easter in November" (L 3.851). Her favorite biblical commandment, she said airily, occurred in a passage from Matthew 6, the only one she ever obeyed (L 3.815):

> And why take ye thought for raiment? Consider the lilies of the field, how they grow; they toil not, neither do they spin:
> And yet I say unto you, That even Solomon in all his glory was not arrayed like one of these.
> Wherefore, if God so clothe the grass of the field, which today is, and tomorrow is cast into the oven, *shall he* not much more *clothe* you, O ye of little faith? (28–30)

To her Aunt Sweetser's gift of lily bulbs in spring 1884, she wrote:

> Thank you for "considering the lilies."
> The Bible must have had us in mind, when it gave that liquid Commandment. Were all it's advice so enchanting as that, we should probably heed it. (L 3.821)

By "liquid" she probably meant that the phrase was intoxicating, like wine. With "enchanting" she implicitly contrasts the aesthetic content of the commandment with the condemnatory harshness of other commandments (especially from the Old Testament). Those she especially repudiated. ("Had but the Tale a warbling Teller," she writes of the Bible in poem 1545, rather than a wrathful one, "All the Boys would come.") With their monklike cowls or bells, lilies had religious connotations. But in their elegance and perfume they stood for beauty, simply. When the gospeler urges her to contemplate beauty ("Consider the lilies") and beauty whose purpose is itself ("they toil not, neither do they spin"), she is glad to obey. She grew red meadow lilies to distinguish her special poetic sensibility—for she was the red-haired, fiery cow lily, not so ascetic as the white one. She sent them as messages to friends.

This method of fashioning a spiritual iconography with flowers, and of studying flowers as they grew and died, was part of the fabric of Emily Dickinson's culture. One of the most popular books of the 1850s was Asa Gray's *Botany for Young People,* which began with the "lesson of the lilies." Dickinson may have read Erasmus Darwin's *The Botanic Garden* (1798), in which flowers are like girls and the lily is "given to secret sighs." As a woman of twenty-nine, she was given Mrs. C. M. Badger's *Wild Flowers Drawn and Colored from Nature* (1859) by Edward Dickinson as a New Year's gift. (Her father's inscription, "To my daughter Emily from her father Edward Dickinson," suggests the tight-lipped reserve of that Whig gentleman.) Mrs. Badger's costly volume presented pictures of the dogwood, wild geranium, ground pink, trailing arbutus, harebell, yellow lily, wild rose, and daisy—all of them (except the dogwood) the subjects of later Dickinson poems. Accompanying the pictures were verses of the most simpering and awkward lassitude, with the exception of an introductory verse that evokes Emily Dickinson's attitude to flowers. It was written by a Mrs. Brainard:

> Who does not love a flower?
> Its hues are taken from the light
> Which summer's sun flings pure and bright,
> In scattered and prismatic hues,
> That shine and smile in dropping dews;
> Its fragrance from the sweetest air,
> Its form from all that's light and fair; –
> Who does not love a flower?

Even this little poem, with its allusion to light that the "sun flings pure," shows the contemporary conception of nature as proof of the divine. Her own fine poem 673 would speak of the glamor of divine love or light as it is radiated in the filaments of noon. Here Dickinson traces the sunlight to its source: it "flings in Paradise."

The watercolors that accompany the Badger text, however, are entirely remote in execution from the intention of the American Pre-Raphaelites. They are neither highly detailed nor refined. Nor do they exhibit a persuasive tension between passionate feeling for the internal, transitory life of the flower and meticulous description of its external form. (It is this tension—between the infinite and ideal and the finite and real—that is stirring in Church's still lifes, and Emily Dickinson's. The cardinal defect of Pre-Raphaelite painting was that, by its meticulousness, it could seem to mummify what it observed.[34]) The Badger flowers are flat, only superficially detailed, and pallid in color. Reminiscent of floral paintings on crude pottery or china, they could not have provided Dickinson with more than aide-mémoires. Like Hitchcock's *Catalogue of Plants Growing in the Vicinity of Amherst* (1829), which she called "Flowers of North America," Badger's book may have consoled her "when Flowers annually died." (She told Higginson she "used to read Dr. Hitchcock's Book" in winter as a child, which "comforted their Absence—assuring me they lived" [L 2.573].) The difference between Dickinson's poetry and the commonplace floral verse of her time is epitomized by the distinction between the Badger/Brainard daisy or fringed gentian and her own. But the sentimental enervation of some of Dickinson's flower poems may also be attributable to infection from such sources.

Badger's readers were reminded by the popular poet Lydia Sigourney in an introduction that these "flowerets . . . can never fade." This was part of the appeal of floral still life to the Victorians. That some flowers were perennials also proved that nature was self-perpetuating, itself a proof of eternal life. Thus Higginson published an essay in the *Atlantic Monthly* (December 1862) entitled "The Procession of the Flowers." He mentions the tradition of still life, but records keener interest in what he calls the "march of the flowers," the pageant of their growth. It is not the Pre-Raphaelite genus or species minutely observed in repose but what Dickinson called "the river in the tree" (L 2.452) that concerns him:

> To a watcher from the sky, the march of the flowers . . . across the year would seem as beautiful as [a] West Indian pageant. These frail creatures, rooted where they stand, a part of the "still life" of Nature, yet share her ceaseless motion. In the most sultry silence of summer noons, the vital current is coursing with desperate speed through the innumerable veins of every leaflet; and the apparent stillness, like the sleeping of a child's top, is in truth the very ecstasy of perfected motion.

In "Nature," Emerson said, "Every appearance in nature corresponds to some state of the mind"; and "The sensual man conforms thoughts to things; the poet conforms things to his thoughts. The one esteems nature as rooted and fast; the other, as fluid, and impresses his being thereon."[35] Higginson's essay shows him contemplating the sequence of the seasons, with their different wildflowers, as proof of the continuance of natural forms. (The sixteen-year-old Emily Dickinson had written Abiah Root, "the ceaseless flight of the seasons is to me a very solemn thought" [L 1.37]). His essay reveals him as both botanist and artist-at-heart, alive to color in particular: "the varying tints of blue upon the same stalk [of the lupine] are a perpetual gratification to the eye." In his gentle response to what seems the personality of each flower—whether it be the "timid" rhodora or the "fastidious" orchid or the "blushing" wild rose—he emphasizes its power to elevate his thoughts. "When June is at its height," he writes, "the sculptured chalices of the Mountain Laurel begin to unfold." There is a holiness in the process of the birth, growth, and death of these flowers. Speaking of the field lilies Dickinson associated with herself, his essay describes a surreal landscape (one thinks of Edvard Munch's *Separation*, for instance, in which flowers are flames and a tree resembles a crucifix): "as I lay and watched the red lilies that waved their innumerable urns around me, it needed but little imagination to see a thousand altars, sending visible flames forever upward to the answering sun."

Higginson's depiction of the lilies as urns—or the mountain laurel as altars—was an inevitable consequence of the American tradition of reverence for nature fostered by Emerson and the English romantics. Thomas Cole's habit of forming the branches of trees in some of his landscapes so that they made a cross was memorialized by Church's *The Cross in the Wilderness* (1857). In many poems Dickinson compares the "Grace – and Hue" (671) of creation to heaven. But her vision of nature, and of flowers in particular, is not always sacramental. Since she associated flowers with herself, her floral portraiture has a variety of moods: gay, irreverent, sentimental, sullen, arch, and, beyond those, the appeal to the infinite. Its range may be suggested by two poems: the brilliantly daring 339 ("I tend my flowers for thee") and the ceremonious and stately 1241 ("The Lilac is an ancient shrub"). Each of these poems transcends still life to make the flowers Dickinson describes emblems of her personality and beliefs.

Emily Dickinson is a daisy in her letters to Bowles and the poems to Master. Sometimes she is but a doll compared to him (481). She sent a pencil stub to Samuel Bowles in 1863, during one of his visits to Sue and Austin, telling Bowles—since he was not writing to her—to draw her a picture of a daisy

> Most as big as I was,
> When it [you] plucked Me? (921)

At a time when Master was away, she sent him a lament from her solitude. Far from being a still-life elegy, its teasing rhythms, until the end, convey a keen and challenging sexuality:

> I tend my flowers for thee –
> Bright Absentee!
> My Fuschzia's Coral Seams
> Rip – while the Sower – dreams –
>
> Geraniums – tint – and spot –
> Low Daisies – dot –

My Cactus – splits her Beard
To show her throat –

Carnations – tip their spice –
And Bees – pick up –
A Hyacinth – I hid –
Puts out a Ruffled Head –
And odors fall
From flasks – so small –
You marvel how they held –

Globe Roses – break their satin flake –
Upon my Garden floor –
Yet – thou – not there –
I had as lief they bore
No Crimson – more –

Thy flower – be gay –
Her Lord – away!
It ill becometh me –
I'll dwell in Calyx – Gray –
How modestly – alway –
Thy Daisy –
Draped for thee! (339)

The evidence of her poem cleverly contradicts Dickinson's wry first line.
She is *not* tending her flowers. A horticulturalist would know that if
her geraniums are turning color and also have the disease called "[black]
spot," she hasn't been stripping the blooms off as they come. In fact,
the whole garden needs attention: the fuchsias and carnations litter it
with pods, the cactus is overgrown, the daisies have not been picked
(so that more might grow). Time has passed since she was a true sower
of seams—her accents are biblical, alluding to Matthew 13:3–9 and the
parable of the sower of seeds. (There is a pun, too, on *sower; that is,*
she should be a *sewer* of the seams of her flowers that rip from neglect.
Here is Dickinson speaking indeed as a woman, one who cultivates
gardens and lovers as a dressmaker finishes a gown.) She has been
dreaming, instead, of her lord. He is the "Absentee [Land] Lord" of
her garden, the garden of herself; in his absence, she loses interest in
life.

Amusing in this poem is the variance between its underlying rhythms
and its statement. The latter seems innocuous, a sentimental confession
of loneliness from one left behind. But at the word "rip," a staccato

rhythm is set up and continued with trochees: "tint – and spot," "tip their spice," "pick up," "splits her beard," "show her throat." The flowers are undressing or—in the case of the hyacinth bulb—filling out. If the poem is a message to an absent man, it is meant to get his attention. Colonel Higginson recalled that when he met Emily Dickinson, he had expected to find her naive. Instead, he discovered in her conversation "skill such as the most experienced and worldly coquette might envy."[36] Since, as she elsewhere insists, "I hide myself within my flower" (903), the flowers are her means in this poem of reminding Master that she has a body as well as a voice.

Just as her landscape poems usually prefer to describe nature in activity, so this poem with its superficial aspect of a still-life garden scene depicts the fluidity of nature and a flood of feeling in herself. While Pre-Raphaelite painters and photographers did careful studies of intricately full-blown roses, Dickinson draws a rose just past its prime and dropping its petals. Even this emblem of romance is in ruins, and its dishevelment, she says, of no interest to the speaker. If, as Emerson wrote, "every appearance in nature corresponds to some state of mind," then Dickinson's roses reflect the careless apathy of one whose lord is away. In the last stanza, she simply acknowledges herself as "thy flower"—Master obviously thinks of her as a daisy. But, unlike the hyacinth bulb that has blossomed, she now is "in Calyx – Gray." She is a daisy in mourning for him. It is a curiously static image suggesting not so much a mourner as a woman-flower (the inevitable connection for the Victorians). And the woman-flower is hidden inside a calyx, draped for her portrait, as the poem becomes emptied of action—a still life indeed—at its close.

Impersonal, severe, but full of wonder, "The Lilac is an ancient shrub" pretends to be a floral still life but is in reality a study of sunset. Even as a landscape, it is not typical of Dickinson but, rather, resembles the emblematic strictness of a shield or crest in needlework or paint. In stately accents Dickinson formulates a vision of permanence:

> The Lilac is an ancient shrub
> But ancienter than that
> The Firmamental Lilac
> Upon the Hill tonight –
> The Sun subsiding on his Course
> Bequeaths this final Plant
> To Contemplation – not to Touch –
> The Flower of Occident.

Of one Corolla is the West —
The Calyx is the Earth —
The Capsules burnished Seeds the Stars
The Scientist of Faith
His research has but just begun —
Above his synthesis
The Flora unimpeachable
To Time's Analysis —
"Eye hath not seen" may possibly
Be current with the Blind
But let not Revelation
By theses be detained — (1241)

Dickinson's lines imagine a lilac flower in the heavens as the sun sub-
sides. One of the flowers of Persian origin that she preferred, the lilac
is ancient and connotes love. But the sunset is even older and, as a
metaphor of death and eternity, a theme for contemplation. Important
in the poem is the connection between what can be touched ("shrub")
and supernal ("Firmamental") reality that transcends touch and must
be contemplated. Gazing at the sky, Dickinson sees it meet with earth
as the points of the flower whose capsules are stars. And though she
uses the appropriate botanical terms, *corolla, calyx,* she separates herself
from scientists (like Darwin and Humboldt) interested in the history of
the earth. The flower in the sky is not vulnerable to analysis. To appreciate it, one must be a "Scientist of Faith," for whom the synthesis of
the sunset's parts is only "just begun" on earth. At the same time, the
passage from her favorite 1 Corinthians 2:9—"Eye hath not seen, nor
ear heard, neither have entered into the heart of man, the things which
God hath prepared for them that love him"—is not wholly appropriate;
for the sunset provides a Revelation each evening to those who see.
Nature is able to provide some of the experience of paradise here, now.
The form of Dickinson's poem 1241 is unusual for her: twenty lines
with no break. She fashions it as a long thesis, a "synthesis," in which
the single flower that expands into the heavens is enlarged at last to
mean eternity.

7

In the fourth act of *Antony and Cleopatra,* the defeated protagonist
(with whom Dickinson associated herself) must acquaint his boy-ser-
vant Eros with his altered fortunes and state. He does so by appealing

to the great Renaissance theme of appearance and reality, marking the distinction between shapes that clouds may propose to the interpretive eye and the clouds themselves:

> Sometime we see a cloud that's dragonish,
> A vapor sometime like a bear or lion,
> A towered citadel, a pendant rock,
> A forked mountain, or blue promontory
> With trees upon't that nod unto the world
> And mock our eyes with air . . .
> That which is now a horse, even with a thought
> The rock dislimns, and makes it indistinct
> As water is in water. (4.14.3–11)

Thus Antony explains that, while he appears to be Antony, he has been so blighted by Cleopatra and his own failure that, like moving clouds, he cannot keep his authority, or "visible shape." (Dickinson's knowledge of this passage is indicated by her quotation of the rare Shakespearean word *dislimn* in a letter to Kate Anthon [L 2.365].) His speech suggests that Shakespeare may possibly have been acquainted with the old painterly habit of looking for "images in the clouds," a practice recorded by Giorgio Vasari in explaining various disciplines in his *Lives of the Most Eminent Painters* (1550). Leonardo was known to have advised this airy study, which he extended to the study of walls in his "Treatise on Painting":

> You should look at certain walls stained with damp, or at stones of uneven colour. If you have to invent some backgrounds you will be able to see in these the likeness of divine landscapes, adorned with mountains, ruins, rocks, woods, great plains, hills and valleys in great variety; and then again you will see battles and strange figures in violent action, expressions of faces and clothes and an infinity of things which you will be able to reduce to their complete and proper forms. In such walls the same thing happens as in the sound of bells, in whose stroke you may find every named word which you can imagine.[37]

Although it is not probable that Emily Dickinson read Leonardo, and only possible that she may have read Vasari (there were allusions to the *Lives* in the *Atlantic*), her landscape poems are versatile evidence of a propensity to distinguish palaces in the sky and faces in the clouds. She was attempting to compose that "infinity of things" which Leonardo said could be drawn from particulars. To Thomas Cole, writing a poem on the cover of his sketchbook in 1829, nature had a face with "sacred features";[38] and he was wont to suggest angelic or divine visages in the skies above his human subjects or his ruined towers, blasted trees, and other spectral romantic presences. In his *Old Age,* whose iconography may have recurred to Dickinson as she herself grew older, the clouds part to reveal the suggestion of a divine Face, set there as she says of God's face in 820 and receptive to the aged voyager. In *Manhood* there are demonic spirits akin to the creatures who "gnashed their teeth" and "swung their frenzied hair" in Dickinson's poem about "an awful Tempest" (198). They may be seen, evoking Satan's power, in the murky, whirling skies above Cole's endangered man. Emerson had said in "The Poet" that the clouds have faces if the artist is conscious enough to see them. This theory supported the influential romantic conception that Nature and human nature were intimately related, even as Wordsworth had proposed. It was the principle that inspired Constable's many cloud studies or those of Turner, described by Ruskin. Moreover, all that was unseen (those forces that Dickinson called "immortality" or "death") congregated below the horizon even on ordinary days and might be perceived and commented on in poetry, provided the poet were attentive to their ghostly reality.

Dickinson's poem 1710 shows facility in seeing shapes in clouds. Here her subject is the difference in aspect one cloud can present:

> A curious Cloud surprised the Sky,
> 'Twas like a sheet with Horns;
> The sheet was Blue –
> The Antlers Gray –
> It almost touched the Lawns.
>
> So low it leaned – then statelier drew –
> And trailed like robes away,
> A Queen adown a satin aisle,
> Had not the majesty.

This seems a fanciful exercise in noting just how different the images made by clouds might be, at one point resembling an animal but at another, a queen.

In poem 194, written around 1860, Dickinson begins by sketching a scene reminiscent of many done by Church and the Luminist painters:

> On this long storm the Rainbow rose –
> On this late Morn – the Sun –

> The clouds – like listless Elephants –
> Horizons – straggled down –

In their efforts to reveal the sublime power of Nature, Church and the others depicted scenes like his dramatic *Storm in the Mountains* or *Blasted Tree* (1847) and *The Harp of the Winds (A Passing Storm)* (1849). Equally effective were scenes in which, as in Dickinson's 194, the terrible anger of nature subsided in ominous calm. Studying the clouds, Dickinson conceives them as "listless Elephants," lumbering and apathetic, their energies temporarily spent. The horizons straggle, to her painterly eye undefined in the aqueous air that results from a storm. The poem does not seem imbued with terror but with relief at first. The second quatrain begins

> The Birds rose smiling, in their nests –
> The gales – indeed – were done –

Then, with a frank "Alas," Dickinson shifts her emphasis and her perspective on the scene she has imagined. It becomes like one of the Luminist seascapes in which the sun rises over a beach dotted with dead bodies after a storm-tossed night:

> Alas, how heedless were the eyes –
> On whom the summer shone!
>
> The quiet nonchalance of death
> No Daybreak – can bestir –
> The slow – Archangel's syllables
> Must awaken *her!*

One person does not survive the storm on which "the Rainbow rose." Emblem of God's covenant with Noah after the flood (Genesis 9:13), the "bow in the cloud" traditionally signifies hope. It is a false image of happiness here, however, for the eyes that should rejoice to see a rainbow are heedless and will open only in heaven. "On this long Storm the Rainbow rose" appears at first, then, to be a landscape poem that also studies shapes in the sky with an artist's perception. But, more specifically, it is a poem in which outer has become inner weather. The long storm, the gales now done, are the protracted suffering and death of *her* whom only the archangels can wake. This translation of the face of nature into the being of a human sojourner under her skies is characteristic both of Emily Dickinson and of the artist who painted *The Voyage of Life*. (So insistent, indeed, is Cole on associating human destiny with the natural forces that both affect and reflect it that he makes diabolic faces in the storm clouds of *Manhood* and angelic ones in the paradisal skies of *Old Age*.)

If the face was an important conceit for many nineteenth-century writers and painters, there was good reason. The age was deeply interested in portrait painting, all the more so because of the challenge to the painter offered by the photographer. Photography was uncreative and, as art, a disaster, according to Ruskin. But Pre-Raphaelites like Rossetti often used it, making daguerreotypes of scenes they would later paint. (Some Pre-Raphaelites were embarrassed to admit that they had painted over the photographs.) There was also considerable interest in phrenology and therefore in the revealing conformation of a subject's features. This absorption affected the descriptions of the novelists. I have said earlier that Dickinson had an obsession with faces. Though it had literary analogues, this obsession was ultimately distinct in character and comprehensiveness.

In *Confessions of an English Opium-Eater* De Quincey complained of "the tyranny of the human face"; for him on his sea of troubles "the sea appeared paved with innumerable faces." In De Quincey's opium reverie, the humanity from which he was separating himself assumed vengeful authority. In other books Dickinson read, the face was similarly significant. Barrett Browning declared in sonnet 7 of her *Sonnets from the Portuguese* that "the face of all the world is changed, I think, / Since first I heard the footsteps of thy soul / Move still, oh still, beside me." In "Any Wife to Any Husband," Robert Browning seemed to echo her connection between face and self in his line "Thy soul is in thy face." Theirs was the conventional expression (especially common to Renaissance poetry) of the biblical association of soul with face made, as we have seen, in Dickinson's often-quoted 2 Corinthians 3:18. In her own love poetry, however, Dickinson imbues the idea of looking on the face with an even more awful power. She asks Master's "Pardon – to look upon thy face," that is, his inmost self, with earthly eyes (788). Looking into the face has the force of Exodus 33:20 where God tells Moses "thou canst not see my face: for there shall no man see me, and live." (This precept states one theme of her poetry, in fact: that to meet each other's soul or face first necessitates death.)

Emily Dickinson's more inclusive representation of a world of faces— one that linked her to the nineteenth-century American landscape painters—was also far more subtle yet specific than the Brownings', and the faces she saw were of great variety. To begin with, for Dickinson, the student of Edward Hitchcock's *Elementary Geology* and Benjamin Silliman's *Elements of Chemistry,* even atoms had faces. That fact reassured her "fractured Trust," encouraging her that she would some day see "the finished Creatures / Departed me" (954). Flowers had "pathos in their faces" (137). Day had a "spotted Face" which she stooped to "the Otter's Window" and laid "at the feet of the old Horizon" before dying (228). The Moon had a "lustral Face" (1672). She imagined an "abyss's face" (1400). The aspect of infinity that worried Emily Dickinson was the fact that, like silence, "Himself have not a face." A prism's face was "ponderous" (652); the saints had "veiled faces" (664). Not only because she so often read the Bible or Shakespeare or the Brownings, wherein face mirrored soul, but because she desired concretion (though, contrapuntally, she liked to "ride indefinite" [661]), Dickinson records the continual passion to see faces. As her life developed after 1862, and she found it harder and harder to withstand the drain of her too-responsive feelings occasioned by seeing people, she nevertheless asked to see photographs. Mary Bowles was chided in 1881 for forgetting to send a photograph of "Mr. Samuel's" child and, when she received it, Dickinson wrote to congratulate her as "the mother of the beautiful face" (L 3.708, 709). Dr. Holland pleased her by sending "the Face of George Eliot" (L 3.693). She pronounced it homely but hung it in her room. She tried to explain the effect on her, finally, even of photographs: "Believing that we are to have no Face in a Farther Life, makes the Look of a Friend a Boon almost too precious" (L 3.792). Nature's face was safest, requiring no response but permitting her to study it, as if it were the study of herself: " 'Nature' is what we see,"

> Nature is what we know —
> Yet have no art to say —
> So impotent Our Wisdom is
> To her Simplicity (668)

The faces she perceived in nature assumed expressions. There was sometimes, for instance, an "eager look – on Landscapes / As if they just repressed / Some Secret" (627). Snow made the world wear a look of composure and youth or, paradoxically, of tranquil death, like the placid surfaces of Thomas Doughty's fanciful landscapes, popular nineteenth-century primitive paintings that resembled samplers:

It fills the Alabaster Wool
The Wrinkles of the Road –

It makes an Even Face
Of Mountain, and of Plain –
Unbroken Forehead from the East
Unto the East again – (311)

In winter, the earth became like people at a death watch, attentive to that "certain Slant of light" which meant "affliction / Sent us of the Air" and preceded the still depths of bitter cold. Then,

the Landscape listens –
Shadows – hold their breath –
When it goes, 'tis like the Distance
On the look of Death – (258)

Sometimes her perception of natural faces akin to the human could be comical. In 1862 she wrote a poem for "Ishmael," a wandering traveler. It made sport of her propensity to see his face everywhere and in everything. The poem was probably written while Bowles was in Europe. In the poem he becomes that proverbial figure, the man in the moon. Though everything changes around her, he remains. Her good-humored poem ends on a serious note, with an allusion to death:

You know that Portrait in the Moon –
So tell me who 'tis like –
The very Brow – the stooping eyes –
A-fog for – Say – Whose Sake?

The very Pattern of the Cheek –
It varies – in the Chin –
But – Ishmael – since we met – 'tis long –
And fashions – intervene –

When Moon's at full – 'tis Thou – I say –
My lips just hold the name –
When crescent – Thou art worn – I note –
But – there – the Golden Same

And when – Some Night – Bold – slashing Clouds
Cut thee away from Me –
That's easier – than the other film
That glazes Holiday – (504)

The man of her portrait has tears ("A-fog") in his eyes in the first quatrain, which correspond to the film over the eyes of the dead in the last. Though parting, like "slashing," is bad, it is better than death. Her poem is gamin ("Say – Whose Sake?"), even coquettish ("since we met – 'tis long"). And is there a pun in the tenth line? Dickinson's whimsical avowal,

> When Moon's at full – 'Tis Thou – I say –
> My lips just hold the name –

permits the reflection that one holds things in bowls. If she intended it, then she means she says "Bowles" with her lips, which are "bowls" consecrated to his radiance. This is the kind of joke to which as a Shakespearean she was no stranger.

8

If the classical artistic discipline of imagining faces in the clouds was practiced with special enthusiasm in the nineteenth century, it was perhaps because nature, art, and personality were intimately related. Reading matter that pretended merely to inform about botany or agriculture also imparted ethical precepts or suggested underlying principles of painterly design observable in God's handiwork, earth.

Emily Dickinson's copy of the *Atlantic Monthly* (August 1861) offered her the following study of design and perspective in the article "Trees in Assemblages":

> The subject of Trees cannot be exhausted by treating them as individuals or species, even with a full enumeration of their details. Some trees possess but little interest, except as they are grouped in assemblages of greater or less extent. A solitary Fir or Spruce, for example, when standing in an inclosure or by the roadside, is a stiff and disagreeable object; but a deep forest of Firs is not surpassed in grandeur by one of any other species. These trees must be assembled in extensive groups to affect us agreeably . . . Nature must be combined with Art, however simple and rude, and associated with human life, to become deeply affecting to the imagination.

"Trees in Assemblages" particularly considered the "picturesque grouping of woods" in the New England landscape, making comparisons between American and European woodland and deciding that the American forest had a "superior tinting." Its preference was for pine woods:

> Their dark verdure, their deep shade, their lofty height, and their branches which are ever mysteriously murmuring, as they are swayed by the wind, render them singularly solemn and sublime.

This essay, with its concentration on the artistic potentiality of trees in arrangements or in isolation, may have lingered in the mind that conceived "Four Trees – upon a solitary Acre" (742) and "By my Window have I for Scenery" (797). The first poem, written probably in 1863, however, observes the apparent designlessness of trees that are *not* grouped in woods, forests, or other "assemblages." So they do not meet the requirements for the beautiful proposed in the *Atlantic* article. Dickinson's lyric 797, on the other hand, finds mystery (as does the essayist) in pine trees, though she selects only one for analysis or, rather, for tribute. Each of these poems shows an attitude to natural phenomena that is different. Taken together, however, they compose the characteristic view of Emily Dickinson: that aesthetically composed or not, nature offers clues about infinity.

Poem 742 begins with the grave detachment and hard clarity of a Pre-Raphaelite landscape. From the landscape, as by meditation, austere conclusions are drawn:

> Four Trees – upon a Solitary Acre –
> Without Design
> Or Order, or Apparent Action –
> Maintain –
>
> The Sun – upon a Morning meets them –
> The Wind –
> No nearer Neighbor – have they –
> But God –
>
> The Acre gives them – Place –
> They – Him – Attention of Passer by –
> Of Shadow, or of Squirrel, haply –
> Or Boy –
>
> What Deed is Theirs unto the General Nature –
> What Plan
> They severally – retard – or further –
> Unknown –

Here the artist's mathematical observation (four trees, one acre) is summoned to make an account of a plan unknown to the speaker and to mathematics itself. Underlying and composing the poem are the antitheses of "Design" and "Without Design"; the trees that catch the speaker's eye because they appear to have sprung up randomly on an acre (or have been left there after a clearing) themselves constitute a design. The trees "Maintain" (and by setting the word off alone on the line, she underscores their structural power). A good botanist, Dickinson knew that trees support themselves by their roots and that they also maintain, or solidify, the soil. Her poem thus establishes an underlying current of paradox: even as it records her suspicions of apparent designlessness, it makes, itself, a design. There is also a design or pattern in the way the land supports the trees while they give to the land itself a point of reference. The trees have no apparent function. They are thus living works of art, and their real function is an artistic one, to establish compositional perspective. Like transcendental anchorites, they are greeted by the sun and wind of a morning; those who notice the trees are, like Dickinson herself, conservationists of secrets unknown to "the General": shadows or squirrels or a boy, all of which usually mean to her flight, independence, or impermanence.

"Four Trees" is a landscape poem, one subject of which is uncertainty. Yet it is still a landscape and, by its own properties, establishes space and boundary. Written in fours and twos, the poem's shorter lines assume a peculiarly instructive authority. The trees *Maintain* (Dickinson's first choice had been *Do reign*) and no one neighbors them *But God*. The last stanza admits that—unlike the writer of "Trees in Assemblages"—she does not discern how these trees contribute to the larger design of nature, and her concluding word *Unknown* is conclusive, really, of that reservation. She cannot say that they have an apparent claim or right—in all their straggly disorder—to participation in a divine plan. All the grouped trees of "Trees in Assemblages" were said to have roles to play in nature's show, and each grouping was also symbolic.

Yet while her poem records her doubt, it also provides what Cynthia Griffin Wolff calls "a sensuous reality." But Dickinson's verb *maintain* is not "simply negation clothed in the superficies of a positive assertion," as Wolff also says in her discussion of 742 as a poem containing "elegant gibberish." Dickinson's use of the transitive verb here is not "vacuous" because it has no object to complete its meaning.[39] Rather, Dickinson's opening and closing words—*maintain* and *unknown*—underscore the two realities her poem contemplates: the *fact* of the trees and the *mystery* of their ultimate function. (Surely "themselves" is the understood object, in any case, of *maintain,* a typically Dickinsonian elision, and effective.) Finally, what Dickinson says primarily of the trees is that they *endure,* or maintain. Nature's dumb endurance is a faculty often so touching that we lament its passing when trees are felled. The tone of this poem is exceptionally reserved and distant. Here is, in fact, the manner called *lâché* in Luminist painting. There is no vivid "I"; the brush strokes or personality of the artist are concealed beneath a tone of subdued reportage. The speaker affirms the trees' daily association with God, nature, and humanity, but her painterly eye regards them as isolated nevertheless.

By contrast, the lonely pine tree at her window in poem 797 calls up a distinctly personal joy because she sees it as a link between the real and the ideal:

> By my Window have I for Scenery
> Just a Sea – with a Stem –
> If the Bird and the Farmer – deem it a "Pine" –
> The Opinion will serve – for them –
>
> It has no Port, nor a "Line" – but the Jays –
> That split their route to the Sky –
> Or a Squirrel, whose giddy Peninsula
> May be easier reached – this way –
>
> For Inlands – the Earth is the under side –
> And the upper side – is the Sun –
> And it's Commerce – if Commerce it have –
> Of Spice – I infer from the Odors borne –
>
> Of it's Voice – to affirm – when the Wind is within –
> Can the Dumb – define the Divine?
> The Definition of Melody – is
> That Definition is none –
>
> It – suggests to our Faith –
> They – suggest to our Sight –
> When the latter – is put away
> I shall meet with Conviction I somewhere met
> That Immortality –
>
> Was the Pine at my Window a "Fellow
> Of the Royal" Infinity?
> Apprehensions – are God's introductions –
> To be hallowed – accordingly –

Since the speaker is looking at her tree from the second story, it seems like a bloom on a stem; or, better, with its branches rippling in the wind, it is a sea. Such vastness cannot be connoted by the word "Pine," but Dickinson introduces the name as a nod to the world of birds and farmers, for whom the tree is an ordinary feature of the scene and not—as for her—a marvel. The tree is so full that it has no port or line, that is, as a sea it offers no ports to birds or lines (customary trade routes) along its thousands of needles. The bluejays, flying in flocks, must part from one another to pass it. Squirrels might quickly swing along a bough. As a sea, however, it does have inlands, and those seem South American, even like the tree's commerce of spice. In order to suggest how transporting she finds the sight, sound, and aroma of the pine, Dickinson appeals to the exotic myth of a prelapsarian Latin America, established by the landscape tradition of the 1860s. Just as her images of volcanoes may derive in part from reports and paintings of the voyages of Church or from *Harper's* articles like "The Volcanoes of Central America" painted by Heade, so her frequent image of the "Peninsula" (Italy?) may have been inspired by her fascination with exotic land and seascapes. There are no peninsulas in Amherst, even as (she says herself) there are no seas, ports, or trade routes. (In her love poems, however, she imagines "My Blue Peninsula" [405] – both desired and feared.) The pine lies between earth and sun and, itself a sea, makes a "giddy Peninsula" for the squirrel.

This importation of the marine is typical of Emily Dickinson, and it too may have partly been affected by her sympathy with the graphic and literary texts of her age. Just as Church includes the motifs of falls and a pool in *The Andes of Ecuador* (1855), water almost invariably appears in a Luminist or Hudson River Valley landscape. Seen by geologists as evidence of the convulsive currents of the prehistoric world, regarded by devout creationists as a mighty sign of God's power in Genesis, water had associations that were profoundly spiritual. In fanciful paintings such as Cole's *Moonlight* (1833–34), in John F. Kensett's serene *Third Beach, Newport* (1869), in Ryder's unquiet *Toilers of the Sea* (ca. 1884), and in Whistler's aesthetic *Symphony in Gray and Green: The Ocean* (1866), water is imagined as an image of inner peace or disturbance and sometimes of deep joy. Of course it gives the promise of voyaging to new shores and new understanding.

In poem 797, the pine makes music that Dickinson finds "divine." Like Coleridge listening to the music of the wind in his aeolian harp, she considers herself dumb by comparison. Nor can she define its melody, since the true music (of nature?) defies definition. The wind in "The Aeolian Harp" spoke to Coleridge of "the one Life within us and abroad," "A light in sound, a sound-like power in light." So too for Dickinson the music in the pine boughs encourages faith, so much so that she declares "When [Sight] is put away"—at death—she "shall meet with Conviction" what she "somewhere met" by faith: the immortality of which the pine itself is an emblem. She asks a rhetorical question at the poem's end, a question that shows how decidedly she regarded nature as of transcendental significance. In saying

> Was the Pine at my Window a "Fellow
> Of the Royal" Infinity?

she is playing on words, saying that the tree was *not* a fellow of the Royal Society but, rather, of Infinity: it does not instruct in the scientific facts known to Newton and other members of that historic group. (This is one of Dickinson's many comments on the limitations of science. She knew, for instance, how important *The Origin of Species* was but observed to Mrs. Holland, "Why the Thief ingredient accompanies all Sweetness Darwin does not tell us" [L 2.485]. That is, science—even sciences interested in first causes—cannot explain why all human pleasures fade.) However solitary it seems, the pine's membership is in the mysterious company of created things that predict the Creator. The pine has given her apprehensions of infinity.

In *The Europeans* (1878), a novel contained in the Dickinson library, Henry James attempts to establish the characters of the American Wentworth family by associating them with Emerson and New England transcendentalism. He places them in "a large square house in the country" outside Boston, an eighty-year-old federalist house surrounded by magnificent trees and flowering shrubs, "basking in the abundant light and warmth" of a still Sabbath morning. Like Emily Dickinson's Emersonian House of Possibility, the Wentworth mansion keeps its doors "wide open, to admit the purifying sunshine." The house and the family are given austere integrity; Dickinson alluded to it in a letter once, saying, "An awkward loneliness smites me – I fear I must ask with Mr. Wentworth, 'Where are our moral foundations?' " (L 2.647). To suggest the devious charm of his European baroness, James associates her with draperies, candlelight, and shadow. But the honorable, ascetic, high-minded Mr. Wentworth dwells in a house any Luminist would be glad of, classic and "shining in the morning air."

Then, when it comes time in the novel to present her American suitor, Robert Acton, in serious conversation with Baroness Eugenia, James depicts them both as they drive through the "wild country" beyond the Wentworth property. Acton wants Eugenia "to think highly of American scenery" and of Americans. So James sketches a scene that in every detail resembles landscapes painted by Cole, Durand, Kensett, or the young Frederic Church:

> One day—it was late in the afternoon—Acton pulled up his horses on the crest of a hill which commanded a beautiful prospect. He let them stand a long time to rest, while he sat there and talked with Madame Münster. The prospect was beautiful in spite of there being nothing human within sight. There was a wilderness of woods, and the gleam of a distant river, and a glimpse of half the hill-tops in Massachusetts. The road had a wide, grassy margin, on the further side of which there flowed a deep, clear brook; there were wild flowers in the grass, and beside the brook lay the trunk of a fallen tree.[40]

Like Church's *Heart of the Andes,* James's landscape is a synthesis of attributes thought to represent the sublime and the beautiful in nature. The hill crest, the woods (described with that key term "wilderness"), the two roads—one made by the river, the other by man—the deep, clear brook, reminiscent of Walden Pond, and the wildflowers (subject of so many poetical articles, such as Higginson's for the *Atlantic*): all are allusions to contemporary landscape painting. The wilderness and wildflowers will presumably acquaint the urbane Eugenia with what is most precious in the United States, its pristine loveliness. Paintings like Church's superb *Twilight in the Wilderness* (1860) had served to illustrate Cole's devout belief that in the American wilderness there might still be seen the evidence of God's hand. "Wild flowers in the grass"— a contrast to the hothouse blooms with which Eugenia (like Hawthorne's Zenobia) is familiar—color the Hudson River and Luminist landscapes, appearing in Cole's *Childhood* and *Youth,* for example. James ends his description with what is an important leitmotif of this painting tradition, "the trunk of a fallen tree." The blasted tree was for Cole and his school a mark of the "terrible and grand,"[41] proof of the awesome energy of nature. The image of a split tree savaged by lightning was also an emblem of death when it was placed in a leafy landscape. John Wilmerding points out that there is a "perhaps surprising correlation between luminist imagery and the early writing of Henry James."[42] James had a passage about landscape in his story "A Landscape Painter," published in the *Atlantic Monthly* (1866) and probably read by Emily Dickinson. The passage above from *The Europeans* shows that, in 1878, James was still quoting the landscape tradition when he needed to define the American experience.

In her own poetic revelations of the beautiful and the sublime, Dickinson also included details that the tradition found representative. A poem she wrote around 1864 presents her attentive eye and unique voice, while its homely, intensely visualized scene full of movement has the eccentric animism and plainspoken mysteriousness of fairy tales. Dickinson did the poem in two versions. The first consists of twenty lines and is a fast-moving account of a rainstorm that ends with a picture of a blasted tree. A revision of the poem made in the same year sets it out in her usual quatrains. This was perhaps a stratagem by which she hoped to emphasize the vital disorder of the event by the contrast inherent in a tighter form. This second version, with its neat stanzas and greater abstraction, is elegant. The opening quatrain, for example, has a lovely plainness and finish:

> The Wind begun to rock the Grass
> With threatening Tunes and low –
> He threw a Menace at the Earth –
> A Menace at the Sky.

But I will give the first version Dickinson wrote, in which she makes more use of figures:

> The Wind begun to knead the Grass –
> As Women do a Dough –
> He flung a Hand full at the Plain –
> A Hand full at the Sky –
> The Leaves unhooked themselves from Trees –
> And started all abroad –
> The Dust did scoop itself like Hands –
> And throw away the Road –
> The Wagons quickened on the Street –
> The Thunders gossiped low –
> The Lightning showed a Yellow Head –
> And then a livid Toe –
> The Birds put up the Bars to Nests –
> The Cattle flung to Barns –
> Then came one drop of Giant Rain –
> And then, as if the Hands
> That held the Dams – had parted hold –
> The Waters Wrecked the Sky –
> But overlooked my Father's House –
> Just Quartering a Tree – (824)

The prevailing imagery in this poem is of hands. The wind has hands; the dust is like hands when it covers and obscures the road; finally, the sky is held together by hands, dams that part and flood it. The first conceit of the wind kneading the grass like women kneading dough is less metaphysical—or Luminist for that matter—than symbolist, fantastical. (One is reminded of such paintings as Walter Crane's *Neptune's Horses* [1893] in which the waves are equine or Gustav Klimt's women as waves in *Moving Waters* [1898].) Peopling the rivers, grass, and sky in art became by the mid-nineteenth century a means of personalizing nature but also of illustrating the presence of dangerous powers that could be invoked against mankind's. The wind is a power in Dickinson's poem even as Aeolus was. It is destructive, destroying the grass and hurling it over the plains and into the sky. No bread is made by this kneading, just as nothing is dressed or preserved. Instead the leaves, which in poem 987 are "like Women," unhook themselves as women do getting out of corsets; or like pieces of clothing, hung on hooks but able to break free. Dickinson's housewifery images of kneading and unhooking are joined when the dust "scoop[s] itself like Hands" to "throw away the Road." This sounds like housecleaning until one considers that, by violent internal contractions, the dust is scooping up and dissipating itself. With its own hands it is destroying itself as a road. Everything else inanimate also springs to life. Wagons quicken or hurry to shelter. (She uses the cognate of *quick*, with its biblical overtones of "the quick and the dead" in Acts 10:42.) Thunder gossips or gives out the secret of the coming storm. Suddenly there is a streak of lightning, such as Heade features in *Thunderstorm over Narragansett Bay* (1868). Dickinson's birds become householders, "putting up the Bars to Nests" just as mothers put up the bars to cribs so that their babies won't tumble out; or just as her schoolmaster in gray put up the "evening Bars" to pen in the sunset (318). Dickinson proves the immanence of the storm by saying that her cattle—the Dickinsons had horses and cows—"flung" into the barns with the speedy ease she usually attributes to smaller creatures such as bees. There is a warning drop of rain and then so much of it that the sky is like a wrecked house by comparison with her own house, which is unharmed.

Of course she calls the homestead "my Father's House," even as the land surrounding it is "my Father's ground" (L 3.460). The phrases rose from pride and punctilio as well as from a sense of insufficiency, perhaps; but there also seems to have been comfort for her in the safety they promised, implying as they did that she was still a protected, dependent child.

The poem ends with a classic nineteenth-century emblem of nature's fury in the line "Just Quartering a Tree." As a foreground or featured element, the quartered tree appeared in hundreds of canvases. Cole's *Manhood*, for example, encloses the turbulent sea with decapitated, shattered trees to the left and to the right. His views of *The Ox-Bow* or *Landscape with Tree Trunks* or *A Tornado* presented what Barbara Novak calls the "ubiquitous gnarled tree" as evidence of the mournful, exciting, dangerous experience that was life.[43] Dickinson's quartered tree as well as her rainstorm may well have been "real"; a great many of her letters report the weather, almost always with a consciousness that it represents more than just itself. The seasons were to her "travel," celestial and terrene (L 2.455), and she noted well their daily aspect. Still, like James in *The Europeans,* she often notes those aspects that the age imbued with significance. Her poem about the storm, like her poems about the stand of trees and the pine alone, contemplates the evidence in finite nature of the infinite.

9

In *Nature* and "The American Scholar" Emerson advised looking at horizons and remarking the slightest nuance of alteration in time and season as a discipline for the artist and a means of proving that natural and human moods correspond. The horizon was a point of order for landscape painters like Church. For poets like Dickinson, it was the point of fusion of this world and the next. The Hudson River and Luminist painters enjoyed presenting twilight or dawn on the horizon. Such scenes were less dramatic than the bonfire (as Dickinson regarded it in 1114) of the sunset, a charged moment that the painters depicted in hundreds of canvases. But dawn and twilight implied stillness, silence, the cloistral harmonies of a Nature attuned to God's will and readying herself to resign her inferior light to his on the Last Day. In the gray-gold or roseate suffusions of light above the dim horizon at dawn or evening could be seen the dim outlines of Jerusalem, the eternal city, even as the Victorian hymns promised in sacred equivalents of Leonardo's descriptions of palaces in the clouds.

Cole's *Voyage* presented the cloud-palace of *Youth,* floating without connection to the horizon and thus illusory and dooming the youth to disappointment. It is paralleled, however, in *Old Age* by the manifestation of descending angels who (as reproductions scarcely show) trace a ladderlike line from God to the wondering voyager. For many Victorian Americans, Cole's *Old Age* was thus the paradigm of that moment at which, accompanied by guardian angels, the soul was conducted into eternity. That instant of spiritual translation was for the Dickinson of "Because I could not stop for Death" of supreme importance. So it was for Cole, whose rivers of life lose themselves in many landscapes at a specific point of infinitude on a sea of eternity. The painterly techniques by which Cole managed (in oils) his fusions of real and ideal were more common to the watercolorists. Reverently adopted by Church, they characterized many of the latter's paintings. Indeed, Church's last important canvas, executed in 1877 after his influence had waned, paid a final tribute to Cole by perpetuating the theme of the river of light. Now called *Morning in the Tropics,* Church first entitled his painting *The River of Light.* The stream of life courses into its ultimate source in the heavens of eternity.

Dickinson's continual identification of life with light and both with the eternal sea shows her knowledge of Wordsworth, Emerson, Cole, and the nature artists of the nineteenth century. Remarkably, the physical disposition of many of her nature lyrics about light reveals methods similar to the painters', as if she were using such methods in words. Consider the following:

> As if the Sea should part
> And show a further Sea –
> And that – a further – and the Three
> But a presumption be –
>
> Of Periods of Seas –
> Unvisited of Shores –
> Themselves the Verge of Seas to be –
> Eternity – is Those – (695)

Analyzing the syntax of this poem, Brita Lindberg-Seyersted observes:

> The whole poem consists of one long and very intricate syntactic structure . . . a series of [implied] *as if*—clauses being strung one onto the other by the connective "and." . . . This is a remarkable example of successful manipulation of sentence structure to achieve poetic meaning. By using a syntactic structure which so to speak gropes its way toward its solution, the poet "imitates" the efforts of the mind to imagine and to formulate the concept of eternity. The aspect of eternity that above all she wished to convey is its immeasurable vastness. This is done by the accumulation of clauses and phrases which are not syntactically resolved, but left "open," not confined. It is also achieved by the gradual change from the singular to the plural form of the crucial noun "Sea."[44]

In Hudson River and Luminist landscapes, the compositional equilibrium achieved by meticulous arrangement of masses, the tonal gradations of light and, especially, the establishment of a foreground element—tree, mountain, ship—were aims and stratagems chosen to incorporate the idea of the supernatural in the earthly. "Sea and sky fuse in a mirrored union in which time stops"[45] and eternity begins. Even the foregrounded element, which was often the blasted tree or floundering sail, led the eye into the painting's apparently endless reaches. Such unlimited spaces Dickinson herself explained as "Vast Prairies of Air" (564).

Dickinson's "As if the Sea should part" has what corresponds to the painters' foregrounded element: the implicit clause "I imagined a final vastness." As in the case of other Dickinson lyrics, its lines then become like the receding levels of light in a Luminist seascape. In another poem, a similar technique appears:

> I cross till I am weary
> A Mountain – in my mind –
> More Mountains – then a Sea –
> More Seas – And then
> A Desert – find –
>
> And My Horizon blocks
> With steady – drifting – Grains
> Of unconjectured quantity –
> As Asiatic Rains – (550)

Certainly Dickinson could have been encouraged in this verbal technique by her knowledge of Cole and, probably, Church; but it may have been additionally stimulated through responsive awareness of other Hudson River and Luminist paintings like Sanford Gifford's *Sunset with Cows,* with its central motif of Cole's river of light.

Two of Dickinson's greatest poems of sublimated or renunciatory love are "There came a Day at Summer's full" (322) and "I cannot live with You" (640). In these poems, landscape or external reality is implied but superseded and then displaced by an austere landscape of the mind. Here *natural* light is not "poetized" through description, as Dickinson once told Sue she sought to do in her art (L 1.181). Instead light is conceptualized as understanding, passion, or grace. Such poems attempt primarily by means of syntax to translate the reader into the clear, windless light of the mind as it reasons or remembers. Dickinson's imagery (which is largely ecclesiastical but invested with meanings of her own) acts boldly to create a symbolic world, a sober theater of decision in which the light of understanding supplants natural light.

In "There came a Day at Summer's full," the natural setting—a garden in bloom?—is almost immediately beset and countermanded by emblems of the speaker's forbidden love: a sealed church, the supper of the Lamb, two decks. The poem's theme is love (its final word) that aspires to marriage in a context other than the earthly Christian one in which the speaker appears to believe:

> There came a Day at Summer's full,
> Entirely for me –
> I thought that such were for the Saints,
> Where Resurrections – be –
>
> The Sun, as common, went abroad,
> The flowers, accustomed, blew,
> As if no soul the solstice passed
> That maketh all things new –
>
> The time was scarce profaned, by speech –
> The symbol of a word
> Was needless, as at Sacrament,
> The Wardrobe – of our Lord –
>
> Each was to each The Sealed Church,
> Permitted to commune this – time –
> Lest we too awkward show
> At Supper of the Lamb.
>
> The Hours slid fast – as Hours will,
> Clutched tight, by greedy hands –
> So faces on two Decks, look back,
> Bound to opposing lands –
>
> And so when all the time had leaked,
> Without external sound
> Each bound the Other's Crucifix –
> We gave no other Bond –
>
> Sufficient troth, that we shall rise –
> Deposed – at length, the Grave –
> To that new Marriage,
> Justified – through Calvaries of Love – (322)

Dickinson's narrative takes place in the summer solstice, June 21–22, the season of weddings. On one hand, it describes a troth on earth that will be binding in a new marriage among the saints of heaven. On the other, it records a ceremony or compact of renunciation, akin to that embraced by those entering into religious life. Thus, when a Victorian novice took final vows, her crucifix was often "bound" or fastened on her breast as a sign of Christian witness but also of her calling as the spouse of Christ. In 322 the speaker and another act as sponsor and sponsored in taking up the cross to wear (instead of a wedding ring: "We gave no other Bond"). They have feelings for each other that— though doomed, apparently, in the temporal world—cannot be explained in any but religious terms, eucharistic and biblical. By the utterance of "Saints" and "Resurrections" the speaker calls on the imagery of Revelation to qualify the rural setting, the human context of her experience. This may have looked like an "accustomed" sunny day when her flowers bloomed as usual, but it has marked her own movement from spring to summer: from girlhood to womanhood, from the old life to the sacred new one.

A flicker of information about a possible human situation resumes when Dickinson's speaker remembers, "The Hours slid fast – as Hours will / Clutched tight, by greedy hands." Then her description moves once again into the symbolic and comparative: "So faces on two Decks, look back." She is on the emblematic sea of life and suffering. The garden sunshine gives way to a scene of separation as of indentured servants "bound to," as well as for, "opposing lands," one that recalls the narrative of "They put Us far apart" (474) wherein the forbidden lovers are executed at sea in sight of each other and paradise. "There came a Day at Summer's full" concludes without alluding again to a specific occasion. The poet's "Each was to each" gives little sense of the lover's personality. He (probably not she: religious imagery appears more frequently for Master) is simply her partner in sublimation and expectation. The poem is not about earthly but heavenly illumination.

In "I cannot live with You" there is no landscape at all and no real place. Dickinson's vision of forms here is wholly emblematic:

> I cannot live with You –
> It would be Life –
> And Life is over there –
> Behind the Shelf
>
> The Sexton keeps the Key to –
> Putting up
> Our Life – His Porcelain –
> Like a Cup –

Discarded of the Housewife –
Quaint – or Broke –
A newer Sevres pleases –
Old Ones crack –

I could not die – with You –
For One must wait
To shut the Other's Gaze down –
You – could not –

And I – Could I stand by
And see You – freeze –
Without my Right of Frost –
Death's privilege?

Nor could I rise – with You –
Because Your Face
Would put out Jesus' –
The New Grace

Glow plain – and foreign
On my homesick Eye –
Except that You than He
Shone closer by –

They'd judge Us – How –
For You – served Heaven – You know,
Or sought to –
I could not –

Because You saturated Sight –
And I had no more Eyes
For sordid excellence
As Paradise

And were You lost, I would be –
Though My Name
Rang loudest
On the Heavenly fame –

And were You – saved –
And I – condemned to be
Where You were not –
That self – were Hell to Me –

So We must meet apart –
You there – I – here –
With just the door ajar

That Oceans are – and Prayer –
And that White Sustenance –
Despair – (640)

In this commanding lyric, whose dark and harrowing logic has made it
a model of poetic argument, there are few images. There is the sexton's
shelf, not only set apart "over there" but locked; there is porcelain *like*
a cup; and both necessarily imply the presence of a church, in which
the sacrament or at least the holy vessels are kept. But once again, as
in 322, these images are metaphors of a spiritual and emotional reality.
The poem's real power derives from its carefully reasoned dismissal or
forfeiture of human life with all of its actual visual forms, and from its
election of a state of mind counter to happiness, even—theologically
speaking—to salvation: Despair. The opening lines "I cannot live with
You – It would be Life" remind us that Dickinson was quite familiar
with the arguments and proposals of Elizabethan poetry ("Come live
with me and be my love") and that she herself was most powerful as a
poet when speaking directly and in a deceptively simple fashion. Her
poem provides an ironic answer to all such blandishments as Christopher Marlowe's, and one feels the speaker's longing, exasperation, and
resignation in each of the lines that follow. Once again the ecclesiastical
imagery of sexton, shelf, and porcelain cup join with the doctrinal
concepts of paradise, heaven, and hell to make this poem describe the
surrender of a love that is morally forbidden. (It is the sexton who locks
up life like a discarded cup, and he it is who keeps order in the church.)
Dickinson's extended comparison of the lovers' life—that is, the life of
their love—to old cups "Quaint – or Broke" implies its unsuitability
but long duration. "A newer Sevres pleases" recalls "A Different Peru"
in her poem for Sue, "Your Riches – taught me – Poverty" (299); it
makes the same claim as that phrase does in the context of 299, observing that "Old [loves] crack" or lose value. Dickinson's life with all
its amorous possibilities is then a eucharistic cup, shelved.

Like "It was not Death, for I stood up" (510), with its trinity of
denials, "I cannot live with You" follows a disciplined pattern of argument so that the misery of the speaker and the ravage of her hopes
are only heightened by her self-control. "I cannot live with You"; "I
could not die – with You"; "Nor could I rise – with You"—these are
inevitably the three experiences the speaker usually imagines sharing
with the one she loves, whether that be Master or the beloved woman.
But this poem, with its focus on the light of the lover's countenance,

eclipsing Christ's, shares in the image patterns assigned to Master. That he is able to outshine the Light of the World is one of the blasphemies that earned Christina Rossetti's censure; but the poem derives great consequence from the speaker's painful, and acknowledged, recklessness. She calls paradise "sordid," its light soiled and vile to her eyes, "saturated" (sighted for one thing only) with passion. Hell and heaven have no meaning for her except as descriptions of the lover's absence or presence. She recognizes these circumstances to be disruptive of all harmony, on earth or in the world of the spirit, and ends her poem with the brilliant paradoxes declaring that passion never dies.

To "meet apart with door ajar" is a concept taken from the very pattern of Dickinson's daily life by 1862. She met people behind doorways; she met them in letters; she met them by sending herself in spirit to their rooms. Here, though, the doors ajar between the lovers are "another" trinity: oceans, prayer, and the white sustenance—like the white communion host—of despair. There are no true visual realities or experiential possibilities in this poem. The speaker's terrible last word is followed by her strategically placed dash, suggesting that her voice is resting and may speak again, even more bleakly still.

Mrs. Todd substituted "pale" for "white" in *Poems* (1890), but the poet intended her allusion to whiteness, an allusion suitable not only to the legend (under construction) of her own life but to the Luminist visions, in which white might mean death of the material and continuity of the celestial. Dickinson's preoccupation with light, with degrees of silence, and with marginal distinctions between life and death, action and repose, was characteristically Luminist, as is apparent in:

> I heard a Fly buzz – when I died –
> The Stillness in the Room
> Was like the Stillness in the Air –
> Between the Heaves of Storm –
>
> The Eyes around – had wrung them dry –
> And Breaths were gathering firm
> For that last Onset – when the King
> Be witnessed – in the Room –
>
> I willed my Keepsakes – Signed away
> What portion of me be
> Assignable – and then it was
> There interposed a Fly –

> With Blue – uncertain stumbling Buzz –
> Between the light – and me –
> And then the Windows failed – and then
> I could not see to see – (465)

Dickinson's audacious opening line demands that her reader listen to the remembrance of a dead person whose consciousness has so survived the transitus that it can describe for us the first step of that journey. The speaker isolates the precise moment of her death as the failure of light: not only of daylight but of the ocular mechanism by which light is received, and (by analogy) of the light of the spirit. Just as this happens, however, and the windows fail—that is, the apertures of the house darken as do those of her body's house, her eyes—she hears a buzzing fly. The sound of it is grotesquely loud amid the stillness of the death-bed scene, whose company of mourners is already wrung dry and ready for the last act, the onset of death. All has proceeded so far with ceremony, even to the willing of keepsakes, while what is expected is the storm of dissolution, the sublime moment of passage. Instead, the speaker relates, the last thing she sees on earth is that household nuisance, a blue-bottle fly, its stupid aimlessness a suggestion of the puzzlement that is life as well as its homely sweetness. In such poems Emily Dickinson investigates the nature of consciousness by analyzing its recession.

The ultimate "recession" that Luminism attempted to describe by its planar harmonies was fusion with what Emerson called the Oversoul. The ultimate sublime for the Luminist (as for painters like Cole) was a stillness that suggested peace after death. Again and again, as in "I heard a Fly buzz," Dickinson describes the moment of translation out of life into eternity. Sometimes she is in bed when it happens; sometimes she is on a road and a carriage stops for her; sometimes she is—on the village green, standing before the houses? in bed imagining them?—in a "place" that is best described as a passage, simply, between light and dark:

> The Sun kept setting – setting – still
> No Hue of Afternoon –
> . . . . .
> The Dusk kept dropping – dropping – still
> No Dew upon the Grass –
> . . . . .
> My Feet kept drowsing – drowsing – still
> My fingers were awake –

Yet why so little sound – Myself
Unto my Seeming – make?

How well I knew the Light before –
I could see it now –
'Tis Dying – I am doing – but
I'm not afraid to know – (692)

Like many of her poems written about the death scenes of other women,
Dickinson's lyric 692 is muted, as if to describe the fading of consciousness. The repetition of "still" conveys the impression of life that only
just persists. Yet the final stillness and tranquility that Luminism sought
to achieve are not conveyed here as they are suggested by poem 456's
"I could not see to see"; for Dickinson's persistent "I" survives the
experience of dying.

Her most ambitious poem about dying describes light and the translated consciousness. Dickinson's poem 721 appears in fascicle 36, together with her ghostly fantasy about death, "Dropped into the Ether
Acre" (665). Both poems are surreal, but 721 has an energy, suavity,
vehemence, and exultation that result in true majesty. Here she is at the
center of her canvas, a voyager like Cole's, but in a landscape even
more dramatic and theatrical than his:

Behind Me – dips Eternity –
Before Me – Immortality –
Myself – the Term between –
Death but the Drift of Eastern Gray,
Dissolving into Dawn away,
Before the West begin –

'Tis Kingdoms – afterward – they say –
In perfect – pauseless Monarchy –
Whose Prince – is Son of None –
Himself – His Dateless Dynasty –
Himself – Himself diversify –
In Duplicate divine –

'Tis Miracle before Me – then –
'Tis Miracle behind – between –
A Crescent in the Sea –
With Midnight to the North of Her –
And Midnight to the South of Her –
And Maelstrom – in the Sky –

Charles Anderson, in a beautifully conceived passage, studies its first stanza to show that the very shape of this poem symbolizes the pattern of Dickinson's best work. "The pure light of immortality," he says,

> shines behind this poem though it never materializes in the text. Taking advantage of an orientation traditional in her civilization, she looks backward towards the east as the source of all light and life, glances towards the west as the soul's ultimate destination, then fixes her attention on the dark span that lies between . . . Over the horizon behind "dips Eternity," the timelessness before her consciousness existed; over the horizon in front looms "Immortality," the future timelessness into which her consciousness will survive. Her gaze is for the moment so fixed on these two radiant zones she has no words for the mortal existence she actually knows. This is lightly bypassed as the "Term between," the allotted three score years of man.[46]

As Anderson says, the poem contains an apocalypse in its central stanza. I would add that in its last stanza it depicts the same images that many painters employed in order to suggest the awful passage from life into eternity. Maelstrom and midnight, a crescent in the sea: these may be seen in scores of Luminist and Hudson River landscapes from Cole's *Ox-Bow* to Church's *Storm in the Mountains (Blasted Tree)* or Heade's *Thunderstorm over Narragansett Bay.*

"Behind Me – dips Eternity" comes also as near as any poem in the Dickinson canon to being a provisional but heroic hymn. With characteristic reservation in the phrase "they say," it repeats as in a chant what Dickinson has learned: that there is a Trinity in which many believe. (And, for the purpose of the poem, she includes herself among the believers.) In her second stanza there is a variation upon the ancient Nicene Creed, which professes the central Christian mysteries. Dickinson's "perfect pauseless Monarchy" renders the creed's one God, "Whose kingdom shall have no end." Her lines "Whose Prince – is Son of None – / Himself – His Dateless Dynasty – / Himself – Himself diversify – / In Duplicate divine" evoke the creed's "one Lord Jesus Christ, the only-begotten Son of God; Begotten of His Father before all worlds, God of God, Light of Light . . . Begotten, not made; Being of one substance with the Father." And her "Kingdoms afterward" inflects (however guardedly) the creed's declaration of "the Life of the world to come."

But Dickinson's poem is more concerned with the cataclysmic fission of body and soul than with any prospect of peaceful rest in paradise. Like the creed or the doxology that celebrates the Trinity, this poem contemplates the association between a terrific but enduring God whose person is "diversified" and the created soul. Yet it is still fascinated by nature, which has been brought to the furthest point of its power to illuminate and reveal: nature, in fact, which has itself become a trinity of aspects—three midnights, North, South, and the horizontal Maelstrom. Dickinson presents her belief here that death is merely one aspect of landscape: "the drift of Eastern Gray, / Dissolving into Dawn away" before the west or afterlife. In this way, and because of her focus on the dateless deity, she writes a lyric akin to Protestant hymns like Isaac Watts's "O God Our Help in Ages Past," with its fourth stanza that rather bleakly contemplates the effacement of all Time's sons in one river of eternity and one evening.

Dickinson's poem as a painting about apocalyptic light inspires awe, for the persona—unlike the speaker (also dying) in the carriage in "Because I could not stop for Death"—is unprotected by any human contrivance from the natural elements which flash and fan out and dissolve against the sky. One understands her body to be pitched anyhow against the translating horizon. She is so defenseless as to be depersonalized into a "Term." As a term, however, she is a "word," related to the "Word . . . made Flesh" of John 1:14—Christ, assumed into the sky; and within the grandeur and terror that compose the sublimity of her experience, there is also rapture. Her self-portrait in poem 721 resembles no nineteenth-century painting so much as it anticipates the disjunctive, surreal paintings of such modernists as Yves Tanguy, abstract and yet figurative. The reader deduces that the poet's consciousness has passed like lightning into a comprehension of eternal revelation.

This was to push landscape painting to its limit, and here Dickinson's dash after "Sky" suggests that "hyphen" (1454) which she conceived death to be. For her—in ways obviously unique—nature and eternity were reflexive and reflective of each other. It was her continual design to observe and report their mutual illumination. She wrote to Helen Jackson in 1884 (L 3.840), "The Summer has been wide and deep, and a deeper Autumn is but the Gleam concomitant of that waylaying Light."

⁓ 6 ⁓

Art as Life

> When Time's course closed, and Death was encountered at
> the end, barring with fleshless arm the portals of Eternity, how
> Genius still held close his dying bride, sustained her through
> the agony of the passage, bore her triumphant into his own
> home—heaven; restored her, redeemed, to Jehovah—her
> maker; and at last, before Angel and Archangel, crowned her
> with the crown of Immortality.
>
> —Charlotte Brontë, *Shirley* (1849)

In April 1884 a statue of John Harvard by Daniel Chester French (1850–1931) was unveiled in Harvard Yard. French was the son of a prominent New England lawyer; as a boy he lived in Amherst. His family were friends of Susan Dickinson, and he himself was a favorite of Emily Dickinson's Norcross cousins. French's statue of *The Minute Man* (1874), commissioned by fellow townsfolk of Concord, made him famous. He would go on to sculpt some of the best-known statues in the United States—not only *John Harvard* but the seated portrait for the *Lincoln* memorial (dedicated in 1922). Sue and the Norcrosses must have kept Emily acquainted with developments in the career of the fifteen-year-old Danny French she once knew. The Dickinsons had affectionate ties with Harvard.[1] When the statue was unveiled, Dickinson was apparently moved by French's success in so distinguished a sphere. She wrote to him,

> Dear Mr. French: –
> We learn with delight of the recent acquisition to your fame, and hasten to congratulate you on an honor so reverently won.
> Success is dust, but an aim forever touched with dew.
> God keep you fundamental!
>
> > Circumference, thou bride
> > Of awe, – possessing, thou

314

Shalt be possessed by
Every hallowed knight
That dares to covet thee.

Yours faithfully,
Emily Dickinson (L 3.822)

Her letter was preserved by French's family and, indeed, it is among the most significant and touching of the letters, especially if one considers her circumstances when it was written. In 1884 she was just two years from death and, for the most part, unknown as a poet. French was only thirty-four, with one triumph behind him and many others ahead. There can be no more public art, perhaps, than commemorative sculpture; unlike some other public art forms—music or theater—it aspires to material continuity and permanence. French's statues would stand in the open, buffeted by winds and snow. They were images whose very purpose was publicity: to proclaim the enduring greatness of a public man. By their nature, then, French's calling and work were distant from the remarkably private life and art of the woman who addressed him. Yet Dickinson's letter salutes French as (he may not have known) a fellow artist. From her triple isolation as a recluse, an elderly and dependent spinster, and a poet whose eccentricities were better known than her verses, she offered him a few words of advice.

Thus: honor was to be "reverently won." She assumes that he has done so, but her earnest phrase reminds him of it. The honor of being chosen to do the statue is conflated with the honor that belongs to artists when they are faithful to the sacred mission of telling all the truth in the "slant" way that is Art itself. To win such honor in poetry, if only in her own mind, Dickinson had worked very hard. She realized that an artist must be satisfied with the artifact; otherwise, its recognition by others is hollow, even nugatory. She had written, about twenty years earlier,

Fame of Myself, to justify,
All other Plaudit be
Superfluous – An Incense
Beyond Necessity –

Fame of Myself to lack – Although
My Name be else Supreme –
This were an Honor honorless –
A futile Diadem – (713)

Such austere advice might appropriately be given to sculptors, who are especially vulnerable to the public taste by a need for commissions; but it implies Dickinson's proud, self-reliant avoidance of any praise that might be earned by a violation of aesthetic vision. And it reminds us once again of the limitations of those who surrounded her when it came to reading her poetry. Of people with literary connections—the essayist Higginson, the editors Samuel Bowles and Josiah Holland, the novelist Helen Hunt Jackson and her sister-in-law Sue—only the two women intuited Dickinson's greatness. Jackson begged Dickinson repeatedly to accept her help in publishing. "You are a great poet," she wrote, accusing her of being stingy in keeping back her poems:

> What portfolios of verses you must have.—
> It is a cruel wrong to your "day & generation" that you will not give them light.—if such a thing should happen as that I should outlive you, I wish you would make me your literary legatee & executor. Surely, after you are what is called "dead," you will be willing that the poor ghosts you have left behind, should be cheered and pleased by your verses, will you not?—You ought to be.—I do not think we have a right to withhold from the world a word or a thought any more than a *deed,* which might help a single soul.[2]

This enthusiasm resulted in the anonymous appearance of "Success is counted sweetest" in *Masque of Poets.* Other poems of the 1860s were "stolen" by Sue or Bowles for the *Springfield Republican.* Just after she married, Sue compared inaugurating Emily's career to launching the ship *Burnside*: she was its promoter but it was taking too much time.[3] Jackson's clever appeal to Dickinson's thoughtfulness for others was matched in later years by requests that she lend poems to charitable publications. From such entreaties Dickinson always fled, securing the intervention and assistance of Colonel Higginson. She asked him on one occasion, "May I tell [Mrs. Jackson] . . . that you dont prefer it?" It seemed to her "sordid" to refuse requests for poems on her own account. (L 2.566). But refuse she must, and did. She seems to have perceived that any interest shown in her poetry by Higginson and Bowles originated, finally, in personal affection. By the mid-1860s Sue's admiration did not include encouragements to publish. And there is evidence that Dickinson recognized the difference between her poetic language and the popular verse of her day:

> Honor is then the safest hue
> In a posthumous Sun –

Not any color will endure
That scrutiny can burn (1671)

In her copy of Emerson's *Poems* she put an X next to "Woodnotes," with its lines

> For this present, hard
> Is the fortune of the bard,
>   Born out of time;
> All his accomplishment,
> From Nature's utmost treasure spent,
>   Booteth not him.

Thus there was a persuasive logic in Dickinson's various allusions to the inner security a poet requires: "Himself – to Him – a Fortune – / Exterior – to Time" (448). Her words to French, "We learn with delight of . . . your fame," came from the same hand that had written, so realistically, a few years earlier,

> Fame is the one that does not stay –
> It's occupant must die
> Or out of sight of estimate
> Ascend incessantly –
> Or be that most insolvent thing
> A Lightning in the Germ –
> Electrical the embryo
> But we demand the Flame (1475)

In this poem she grouped herself, as usual, with the "we" who are not famous or, as in "This was a Poet" (448), not artists. Yet I think she may have hoped that she was the lightning in the germ of another age; hence she left no instructions to her sister Lavinia to destroy the locked box containing seven hundred poems. The famous letter she sent to Higginson when he told her to "delay 'to publish'" is tinged with romantic grandiosity, as well as Puritan reserve, but it seems wholly sincere:

> If fame belonged to me, I could not escape her – if she did not, the longest day would pass me on the chase – and the approbation of my Dog, would forsake me – then – My Barefoot-Rank is better (L 2.408)

She had great belief in herself, if we take her first sentence seriously. Yet she must also have known her art to be "insolvent" in such a marketplace as the Boston or New York of her lifetime. There Bowles's associate Holland, who also recommended that Dickinson not publish, had been able to sell to *Scribner's* the following lines for his dog. Dickinson read them aloud in 1881 to her delighted mother and Vinnie "at their request" (L 3.706):

> Did I sit fondly at His feet,
> As you, dear Blanco, sit at mine,
> And watch Him with a love as sweet,
> My life would grow divine!

Her only acknowledgment of the verse's bathos was a witty remark to Elizabeth Holland, "Doctor's betrothal to 'Blanco' I trust you bear unmurmuringly" (L 3.706).

"Success is dust," she tells French, "but an aim forever touched with dew." This line, like the remaining sentences in her letter, contains words she endowed with special meaning. Perhaps her most anthologized poem would be the clear-sighted and bittersweet "Success is counted sweetest / By those who ne'er succeed" (67). When *Poems* (1890) appeared, it was placed on the first page. It drew its imagery from two wars: the Civil War and that war—also "civil" or between two compulsions or forces—fought by those "Who charge within the bosom / The Cavalry of Woe" (126). "Success is counted sweetest" was probably written when Dickinson was only twenty-nine. Its sad wisdom embraces her remark to French a quarter of a century later. Success is dust because it is as capricious as fame; it is associated with death, since only the ruined and dying really understand or (vicariously) experience it:

> Not one of all the purple Host
> Who took the Flag today
> Can tell the definition
> So clear of Victory
>
> As he defeated – dying –
> On whose forbidden ear
> The distant strains of triumph
> Burst agonized and clear!

Nevertheless, success is "an aim forever touched with dew," and *dew* is a word that Dickinson had long associated with creativity. Artists want to be successful; it is only natural. "Dew" belongs to fresh mornings full of new chances; it is akin to inspiration; it is nature's baptismal grace. Dickinson's letter cautions French that success may fade and is valuable only as an aim, an incitement to creation. Still (living in the America of Horace Greeley) she recognizes it to be a lure "forever."

If French had read her poems, as is unlikely, Dickinson's prayer "God keep you fundamental" might have seemed to him especially persuasive. *Fundamental* is one of her touchstones for poetry; she uses it revealingly in five poems (997, 1106, 1205, 1295, 1744). To be fundamental means to be essential, to remember the foundations of things, to look into their component parts and disclose the harmony of the whole. Her choice of the word in this specific instance, in speaking to a sculptor, is wonderfully apt. She tells French to remember the basic materials with which he works. Marble, brass, or stone, they are all describable in the end as "earth." She hopes he will be an honest artist, true to the humble elements he must employ, and true to life.

Her deeply felt exclamation leads to a verse that includes several other critical Dickinson terms: circumference, bride, awe, knight. From her isolation she addresses the famous youth in words that show her own long intimacy with the muse:

> Circumference, thou bride
> Of awe, – possessing, thou
> Shalt be possessed by
> Every hallowed knight
> That dares to covet thee.

I have said that it is characteristic of Dickinson to trace artistic inspiration to love. Even more, she associates it with marriage. Her word "circumference" generally means either poetry itself or the significance of all that exists, on earth and in heaven. She marries it here to awe: the respectful fear or veneration that should be chief dweller in God's universe. The poetry or circumference of things possesses every knight— art, like chivalry, is a noble venture—who dares to know it, in the biblical (sexual) sense of coveting. Yet this coveting and possession of the bride Circumference are not wrong, for the knight is hallowed, honorable. Her words, then, tell French that he must be honorably married to the muse, to "poetry" or beauty and truth. She signs her letter with the rare "Faithfully," a word that implies commitment, not only to her friend French but to the ideals expressed in her letter.

In her last years, speaking of aesthetics, she talked with authority. Love was increasingly her subject, love as the essential element in all understanding. To her nephew Ned, on vacation in the Adirondacks, she wrote, "Your intimacy with the Mountains I heartily endorse – Ties

more Eleusinian I must leave to you – Deity will guide you – I do not
mean Jehovah – The little God with Epaulettes" (L 3.880). Eros with
his bow and arrows would come to Ned's aid; she hoped he would
marry. But nature, art, and love were commingled for her; whether
advising nephews or sculptors, she insisted on the connection. Much of
her advice was given to young men. Samuel Bowles Jr. was marrying
in 1883. She congratulated him with words echoing Revelation 21:21
that included her old symbol for bliss associated with his father, Eden:
"Every several Gate is of one Pearl" (L 3.796). A poem she sent him
resembles her lines for French. Written within a few months of one
another, each lyric declares the importance of love to life and art. Her
poem for Bowles's son—a writer and journalist and therefore an aspi-
rant to the artistic life—enjoins,

> Lad of Athens, faithful be
> To Thyself,
> And Mystery –
> All the rest is Perjury (L 3.797)

As she did with French, Dickinson exhorts Bowles to be true to his
own vision and yet to the mystery of creation. Athens was the great
seat of classical civilization, the home of everyone who loved learning.
The subtext of her poem is another, however, which was written by
Lord Byron in 1810:

> Maid of Athens, ere we part,
> Give, oh give me back my heart!
> Or, since that has left my breast,
> Keep it now, and take the rest!

Byron's pledge to his Greek maid is "My life, I love you." By appealing
to it in her poem for young Bowles, Dickinson is alluding once again
to the metaphor of passionate vows that orders her poem for French.
To all her "Kingdom of [young] Knights" (L 3.876), with their futures
before them, the aging Emily Dickinson wrote that love and honor are
requisite to artistic endeavor.

2

Yet Dickinson herself was not a knight and, despite her many allusions
to Emily as a boy or to poets as *he,* it was as a woman writer that she
had to confront herself. In the 1860s she wore her hair in side curls, as

Elizabeth Barrett Browning did. Her elegies for her and for Charlotte
Brontë show the ardor of her respectful identification with them. Cynthia Griffin Wolff offers the moving irony that the homestead built and
kept by those overbearing and officious Dickinson men, Emily's father
and grandfather, is now called the *Emily* Dickinson House, a translation
wrought by the art of a woman. In the last decade in particular, important attention has been paid to Dickinson's perception of herself as
a woman writer with ties of love and thought and (sometimes) shared
anger to other women writers in a tradition that includes her favorites:
not only the Brontës and Barrett Browning but George Eliot and George
Sand.

Dickinson marked a passage in Barrett Browning's *Aurora Leigh*
that, like so many of her flagged passages, seems apposite to her own
life:

> I may love my art.
> You'll grant that even a woman may love art,
> Seeing that to waste true love on any thing
> Is womanly, past question. (2.494–497)

The irony and sarcasm in this passage were surely not "wasted" on
Dickinson. Other lines in that feminist poem were similarly marked:

> By the way,
> The works of women are symbolical.
> We sew, sew, prick our fingers, dull our sight,
> Producing what? A pair of slippers, sir,
> To put on when you're weary, or a stool
> To stumble over, and vex you – "Curse that stool!"
> Or else, at best, a cushion, where you lean
> And sleep, and dream of something we are not,
> But would be for your sake. Alas, alas!
> This hurts most, this – that after all we are paid
> The worth of our work, perhaps. (1.455–465)

One can only guess how much subtle damage may have been done
to Dickinson's ambition by the usual Victorian assumption that a lady's
place was at her embroidery, not her desk; or that if she painted or
wrote, it should be for decoration or moral suasion. She read Emerson's
essays repeatedly at the outset of her career. What was the subliminal
effect of always encountering the masculine pronoun without variation:
"The poet . . . He is a sovereign, and stands on the centre"? Emerson's
essay "The Poet" acknowledges nothing female but nature. Higginson,

at least, included women among his poetic "Young Contributors," although he did so reluctantly.[4]

Susan Dickinson was to write Colonel Higginson after the appearance of *Poems* (1890) that her sister-in-law had not published because "in her own words (after all the intoxicating fascination of creation) she as deeply realized that for her as for all us women not fame but 'Love and home and certainty are best.'"[5] Publication was an auction that gentlewomen did not supply; it was all right to create but not to "invest – Our Snow" (709). Sue herself, of course, attempted to sell as many of Emily's poems in her possession as she could after 1890, competing with Lavinia, who received royalties on the first three volumes. She observed to Higginson, even as she sent off one poem after another, "I sometimes shudder when I think of the world reading her thoughts minted in deep heartbroken convictions . . . I find myself always saying 'poor Emily.'" As the wife of a wealthy lawyer—one who never denied her material comforts though he no longer loved her—Sue did not need the occasional fifteen dollars paid her by magazines like the *Century* for a Dickinson poem. But she did need to lay claim to the poet. As she said, "I think this much is due myself—my life long intimacy with Emily, my equally long deep appreciation of her genius." That appreciation had not been expressed in pressure to publish after the early 1860s; nor did she take any step to bring the poems to print until Lavinia—and Austin, helped by Mabel Todd—had done so. Stung into rivalry with the other Dickinsons, Sue wrote a revealing sentence to Higginson: "'The Poems' will ever be to me marvellous whether in manuscript or type." To have written them, she meant, was enough. Dickinson's poems themselves make such a point repeatedly. Such idealism, however, was as much the result of Dickinson's temperament and circumstances as of rooted conviction.

Dickinson wrote, probably in 1877,

> To earn it by disdaining it
> Is Fame's consummate Fee –
> He loves what spurns him –
> Look behind – He is pursuing thee (1427)

It was a sibylline observation, for the posthumous publication of *Poems* was attended by extraordinary success. One might argue that Dickinson did what she could, given the censure of Higginson and the rest, to ensure for herself some portion of immortality. (Not for fame but for immortality she expressed a deep wish.[6]) Sending her poems to so many different people may have been one stratagem for achieving it. As Karen Dandurand has discovered, it resulted in wider publication of Dickinson's poetry during her lifetime than was earlier supposed; friends took lyrics from her letters and submitted them to local newspapers.[7] Did she hope they would?

When Dickinson spoke about poetry and its composition, moreover, she spoke as an authority, for all her modesty; and, ironically, she spoke in images associated with women and women's lives. Thus three of her most important poems about the nature of literary art take power from women's experiences. In poem 675, for example, she might be describing her own poetic method of compression and the necessity for the specific image. But her metaphysical metaphors come from the world of perfumes and sachet:

> Essential Oils – are wrung –
> The Attar from the Rose
> Be not expressed by Suns – alone –
> It is the gift of Screws –
>
> The General Rose – decay –
> But this – in Lady's Drawer
> Make Summer – When the Lady lie
> In Ceaseless Rosemary (675)

The poem begins, as Dickinson often likes to begin, with a thesis: to get at what's essential, there must be a cutting away of superfluities; such emphasis or condensation involves pressure or, by analogy, pain. To make perfume from roses—to capture life's beauty in the permanency of a poem—one needs not only to be inspired ("suns") but formal ("screws"). There is, the poem implies, good reason to make such costly effort. For art transcends nature by endowing it with lasting life. Roses decay in a continuous present that nature cannot escape. This art of perfume (or of her poem), however, preserves the essence of roses. Though a lady lies in her grave, the sachet lying in her drawer smells of the summers she knew when alive. Poems, like sachet, ensure "Ceaseless Rosemary": endless remembrance—since rosemary connotes this in the language of flowers—for women, as for roses.

In "This was a Poet" Dickinson also speaks of making poems as distilling perfume. Her well-known poem indirectly attributes artistry to men by speaking of the poet, finally, as "He." Its accents evoke Emerson's "The Poet." Yet they were her own accents, her own terms, as well. One critic argues that her suppressed discomfort with such a prejudice in gender results in the awkward "It is That" of her opening line.[8] I think, rather, that it reflects her definition of the poet as a nearly suprapersonal asexual force. She was not troubled by the classical use of the masculine gender merely as the first of two sexual possibilities. Like most brilliant and ambitious women (in and before her time and even now), she would have read "she" for "he." More than for most women poets, that was easy for Emily Dickinson to do. The artist, however, transcends sex in this poem. Still the wearing, if not the making, of perfumes is usually thought of as feminine and, as in the case of 675, the beautiful is associated with women. So is art ("sense" with "scents"):

> This was a Poet – It is That
> Distills amazing sense
> From ordinary Meanings –
> And Attar so immense
>
> From the familiar species
> That perished by the Door –
> We wonder it was not Ourselves
> Arrested it – before (448)

The familiar species, Dickinson's wildflowers and gentians, dotting the grass of dooryards are the homely reality that poetry renders full of wonder. Poets are able to arrest such reality (she often regards beauty as worthy of "chase"), and thus they make the familiar, even the "perished," imperishable. Though her third quatrain declares,

> The Poet – It is He –
> Entitles Us – by Contrast –
> To ceaseless Poverty –

it is once again women who come to mind with flowers and perfumes, so that they are also associated with the preservation and refinement of simple truths. But her line "The Poet – It is He," with its curiously legalistic and determined syntax, achieves an almost neutral definite.

Finally, her lyric "The Poets light but Lamps," with its declaration of faith in the endurance of true art, has for a central conceit the feeding of oil lamps. This was usually a Victorian woman's task, and in her father's house it was often Dickinson's:

> The Poets light but Lamps –
> Themselves – go out –

The Wicks they stimulate –
If vital Light

Inhere as do the Suns –
Each Age a Lens
Disseminating their
Circumference – (883)

Like many others, this poem associates light on earth and the light of
art with the light of truth. Poets die, "go out," but they leave behind
the wicks or twisted fibers by which oil may be conducted, bringing
flame to other lamps. That is, they are inspirations to other poets. The
lens or prismatic glass surrounding a lamp is the enlargement in reputation the good poet experiences in "Each Age." Her symbol of circumference concludes the poem: the circle of light cast by a lamp is likened
to poetry, the sum of meaning. Set in the larger context of Dickinson's
oeuvre, this poem is touching; for in "I was the slightest in the House"
(486), she described herself, as I have said, with "my little Lamp, and
Book," working with great industry, yet "noteless[ly]."

In a poem that includes a dream vision about the practical act of
sewing, Dickinson gives us insight into the woman writer who marked
Aurora Leigh's passage about needlework: "We sew, sew . . . " Her
speaker has made blunders at her sewing because, like the lovesick
gardener of 339, she is preoccupied, perhaps aggrieved. The poem
contrasts the precision that sewing requires with the disorientation of
the speaker. It begins by protesting that she really *will* return to life as
it should be led. She tries to stop someone from laying away her sewing
articles:

Don't put up my Thread & Needle –
I'll begin to Sow
When the Birds begin to whistle –
Better Stitches – so –

These were bent – my sight got crooked –
When my mind – is plain
I'll do seams – a Queen's endeavor
Would not blush to own – (617)[9]

This persona is well acquainted with the skill of sewing: she can do
straight seams and fine hems with sightless knots; she knows tucking
and how to fetch a seam. She'll do it all when morning, or happiness,
comes back. A great many of Dickinson's poems eschew specific gender;

the persona speaks with sexless freedom. But poems like this one remind us of the womanliness that Emily Dickinson's speaker may candidly acknowledge.

Her characteristic punctuation in poem 617 also provokes some conjecture. When Thomas Johnson presented the *Complete Poems* to the public, he restored not only the capital letters used by the poet so liberally but the unorthodox punctuation for which she is now well known. Previous Dickinson texts had universally regularized the grammar and appearance of her poems. Indeed, so intrusive was the meddling of Mabel Todd and Martha Dickinson Bianchi that some Dickinson poems were published shorn of lines and even stanzas, while exact rhymes were substituted for the poet's off-rhymes with occasional execrable defeats of meaning.[10] Since the publication of Johnson's text, Dickinson's "dashes" have been taken seriously. R. W. Franklin reminds us that they are not precisely dashes but marks "of various lengths resembling a dash that tilt up and down as frequently as [they are] level." Furthermore, "because of her handwriting, it is often difficult to tell a comma from a dash and a dash from a lengthened period. Such punctuation cannot be reproduced exactly in type."[11]

Discerning the possible distinction between the dash-as-comma/period and the dash-as-dash is only one of many problems encountered by someone working with the manuscripts of this "poet of the portfolio."[12] Some critics maintain that, had she seen her poems through to publication, Dickinson herself would have regularized their appearance. I wonder whether she would have done this willingly. The bases for my skepticism are poems such as 617; a few of Dickinson's letters about literature as marking/signing/sewing; and her complete pleasure in idiosyncrasy. Dickinson's slanted marks, when scrutinized in manuscripts, have for the most part the appearance of dashes. But they also conspire with her words to make designs. In a poem discussed earlier, "Just so – Christ – raps" (fig. 8), for instance, the short marks in the first line especially, but throughout the poem as well, seem related to the longer mark that underlines and ends it.[13] Edith Perry Stamm's hypothesis that Dickinson's dashes were elocutionary marks, directions for reading her poems aloud,[14] is sometimes still invoked for poems like this one, where the dash might be taken to imitate rapping. Frequently the dashes do indeed seem mimetic, as in "Quick – like a Liquor – / Gay – like Light" (473). As Franklin points out, Dickinson wrote cake recipes using dashes. Still more important, when she made a transcript of George Herbert's poem "Matins," working from the printed page, she trans-

8. Page from fascicle 11, "Just so – Christ – raps." Variant of poem 317 (addressed to Sue), handwriting of the early 1860s.

lated it into her own characteristic copy: words intermingled with dashes.[15]

Thus, in reading another's poem, she made it hers by her system of notation. For someone like Dickinson, given to sending poems accompanied by sketches; for someone interested in drawing; who spoke of her own words as marks/symbols on the page and who referred to poetry as "needlework"[16]—was the dash or slanted mark part of a spontaneous design? Sometimes she sent woven articles or pieces of embroidery to accompany her poems.[17] Her custom gives rise to possibilities: she may have been "justifying" her poetry by associating it with women's accomplishments (even as she said she justified her face by holding a flower); indeed, she may have been declaring the unity of creative endeavor in which embroidery and poetry are both artistic so that, by extension, the female artist is related to the male. Van Wyck Brooks wrote of her telegraphic poems;[18] she herself called them bulletins from immortality (827). So they stand on the page, like wireless messages that she also meant to look lively. Many of Dickinson's poems approach the making of shapes, poetry in figures such as Herbert's own "Easter Wings." In "Banish Air from Air" (854) for example, her placement of the word "Fit" describes the union of two streams of air in one word, like a period:

> Banish Air from Air –
> Divide Light if you dare –
> They'll meet
> While Cubes in a Drop
> Or Pellets of Shape
> Fit.

She was probably experimenting with poetry in form. Her dashes, though they are used with apparent caprice, seem the result of an instinct to personalize her texts, to make them visually vivid. It is also interesting to note that certain consonants, the *y*'s and *s*'s and *l*'s, of the manuscript poems are given wide scriptorial latitude so that they often appear to be designs. The dash, for Victorians, was the most used and abused of punctuation marks.[19] But it is also the closest to a brushstroke. Like the "symbolical" works mentioned in *Aurora Leigh,* Dickinson's poems were the works of a woman. Perhaps their superficial appearance declared them that of a woman artist. Her final association between sewing and poetry was provided when she sewed her fascicle poems together with thread.

3

In Dickinson's best-known poem of the transitus, "Because I could not stop for Death," she envisions Death as a beau, picking her up for a buggy ride and setting her down in eternity. Allen Tate called this poem one of the greatest in the English language though, when he said so, he had only seen the marred and emended Todd-Higginson version.[20] The concept of (in Whitman's words) "Death, the deliveress"[21] became current in late Victorian iconography, as in Vedder's *Cup of Death* (1886). But when Dickinson wrote her poem, around 1862, the usual conception of Death was of a skeletal marauder-thief with a scythe and a grimace. There was also an iconographic theme relating to the death of artists that, surviving from classical art, persisted in Victorian painting. This was the conceit of the artist carried to heaven in Apollo's chariot. It was a form of translation, body and soul, that—like the Assumption of the Virgin Mary, also often portrayed—constituted a reward for exceptional beatitude.[22] Dickinson's poem owes nothing to the flossy heroic paintings that illustrate this theme, but Higginson may have been acknowledging them by calling her poem "The Chariot." His title is at variance with the tone and language of the poem:

> Because I could not stop for Death –
> He kindly stopped for me –
> The Carriage held but just Ourselves –
> And Immortality.
>
> We slowly drove – He knew no haste
> And I had put away
> My labor and my leisure too,
> For His Civility –
>
> We passed the School, where Children strove
> At Recess – in the Ring –
> We passed the Fields of Gazing Grain –
> We passed the Setting Sun –
>
> Or rather – He passed Us –
> The Dews drew quivering and chill –
> For only Gossamer, my Gown –
> My Tippet – only Tulle –
>
> We paused before a House that seemed
> A Swelling of the Ground –

The Roof was scarcely visible –
The Cornice – in the Ground –

Since then – 'tis Centuries – and yet
Feels shorter than the Day
I first surmised the Horses' Heads
Were toward Eternity – (712)

In Dickinson's poem there can be no doubt that the persona, the speaker-artist, carried to heaven is a woman. Much is made of her feminine clothing in the fourth quatrain, deleted by Todd and Higginson; and Death's approach to her is kindly and marked by the civility a suitor should show. Like the woman's sewing that is nearly "put up" in 617, the speaker's life has been "put away"; so busy was she that Death had to overtake and stop for her on the road. A Dickinsonian equivalent of the heroic conception of Apollo rewarding the artist is the presence of Immortality in the carriage.

The poem begins almost immediately to compress time and space in order to dramatize the difference between life and death, time experienced and time conceptualized. Death drives slowly, knowing no haste. Why should he? He is a force outside time who enters it briefly to depart again. But in the third quatrain—though her reaction to the fact, since she is dead, is not intense—she reports in a triple repetition ("We passed") that she has just surveyed and passed by three stages of human life. As if in accord with the theory that one's life flashes in various sequences before the soul as it leaves the body, Dickinson describes childhood (when ring games are played), maturity (fields of grain), and old age (the setting sun). This quatrain is particularly effective, acknowledging that in this hard life even children are forced to strive at what ought to be recess. And they compete "in the Ring," an image that recalls the ring games like Farmer in the Dell, played in New England, but that also has a dark undercurrent of dangerous games in rings: the contests of gladiators, boxers, or wrestlers. But in the fourth quatrain the poem proceeds to show that time's periods are irrelevant to a passenger in Death's carriage. So the sun, arbiter of earthly time, is made to pass them, and the speaker is in no place and out of time. Cold as a corpse, dressed with weirdly appropriate inappropriateness in the silk mesh suitable for a wedding or a ball, she feels the dews of what could be morning or evening.

The house to which Death brings her, like a bridegroom conducting his bride to her new home, is a new-made grave. Yet she perceives that the roof (the tombstone) is scarcely visible, being covered over (with grass?). The cornice, or rectangular upper edge of the tombstone, is sunken. Therefore, arriving at her grave, Dickinson also realizes that she has been buried for many years. Her perfect rhyme "Ground" and "Ground" in stanza five shows her complete assurance in this great poem; in *Poems* (1890) Mrs. Todd altered it to "Ground"/"Mound," thus making the rectangular cornice a different shape and thing. The perfect rhyme, however, was bravely paradoxical, for the speaker's grave here is an airless vacuum, out of nature. The repeated "Ground" points out that irony.

At the poem's end, Dickinson's speaker is content in a completed nonexistence that has nullified temporal awareness, except to leave her with the surreal conviction that centuries are shorter than a day. Her last image is apocalyptic: the horses going toward eternity, where she and Death pause but never stop. For at the end of her poem she has achieved eternity, followed by the dash that declares it to be unending immortality. The poem is thus her supreme assertion of the continuance of the soul or self. It may be a tribute to herself as poet. The concluding dash appropriates the powerful artistic function of suggesting continuity. Once again she associates death with a hyphen, but here it too has undergone the transitus into infinity.

During the 1860s, when she was remembered for holding interviews like the newly widowed Queen Victoria behind half-open doors, Dickinson was reading the queen's favorite poet, Tennyson. She later judged that—"once so rare"—his powers were declining (L 2.571). But she always kept a faithful affection for his poetry. In 1883, when for her there had been too many "snows" or deaths, she quoted *In Memoriam* and "Love and Duty" (L 3.760). Her citation of the latter poem was especially poignant: "Of Love that never found it's earthly close, what sequel?" During their girlhood years when *The Princess* served her and Sue as a "feast in the reading line," what seems to have drawn her to Tennyson was not only his lyricism but the provocative antifeminist theme of that poem. Dickinson's double-line markings in a copy of *The Princess* inscribed S. H. Gilbert and dated 1858 are noteworthy. The poem includes these lines in the prologue, uttered by Lilia ("Lily") who longs for the education of women:

> You men have done it: how I hate you all!
> Ah! were I something great! I wish I were
> Some mighty poetess, I would shame you then. (130–132)

There are many markings set down in Sue's *Tennyson* in the delicate strokes of Emily Dickinson. They may record her response to Tennyson's myopic, limited, but at least engaged debates about the role of the sexes. It is easy to suppose that some of these scorings imply her reaction to the poem's facile generalizations about women's lives. This formula, for instance, is marked:

> Man for the field
> Man for the sword
> Man for the head (5.437–439)

And the concluding line of the quatrain is even parenthesized: "Man to command, and woman to obey." To such a formula, Dickinson's art does no service.

Yet it was characteristic of her ability to be fair, loyal, and perceptive that Dickinson preserved her regard for the poet laureate of the age. In her favorite among his poems, *In Memoriam,* he showed himself to be a great poet of eternal love, eternal life. As she did, he made art from his conflicts and triumphs, art that similarly mirrored the culture of his time. Near the end of her life she quoted *Idylls of the King,* declaring "to fall asleep in Tennyson's Verse, seems almost a Pillow" (L 2.585). In part her sentence may allude to his lush sonorities, so different from her own spare meters. But she was probably speaking too of Tennyson's comforting vision of Avilion, paradise. At the close of the *Idylls,* King Arthur is rowed there, like Cole's voyager in *Old Age,*

> Down that long water opening on the deep
> Somewhere far off, [to] pass on and on, and go
> From less to less and vanish into light.

Quoting Tennyson's last line about Queen Guinevere, who passes from her seclusion into heaven, Dickinson associated it with her own desire for eternity: that place "where beyond these voices there is peace" (L 2.585).

During her lifetime, she seemed (said Higginson) "surrounded by a fiery mist."[23] Close study of her life in art, of the art she wove from life, illumines such mystery. The sophisticated allusiveness of her literary sensibility helped to contrive it, as well as the difficulty that many find in believing that so "stern and simple"[24] an existence could give life to such poems as hers. In one lyric Emily Dickinson writes, "I take – no less than skies." She introduces her thought by admitting, "perhaps I asked too large," and adds three lines that explain both her nature and her art:

My Basket holds – just – Firmaments –
Those – dangle easy – on my arm,
But smaller bundles – Cram. (352)

She desired much: what she called the honor of an artist, the shortest route to immortality. To attain it, she led her productive life, leaving us the poems that disclose her vision of time in eternity and eternity in time.

Appendix

Notes

Acknowledgments

Index of First Lines

Index

Abbreviations

(1 . . . 1775)	Numbers in parentheses after ED lines refer to poem numbers in *The Poems of Emily Dickinson*, 3 vols., ed. Thomas H. Johnson (Cambridge: Harvard University Press, 1955)
CW	*The Collected Works of Ralph Waldo Emerson*, vols. 1–3, ed. Alfred R. Ferguson et al. (Cambridge: Harvard University Press, 1971, 1979, 1983)
L 3.906	Volume and page number in *The Letters of Emily Dickinson*, 3 vols., ed. Thomas H. Johnson (Cambridge: Harvard University Press, 1958)
Leyda	Jay Leyda, *The Years and Hours of Emily Dickinson*, 2 vols. (New Haven: Yale University Press, 1960)
Sewall, *Life*	Richard B. Sewall, *The Life of Emily Dickinson* (New York: Farrar, Straus and Giroux, 1974)

Appendix

POEMS FOR SUE AND POEMS FOR MASTER

This arrangement of the poems I take to be for or about Sue and those for or about Master is made provisionally. My aim is to show the extent and contiguity of these poems as well as to suggest characteristics in each grouping or cycle that make it distinct. It has been observed that the lyrics for the beloved woman and those for the loved man are sometimes much alike. This is especially true in love-and-burial poems, such as 1666. Although Dickinson imagines herself and Master sharing paradise or a grave, she uses a similar trope for Sue. She writes to her, "we will lie side by side in the kirkyard," "'neath one willow tree" (L 1.201, 195); and Sue was sent poem 1666, which begins "I see thee clearer for the Grave" and ends with the nest imagery associated with her. Nevertheless, the two groupings have distinctive qualities, marked by the rescuing powers of Master as opposed to the troubling, forbidden appeal of the undependable woman (my list does not include the many poems sent to Sue on general topics).

In parentheses after the poem's first line—listed here without regard for exact punctuation or capitalization—are the Johnson poem number; the Franklin fascicle/set number; the volume and page from the Johnson letters (L).

Poems for Sue

Date	Poem
1853	On this wondrous sea (4; F1; L 1.226)
1854	I have a bird in spring (5; L 1.306–307)
1858	There is a word (8; F2)
1858	Through lane it lay, thro' bramble (9; F2)
1858	One sister have I in our house (14; F2; L 2.342–343)
c. 1858	Distrustful of the gentian (20; F1)
1858	I had a guinea golden (23; F1)
c. 1858	It did not surprise me (39; F2)
c. 1858	Once more, my now bewildered dove (48; F2)

c. 1858	I often passed the village (51; F3)
c. 1859	Going to heaven (79; F6)
c. 1859	Her breast is fit for pearls (84; F5)
c. 1859	My friend must be a bird (92; F3)
c. 1859	For every bird a nest (143; F4)
c. 1860	Two swimmers wrestled on the spar (201; F15)
c. 1860	You love me, you are sure (156; F9)
c. 1860	Dying! Dying in the night (158; F9)
1861	Is it true, dear Sue (218; L 2.373)
c. 1861	Could I then shut the door (220)
c. 1861	I held a jewel in my fingers (245; F11)
c. 1861	Over the fence (251; F11)
c. 1861	You see I cannot see your lifetime (253; F13)
c. 1861	One life of so much consequence (270; F10)
1862	Your riches taught me poverty (299; F14)
c. 1862	For largest woman's heart I knew (309; F28)
c. 1861	Just so Jesus [Christ] raps (317; F11)
c. 1861	We grow accustomed to the dark (419; F15)
c. 1862	Removed from accident of loss (424; F14)
c. 1862	I'll clutch and clutch (427; F19)
c. 1862	Taking up the fair ideal (428; F19)
c. 1862	It would never be common more, I said (430; F19)
c. 1862	Knows how to forget (433; F19, S7)
c. 1862	Forget! The lady with the amulet (438; F29)
c. 1862	I showed her heights she never saw (446a; F16)
c. 1862	The Malay took the pearl (452; F21)
c. 1862	Like eyes that looked on wastes (458; F32)
c. 1862	She dealt her pretty words like blades (479; F22)
c. 1862	Going to her (494b)
c. 1862	Her smile was shaped like other smiles (514; F12)
c. 1862	Her sweet weight on my heart a night (518; F29)
c. 1862	Sweet, you forgot but I remembered (523; F31)
c. 1862	She's happy with a new content (535; F25)
c. 1862	'Tis true they shut me in the cold (538; F30)
c. 1862	I took my power in my hand (540; F30)
c. 1862	We learned the whole of love (568; F28)
c. 1862	Ourselves were wed one summer, dear (631; F26)
c. 1862	The first day when you praised me, sweet (659; F22)
c. 1862	Of all the souls that stand create (664)
c. 1863	Ah, Teneriffe (666; F36)
c. 1863	Shells from the coast mistaking (693; F35)
c. 1863	I could bring you jewels, had I a mind to (697; F35)
c. 1863	No matter now, sweet (704; F35)

c. 1863	Precious to me she still shall be (727; F36)
c. 1863	Let us play yesterday (728; F36)
c. 1863	She rose to his requirement, dropt (732; F38)
c. 1863	It dropped so low in my regard (747; F37)
c. 1863	You constituted time (765; F23)
c. 1863	Two were immortal twice (800; F38)
c. 1863	I play at riches to appease (801; F38)
c. 1863	This bauble was preferred of bees (805; F38)
c. 1864	I could not drink it, sweet (818; S5)
1865	An hour is a sea (825; L 2.446)
c. 1864	This chasm, sweet, upon my life (858; S6b)
c. 1864	That distance was between us (863; S5)
c. 1864	Because the bee may blameless hum (869; S5)
1865	Unable are the loved to die (L 2.441)
1869	Her sovereign people (1139; L 2.465)
c. 1870	Distance is not the realm of fox (1155)
c. 1870	Lest any doubt that we are glad (1156; L 2.484)
c. 1871	Of so divine a loss (1179; L 2.489)
1872	Now I knew I lost her (1219; S11)
c. 1873	The most pathetic thing I do (1290)
c. 1873	Art thou the thing I wanted (1282)
c. 1873	Frigid and sweet her parting face (1318; S10)
c. 1877	To own a Susan of my own (1401)
c. 1877	But Susan is a stranger yet (1400[var.] L 2.598)
c. 1878	Sister of Ophir (1366b; L 2.632)
c. 1880	Birthday of but a single pang (1488; L 3.684)
c. 1880	The pile of years is not so high (1507)
c. 1881	'Tis seasons since the dimpled war (1529)
c. 1882	Follow wise Orion (1538; L 3.734)
c. 1883	To be forgot by thee (1560)
1883	The heart has many doors (1567)
c. 1883	Cosmopolites without a plea (1589)
Oct. 1884	Some arrows slay but whom they strike (1565; L 3.842)
c. 1884	Though the great waters sleep (1599; L 3.828)
c. 1884	Declaiming waters none may dread (1595; L 3.829)
c. 1884	Show me eternity and I will show you memory (L 3.830)
c. 1884	The farthest thunder that I heard (1581)
?	I see thee clearer for the grave (1666)
?	That she forgot me was the least (1683)
?	Volcanoes be in Sicily (1705)
?	When we have ceased to care (1706)
?	To lose thee, sweeter than to gain (1754)

Poems for Master

Date	Poem
1858	I would distil a cup (16; L 1.339)
c. 1858	Summer for thee, grant I may be (31; F1)
c. 1858	When roses cease to bloom, sir (32; F1)
c. 1858	If recollecting were forgetting (33; F1)
1858	If she had been the mistletoe (44; F2)
c. 1858	Heart! We will forget him (47; F2)
c. 1859	Sexton! My master's sleeping here (96; F3)
c. 1859	The daisy follows soft the sun (106; F2)
c. 1859	Mute thy coronation (151)
c. 1860	What shall I do, it whimpers so (186; F9)
c. 1860	He was weak, and I was strong then (190; F9)
c. 1860	For this accepted breath (195; F9)
c. 1860	I'm wife, I've finished that (199; F9)
c. 1860	I stole them from a bee (200; F9)
c. 1860	He forgot and I remembered (203; F9)
c. 1860	With thee in the desert (209; F10)
c. 1860	Come slowly, Eden (211; F10)
c. 1860	Least rivers, docile to some sea (212; F10)
1861	Savior! I've no one else to tell (217; F12)
c. 1861	I came to buy a smile today (223; F11)
c. 1861	I've nothing else to bring, you know (224; F10)
1861	Should you but fail at sea (226; L 2.393)
c. 1861	If he dissolve then there is nothing more (236)
c. 1861	Kill your balm and its odors bless you (238; F14)
c. 1861	Ah! Moon and star (240; F11, 14)
c. 1861	Forever at his side to walk (246; F11)
c. 1861	What would I give to see his face (247; F11)
c. 1861	Wild nights, wild nights (249; F11)
c. 1861	I shall keep singing (250; F11)
c. 1861	If I'm lost now (256; F13)
c. 1861	Read, sweet, how others strove (260; F13)
c. 1861	He put the belt around my life (273; F12)
c. 1861	Doubt me! My dim companion (275; F12)
c. 1861	What if I say I shall not wait (277; F14)
c. 1861	The drop that wrestles in the sea (284; F11)
c. 1861	I got so I could take his name (293; F12)
c. 1861	One year ago jots what (296; F12)
c. 1861	There came a day at summer's full (322; F13)
c. 1862	The face I carry with me last (336; F19)

c. 1862	I tend my flowers for thee (339; F18)
c. 1862	Although I put away his life (366; F20)
c. 1862	How sick to wait in any place but thine (368; F20)
c. 1861	No rose yet felt myself a'bloom (L 2.375)
c. 1861	Take your heaven further on (388; F30)
c. 1862	'Twas love, not me (394; F27)
1862	The loss by sickness, was it loss (L 2.418)
c. 1862	I had not minded walls (398; F27)
c. 1862	A tongue to tell him I am true (400; S1)
c. 1862	Sunset at night is natural (415; F15)
c. 1862	Not in this world to see his face (418; F15)
c. 1862	More life went out when he went (422; F14)
c. 1862	I tie my hat, I crease my shawl (443; F24)
c. 1862	He showed me hights I never saw (446b; F16)
c. 1862	Could I do more for thee (447; F21)
c. 1862	So well that I can live without (456; F32)
c. 1862	A wife at daybreak I shall be (461; F32)
c. 1862	Why make it doubt, it hurts it so (462; F32)
c. 1862	I live with him, I see his face (463; F32)
c. 1862	The power to be true to you (464; F32)
c. 1862	'Tis little I could care for pearls (466; F26)
c. 1862	I am ashamed, I hide (472; F33)
c. 1862	They put us far apart (474; F33)
c. 1862	"Why do I love" you, sir (480; F22)
c. 1862	The Himmaleh was known to stoop (481; F22)
c. 1862	The world stands solemner to me (493)
c. 1862	Going to him! Happy letter (494)
c. 1862	I envy seas whereon he rides (498; F18)
c. 1862	You know that portrait in the moon (504; S1)
c. 1862	He touched me, so I live to know (506; F17)
c. 1862	I'm ceded, I've stopped being theirs (508)
1862	If you were coming in the fall (511; F17)
c. 1862	Me prove it now whoever doubt (537; F31)
c. 1862	Some such butterfly be seen (541; F30)
c. 1862	That I did always love (549; F31)
c. 1862	My first well day since many ill (574; F28)
c. 1862	If I may have it when it's dead (577; F15)
c. 1862	I gave myself to him (580; F19)
c. 1862	Empty my heart of thee (587; F19)
c. 1862	He found my being, set it up (603; F24)
c. 1862	I see thee better in the dark (611; F21)
c. 1862	I rose because he sank (616; F21)
c. 1862	'Twas a long parting but the time (625; F32)

c. 1862	To my small hearth his fire came (638; F33)
c. 1862	I cannot live with you (640; F33)
c. 1862	I could suffice for him, I knew (643; F33)
c. 1862	You left me, sire, two legacies (644; F33)
c. 1862	I think to live may be a bliss (646; F34)
c. 1862	Promise this when you be dying (648; F34)
c. 1862	Again his voice is at the door (663)
c. 1861	I'll send the feather from my hat (687)
1862	Speech is a prank of parliament (688; L 2.395)
c. 1862	The zeroes taught us phosphorus (689; F35; L 2.426)
1863	Victory comes late (690; F34)
1861	Would you like summer, taste of ours (691; L 2.371)
c. 1863	Where thou art, that is home (725; F36)
c. 1863	Alter! When the hills do (729; F36)
c. 1863	If he were living, dare I ask (734; F35)
c. 1863	You said that I was great one day (738; F35)
c. 1863	You taught me waiting with myself (740; F37)
c. 1863	My worthiness is all my doubt (751; F37)
c. 1863	My life had stood a loaded gun (754; F34)
c. 1863	To wait an hour is long (781; F39)
1862	Through the strait pass of suffering (792; F36; L 2.395)
c. 1864	So set its sun in thee (808; S7)
c. 1864	Unable are the loved to die (809; L 2.441)
c. 1864	An hour is a sea (825: L 2.446)
c. 1864	Each scar I'll keep for him (877; S5)
c. 1864	I make his crescent fill or lack (909; F40)
c. 1864	I cannot be ashamed (914; S7)
c. 1864	If it had no pencil (921)
c. 1864	Struck was I not yet by Lightning (925; 54a)
c. 1864	Wert thou but ill that I might show thee (961; F40)
c. 1864	All forgot for recollecting (966; F40)
c. 1864	Fitter to see him I may be (968; F40)
c. 1865	Too scanty 'twas to die for you (1013; S4)
c. 1864	'Twas my one glory (1028; S7)
c. 1865	Sang from the heart sire (1059; S6b)
c. 1862	Title divine is mine (1072; L 2.394)
c. 1866	Ended ere it begun (1088; S7)
c. 1866	Themself are all I have (1094; S7)
c. 1870	He is alive this morning (1160; L 2.472)
c. 1872	Had I not seen the sun (1233)
c. 1872	My heart ran so to thee (1237)
c. 1873	Because that you are going (1260)
1878	These held their wick above the west (1390; L 2.606)

c. 1877	I have no life but this (1398; L 2.589)
1878	Not that he goes we love him more (1435; L 2.601)
1882	The pattern of the sun (1550)
1884	Who abdicated ambush (1616; L 3.839)
?	He was my host, he was my guest (1721)
?	Rearrange a wife's affection (1737)
?	The grave my little cottage is (1743)

Notes

1. The Hidden Face

1. Austin Dickinson's description in his diary entry for May 15, 1886. Leyda, II, 471. See Daniel Lombardo, *Tales of Amherst* (Amherst: Jones Library, 1986), p. 111, for ED's funeral.
2. Ibid., pp. 474, 357.
3. Ibid., p. 476.
4. Quoted in L 2.473, letter 342a.
5. Leyda, II, 475.
6. Richard Rudisill, *Mirror Image* (Albuquerque: University of New Mexico Press, 1971), p. 32.
7. Leyda, II, 473.
8. Martha Dickinson Bianchi, *The Life and Letters of Emily Dickinson* (Boston: Houghton Mifflin, 1924; New York: Biblo and Tannen, 1971), p. 101.
9. Leyda, II, 475.
10. From Higginson's recollections of ED in the *Atlantic Monthly* 68 (October 1891), quoted in L 2.476: "The impression undoubtedly made on me was that of an excess of tension, and of an abnormal life . . . She was much too enigmatical a being for me to solve in an hour's interview."
11. Leyda, II, 471.
12. Ibid., pp. 472–474.
13. Professor Martha Nell Smith at the University of Maryland reminds me that this is true. Sue's attitude to Dickinson's poems, especially in the later years, was highly possessive. Perhaps she found it more than usually acceptable to share these lines with the general public because she herself had established the context in which they appear.
14. Reported in Sewall, *Life*, p. 268.
15. Sue began by urging ED to publish. But by 1890 she was telling Higginson that the publication of the poems made her "sometimes shudder." Still she herself attempted to sell several poems after the success of the first series of *Poems by Emily Dickinson* (1890). Angry competition between her and Lavinia Dickinson over who best knew and valued the poet and her poems complicates discernment of Sue's true feelings about women who published. Sue wrote William H. Ward, editor of the *Independent*, "I wish I could persuade my daughter to send you an Easter poem she has just written—but she is immovable, having a most feminine horror of print." In *Ancestors' Brocades: The Literary Début of Emily Dickinson* (New York: Harper, 1945), Millicent Todd Bingham observes that "Sue was more interested in

her daughter's literary career than in Emily's poetry" (p. 59); but the word *feminine* repeats the word reputedly used—to excuse her from publishing—by ED herself.

16. Matthew Arnold, *Essays in Criticism* (Boston: Ticknor and Fields, 1866), p. 98. Houghton Library's catalogue lists books marked "probably" by ED; subjects and method argue the certainty.

17. Sue had an interesting preference for Dickinson's poems of forbidden love, as 792 might be interpreted. The first poem she sent out (to Scribner's) among those in her possession was "There came a Day at Summer's full."

18. *The Journal of Louisa May Alcott,* ed. Joel Myerson and Daniel Shealy (Boston: Little, Brown, 1989), p. 89.

19. Sewall, *Life,* p. 4.

20. I shall return frequently to this favorite ED word, used more than 150 times in the poems alone. In her biography *Emily Dickinson* (New York: Knopf, 1986), Cynthia Griffin Wolff argues that Dickinson's deprivation of intimate contact with her depressed mother in infancy resulted in her "Fall into Language" as a poet (pp. 52–54). I am not unsympathetic to this view. But my interest in ED's interest in faces focuses primarily on its scriptural roots and cultural analogues rather than on psychology.

21. See Higginson's memoir of meeting Dickinson for the first time: "She makes all the bread for her father only likes hers and says '& people must have puddings' this *very* dreamily, as if they were comets—so she makes them" (L 2.474).

22. Rudisill, *Mirror Image,* p. 23.

23. Ibid., p. 43.

24. "She had a dramatic way of throwing up her hands at the climax of a story, or one of her own flashes . . . Her spirit seemed merely playing through her body." Bianchi, *Life and Letters,* pp. 50–51.

25. Rudisill, *Mirror Image,* p. 19.

26. Recollection of "Miss Marian," a seamstress who made dresses for Emily Dickinson. Leyda, II, 480.

27. Reproduced in Sewall, *Life,* p. 114.

28. Quoted in Michael Bertram, *The Pre-Raphaelite Camera* (Boston: Little, Brown, 1985), p. 132.

29. Quoted in Rudisill, *Mirror Image,* p. 50.

30. Jane Donahue Eberwein, *Dickinson: Strategies of Limitation* (Amherst: University of Massachusetts Press, 1985), p. 24. This discussion of the poet's life as a solitary by choice has both sensitivity and humor.

31. In *Emily Dickinson's Home: Letters of Edward Dickinson and His Family* (New York: Harper, 1955), for instance, Mrs. Bingham says that ED's "gradual withdrawal [was] a natural response—given her genius—which she could have made to a world in which, as she said, there was so much matter-of-fact" (p. xv).

32. Sewall, *Life,* p. 128.
33. William James, "Address at the Emerson Centenary in Concord" (1903), in F. O. Matthiessen, *The James Family* (New York: Vintage, 1980), pp. 454, 455.
34. Leyda, I, xlvii.
35. Ibid., p. 377.
36. Mabel Todd thought at first that Emily's "curious leaving of outer life never seemed unnatural to [Austin] . . . Her life was perfectly natural." Later her daughter reported that Mrs. Todd had cited, as proof of Austin's imperfect understanding of Emily, his view "that she withdrew because she knew 'how plain she was.'" *Ancestors' Brocades,* pp. 12, 235.
37. Leyda, II, 77.
38. Poem 1589, about the worldliness of socialite-travelers, was composed on the verso of a strip of paper used to draft a message to Sue as she left on a trip in October 1882. See my discussion in Chapter 2, p. 83.
39. Bianchi tells this story in *Life and Letters,* saying that Emily "dropped and disappeared before him like the dew, but with a wicked glance" (p. 64).
40. The note indicates that Dickinson made Wadsworth a confidant of her anguish in the Master period. While it reveals his deeply pastoral, even friendly concern, however, it also suggests that they were not intimates: "My Dear Miss Dickenson   I am distressed beyond measure at your note, received this moment,—I can only imagine the affliction which has befallen, or is now befalling you. Believe me, be what it may, you have all my sympathy, and my constant, earnest prayers. I am very, very anxious to learn more definitely of your trial—and though I have no right to intrude upon your sorrow yet I beg you to write me, though it be but a word" (L 2.392).
41. Leyda, II, 34.
42. Thomas H. Johnson, *Emily Dickinson: An Interpretive Biography* (Cambridge: Harvard University Press, 1955), p. 81.
43. See, in order: for agoraphobia, Martha Dickinson Bianchi, *Life and Letters* (1924); for Edward Dickinson's influence, Vivian Pollak, *Dickinson* (1984); for separation anxiety, John Cody, *After Great Pain* (1971) and Cynthia Griffin Wolff, *Emily Dickinson* (1985); for retreat as a religious act, Charles R. Anderson, *Emily Dickinson's Poetry* (1960); for guilty lesbianism, Rebecca Patterson, *The Riddle of Emily Dickinson* (1955); for plagiarism, John Evangelist Walsh, *The Hidden Life of Emily Dickinson* (1971); for anorexia, Heather Kirk Thomas, "Emily Dickinson's 'Renunciation' and Anorexia nervosa" in *On Dickinson* (1990); for pregnancy, William Shurr, *The Marriage of Emily Dickinson* (1983). I find Thomas' essay on anorexia appealing for itself, though not necessarily as an explanation of ED's retirement.
44. Reported in Sewall, *Life,* pp. 128, 153.

45. Thomas à Kempis, *The Imitation of Christ* (Chicago: Moody Press, 1958), p. 36.

46. Dickinson sometimes signed herself to Higginson, "Your Scholar." On other occasions she wrote to him as "your gnome." A gnome may be a dwarf who guards gold in a cave, or it may be a maxim. The phrase was selected probably to indicate the nature of her gifts: her angels or muses were gnomic, aphoristic.

47. Marina Warner, *Monuments and Maidens* (New York: Atheneum, 1985), p. 331.

48. Sewall records this "message" for ED, sent to the Austin Dickinsons in 1863, and comments, "If [it] ever reached Emily, it might well have hurt her deeply" (*Life*, p. 474).

49. The term "Hudson River School" was disparagingly applied by the *New York Tribune* (1879) to the American landscape tradition of 1840–1880. Inspired by Thomas Cole who began painting at Catskill, New York, the group included Asher Durand, Frederic Church, Albert Bierstadt, Sanford Gifford, and Jasper Cropsey. "Luminism"—in which brilliant austerity is preferred to colorful grandeur—is regarded either as an alternative tradition to Hudson River painting or as its culminating phase. See Kevin J. Avery, "A Historiography of the Hudson River School," in *American Paradise: The World of the Hudson River School* (New York: Metropolitan Museum of Art, 1987), pp. 3–20.

50. See "There came a Day at Summer's full" (322) in which she describes a sacramental communion between proscribed lovers. "Each was to each The Sealed Church" means that each represented the closed church on Good Friday. Each was like the shut place of the eucharist, of love, on a day that stands for supreme suffering. See also my discussion in Chapter 5.

51. Anna Mary Jameson, *Legends of the Madonna as Represented in the Fine Arts* (London: Longman, Green, 1864), p. xix.

52. David H. Dickason, *The Daring Young Men: The Story of the American Pre-Raphaelites* (Bloomington: Indiana University Press, 1953), p. 63.

53. Quoted in Willis J. Buckingham, ed., *Emily Dickinson's Reception in the 1890s: A Documentary History* (Pittsburgh: University of Pittsburgh Press, 1989), pp. 208–209.

54. George Frisbee Whicher, *This Was a Poet: A Critical Biography of Emily Dickinson* (New York: Scribner's, 1938), p. 55.

55. Sandra M. Gilbert and Susan Gubar, *The Madwoman in the Attic* (New Haven: Yale University Press, 1979), p. 621.

56. Austin Dickinson comments in a letter to Susan Gilbert on September 25, 1851, that Boston convinced Emily of the "hollowness & awfulness of the *world*" (Leyda, I, 213). Apparently the italicized word, often denoting secularism and vanity, was current with her. See Chapter 3, p. 117.

57. Emerson, "The Over-Soul." *CW*, II, 167, 170.

58. *The Idylls of the King*, "Lancelot and Elaine," lines 877–879: "Full often the bright image of one face, / Making a treacherous quiet in his heart, / Dispersed his resolution like a cloud." In a note to "Crossing the Bar" in *Tennyson. A Selected Edition* (Berkeley: University of California Press, 1989), Christopher Ricks compares Tennyson's "I hope to see my Pilot face to face" with lines from *In Memoriam,* 121: "And come to look on those we loved / And that which made us, face to face" (p. 666). I find that ED's appeal to the conceit of the face, seen as the soul, is very like Tennyson's in many poems. Both poets take the image, finally, from ED's favorite 1 Corinthians 13:12: "For now we see through a glass, darkly; but then face to face."

59. Thomas à Kempis, *Imitation of Christ,* pp. 184, 190, 133.

60. Emerson, "The Over-Soul, *CW,* II, 172.

2. Solitary Mornings on the Sea

1. Sewall, *Life,* pp. 54, 468. ED may be indicating her association of Emerson's works with the magic of poetic inspiration by using the phrase in 371 about "an Antique Book" that "tell[s] you all your Dreams – were true – / He lived – where Dreams were born."

2. In her copy of Emerson's "Circles," for example, ED would have read these lines that contrast the folly of women in financial matters with the prudent foresight of men: "A rich estate appears to women a firm and lasting fact; to a merchant, one easily created out of any materials, and easily lost" (*CW,* II, 180).

3. Thomas Wentworth Higginson, "A Letter to a Young Contributor" (1862), reprinted in *Atlantic Essays* (Boston: Lee and Shepard, 1882), pp. 78, 85, 92.

4. "You think my gait 'spasmodic' – I am in danger – Sir" (L 2.409), ED's letter of June 7, 1862, to Higginson. Higginson may have told her she was a "spasmodic," that her poems resembled those of Sydney Dobell or Alexander Smith, author of *Dreamthorpe* (1863). Passionate to the point of incoherence, they were said to have influenced Tennyson's *Maud.*

5. See Higginson's listing in *Book Buyer* (March 1893) of his favorite heroines in fiction: "Alcestis, Portia, Cleopatra, Mrs. Poyser." Reproduced in Buckingham, *Emily Dickinson's Reception,* p. 27.

6. Emerson, "Spiritual Laws," *CW,* II, 95.

7. Emerson, "Nature," *CW,* I, 45.

8. Leyda, II, 149.

9. Robert Rosenblum and H. W. Janson, *19th-Century Art* (New York: Abrams, 1984), p. 276.

10. Ibid., p. 180.

11. Emerson, "Nature," *CW,* I, 44.

12. Harold Bloom, *The Visionary Company* (Ithaca: Cornell University Press, 1961), p. 154.

13. ED's conception of her physical size and stature seems to have been affected by her image of personal importance: slight. Thus, when she invited Higginson to Amherst on March 17, 1866, she told him, "You would find a minute host but a spacious Welcome" (L 2.450). Begging him to take her on as a poetic pupil, she conflates her lack of fame with lack of stature: "I have a little shape – it would not crowd your Desk" (L 2.409). Again, of her inability to serve as her own critic: "I could not weight myself – Myself – My size felt small – to me" (L 2.405). It is difficult to harmonize others' reports of her figure. That her coffin measured 5′6″ is an indication that she was not short, especially in Victorian America. But there are many descriptions of her childlike appearance and slender frame. The white, pleated morning dress preserved in her room at the Homestead was made for a petite, trim figure: I would guess a contemporary size 4. Helen Hunt Jackson, who admitted that she herself—an "ox"—weighed 170 pounds (at 5′1″), understandably found ED like a "wh[ite] moth" (see L 2.565; 3.841). But ED did cast herself as "Emily 'Jumbo'" during her courtship by Otis Lord (L 3.747).

14. The *Atlantic Monthly* presented well-written essays on topics of deep interest to ED. Many, like Higginson's "The Life of Birds" (September 1862), seem the raw material for some of her poems.

15. Joseph B. and Laura E. Lyman, *The Philosophy of Housekeeping* (Hartford: Goodwin and Betts, 1867), pp. 409–410.

16. Charles Knight, ed., *The Comedies, Histories, Tragedies and Poems of William Shakespeare* (Boston: Little, Brown, 1853), II, 137.

17. Lines 1018–1019. This poem was called "Elaine" when published in 1859 and retitled "Lancelot and Elaine" in 1870. It is a rich trove of conceits and images similar to ED's. Elaine's "Song of Love and Death" (l. 998); a phrase like "Love, thou art bitter" (l. 1004) with its cadence reminiscent of ED's "Love – thou art high" (453); and the poem's concentration on faces—"So dwelt the father on her face" (l. 1023) and "the bright image of one face" (l. 877).

18. Jonathan Edwards, "Narrative of His Conversion," in Samuel Hopkins, ed., *The Life and Character of the Late Rev. Mr. Jonathan Edwards,* extracted in *The Norton Anthology of American Literature* (New York: Norton, 1986), p. 106.

19. ED's profound admiration for "gigantic Emily Brontë" was well known during her lifetime (L 3.721). It increased as she grew older; to "No coward soul is mine," she returned repeatedly in the 1880s, quoting the memorable line "Every Existence would exist in thee" (L 3.803). There are many similarities in the two women's lives. ED's poem 298, "Alone, I cannot be – / For Hosts – do visit me," describes artistic creation as Brontë does

in "The Visionary": "What I love shall come like visitant of air"; "He for whom I wait, thus ever comes to me; / Strange Power! I trust thy might; trust thou my constancy."

20. Wendy Barker, *Lunacy of Light: Emily Dickinson and the Experience of Metaphor* (Carbondale: Southern Illinois University Press, 1987), p. 26. Barker interprets ED's use of light/dark metaphors to discuss her development as a woman poet who, unlike Emerson and Thoreau, felt she had "no place in the world of the sun" and preferred darkness as "a familiar place of truth, dream, and nightmare" (pp. 17, 20). This seems to me too systematic a view: for artists of both sexes, darkness has traditionally been associated with the powers of creativity, nourished by the subconscious mind. My own view is that ED used light imagery on many occasions exactly as Emerson did.

21. "Before Sunrise," published as "Just before Sunrise," appears in Marshall B. Tymn, ed., *Thomas Cole's Poetry* (York, Penn.: George Shumway, 1972), p. 166. His essay on sunrise and the poem "Morning" are quoted in Matthew Baigell, *Thomas Cole* (New York: Watson-Guptill, 1985), p. 36.

22. Dickinson copied Herbert's "My God, what is a heart?" after it appeared in the *Springfield Republican,* October 28, 1876 (see Leyda, II, 260). For a discussion of Dickinson's knowledge of Herbert's *Temple,* see Judith Farr, "'Compound Manner': Emily Dickinson and the Metaphysical Poets" (1961), reprinted in Edwin H. Cady and Louis J. Budd, eds., *On Dickinson* (Durham: Duke University Press, 1990), pp. 52–68.

23. ED's Bible may be seen in the Houghton Library, Harvard University.

24. Sewall describes this curriculum in *Life,* "Schooling," pp. 335–367.

25. See Edward Hitchcock, ed., *Memoir of Mary Lyon: The Power of Christian Benevolence Illustrated in the Life and Labors of Mary Lyon* (Northampton, Mass.: Hopkins, Bridgman, 1851), p. 329. Mary Lyon to Mrs. Porter of South Hadley, October 27, 1848: "None but God knows how the responsibility of giving religious instruction to those candidates for eternity weighs on my heart."

26. Ibid., p. 293.

27. Emerson, "The Poet," CW, III, 11.

28. Although for Cole landscape was imbued with the divine presence, certain of his landscapes portray "a sterner, harsher view of God than is seen in the poetry" or, indeed, in other paintings (see Tymn, *Thomas Cole's Poetry,* p. 20). *Moses on the Mount* (ca. 1828) presents that prophet in a turbulent setting that suggests his solitary contest with supernal power and with the God who denied him Canaan. ED wrote four poems that mention Moses. In 168 she asks "Could we stand with that old 'Moses' – / 'Canaan' denied." In 597 she debates the issue of God's will with respect to him: "It always felt to me – a wrong / To that Old Moses – done – / To let him see – the Canaan – / Without the entering."

29. See Darrel Sewall, "Thomas Cole: The Voyage of Life," in Theodore E. Stebbins, Jr., ed., *A New World: Masterpieces of American Painting, 1760–1910* (London: Mansell, 1983), p. 226.

30. Mary Lyon's establishment and decoration of her seminary coincided with the publication of copies of the first *Voyage of Life*. This *Voyage*, particularly in *Manhood*, emphasizes the dynamic powers that Cole saw in nature.

31. In a letter to Mrs. Thomas P. Field: "Expulsion from Eden grows indistinct in the presence of flowers so blissful, and with no disrespect to Genesis, Paradise remains" (L 2.610).

32. Barton Levi St. Armand, *Emily Dickinson and Her Culture: The Soul's Society* (London: Cambridge University Press, 1984), p. 278.

33. "We are still in Eden; the wall that shuts us out of the garden is our own ignorance and folly." Quoted in Oswaldo Rodriguez Roque, "The Exaltation of American Landscape Painting," in *American Paradise*, p. 30.

34. Thus in 1851 she tells Austin: "Home is a holy thing . . . here seems indeed to be a bit of Eden which not the sin of *any* can utterly destroy (L 1.150–151). In 1873 she writes Mrs. Holland of her meadows, which are "intimate" with the sun: "Eden, always eligible, is peculiarly so this noon" (L 2.508).

35. Doreen Bolger and Kathleen Motes Bennewitz, "Thomas Cole's *Garden of Eden*," *Antiques* 137 (July 1990), 110.

36. See St. Armand, *Emily Dickinson and Her Culture*, p. 251, for a list of the Austin Dickinsons' paintings. They included *Autumn in the White Hills* (1858) by Sanford Gifford and *Sunset with Cows* (1856) by John Kensett.

37. Rosenblum and Jackson, *19th-Century Art*, p. 273.

38. Quoted in Stebbins, *A New World*, p. 227.

39. Baigell, *Thomas Cole*, p. 62.

40. Quoted in Tymn, *Thomas Cole's Poetry*, pp. 145–160.

41. Jack L. Capps's phrase in *Emily Dickinson's Reading, 1836–1886* (Cambridge: Harvard University Press, 1966), p. 76. For a feminist treatment of Dickinson and the romantics, see Joanne Feit Diehl, *Dickinson and the Romantic Imagination* (Princeton: Princeton University Press, 1981).

42. Some of Dickinson's "Victorian" attributes are traced by St. Armand in his study of her debt to the culture of her time. Farr in "Compound Manner" (1961) and Louis L. Martz in *The Poem of the Mind* (New York: Oxford University Press, 1966) discuss Dickinson's metaphysical qualities. William Robert Sherwood in *Circumference and Circumstance: Stages in the Mind and Art of Emily Dickinson* (New York: Columbia University Press, 1968) comments on her use of medieval images.

43. See, for example, Brita Lindberg-Seyersted, *The Voice of the Poet* (Cambridge: Harvard University Press, 1968).

44. John Evangelist Walsh, *The Hidden Life of Emily Dickinson* (New York: Simon and Schuster, 1971).

45. Edmund Burke, *On the Sublime and Beautiful,* in Charles W. Eliot, ed., *The Harvard Classics* (New York: Collier, 1909), part 2. "Of the Passion Caused by the Sublime," pp. 49, 58. ED's word "transport" in poem 167 ("To learn the Transport by the Pain") describes the Burkean sublime. Several critical works, inspired by the Freudian gender criticism of Harold Bloom, anatomize ED's attitude toward the sublime as antitraditional. See, for example, Joanne Feit Diehl, *Women Poets and the American Sublime* (Bloomington: Indiana University Press, 1990), pp. 26–43; or Gary Lee Stonum, "Emily Dickinson's Calculated Sublime," in Mary Arensberg, ed., *The American Sublime* (Albany: State University of New York Press, 1986), pp. 101–129, and *The Dickinson Sublime* (Madison: University of Wisconsin Press, 1990).

46. Burke, *On the Sublime and Beautiful,* "Infinity," p. 62.

47. Ibid., 4, "Of Delight and Pleasure as Opposed to Each Other" (p. 33), and 6, "Privation" (p. 60).

48. Leyda, II, 211.

49. Ryder's intensely literary art with its absorption in the otherworldly is not stylistically like ED's—his poetry is softly molded—but its conceptions recall hers. His painting *The Poet on Pegasus Entering the Realm of the Muses* (ca. 1918) is a haunting evocation of the themes in "Because I could not stop for Death." See Elizabeth Broun, *Albert Pinkham Ryder* (Washington, D.C.: Smithsonian Institution Press, 1989).

50. Barbara Novak, *Nature and Culture* (New York: Oxford University Press, 1980), p. 134.

51. [Charles Goodrich Whiting], "The Literary Wayside," *Springfield Republican,* November 16, 1890: review of *Poems* (1890). Quoted in Buckingham, *Emily Dickinson's Reception,* p. 21.

52. See my discussion of this poem in Chapter 7.

53. Bianchi reports this "repeated cry" as "Where is he? I can't find him," saying that no one "could ever forget it, or those days of abyss when her face wore a stricken expression of surprise." *Life and Letters,* p. 84). Leyda, however, reports the line as "Where is he? Emily will find him!" (II, 227).

54. In *Sexual Personae: Art and Decadence from Nefertiti to Emily Dickinson* (New Haven: Yale University Press, 1990), Camille Paglia presents a revisionist overview of the poet. Writing that "the brutality of this belle of Amherst would stop a truck," Paglia complains that "Dickinson scholars are tone-deaf" to the poet's masochism and the "maniacal glee in her sepulchral letters" (pp. 624, 660, 665). She finds ED's elegies sadistic and "in questionable taste" (p. 664). That ED was too complex a woman to be captured by her own childish epithet "the belle of Amherst" (L 1.13) is incontestable. But most scholars acknowledge that the poet accepts pain as a condition of "transport." And it is impossible to see "maniacal glee" in the tone of her elegies for her nephew or others. Paglia compares ED to Mark Twain's dotty elegist, Emmeline Grangerford, who arrives with her

verses before the body is cold. But ED sometimes had to apologize for sending belated condolences. She wrote this message to Mrs. James S. Cooper: "Is it too late to express my sorrow for my grieved friend? Though the first moment of loss is eternity, other eternities remain" (L 3.898). Not only was Dickinson the older woman in her household and thus responsible for writing to the bereaved; she was one whose deep intimacy with feeling— with sorrow—and whose reliance on artistic language as a restorative would naturally lead her to communicate with grieving friends. Paglia herself may be "tone-deaf" to the unique Dickinson voice with its fusion of tough realism and tender empathy.

55. Letter of Mrs. Jameson (a neighbor), October 14, 1883. Leyda, II, 408.

3. The Narrative of Sue

1. Thus Cole defended his belief that in the American wilderness poets and painters were presented with a new subject whose unspoiled naturalness was implicitly divine. See Oswaldo Rodriguez Roque, "The Exaltation of American Landscape Painting," *American Paradise*, (New York: Metropolitan Museum of Art, 1987), p. 30. Did ED read Cole's "Essay on American Scenery" (1835)? Certainly she seems to have known about the painting *Expulsion from the Garden of Eden*, and her words in a letter to Mrs. Thomas P. Field approximate his: "Expulsion from Eden grows indistinct in the presence of flowers so blissful, and with no disrespect to Genesis, Paradise remains" (L 2.610). The Darwinian controversy occasioned by *The Origin of Species* (1859) heightened the appeal to Eden as a myth. It appears frequently in Dickinson's letters as emblematic of deep happiness or remembered pleasure. The last is especially true at the close of her life: "Were we more fresh from Eden we were expecting him – but Genesis is a 'far journey'" (L 3.691).

2. In *Emily Dickinson's Imagery* (Amherst: University of Massachusetts Press, 1979), Rebecca Patterson discusses Dickinson's "eastern" images (pp. 156–161, 193–198) though not their connection with an Edenic past.

3. Vivian Pollak, in *Dickinson: The Anxiety of Gender* (Ithaca: Cornell University Press, 1984), speaks of the poet's "suppression of a complex homosexual identity" and decides, "'Carnality,' however, was not the major focus of her relationship with Sue" (pp. 133, 79). Other critics assume what Pollak assumes: that there was no physical relationship between Dickinson and her sister-in-law. A growing number of writers, such as Judy Grahn (*The Highest Apple: Sappho and the Lesbian Poetic Tradition* [San Francisco: Spinster's, 1985]) and Paula Bennett (*Emily Dickinson, Woman Poet* [Iowa City: University of Iowa Press, 1990]), emphasize what they regard as Dickinson's lesbian identity.

4. Vinnie's allegation, reported in Sewall, *Life*, p. 229.

5. Lillian Faderman, "Emily Dickinson's Letters to Sue Gilbert," *Massachusetts Review* 28 (Summer 1977), 205. Also her *Surpassing the Love of Men: Romantic Friendship and Love between Women from the Renaissance to the Present* (New York: Morrow, 1977), p. 15.

6. Bram Dijkstra, *Idols of Perversity, Fantasies of Feminine Evil in Fin-de-Siècle Culture* (New York: Oxford University Press, 1986), p. 150. Dijkstra's fifth chapter, in particular its sections "The Mirror of Venus" (pp. 129–146) and "The Lesbian Glass" (pp. 147–159), provides an illuminating discussion of nineteenth-century conceptions of woman as either "the moon of reflected light" or "the moon of [narcissistic] circularity" (p. 148). He also observes that "the exchange of imagery between painters and writers was intense. The painters raided literature, while the writers were endlessly describing and transliterating the paintings they had seen" (p. 150).

7. Leyda, I, 319.

8. Sewall, *Life,* p. 380.

9. Ibid., p. 383.

10. Thomas H. Johnson, *Emily Dickinson* (Cambridge: Harvard University Press, 1955), p. 57.

11. Sewall, *Life,* p. 383.

12. Martha Dickinson Bianchi, Editor's Preface, *The Single Hound* (Boston: Little, Brown, 1914), p. v.

13. See Millicent Todd Bingham, *Ancestors' Brocades: The Literary Début of Emily Dickinson* (New York: Harper, 1945), p. 383: "in the original volumes of letters all reference to Sue was omitted at her husband's request."

14. See Polly Longsworth, *Austin and Mabel* (New York: Farrar, Straus and Giroux, 1984), p. 69.

15. See Robert Weisbuch, *Emily Dickinson's Poetry* (Chicago: University of Chicago Press, 1975), p.183.

16. See Gary Lee Stonum, *The Dickinson Sublime* (Madison: University of Wisconsin Press, 1990), pp. 40, 41.

17. In her third letter to Higginson (July 1862), ED writes, "When I state myself, as the Representative of the Verse – it does not mean – me – but a supposed person" (L 2.412).

18. This theory is advanced by John Cody, *After Great Pain: The Inner Life of Emily Dickinson* (Cambridge: Harvard University Press, 1971), Barbara Antonina Clarke Mossberg, *Emily Dickinson: When A Writer Is a Daughter* (Bloomington: Indiana University Press, 1982), and Cynthia Griffin Wolff, *Emily Dickinson* (New York: Knopf, 1986).

19. Quoted in Longsworth, *Austin and Mabel,* p. 70.

20. I am indebted to Longsworth's *Austin and Mabel,* chap. 2, for much of my information about Sue's childhood. These words appear on p. 70.

21. Ibid., p. 76.
22. Mabel Todd's phrase, quoted in Sewall, *Life*, p. 278. "Queen of Pelham" is Bowles's salutation of Sue in an unpublished letter in the Dickinson Papers, Houghton Library.
23. Bingham, *Ancestors' Brocades*, p. 86.
24. Quoted in Longsworth, *Austin and Mabel*, p. 75.
25. Ibid., p. 81.
26. Quoted in Leyda, I, 213.
27. Ibid., p. 203.
28. Quoted in Longsworth, *Austin and Mabel*, p. 106. Note Dickinson's letter to Austin of April 12, 1853: "I wish we were children now. I wish we were *always* children, how to grow up I dont know" (L 1.241).
29. Quoted in Leyda, I, 292–293.
30. Louisa May Alcott, *Little Women* (New York: Grosset and Dunlap, 1947), p. 255.
31. Recollection of Mrs. Jeanie Ashley Bates Greenough, who met ED at Willard's Hotel, Washington, D.C., in January 1855. Edward Dickinson was then in Congress. Leyda, I, 328.
32. Ibid., p. 342. The wedding took place on July 1 but had been scheduled for June 30. ED's poem "Ourselves were wed one summer – dear" (631) alludes to the beloved woman's wedding thus: "You – were crowned in June," "Your Vision – was in June." June is the symbolic month for weddings; literalist objections that Sue's marriage took place in July, so that she could not have been the subject of this poem, may be easily countered. Poets need not honor calendar facts absolutely; at the same time, the wedding had been planned for June over a two-year period. That ED is contrasting *her* "Vision" (and "Veto" in 528) with Sue's "Vision" is demonstrated by "But" in the last line. Both "were Queens" one summer but Sue was a "crowned" queen, while the poet was a queen in secret.
33. Quoted in Longsworth, *Austin and Mabel*, p. 96.
34. Their withdrawn lives and single state, the rumor of their renunciations of love, and the ardent intensity and self-awareness of their poems have caused frequent comparisons to be made between Rossetti and ED. But there are important differences in the poetry that make the comparison improper. For example, the religious faith, conservative views, and moral piety of Christina Rossetti are absolute; she maintains no ironic distance between her speakers' voices and the employment of sacred or traditional iconography. ED, on the other hand, often puts quotational images in relief so that they become the means of achieving heightened pathos, comedy, or irony. Here is Rossetti's solemn poetic allusion in "Until the Day break" to the parable of the sower:

> When will the day bring its pleasure?
> When will the night bring its rest?

> Reaper and gleaner and thresher
> Peer toward the east and the west:
> The Sower He knoweth, and He knoweth best

Contrast this poem with ED's 1237. In what is for her a *most* unusual poem in dimeter, fully rhymed (and therefore more akin to Rossetti's lyrical line than many), she alludes to Christ's birthplace as a final metaphor for joy in the advent of the beloved. Religion is a means here, not an end:

> My Heart ran so to thee
> It would not wait for me
> And I affronted grew
> And drew away . . .
> Not in malignity
> Mentioned I this to thee –
> Had he obliquity
> Soonest to share
> But for the Greed of him –
> Boasting my Premium –
> Basking in Bethleem
> Ere I be there –

ED's speaker, furthermore, usually embraces renunciation of passion precisely because it excites her, intellectually and emotionally, to do so. Rossetti's speakers—such as "Soeur Louise de la Miséricorde"—embrace it as "disenkindled fire" and lament the loss of desire while reviling it: "Alas, my rose of life gone all to prickles, – / Oh vanity of vanities, desire!" ED's publisher, Thomas Niles, sent a presentation copy of *Poems* (1890) to Rossetti. She replied that it was "a very remarkable work of genius,— though I cannot but deplore some of the religious, or rather irreligious pieces." Quoted in Klaus Lubbers, *Emily Dickinson: The Critical Revolution* (Ann Arbor: University of Michigan Press, 1968), p. 30.

35. Clara Bellinger Green remembered ED as "a tiny figure in white," "a little body, quaint, simple as a child and wholly unaffected" (Leyda, II, 273). Bowles's letters to Sue and Austin in the Harvard collection sometimes allude to the Newman sisters as "the Girls" but sometimes to "the girls next door." Sue was reported to be "a bit ashamed to acknowledge the relationship [with Emily and Vinnie] and treated them as strangers or worse" toward the close of ED's life. See Sewall, *Life*, p. 229.

36. Victorian poems such as Robert Browning's "Women and Roses" reestablished the long literary association of the rose with amorous feeling. Edmund Blair-Leighton's painting *Until Death Do Us Part* (1878–79) was a typical Victorian rendering of the American bride. She is escorted by her father and observed by a downcast and cast-off lover; the aisle of the church is strewn with roses and the bride carries roses as a bouquet.

37. Pollak, *Dickinson*, p. 144.

38. Quoted in Longsworth, *Austin and Mabel,* p. 154.
39. Said of her by Sue's brother-in-law, Julius Learned. Ibid., p. 79.
40. See Pollak, *Dickinson,* p. 78. Richard Sewall cautions that none of the Dickinsons' friends or relations recorded any worry about Emily's health at this time: had she suffered from severe, prolonged depression, would they not have done so? His point is well taken. Still, ED's language in poems and letters suggests that she is familiar with depression.
41. Quoted in Sewall, *Life,* p. 280.
42. Ibid., p. 281.
43. Ibid., p. 282.
44. Ibid., p. 284.
45. Ibid., p. 281.
46. Millicent Todd Bingham remembers this about her mother. Ibid., p. 298.
47. Longsworth, *Austin and Mabel,* p. 120.
48. I have set in an appendix to this book a list of poems (together with their numbering in the fascicles) that I consider to be probably written for or about Sue. This is a risky venture because ED writes poems, particularly elegies, for or about women who clearly are not Sue. Furthermore, as Adelaide Morris observes, "the material for Sue and the material for 'Master' are similar," involving a "struggle to maintain wholehearted, blind devotion to someone not usually worshipped, to someone in fact probably not worthy of worship"—"The Love of Thee—a Prism Be,'" in *Feminist Critics Read Emily Dickinson,* ed. Suzanne Juhasz (Bloomington: Indiana University Press, 1983), p. 101. It is the latter condition, however, which I think *does* distinguish the Sue cycle from the Master poems because Master, while sometimes heedless, is not malicious or triumphant in giving pain, as the beloved woman sometimes is. I include my list in order to suggest as well the probable broad extent of the Sue materials, their complexity, and the fact that powerful love poems for the beloved woman appear in the same contexts as the poetry for Master. ED's conception of love was founded on two major experiences, which the fascicles draw upon simultaneously.
49. The phrase is Pollak's subtitle to her book on ED.
50. In his edition of the *Letters,* Johnson records that this poem was sent to Samuel Bowles (I, 69). Pollak offers that it "was apparently intended for his wife Mary" (*Emily Dickinson,* p. 135). Possibly it was, within the context of that letter; but even there it may allude to her feelings for Sue, which she would try to reveal to Bowles in "Two swimmers wrestled on the spar" (L 2.363).
51. Thus Lavinia writes to Austin on March 28, 1854, as "Dear *Rooster*" and signs herself "Vinnie alias, Chick." The epithet was his as the red-haired male between his sisters, chickens. He was also fond of one of the Dickinson birds. ED writes Jane Humphrey on May 11, 1842: "you know that Elegant

old Rooster that Austin thought so much of – the others fight him and killed him." Leyda, I, 301, 77.

52. In a letter (L 3.738) of summer 1882 to Higginson, enclosing a turquoise brooch for his baby daughter Margaret.

53. Her lightly penciled words are still visible in Franklin, ed., *The Manuscript Books*, I, 5. Thomas Johnson writes in *Poems* (I, 22), "The dash in the fifth line may suggest [a] blank to be filled in with whatever name was appropriate if she enclosed [the poem] to a friend." But the idea of singing while trudging through snow or of associating the missing beloved with paradise appears in the literature for Sue.

54. In *Poems* (I, 220) Johnson writes, "It has been plausibly suggested that this poem was written in memory of Benjamin Franklin Newton." Three years later he observes that the poem might also be for someone "ED feels that she has lost, perhaps Sue herself" (L 2.401–402). For a pearl to slip through the fingers, it must have been once held. Newton, though a friend, had never been on such terms of intimacy with her.

55. See the pamphlet in Harvard's Houghton Library, *The Emily Dickinson House* (1966): ED's writing table "was known to be near windows looking south and west, giving a view of Main Street—the world passing by—and of the Evergreens next door—housing part of the 'beloved family.'"

56. This is the imprisonment of those cast adrift (possibly the source of some of ED's poems about drowning), of those forgotten. Just as the line preceding 299, "You see I remember," establishes the claim of fidelity, so many poems in the Sue cycle point out that while the speaker is a prisoner of memory, the beloved woman has forgotten her. See, for example, poems 433, 523, 535, 727, and the appendix listing.

57. Rebecca Patterson, *The Riddle of Emily Dickinson* (Boston: Houghton Mifflin, 1951), associates Goliath with Kate Scott Anthon (p. 190). Most critics interpret "Goliath" or "Goliah" as an impersonal synonym for the world. Thus Eberwein in *Dickinson* (p. 80): "Her effort to emulate David led to her felling herself with her own pebble [in 540]." But ED's use of the name Goliah as an apostrophe in a specific situation (1290) makes it evident that she did not regard it as a general term.

58. The Dickinson family thought of 1705 as intended for Sue: "A Crater I may contemplate / Vesuvius at Home."

59. Patterson, *The Riddle of Emily Dickinson*, pp. 258–260.

60. Theodora Van Wagenen Ward, *The Capsule of the Mind: Chapters in the Life of Emily Dickinson* (Cambridge: Harvard University Press, 1961), pp. 62–64.

61. Eleanor Wilner, "The Poetics of Emily Dickinson," *ELH* 38 (March 1963), 143–144.

62. Weisbuch, *Emily Dickinson's Poetry*, p. 58.

63. Pollak, *Dickinson*, p. 156.

64. Jack L. Capps, *Emily Dickinson's Reading, 1836–1886* (Cambridge: Harvard University Press, 1966), p. 90.

65. Thomas De Quincey, *Confessions of an English Opium Eater,* in David Masson, ed., *The Collected Writings* (Edinburgh: Adam and Charles Black, 1890), vol. 3, pp. 404, 442, 443. There is a 12-volume set of De Quincey among the Dickinson books in the Harvard collection. Vol. 1 is marked by the light pencil marks characteristic of ED.

66. Quoted in Longsworth, *Austin and Mabel*, p. 88.

67. Sewall, *Life,* p. 214. Also, "the loving and fruitful relationship Emily hoped for [with Sue] did not materialize" (pp. 197–198). In a benign sense, this was largely true; as an incitement to poetry, the complex relationship was always fruitful, as Sewall himself makes clear.

68. Ibid., p. 201.

69. L 2.379–380. I have profited from Anthony Hecht's remark to me that Sue did not perceive the wit in Dickinson's own choice of a second stanza for 216. Lines such as "Light laughs the breeze . . . Babbles the Bee" provide a counterpoint to the gravity of stanza 1. Sue, typically, liked grandeur; Dickinson was being compensatory perhaps in showing that life persists, in all its haplessness, even at graves.

70. Emerson, "The Poet," *CW*, II, 7.

71. See Leyda, II, 111.

72. *Jane Eyre* was another code work for Dickinson. (See Chapter 4.) "I rose because he sank" (616) describes such an experience as the heroine's, who at the end of book 1 must "rise" and leave Thornfield Hall and its master. As does ED's speaker in 616, Jane has tried to serve her "master" as a moral exemplar and helpmeet.

73. ED had a framed portrait of Elizabeth Barrett Browning in her bedroom, wrote elegiacally about her, and saw her as having provided the "witchcraft" that "enchanted" her to write (593). In 312 she imagines herself the poet's "bridegroom." This perhaps has enabled the hypotheses— most recently proposed by Stonum in *The Dickinson Sublime* (p. 42)—that marriage poems like "Ourselves were wed one summer – dear" are for Barrett Browning. John Evangelist Walsh finds 518 an elegy for her, in *The Hidden Life of Emily Dickinson* (New York: Simon and Schuster, 1971), p. 255.

74. Cynthia Griffin Wolff, *Emily Dickinson* (New York: Knopf, 1986), pp. 52–54.

75. See Dijkstra, *Idols of Perversity*, pp. 152–153.

76. Quoted in Leyda, I, 302–303.

77. ED called reading *The Princess* "a feast" (L 1.66). Sue's copy in the Harvard collection is inscribed "Susan H. Gilbert . . . Dec. 22, 48." Although the poem considered education for women, some of its sexist generalizations also seem to have provoked ED's scorn. See Chapter 6.

78. Quoted in Richard B. Sewall, *The Lyman Letters: New Light on Emily Dickinson and Her Family* (Amherst: University of Massachusetts Press, 1965), p. 76.

79. For a more complete account, see Judith Farr, "Emily Dickinson's 'Engulfing' Play: *Antony and Cleopatra*," *Tulsa Studies in Women's Literature* 9 (Fall 1990), 231–250.

80. Margaret Lamb reports, in *Antony and Cleopatra on the English Stage* (Rutherford: Fairleigh Dickinson Press, 1980), that "Before Sir Arthur Quiller-Couch became professor of English at Cambridge University before World War I, *Antony and Cleopatra* was not even admitted into the English tripos at Cambridge, on the ground that it was not morally edifying" (p. 189n).

81. Patterson observes in *Emily Dickinson's Imagery* (p. 154): "In her quotations [from *Antony and Cleopatra*] she appears always to take the role of 'entangled Antony,' and her Cleopatra seems to be her sister-in-law, Susan Dickinson."

82. See Sewall, *Life,* p. 191. Austin could use this phrase in 1882 even though his home was widely admired for its elegance and Sue was considered an imaginative hostess.

83. Mrs. [Anna] Jameson, *Shakespeare's Heroines* (New York: Dutton, 1901), p. 242.

84. Sewall, *Life,* p. 279.

85. Ibid., p. 232.

86. Many of the Master poems, such as "To my small Hearth His fire came" (638), were sent to Sue.

87. See Sewall, *Lyman Letters,* pp. 19–53, and *Life,* p. 140. Joseph Lyman, a young man habitually more in love with himself than anyone else, it seems, gloated on his memory of the adolescent Vinnie's kisses to his fiancée Laura Baker. Vinnie was a type of Tennyson's Maud, he thought, from whom he managed to escape.

88. One of the most famous nineteenth-century Cleopatras was Janet Achurch, called by Bernard Shaw "the only tragic actress of genius we now possess." While she was upright and glassy-eyed in Cleopatra's death scene, she played earlier scenes in the reclining position that was depicted in her publicity photos. See Lamb, *Antony and Cleopatra on the English Stage,* pp. 86–87.

4. The Narrative of Master

1. "Doubt me! My dim Companion!" (275) appears in *Poems* (1890), p. 47, entitled "Surrender." But Todd and Higginson omitted the final stanza, which—asking the lover to scrutinize the speaker closely without taking

the virginity kept (for him) until paradise—probably struck them as indecorous:

> Sift her, from Brow to Barefoot!
> Strain till your last Surmise –
> Drop, like a Tapestry, away,
> Before the Fire's Eyes –
> Winnow her finest fondness –
> But hallow just the snow
> Intact, in Everlasting flake –
> Oh, Caviler, for you!

"Caviler" was altered to "cavlier" and stanza 3 arranged as two quatrains
when the poem appeared in *Bolts of Melody* (1945), printed from a
typescript of Mrs. Todd's (see Johnson, *Poems*, I, 197). The suppression of
the stanza is one of many examples of the Todd-Higginson anxiety
regarding the frequently erotic specificity of ED's language. The poem is
about *caviling*, doubting; so the change to *cavalier* is a reduction in
meaning.

2. George S. Merriam's *The Life and Times of Samuel Bowles* (New York:
Century, 1885), a two-volume biography, described itself as a sketch "of a
nation's story as part of the story of a journalist's life" (I, iii).

3. Poem 792 has an interesting history, revealing of the bitter squabble among
the divided Dickinsons—Lavinia and Mabel Todd on one side, Susan Dickinson on the other—as ED's poems began to appear in the 1890s. William
Hayes Ward, editor of the New York *Independent,* had published a review
(December 11, 1890) of the first volume and later wrote asking Mrs. Todd
if she could furnish other ED poems for publication in the newspaper. She
and Lavinia selected and sent a few; they appeared in the issue of February
5, 1891. On February 8, Ward received a letter from Susan Dickinson,
who—though she gave another reason—had apparently been spurred into
competition with her husband's mistress, who was gaining fame (and modest remuneration) as ED's editor. Sue sent Ward what she called "the poem
on the Martyrs—clean and crisp as rock crystal to me," telling him, "If
you will print it for a money compensation I should be glad and will reserve
others for you which have never been seen." But she added, "I would like
this confidential as the sister is quite jealous of my treasures." Millicent
Todd Bingham, *Ancestors' Brocades: The Literary Début of Emily Dickinson* (New York: Harper, 1945), p. 115.

4. Merriam, *Life and Times,* I, 380.

5. In "Bookishness," *Life* 16 (November 17, 1890), 304. Quoted in Willis J.
Buckingham, ed., *Emily Dickinson's Reception in the 1890s* (Pittsburgh:
University of Pittsburgh Press, 1989), p. 40.

6. Sewall, *Life,* p. 77.

7. Margaret H. Freeman, Introduction to Rebecca Patterson, *Emily Dickinson's Imagery* (Amherst: University of Massachusetts Press, 1979), p. vi.

8. Sewall's *Life* (p. 511) provides the worksheet draft ending—"the loving you"—of poem 1398, which was printed in the single-volume Johnson edition as the more circumspect "the Realm of you."

9. See Merriam, *Life and Times*, I, 419. Bowles wrote Maria Whitney in 1865, "Last night . . . I was hungry . . . and turned to my old friend 'Shirley' for relief. I believe I like to read the last few chapters at least twice a year."

10. Katherine Emma Manthorne, *Tropical Renaissance: North American Artists Exploring Latin America, 1839–1879* (Washington, D.C.: Smithsonian Institution Press, 1989), writes an instructive account of the interrelation between the geological and biological sciences and arts in ED's time. I am indebted to Manthorne and to the discussion of the connection between the painting of Church and the work of Humboldt in Franklin Kelly et al., eds., *Frederic Edwin Church* (Washington, D.C.: National Gallery of Art and Smithsonian Institution Press, 1989).

11. Tennyson, "In Memoriam," 9.18: "Till all my widowed race be run." Tennyson's sister Emily was to marry Hallam, so he may have been thinking of her as the widow. Elsewhere he alludes to "tears of the widower" as like his own (13.1).

12. Quoted in Leyda, II, 72.

13. Bowles's hand—a broad scrawl, often on writing paper topped by the American flag or the red Jacobin cap (for the *Republican*)—provides a vivid index to his personality. In 1863 he reports himself "getting more & more *red*: I shall worship Danton & Robespierre soon." Ibid., II, 76.

14. Bowles Papers, Houghton Library.

15. Sewall, *Life*, p. 264. See also the memoir of Mary A. Jordan (November 1934), reported in Sewall (*Life*, p. 263): "When it comes to Sue, she was a lady who was known to have doubtful relations with other men besides Samuel Bowles."

16. Letter to Mrs. Elizabeth Holland, June 1884 (L 3.824): "I am glad if Theodore balked the Professors – Most such are Manikins, and a warm blow from a brave Anatomy, hurls them into Wherefors." Memoir of Martha Dickinson Bianchi: "he is pretty as a cloth Pink!" (editor's Preface, *The Single Hound*, p. xv).

17. See Longsworth, *Austin and Mabel*, p. 114, and Sewall, *Life*, pp. 191–192.

18. Merriam, *Life and Times*, II, 444: Josiah Holland's phrase. Another friend spoke of Bowles's "virginity of . . . nature" (II, 446).

19. Ibid., I, 337; from a letter to Maria Whitney of January 1862. This letter is a great outpouring of affection and even dependency. That it is written to Maria during ED's Master letter period is noteworthy; it might have been difficult for Bowles to have *two* friendships of such magnitude as the one with Maria. He confides to her in this letter that he has "run away from my religious life" (p. 339).

20. Ibid., I, 210. He also suffered from insomnia, rheumatism, abscesses in the hands, and other ailments that suggest delicacy of constitution.

21. Ibid., II, 415.
22. See Bingham, *Ancestors' Brocades*, p. 30.
23. See the appendix for a list of poems I regard as probably for Master.
24. See ED's well-known letter to Susan Gilbert on the subject of marriage and women about to marry: "How dull our lives must seem to the bride, and the plighted maiden . . . but to the *wife*, Susie, sometimes the *wife forgotten*, our lives perhaps seem dearer than all others in the world; you have seen flowers at morning, *satisfied* with the dew, and those same sweet flowers at noon with their heads bowed in anguish before the mighty sun . . . they know that the man of noon, is *mightier* than the morning and their life is henceforth to him. Oh, Susie, it is dangerous, and it is all too dear, these simple trusting spirits, and the spirits mightier, which we cannot resist!" (L 1.210).
25. See Vivian Pollak, *Dickinson: The Anxiety of Gender* (Ithaca: Cornell University Press, 1984), p. 157.
26. Elizabeth I habitually referred to herself as a "prince" after she became queen.
27. Quoted in Millicent Todd Bingham, *Emily Dickinson: A Revelation* (New York: Harper, 1954), p. 90.
28. In *The English Gentleman. The Rise and Fall of an Ideal* (New York: Morrow, 1982), Philip Mason studies the development of the conventions of gentlemanliness and courtesy from the old order of chivalry. Victorian artists and sculptors frequently represented contemporary figures in medieval dress to suggest the knightly conventions. Mark Girouard, *The Return to Camelot: Chivalry and the English Gentleman* (New Haven: Yale University Press, 1981), studies the presence of Arthurian legends in Victorian art. The paintings of the Pre-Raphaelites, in particular, cherished a passionate vision of knight and lady. In ED's time, Edward Burne-Jones's *Sir Galahad* (1858) and George Frederic Watts's *Una and the Red Cross Knight* (1869) were among countless works of art celebrating the Christian mission of the English knight.
29. Rebecca Patterson, *Emily Dickinson's Imagery* (Amherst: University of Massachusetts Press, 1979), p. 129. Poem 603 is a perfect example of ED's frequent fusion of divine and human lovers. It might easily be read as a response to Christ's Second Coming.
30. "Father liked yellow in almost everything; he liked to wear yellow gloves; and his idea of handsome dress was to adorn himself with white trousers and yellow gloves,—then he would say, '*Voilà!*'." Merriam, *Life and Times*, II, 410.
31. There are several women who patronize and disparage Jane Eyre; Blanche Ingram and Aunt Reed are the cruellest. Although the beloved woman does not always devalue ED's speaker, many of the poems I take to be in the Sue cycle present her as condescending to an inferior or wounding her directly (for example, 479 or 704).

32. Joseph A. Kestner writes of the "Apollonian/solar myth" in "The Solar Theory and Female Oppression in Nineteenth-Century British Art," *Victorians Institute Journal* 17 (1989), 105–124. The sun and the sunflower were among its several expressions. Frederick Leighton did paintings of "the male as light-bearer" (Kestner, p. 107) and in his most famous portrait of a woman, *Flaming June* (1895), represents a sleeping girl whose body makes a circle of filmy orange drapery and flesh that seems to echo the sunlight and yet be enervated by it.

33. Margaret Homans makes this etymological note in the service of a different argument, in *Women Writers and Poetic Identity: Dorothy Wordsworth, Emily Brontë, and Emily Dickinson* (Princeton: Princeton University Press, 1980), p. 118.

34. That ED uses much legal imagery, especially in the love poems to Master, has often been pointed out. Since her father and brother were lawyers, she was accustomed to legal argumentation and naturally associated men with the law. Shakespeare's sonnets also use legal imagery, in similar way.

35. See Sewall, *Life,* pp. 442, 467.

36. In *Charlotte Brontë: The Evolution of Genius* (Oxford: Oxford University Press, 1967), Winifred Gérin presents a moving account of Charlotte's unanswered letters to Heger, sent to him in Brussels after she returned to her family in Haworth. The letters attempt to conceal her passion (even from herself) by making other claims on him as her former teacher and as an educator who might advise her on founding a school. Heger (and Mme. Heger, who becomes the crafty Mme. Beck in *Villette*) shredded the letters but pieced them together again as proof of Heger's moral circumspection after Charlotte became famous. When, after years, her letters went unanswered, Charlotte wrote Heger a farewell, with a postscript in English, that is a masterpiece. Heger used this last letter to scribble a few notes to himself, including the address of his shoemaker. See Rebecca Fraser, *The Brontës* (New York: Fawcett Columbine, 1988), p. 243.

37. William H. Shurr, *The Marriage of Emily Dickinson* (Lexington: University of Kentucky Press, 1983), p. 181.

38. R. W. Franklin, ed., *The Master Letters of Emily Dickinson* (Amherst: Amherst College Press, 1986), p. 5.

39. Charlotte Brontë, *Jane Eyre,* ed. Richard Dunn (New York: Norton, 1971), pp. 133, 221; page numbers hereafter cited in text.

40. But Dickinson's use of Brontë's works has not been seen as coding. Rather, John Evangelist Walsh, *The Hidden Life of Emily Dickinson* (New York: Simon and Schuster, 1971), lists plagiaristic "borrowings" from *Jane Eyre* (p. 262).

41. The use of the French "Maître" and ED's use of "Master" differs in one way, since the former lacked association with Christ but was a commonplace word for a schoolmaster.

42. See Sandra M. Gilbert and Susan Gubar, *The Madwoman in the Attic* (New Haven: Yale University Press, 1979), pp. 594–606.

43. Reported in Sewall, *Life,* p. 264.

44. Quoted in Gérin, *Charlotte Brontë,* p. 292.

45. Merriam, *Life and Times,* II, 445.

46. Ibid., p. 74.

47. Ibid., p. 413.

48. Letter in the Bowles Papers, Houghton Library.

49. Quoted in Leyda, I, 366.

50. Ibid., II, 86.

51. Leyda, p. 101.

52. Ibid., p. 129.

53. Merriam, *Life and Times,* I, 216. Merriam's biography is itself interesting as a Victorian document. It is remarkable, for example, to note the frequency with which the words "feminine" or "woman" are used to characterize Bowles as an empathetic man. This is typical: "He bore into his public life the soul of a high-minded, sensitive, and high-strung woman; flaming out against evils of which good men of another type are too tolerant; like the noblest woman, smitten now and then with admiring hero worship for men who doubtless in another world will justify the prophecy of their good angels who have glorified and loved them in this. He who went after the woman in him often found the sternest, most reticent, and exclusive of able men" (II, 453). Merriam's biography is at ease with the sort of metaphoric androgyny that appears in ED's oeuvre.

54. Merriam, I, 217. That the identity of this writer (whose accents are Emily's) is not divulged—although Merriam reports the identities of others in his memoir—suggests that he was respecting a privacy.

55. Martha Dickinson Bianchi, *The Life and Letters of Emily Dickinson* (New York: Biblo and Tannen, 1971), p. 81.

56. Pollak, *Dickinson,* pp. 91–92.

57. ED occasionally writes that, when she cannot obtain "a bodily interview" with her friends, she will visit them in spirit (L 1.19). This was sometimes conceived of quite literally. Her friend Helen Jackson wrote the publisher Thomas Niles in 1885, when she was dying, "I shall look in on your new rooms some day be sure—but you won't see me—Good bye—Affy, forever." Niles shared her words with Dickinson (see L 3.884).

58. Mark Spilka, "Turning the Freudian Screw: How Not to Do It," in Robert Kimbrough, ed., *The Turn of the Screw* (New York: Norton, 1966), p. 251.

59. Sewall in his *Life* and David Higgins in *Portrait of Emily Dickinson: The Poet and Her Prose* (New Brunswick: Rutgers University Press, 1967) declare for Bowles. Ruth Miller in *The Poetry of Emily Dickinson* (Middletown: Wesleyan University Press, 1968) presents a lengthy argument for

Bowles as Master. Walsh hypothesises that Judge Lord held Emily on his lap as an infant (*Hidden Life,* p. 185).

60. Charlotte Brontë, *The Professor* (London: Oxford University Press, 1968), chap. 23, p. 324. In *My Emily Dickinson* (Berkeley: North Atlantic Press, 1986), Susan Howe says that the third Master letter is influenced by the letter Little Emily leaves in *David Copperfield* upon her elopement with Steerforth (p. 35). "Low at the knee" Howe thinks an echo of Barrett Browning's "She told me she loved upon her knees / As others pray" (p. 26).

61. The poet-critic Alicia Oistraker, for example, in a winning lecture at Georgetown University on June 21, 1990.

62. Richard Wilbur, " 'Sumptuous Destitution'," in Richard B. Sewall, ed., *Emily Dickinson: A Collection of Critical Essays* (Englewood Cliffs: Prentice-Hall, 1963), p. 133.

63. Quoted in Manthorne, *Tropical Renaissance,* p. 15.

64. See John Ruskin, *Complete Works* (New York: Kelmscott Society, n.d.), vol. 7: *Modern Painters,* 6.21.

65. Albert Pinkham Ryder's moonlit marine paintings, while they lack the sharp specificity of ED's art, promote feelings of weird terror or amazing joy like her own marine poems. *The Lovers' Boat,* with its suggestions of desolation and yet fulfillment on a sea lit by a low-hanging moon, is evocative of "Wild Nights" (see Broun, *Ryder,* p. 71). It is improbable that Dickinson knew of Ryder.

66. Jack L. Capps, *Emily Dickinson's Reading, 1836–1886* (Cambridge: Harvard University Press, 1966), p. 31.

67. Manthorne, *Tropical Renaissance,* p. 11. See the discussion of *Heart of the Andes* in Kelly, *Church,* pp. 57–58.

68. See my discussion of ED's probable knowledge of this painting in Chapter 5.

69. Emerson, "The Poet," *CW,* III, 6: "[the poet] does not stand out of our low limitations, like a Chimborazo under the line . . . but this is the landscape garden of a modern house, adorned with fountains and statues."

70. Theodore Winthrop, *A Companion to the Heart of the Andes* (New York: Appleton, 1859), p. 16, reproduced in facsimile by the Olana Gallery (New York, 1988). This pamphlet was Winthrop's first of many subsequent publications, the most famous of which was *Cecil Dreeme* (1861) in which the heroine is a painter.

71. Unpublished letter in the Bowles Papers, Houghton Library; and see Merriam, *Life and Times,* II, 77.

72. "I taste a liquor never brewed" (214), "Blazing in gold, and quenching in purple" (228), "Safe in their Alabaster Chambers" (216). "A narrow Fellow in the Grass" (986) were published anonymously on the front page on February 14, 1866. ED wrote to Higginson on March 17: "Lest you meet

my Snake and suppose I deceive it was robbed of me – defeated too of the third line by the punctuation. The third and fourth were one" (L 2.450). Her words are important for several reasons. First, she disavows publication as "ostensible" in the letter. Second, she implies that others forced it on her. Most of all, her words make clear the fact of Bowles's—or Holland's— insensitivity to her own feelings about her poetry and to the poetry itself. Thus the third and fourth lines of 986 properly read "You may have met Him – did you not / His notice instant is." Her objection to the addition of a comma after *not* reveals the surety of ED's judgment. She had intended to say: if you don't notice a snake, he suddenly gives you notice of himself. Editing reduced that to filler for the line.

73. He also asks, "How does she do this summer!" (Leyda, II, 68). Bowles also wrote Austin in October 1861, "thank Emily & Vinnie, with my love, for their little pleasant notes" (Leyda, II, 34).

74. Quoted in Sewall, *Life*, p. 510.

75. In "Americanism in Literature" (1870), *Atlantic Essays* (Boston: Lee and Shepard, 1882), p. 57. Higginson continues, "How tame and manageable are wont to be the emotions of our bards, how placid and literary their allusions! There is no baptism of fire; no heat that breeds excess. Yet it is not life that is grown dull, surely; there are as many secrets in every heart, as many skeletons in every closet, as in any elder period of the world's career."

76. Adrienne Rich, "Vesuvius at Home: The Power of Emily Dickinson," in *Critical Essays on Emily Dickinson*, ed. Paul J. Ferlazzo (Boston: G. K. Hall, 1984), pp. 175–195. Albert Gelpi, "Emily Dickinson and the Deer-slayer: The Dilemma of the Woman Poet in America," in Sandra M. Gilbert and Susan Gubar, eds., *Shakespeare's Sisters: Feminist Essays in Women Poets* (Bloomington: Indiana University Press, 1979).

77. Sharon Cameron's reading of "My Life had stood – a Loaded Gun" in her chapter "The Dialectic of Rage" from *Lyric Time* (Baltimore: Johns Hopkins University Press, 1979) concludes by saying "the problem with [this] poem . . . is not that it is devoid of meaning but rather that it is overwhelmed by it . . . Its phenomena surpass, seem larger than, their explanations" (p. 68). Her account of the many problematic features of this poem is complex. Yet the poem is not, I think, "overwhelmed" aesthetically but remains successful as a ballad. It calls to mind the "pure poems" of the late medieval and Tudor periods, though the last quatrain is metaphysical.

5. A Vision of Forms

1. Cole's effort as a devout Christian to associate the American wilderness with God's grace appears in works like *Saint John in the Wilderness* (1827), where a cross sanctifies an imaginary landscape that looks South American,

not Palestinian. His belief that "that voice [of God] is YET heard among the mountains" expressed itself in, among other motifs, the crosses that sanctify his landscapes and are often suggested by crossed branches or other natural features. See Earl A. Powell, "Luminism and the American Sublime," in John Wilmerding, ed., *American Light: The Luminist Movement, 1850–1875* (Washington, D.C.: National Gallery of Art, 1980), p. 69.

2. David Porter, *Dickinson: The Modern Idiom* (Cambridge: Harvard University Press, 1981), pp. 152, 181, 160, and chaps. 5–7. Yet Porter treats individual poems with authority and perspicacity and with admiration for the texture of the verse.

3. "Miss Emily was apt with a pencil and in a tiny sketch of Amherst, sent my mother, everything was covered with snow except [our] parsonage. With it came a line saying 'I omitted the snow on the roof, distrusting the premonition, Emily.'" Quoted in Leyda, II, 284. Sue wrote to William H. Ward, editor of the *Independent,* "I have a little article in my mind, with illustrations of her (Emily's) own, showing her witty humorous side." See Millicent Todd Bingham, *Ancestors' Brocades: The Literary Début of Emily Dickinson* (New York: Harper, 1945), p. 118.

4. Emerson liked to speak of the poetry of landscape. In that tradition, Lavinia was heard to say that "there is no landscape since Austin died." See Millicent Todd Bingham, *Emily Dickinson's Home* (New York: Harper, p. 477.

5. *Modern Painters* (volume 1 appeared in the United States in 1847) was being reviewed in the *Atlantic Monthly* when ED was at the height of her creativity. William Stillman, the Pre-Raphaelite painter/editor of *The Crayon,* reviewed volume 5 in August 1860, saying that the first volume "fell upon the public opinion of the day like a thunderbolt from a clear sky." *Modern Painters* is not among the Dickinson books, but internal evidence suggests that she read it. Her remark to Higginson about her literary preference, "For Prose—Mr. Ruskin," since it was made in 1862, would probably have been read as an allusion to *Modern Painters.*

6. Made with whatever intentions, the dashes are like brushstrokes. See Chapter 6 for hypotheses about these signs.

7. Quoted in Louis Le Grand Noble, *The Course of Empire, Voyage of Life and Other Pictures of Thomas Cole, N.A.* (New York: Cornish, Lamport, 1853), pp. 263–264.

8. Gary Lee Stonum, *The Dickinson Sublime* (Madison: University of Wisconsin Press, 1990), p. 110.

9. See Camille Paglia, *Sexual Personae: Art and Decadence from Nefertiti to Emily Dickinson* (New Haven: Yale University Press, 1990), pp. 624, 625, 628, 637, 633.

10. Leyda, II, 386.

11. Ibid., II, 41.

12. Martha Dickinson Bianchi, *Emily Dickinson Face to Face* (Boston: Houghton Mifflin, 1932), p. 126.

13. Barton Levi St. Armand, *Emily Dickinson and Her Culture* (New York: Cambridge University Press, 1984), p. 282.

14. Leyda, II, 395.

15. Betty Ring writes that "the elegance of Massachusetts embroidery [was] unsurpassed. In Boston alone in 1826 there were 2,004 girls enrolled in private [needlework] schools." *Needlework: An Historical Survey* (Pittstown, N.J.: Main Street Press, 1984), p. 82. Judith Reiter Weissman and Wendy Lavitt in *Labors of Love* (New York: Knopf, 1987) record, however, that by 1840 "academic subjects were fast replacing skills like painting and needlework in young ladies' schools and the direction of women's education was changing rapidly" (p. 131). Mary Lyon included needlework among secondary skills taught her pupils.

16. At fifteen, she writes to Abiah Root, "I have been working a beautiful book mark to give to one of our school girls . . . it is an arrow with a beautiful wreath around it." She complains, "I get but very little time to work now days, there are so many other things to be done" (L 1.18). There are a number of allusions to sewing, darning, embroidering, even doing "humblest patchwork" (618) in the poems and letters. Her poem "Death sets a Thing significant" (360) discriminates the pastimes of the sexes in true Victorian fashion. "Perished Creature[s]" who are women leave "little Workmanships / In Crayon, or in Wool" for the world to note. But a man leaves books that have been marked at "The place that pleased Him." Dickinson herself left both.

17. He explains that the word *Nature* "refers to essences unchanged by man" while "*Art* is applied to the mixture of his will with the same things, as in a house, a canal, a statue, a picture" ("Nature," *CW*, I, 8). But in "The Poet" he closes the distance between them (II, 15).

18. Paglia, *Sexual Personae*, p. 624.

19. See *Poems (1890–1896) by Emily Dickinson: A Facsimile Reproduction* (Gainesville, Fla.: Scholar's Facsimiles & Reprints, 1967), *Poems Second Series*, p. 6.

20. Barbara Novak, *American Painting of the Nineteenth Century* (New York: Praeger, 1969), p. 91.

21. John Ruskin, *Complete Works* (New York: Kelmscott Society, n.d.), *Modern Painters*, 3.45.

22. St. Armand, *Emily Dickinson and Her Culture*, p. 239.

23. See Barbara Novak, *Nature and Culture* (New York: Oxford University Press, 1980), p. 79.

24. Ibid., p. 98.

25. Hawthorne was well acquainted with Pre-Raphaelitism; he admired and was discomfited by the carefulness of its techniques.

26. See Susan P. Casteras, "The 1857–58 Exhibition of English Art in America and Critical Responses to Pre-Raphaelitism," in Linda S. Ferber and William H. Gerdts, *The New Path and the American Ruskinians* (New York: Schocken, 1985), p. 116. See also Casteras, *English Pre-Raphaelitism and Its Reception in America in the Nineteenth Century* (Rutherford: Fairleigh Dickinson University Press, 1990), pp. 102–113.

27. Ruskin, *Modern Painters*, 3.67. This exegesis was reprinted in *Knickerbocker* magazine (January 1858), p. 54. Since Austin Dickinson was a collector, it is difficult to think he did not read the *Knickerbocker*, as well as the *Crayon* and the *Photographic and Fine Arts Journal*, each of which described the painting. Susan Dickinson owned the work of John Jarves, whose "Art Hints" previewed the painting in the *Crayon* issue of August 1855. The Boston press and the *Christian Register*, read by ED, featured descriptions and cartoons of it in winter 1857 and spring 1858.

28. See William H. Gerdts, "Through a Glass Brightly: The American Pre-Raphaelites and Their Still Lifes and Nature Studies," in Ferber and Gerdts, *The New Path*, pp. 39–77.

29. Ibid., "Dead Blue Jay," p. 183.

30. Ibid., p. 287.

31. In *Emily Dickinson, Woman Poet* (Iowa City: University of Iowa Press, 1990), Paula Bennett associates ED's floral still lifes with "books of poems and pictures produced by Victorian women" (p. 94). She finds ED writing "within [a] female poetic and artistic tradition" (p. 96) typified by such books as Mrs. C. M. Badger's *Wild Flowers Drawn and Colored from Nature* (see my discussion of Badger's book later). It is probably true that "the tradition which led women to put together calendars and dictionaries of flowers" as well as to write floral poems made ED's still lifes more inevitable (p. 94). But the tradition was by no means expressly female. The artist Jasper Cropsey, for example, used Mrs. Loudon's *Botany for Ladies* (1841), but also the botanist Daniel Cady Eaton's *Beautiful Ferns* (1882), to do careful representations of flora. Like the Pre-Raphaelite artists in my discussion above, most of them male, he did not scorn the small or insignificant detail, as Bennett claims of men by contrast with women. Thoreau's remark in the *Journals* (May 15, 1853) that "At one leap I go from the just opened buttercup to the life everlasting" makes gender distinctions perilous in this regard. Bennett writes, "[Lydia] Sigourney and other women poets learned to look to nature's small and seemingly insignificant moments (the kind they were most likely to sketch) for their intimations of immortality" while male artists searched for *grandeur* (p. 96). Also: "Individual studies of birds, beasts and flowers are in fact relatively rare in the poetry of nineteenth-century men" (p. 103). But among the works of male artists in Victorian England and America, there were thousands of scrupulously done paintings of tiny buds as well as great mountains, while ED's admired

Tennyson characteristically attributes immortality to small flowers. As a group, the Pre-Raphaelites' depictions of pansies, eggs in nests, and shrinking rabbits recall Tennyson's famous sentiment in "Flower in the crannied wall."

32. Because Ruskin considered art an instrument of moral power, his principles, like Emerson's, legislated virtue in the artist and the artifact. The virtue of the artifact was its fidelity to fact. See Ferber and Gerdts, *The New Path*, pp. 196, 33. The American Pre-Raphaelites called their brotherhood the Association for the Advancement of Truth in Art.

33. Bianchi, *Emily Dickinson Face to Face*, quoted in Leyda, II, 413.

34. In Susan Dickinson's copy of James Jackson Jarves' *Art Thoughts* (1869), the author reproves American Pre-Raphaelites like Thomas Farrer because "their art thus far relies too much on . . . exactitude of representation, and too little on the sentiment of nature or on the language of color . . . It is based on a misconception of high art, which has a deeper purpose in view than mere truthful representation of external nature, though it demands that." Quoted in Ferber and Gerdts, *The New Path*, p. 40.

35. *CW*, I, 9, 31.

36. Thomas Wentworth Higginson, "An Open Portfolio," *The Christian Union* 42 (September 25, 1890), 392–393.

37. Quoted in E. H. Gombrich, *Art and Illusion* (New York: Pantheon, 1960), p. 188.

38. From a sonnet written in 1829 and quoted in Louis Le Grand Noble, *The Course of Empire. Voyage of Life and Other Pictures of Thomas Cole, N.A.* (New York: Cornish, Lamport, 1853), p. 107.

39. Cynthia Griffin Wolff, *Emily Dickinson* (New York: Knopf, 1986), pp. 461, 460.

40. Henry James, *The Europeans* (New York: New American Library, 1964), p. 81.

41. Cole writes, "In the terrible and grand . . . when the mind is astonished, the eye does not dwell upon the minute but seizes the whole. . . . The finest scene in the world [however] . . . is made up of minutest parts." The blasted tree, "a splendid remnant of decaying grandeur," was quintessentially sublime. Quoted in Novak, *American Painting of the Nineteenth Century*, p. 77.

42. "The Luminist Movement: Some Reflections," in Wilmerding, *American Light*, p. 101.

43. Novak, *American Painting*, p. 77.

44. Brita Lindberg-Seyersted, *The Voice of the Poet* (Cambridge: Harvard University Press, 1968), pp. 259–260.

45. Earl A. Powell, "Luminism and the American Sublime," *American Light*, p. 78.

46. Charles R. Anderson, *Emily Dickinson's Poetry: Stairway of Surprise* (New York: Holt, Rinehart and Winston, 1960), p. 281.

6. Art as Life

1. Sewall reports Edward Dickinson's "lifelong loyalty" to Yale College, where he graduated in the class of 1823 (*Life*, p. 45). His son Austin, however, was sent to Amherst College, graduating in the class of 1850. He then went to Harvard Law School, graduating in July 1854. This connection seems to have displaced the Yale tie, and the Dickinson papers in the immediate family's possession went to Harvard.

2. Leyda, II, 431.

3. Sue sent a message to ED after the publication in the *Republican* of "Safe in their Alabaster Chambers" on March 1, 1862: "*Has girl read Republican? It takes as long to start our Fleet as the Burnside.*" Leyda, II, 48.

4. T. W. Higginson, *Atlantic Essays* (Boston: Lee and Shepard, 1882), p. 71.

5. Sue's letter quoted in Millicent Todd Bingham, *Ancestors' Brocades: The Literary Début of Emily Dickinson* (New York: Harper, 1945), p. 86.

6. Lois Ella Cowles Ellis, a relation of Edward Dickinson's, remembered "the young Emily [said]: 'I have a horror of death; the dead are so soon forgotten. But when I die, they'll have to remember me'." Leyda, II, 481.

7. See Karen Dandurand, "New Dickinson Civil War Publications," *American Literature* (March 1984), 17–28.

8. Christanne Miller, *Emily Dickinson: A Poet's Grammar,* (Cambridge: Harvard University Press, 1987), p. 119.

9. Johnson writes about 617, "the spelling of 'Sow' and 'sowing' (lines 2 and 17) is undoubtedly a mistake for 'sewing' (pp. 2, 475)." The verb *sew*, from Old English *seowan*, was regularly spelled *sow* in the nineteenth-century; ED would also have found it in Shakespeare.

10. There are many instances of this well-meant but destructive editing. It was practiced by Todd somewhat more than Bianchi, perhaps, because when the latter's volumes were brought out, the public was accustomed to ED's style and many welcomed her eccentricities. The changes Todd made in poem 1057 ("I had a daily Bliss") are typical: she substituted for the final *estimate* the word *right* to rhyme with *sight* in the preceding quatrain. This required the recasting of the whole stanza and the sacrifice of its mournful message of unfulfillment, together with the double meaning of the last line. Thus ED's quatrain reads "Till when around a Height / It wasted from my sight – / Increased beyond my utmost scope / I learned to estimate." In Todd's version it becomes the far more conclusive "Till when, around a crag, / It wasted from my sight / Enlarged beyond my utmost scope / I learned its sweetness right."

11. R. W. Franklin, *The Editing of Emily Dickinson: A Reconsideration* (Madison: University of Wisconsin Press, 1967), p. 117.

12. Higginson's phrase, borrowed from Emerson, and used in his essay "An Open Portfolio" in *Christian Union* 42 (September 25, 1890), 392.

13. Curious effects are produced by the arrangement of the dashes, as in the

third and fourth lines. There the dashes after "he" and "weary," after "First" and "Knocker," seem designed to decorate and fill the line. The *y*'s and *t*'s in this poem, as in others, are also decorative rather than merely utilitarian.

This book does not take up questions raised by the recent work of textual critics, especially Susan Howe, in comparing ED's manuscripts with printed copies of the poems. A strong groundswell of feeling against Johnson's edition as misrepresentative of the poet's metrical/scriptorial intentions has existed since the early 1980s, particularly among critics who regard ED as subversive of her own culture or as a lesbian poet whose work cannot be faithfully regarded as part of a patriarchal tradition. I agree with Paula Bennett (*Emily Dickinson, Woman Poet*) that the "only edition of Dickinson's poetry which will accurately represent what she wrote *the way she wrote it* will be one that duplicates all the idiosyncrasies of her manuscripts" (p. 193). On the other hand, Johnson's normalizations do not seem to me merely to reflect "his preappointed Plan [of] a strained positivity," as Howe says in "Some Notes on Visual Intentionality in Emily Dickinson," *HOW(ever)* 3.4 (n.d.), 11. Johnson's understandable assumption was that Dickinson's short lines flush left (as in "Dew – is the Freshet in the Grass," with "the Grass" set out as an independent second entry) filled out her meter and were accidental, turnover lines caused by inadequate space on the paper. Many manuscript poems suggest that he was right: to fit words in, she would have had to cramp or alter the size of her script. In some instances, however, the poet's flush-left lines appear—especially to eager modern readers—intended. Some words carried over, such as "itself" or "Hound" in 822, appear to deserve their isolation and heightening because of the poem's meaning. When ED sent Sue a copy of those lines without the rest of the poem in 1864, however, she observed the traditional quatrain formation. So did she in sending other poems. Since she shared other poetic experiments with Sue, why not such crucial ones? While I am most sympathetic to efforts to read Dickinson's texts as she meant them to be read, I am dubious about the supposedly modernist character of her intentions. In our time—after Pound, cummings, and Williams—we are used to recognizing the complicated significances created by linear arrangements. (Marianne Moore once said to me in a private conversation in 1957 that everything in her own poetry was intended and that *nothing* could be moved without distortion, not so much as a comma.) But the danger is that in this, as in other matters, we may ascribe to ED a premonitory iconoclasm that was not actually hers. Yet we do need a representative printed text of the fascicle poems; this would greatly reward continued study of the poet's verbal choices as well as her lineation.

14. "Emily Dickinson: Poetry and Punctuation," *Saturday Review* 46 (March 30, 1963), 26–27, and "The Punctuation Problem," *Saturday Review* 46 (May 25, 1963), 23.

15. See Bingham's account of her discovery that she had published Herbert's "Matins" as a Dickinson poem (in *Bolts of Melody*): *Emily Dickinson's Home* (New York: Harper, 1955), p. 572.

16. In a letter (unsent?) quoted in Leyda, II, 395. Gilbert and Gubar declare Dickinson's "commitment to another central female metaphor: sewing" (*The Madwoman in the Attic*, p. 638). But their discussion of "the stitch of art" in ED versus the "stitch of suicide" in the poetry of Sylvia Plath is impressionistic.

17. In 1859, for example, ED threaded together two engravings from *The Old Curiosity Shop* and sewed them to a poem for Sue, "A Poor – torn Heart – a tattered heart" (78). She sent "My country need not change her gown" (1511) along with "a flag of her own making – three bits of braid, red, white, and blue, pinned together with a thorn!" Leyda, I, 379; II, 349.

18. Van Wyck Brooks, "Emily Dickinson," *New England: Indian Summer, 1865–1915* (New York: Dutton, 1940), pp. 316–329. This appreciative essay, now largely forgotten, provides valuable information: for example, that Sue and Austin knew Frederick Olmsted, who designed Central Park and who used their gardens as a source of horticultural study. (Another tie between ED and Sue was probably their semiprofessional interest in gardening.) Brooks also records Bowles's friendship with Dickens and Charles Kingsley.

19. In *The Editing of Emily Dickinson*, Franklin notes the prolificacy of dashes in the correspondence of twenty-four different writers "associated with the nineteenth-century editing of the Dickinson poems" (p. 124).

20. See Allen Tate, "Emily Dickinson," *Essays of Four Decades* (New York: Swallow Press, 1968), p. 290.

21. "Approach strong deliveress," "Dark mother always gliding near with soft feet": from "When Lilacs Last in the Dooryard Bloom'd," lines 147, 143.

22. An occasional subject in nineteenth-century painting was Phoebus Apollo driving his chariot across the heavens. As the patron of artists, Apollo made his ascent into the sky in an aura of power and godliness, seen to be related to that of Christ and the Virgin. Sometimes the dead artist was a passenger in Apollo's chariot. Those paintings were related by theme to such canvases as Albert Pinkham Ryder's studies of Pegasus, the poet's steed: *The Poet on Pegasus Entering the Realm of the Muses* (1883) and *Pegasus Departing* (1901). Thomas Cole's triumphant leader riding in a chariot in the victory procession of *The Consummation of Empire* (1836) was an influential American version of this trope of the voyage as fulfillment.

23. Quoted in Sewall, *Life*, p. 567.

24. Written to Higginson in June 1869 in a letter that praises the "spectral power" of the written word (L 2.460).

Acknowledgments

I have many to thank. My parents, Frances and Russell Banzer, first gave me Dickinson's poems; thereafter, they traveled much in Amherst for my sake. Mrs. Hervey Parke permitted a child to spend hours in the poet's house and room. Charles R. Green of the Jones Library taught me to read a Dickinson manuscript.

Later, Richard Sewall nourished the enthusiasm of a Yale graduate student. He has remained a candid mentor, whose wonderful generosity and keen criticism have earned my deep gratitude. To Sewall and to the authors of the chief scholarly texts—Thomas Johnson, Jay Leyda, and Ralph Franklin—all writers on the poet owe, as do I, an immense debt. In achieving the special character of this study, I was sustained by the work of art historians, John Wilmerding and Barbara Novak in particular.

My graduate and undergraduate students at Georgetown University have cheered this book on. Former teachers—Maynard Mack, Cleanth Brooks, Martin Price, John Pope, A. Dwight Culler, Joseph P. Clancy, and most of all, Louis Martz—all discussed Dickinson with me over the years. Jean Armstrong of Montclair State College contributed to my ideas about Susan Dickinson. James A. Devereux, S.J., commented on an early draft. From the scholars and membership of the Emily Dickinson Society of Washington, D.C., now part of the Emily Dickinson International Society, I had stimulus. My colleagues at Georgetown took an interest: Michael Ragussis, Elias Mengel, John Pfordresher, Joan Holmer, Leona Fisher, John Glavin, Paul Betz, John Hirsh, Jim Slevin, and the late, loved O. B. Hardison and Thomas Walsh. Anthony Hecht counseled, inspired. My devoted son Alec served loyally as an Everyman reader.

Several libraries have been home to me in my research. I extend warm thanks to the staffs of the Pierpont Morgan Library, the Beinecke Rare Book Library of Yale University, and the Berg Collection of the New York Public Library. To John Lancaster, Curator of Special Collections at the Amherst College Library, and to his staff, I owe thanks. I was assisted by the reference library staff of the National Gallery of Art, Washington, D.C. Patricia Serafini of the Munson-Williams-Proctor Institute and Kimberly Cody of the National Museum of American Art,

Smithsonian Institution, were especially helpful. David Black of the Cooper-Hewitt Museum, Smithsonian Institution, gave me special assistance in obtaining reproductions. The librarians of Lauinger Library, Georgetown University, guided me in many matters. The kind staff of the Houghton Library, Harvard University, made the opening of Houghton's doors a metaphor of pleasure.

My friend Joan Reuss prepared the manuscript with care, patience, and finesse. Gayle McDermott typed early drafts. At Harvard University Press, Beth Kiley Kinder, permissions manager, spared me much effort; the senior editor, Joyce Backman, made excellent suggestions that improved the form of the book; and Maud Wilcox, editor-in-chief emerita, encouraged me to write it in the first place.

Thanks to Georgetown University, I received a Summer Research Grant and a publication stipend. The American Council of Learned Societies gave me a travel grant. The American Philosophical Society funded my research in Amherst. For all this generous aid, I am grateful.

Finally, two people did most to see this book through. My chief editor at Harvard, Thomas D'Evelyn, shared his own understanding of Emily Dickinson's poetry and exacted ever more from my own. He took extraordinary pains as a reader of the manuscript. My husband, George F. Farr, Jr., has spent many hours, over thirty years, talking with me about Dickinson. I owe more than can be said to his advice, support, and love.

Index of First Lines

A cloud withdrew from the sky 81
A curious cloud surprised the sky 288
A death blow is a life blow to some
  131
A loss of something ever felt I 83
A poor torn heart, a tattered heart 81
A shady friend for torrid days 192–193
A solemn thing it was I said 32–34, 36,
  42, 150
A solemn thing within the soul 62–63,
  67
A something in a summer's day 16
A toad can die of light 56
A wife at daybreak I shall be 58, 136
A word made flesh is seldom 23
A wounded deer leaps highest 182
Adrift! A little boat adrift 79–80
Ah, Teneriffe 146–147
All circumstances are the frame 288
Alone I cannot be 31–32, 86
An awful tempest mashed the air 288
Angels in the early morning 80
As if the sea should part 303–304
At last to be identified 55
Banish air from air 328
Because I could not stop for death 92–
  93, 303, 329–331
Because the bee may blameless hum
  228
Behind me dips eternity 311–313
By my window have I for scenery 296–
  298
Circumference thou bride of awe 314–
  315, 319
Come slowly, Eden 225–228
Cosmopolites without a plea 85, 165
Did the harebell loose her girdle 193
Distrustful of the gentian 139
Dont put up my thread and needle
  325–326
Doubt me! My dim companion 180
Down time's quaint stream 79

Dropped into the ether acre 311
Dying! Dying in the night 135–136
Essential oils are wrung 323
Fame is the one that does not stay
  317–318
Fame of myself to justify 315–316
Forever at his side to walk 232–233
Four trees upon a solitary acre 294–
  296
Go not too near a house of rose 57
Going to him! Happy letter 159, 189
He found my being, set it up 193–194
He put the belt around my life 31–32
He showed me hights I never saw. See I
  showed her hights she never saw
He touched me, so I live to know 191,
  212, 237–238
He was my host, he was my guest
  191–192
Heart! We will forget him 183
Her breast is fit for pearls 133–134
Her "last Poems" 11
Her sweet weight on my heart a night
  160
Here where the daisies fit my head 279
His bill is clasped, his eye forsook
  272–274
How sick to wait in any place but thine
  237
I am ashamed, I hide 212, 326
I cannot live with you 38, 124–125,
  182, 212, 306–308
I cross till I am weary 304
I dwell in possibility 50
I felt a funeral in my brain 84, 90–91
I gave myself to him 191
I had been hungry all the years 173
I had not minded walls 16
I have a bird in spring 122–127
I have never seen 'Volcanoes' 213–215
I have no life but this 184
I heard a fly buzz when I died 309–310

I held a jewel in my fingers   142, 232
I hide myself within my flower   285
I learned at least what home could be
   58
I live with him, I see his face   44–46
I made slow riches but my gain   56
I make his crescent fill or lack   211
I often passed the village   138–139
I play at riches to appease   142–143
I prayed at first a little girl   193
I rose because he sank   159–160
I saw no way, the heavens were stitched
   83
I see thee better in the dark   215, 246
I see thee clearer for the grave   215
I send two sunsets   260–261
I showed her hights she never saw   132,
   158–160
I taste a liquor never brewed   31
I tend my flowers for thee   283–285,
   325
I took my power in my hand   145–146
I was the slightest in the house   52–53,
   325
I would not paint a picture   253–254
If he dissolve, then there is nothing more
   196–197
If I may have it when it's dead   97
If it had no pencil   195, 283
I'll tell you how the sun rose   49
I'm "wife", I've finished that   193
Image of light, adieu   261–262
Is it true, dear Sue   168
It did not surprise me   137
It might be lonelier   44
It sifts from leaden sieves   291–292
It was a quiet way   7, 191
It was not death, for I stood up   308
It's thoughts and just one heart   132
Judgment is justest   316–317
Just lost, when I was saved   192
Just so Jesus [Christ] raps   232, 267–
   270
Lad of Athens, faithful be   320
Least rivers docile to some sea   225
Let us play yesterday   55, 143–44
Like eyes that looked on wastes   68,
   132, 160–163, 166–167, 192, 211

Long years apart can make no   164
Longing is like the seed   278–279
Love thou art high   234
Me, change! Me, alter   231
Mine by the right of the white election
   38, 129
Morning that comes but once   82
Morns like these we parted   11
My friend must be a bird   122
My life has stood a loaded gun   241–
   244
My river runs to thee   230
Myself was formed a carpenter   61–62
"Nature" is what we see   291
No matter now, sweet   137–138, 148
No matter where the saints abide   263
None who saw it ever told it   167
Nor mountain hinder me   231–232
Not in this world to see his face   43–44
Not with a club the heart is broken
   205
Now I knew I lost her   156, 165–167
Of all the souls that stand create   58,
   153
Of so divine a loss   227
Of tribulation these are they   41–42,
   180, 219
On my volcano grows the grass   214–
   215
On this long storm the rainbow rose
   288
On this wondrous sea   80
One crucifixion is recorded only   239
One life of so much consequence   152–
   153, 227–228
One sister have I in the house   119–
   120, 129, 166
Only a shrine, but mine   36
Our lives are Swiss   58
Ourselves were wed one summer, dear
   110–111, 122, 129, 133, 141, 183,
   245–246
Over the fence   233
Perhaps I asked too large   332–333
Portraits are to daily faces   21
Precious to me she still shall be   162,
   164–165, 180–181
Publication is the auction   180, 322

Rearrange a "wife's" affection   233

Recollect the face of me   65–66

Removed from accident of loss   150–151

Safe in their alabaster chambers   49, 156–157, 249

She dwelleth in the ground   96–97

She rose to his requirement, dropt   226

She sights a bird, she chuckles   274

Shells from the coast mistaking   151–152

She's happy, with a new content   154–155, 160

Sleep is supposed to be   54–55

So from the mould   278

Some work for immortality   110

Struck was I, nor yet by lightning   189, 239–240

Success is counted sweetest   48, 316, 318

Sunset that screens reveals   262–263

Sweet mountains, ye tell me no lie   37

Take your heaven further on   34–36

The angle of a landscape   60

The Bible is an antique volume   64–65, 280

The birds begin at four o'clock   59–60

The daisy follows soft the sun   21, 194–195

The day came slow till five o'clock   58–59

The drop that wrestles in the sea   215

The face I carry with me last   219

The first day's night had come   89–90

The Himmaleh was known to stoop   283

The immortality she gave   96

The lilac is an ancient shrub   285–286

The Malay took the pearl   133–134, 147–150, 160

The martyr poets did not tell   131

The most pathetic thing I do   146

The nearest dream recedes unrealized   49

The one who could repeat the summer day   260

The only news I know   326

The poets light but lamps   324–325

The power to be true to you   211

The soul selects her own society   84–85, 153, 268

The soul should always stand ajar   86

The soul unto itself   86–87

The soul's distinct connection   71

The sun and moon must make their haste   67–68

The sun kept setting, setting still   310–311

The trees like tassels hit and swung   258–259

The wind begun to knead the grass   300–302

The world stands solemner to me   191, 193

There came a day at summer's full   212, 304–306

There is a solitude of space   83

There's a certain slant of light   263–265, 292

There's been a death in the opposite house   159

They put us far apart   190, 219–220, 306

This consciousness that is aware   87–88

This docile one inter   95–96

This was a Poet. It is that   261, 317, 323–324

Three times we parted, breath and I   215

Through the dark sod, as education   275–279

Through the strait pass of suffering   13, 181, 277

'Tis little I could care for pearls   190–191, 233

'Tis opposites entice   160

'Tis so appalling, it exhilirates   80–81

'Tis true they shut me in the cold   155–156

Title divine is mine   178–180

To earn it by disdaining it   322

To fight aloud is very brave   318

To hear an oriole sing   254

To love thee year by year   160

To make one's toilette after death   192

To my small hearth his fire came 195–196

To the bright east she flies 94–95

Today or this noon 93–94

'Twas comfort in her dying room 94

'Twas my one glory 242–243

Two swimmers wrestled on the spar 192

Unto my books so good to turn 78, 162

Volcanoes be in Sicily 214

We, bee and I, live by the quaffing 226

We grow accustomed to the dark 56

We learned the whole of love 191

We play at paste 49

We see comparatively 231

Wert thou but ill, that I might show thee 221

What shall I do, it whimpers so 197

What twigs we held by 225

When diamonds are a legend 138

Where thou art, that is home 180–181

Whether my bark went down at sea 80

Why do they shut me out of heaven 232–233

Why make it doubt, it hurts it so 44

Wild nights, wild nights 80, 223, 228–229, 232–234

Will there really be a "Morning" 60, 81

You know that portait in the moon 292–293

You love me, you are sure 135

Your riches taught me poverty 140–143, 150, 182, 233, 308

Index

Abbott, Mary, 38
Aesthetic art, 92
Agassiz, Louis, 35, 91
Alcott, Louisa May, 15, 103, 118, 230
Alexander, C. R., 258–259
Amherst, Mass., 12, 97, 116, 119, 270
Amherst Academy, 63, 66, 104, 113, 141
Amherst College, 1, 12, 66, 130, 140, 199
Anderson, Charles, 312
androgyny, 43, 97, 159–160, 185
Anthon, Catherine (Kate) Scott, 20, 42, 147, 198, 202, 287
Apollo, 329
Arnold, Matthew, 13
Atlantic Monthly, 14, 24, 46, 48, 53, 58, 141, 174, 236, 240, 282, 287, 293, 299

Badger, Mrs. C. M., 280–282, 371n31
Baigell, Matthew, 76
Barker, Wendy, 351n20
Bartlett, Rev. Samuel, 118, 154, 167
bee, as symbol, 122, 226, 228
Bennett, Paula, 354n3, 371n31, 375n13
Bianchi, Martha Dickinson, 11, 17, 29, 87, 130, 256, 278; as editor, 108–109, 120, 236, 238, 326
Bible, 6, 8, 23, 31, 35, 60, 62, 63–65, 74, 86, 138, 230, 238, 244, 267, 279–280, 289, 301, 313; ED's poem on, 64–65; Corinthians, 30–31, 68, 78, 115, 286, 290; Matthew, 8, 61, 62, 63, 65, 85, 152, 197, 280, 284; Revelation, 40–41, 59, 78, 88–89, 219, 267, 268, 269, 276, 306, 320
Bierstadt, Albert, 264
Bingham, Millicent Todd, 23, 129, 130, 199
bird imagery, 94–95, 120–122, 125–126, 137, 143, 152, 205, 248, 254, 269, 272–274

Blake, William, 91, 245, 248
boat, 229. *See also* ships
Bowdoin, Elbridge, 203
Bowles, Mary, 181, 185–186, 188, 207, 208; letters to, 179, 198, 216, 230, 291
Bowles, Samuel, 27–28, 35, 154, 159, 163, 171, 184, 186 (illus.), 205–209, 215–225 passim, 233, 238–239, 248–249, 256, 283; as Austin's friend, 27–28, 130, 179, 185, 207, 221, 249, 256; character and personality, 27–28, 179, 180, 186–188, 205–207; death, 114, 179, 185, 187–188, 197, 208, 244, 245, 278; depressions, 188, 202, 208; as ED's confidant, 27, 178–183, 198, 201; health, 154, 181, 188, 198, 202, 208, 216; as husband and father, 186, 188, 198, 207; as journalist, 27, 178, 179, 185, 216; and Maria Whitney, 198, 206, 207–209; as Master, 28, 183–184, 186, 218–219, 221; and Sue, 30, 108, 163, 179, 185–187, 189, 207, 208, 215, 223; travels, 179, 185, 202, 215, 216, 217–218, 236, 248; and women's rights, 187, 206; mentioned, 6, 9, 11, 12, 16, 41, 108, 109, 250–251, 292, 316
Bowles, Samuel, Jr., 179, 183, 194, 225, 244, 320
Brandegee, Robert, 272, 275
Bridges, Fidelia, 275
Bridges, Robert ("Droch"), 182
Brontë, Charlotte, 198, 203–204, 209, 229, 314, 321; *Jane Eyre*, 159, 184, 194, 197, 198, 202–204, 207, 209, 211–213, 217–218, 221, 222, 224; *The Professor*, 222; *Villette*, 184–185, 198, 202, 211, 223
Brontë, Emily, 56, 78, 203, 229; *Wuthering Heights*, 138, 229
Brooks, Van Wyck, 328

Brown, Ford Madox, 206
Browning, Elizabeth Barrett, 11, 30, 111, 122, 160, 165, 290, 321; *Aurora Leigh,* 52, 234, 279, 321, 325, 328
Browning, Robert, 2, 111, 121, 136, 148, 290
Bryant, William Cullen, 70
Bullard, Otis, 21
Bunyan, John, 76
Burke, Edmund, 82–83, 254
Byron, George Gordon, Lord, 212, 320

Cameron, Julia Margaret, 21
Cameron, Sharon, 368n77
Capps, Jack L., 148, 352n41
Carlo, 197
Cassatt, Mary, 262
Catlin, George, 227
Century, 322
Christ, 23, 28, 61, 85, 136, 183, 197, 266–269. *See also* God
Church, Frederic Edwin, 55, 56–57, 71–74, 81, 185, 227, 229, 231, 248, 264, 265, 266, 270, 274–275, 283, 289, 297, 302, 303, 304, 312; *Cardamum,* 275, 277 (illus.); *Chimborazo,* 158, 235; *Cotopaxi,* 190; *The Heart of the Andes,* 213, 231, 232, 234–237 (illus.), 266, 299; *Morning,* 56; *Ox-Bow (after Thomas Cole),* 74; *Twilight in the Wilderness,* 162, 299
circle, circular imagery, 103, 108, 134, 161
Clark, Charles H., 66
Clark, James D., 16
Claude Gellée (Lorrain), 71, 265
coded language: in Master materials, 184, 197, 198; in Sue cycle, 126, 134, 141, 146
Cole, Thomas, 57, 58, 62–63, 67, 68–82, 100, 157, 201, 227, 229, 245, 252–253, 264, 265, 283, 287–288, 290, 297, 299, 302, 304, 312; *Expulsion from the Garden of Eden,* 69–70, 81, 82, 227, 229, 230, 253; *Tintern Abbey,* 71, 76; *View from Mt. Holyoke (The Ox-Bow),* 71, 162, 302; *The Voyage of Life* series, 53, 68–71, 74–82, 98, 126, 185, 198, 223, 225, 235,

247, 253, 288, 290, 299, 302–303, 332. *See also* plates 2–5, 8
Coleman, Eliza, 104
Coleridge, Samuel Taylor, 76, 77, 297
Collins, Charles Allston, 34, 36. *See also* plate 1
Constable, John, 264, 265, 288
Crane, Walter, 301
Crayon, The, 38, 266
Cropsey, Jasper, 63, 264, 371n31
Cutler, Harriet and William, 113, 114, 118, 187

daguerreotypes, 2, 17, 20, 21, 23, 101–102. *See also* photography
Daisy, in Master letters, 194, 195, 209, 215, 221, 224
Dandurand, Karen, 323
Darwin, Charles, 35, 226, 230–231, 298
dashes, 252, 326–328
dawn, 8–9, 54–55, 59. *See also* morning
dead, poems for the, 93–99
death, 14–15, 93; ED's preoccupation with, 3–7, 14; as theme, 3–4, 7–9, 45, 88–89, 93–99, 245, 309–313, 329–330
Depression, 5. *See also under* Bowles and ED
De Quincey, Thomas, 76, 148–149, 150, 202, 290
Deverell, Walter Howell, 121
Dewing, Margaret Aurelia, 17, 19 (illus.), 20
Dickens, Charles, 179, 188, 209, 221
Dickinson, (William) Austin, 7, 12, 25, 27, 30, 107, 108, 109, 116–118, 120, 134, 140, 197; interest in art, 36, 74, 235, 248, 256; character and personality, 117; courtship of Sue, 107, 116–118, 127, 173, 247; and Mabel Todd, 11, 27, 117, 130, 167–168, 173, 176; as "Malay," 147–151; marriage, 28, 30, 101, 108, 112, 113, 118–119, 126–127, 128–131, 147, 154–155, 173; mentioned, 1, 9, 213, 251, 322
Dickinson, Edward (father), 20, 37, 94, 115, 116, 117, 119, 167, 187, 251, 255, 257, 280–281; death, 7, 94
Dickinson, Emily, 18 (illus.); interest in art, 69, 82, 245–265 passim, 269;

biblical knowledge, 8, 30–31, 59, 61, 63–65, 66, 197, 232, 268, 279–280, 286, 290; as boy, 64, 65, 79, 137, 159, 197, 242, 320; death and funeral, 1–3, 6, 7, 167–168; depressions, 127–128; domestic pursuits, 50, 255, 257, 324–325, 328; education, 4, 63, 66–67, 70, 113, 249, 257; eye disorder, 60, 110, 170, 271; and father, 20, 94, 280–281; girlhood friends, 4–5, 9, 25–27, 103–107; handwriting, 200, 217, 326, 327; health, 1, 4, 60, 110, 127–128, 170, 223; interest in horticulture, 12, 25, 28, 275–286, 295; literary tastes, 13–14, 31, 63–64, 82, 101; attitude toward marriage, 12–13, 34, 42, 103, 193–194, 211, 319; and mother, 95, 112, 245; interest in needlework, 257–258, 328; as neurotic, 12, 25, 29, 31; obituary, 2, 9–13; attitude toward publication, 11, 180, 246, 316–318, 322; reclusion, 1, 2–3, 12, 13, 15–16, 23–33, 35, 46, 50, 109, 128, 154, 291, 309, 315; religious views, 6, 13, 30, 35, 63–68, 106, 124–125, 210–211, 250, 268; and sexuality, 37, 43, 101, 110, 145, 148, 150, 192, 193, 198; attraction to solitude, 24–27, 29–30; white clothing, 17, 29, 34, 37, 38, 40, 219, 220, 276; as woman writer, 30, 320–328; working habits, 16, 52, 58, 65

Dickinson, Emily Norcross (mother), 94–95, 112, 245, 255

Dickinson, (Thomas) Gilbert, 4, 13, 97–99, 112, 164, 168

Dickinson, Lavinia (Vinnie), 1, 2, 3, 4, 9, 11, 53, 107, 109, 113, 115, 117, 120, 124, 130, 160, 167, 177, 271, 273, 322; on ED's reclusion, 23, 29; and locked box, 4, 317; and Master letters, 199, 213

Dickinson, Martha. See Bianchi, Martha Dickinson

Dickinson, Ned (Edward), 64, 130, 154, 168, 176, 204, 319–320

Dickinson, Susan Huntington Gilbert (Sue), 11–12, 112–119, 129 (illus.), 252, 256, 276; interest in art, 12, 36, 74, 235, 248, 256; as author of ED's obituary, 2, 9–13, 176; love of books, 114–115, 256; and Bowles, 30, 108, 130, 163, 179, 185–186, 187, 189, 207, 208, 215, 223, 244; character and personality, 108, 110, 113, 116, 117–118, 122, 127, 128–129, 145, 158, 167–168, 176, 187; childhood, 12, 112–114, 186; as Cleopatra figure, 21, 101, 119, 128, 146, 155, 171–174; courtship by Austin, 107, 116–118, 127, 173, 247; as critic of ED's poems, 49, 156–157, 316, 322; and ED's reclusion, 2, 12, 13, 25, 28–29, 109; love of entertaining, 28, 41, 110, 141, 155, 173, 189; estrangement from ED, 11, 13, 25, 30, 100, 109, 114, 123, 126–27, 136, 156, 163–166, 268; as girlhood friend, 9, 101, 109, 113, 115–116, 159; health, 118, 127–128, 168; marriage, 28, 30, 101, 108, 112, 113, 118–119, 126–131, 154–155, 168, 176; as mother, 97, 130, 164, 168; and publication of ED's poems, 101, 115, 316, 322; relationship with ED, 9, 25, 30, 97, 100–101, 103, 107–111, 113, 119–127 passim, 131–177 passim, 244, 247–248, 268, 322; and religion, 13, 36, 113, 124–125; sexuality and, 118, 128–129; snobbery, 12, 110, 117, 130; and Sue cycle, 110–112, 119–170 passim, 177, 188, 189, 223, 228, 247; view of women's role, 11, 12, 322; mentioned, 1, 26, 70, 79, 89, 239, 250, 251, 304, 314, 316

Diehl, Joanne Feit, 352n41, 353n45

Dijkstra, Bram, 103

Domenichino (Domenico Zampieri), 71

Donne, John, 161

Doughty, Thomas, 291

Durand, Asher, 71–74, 265, 266

Durand, John, 38, 266

Eakins, Thomas, 229

Eastern and oriental imagery, 101, 122, 133

Eberwein, Jane Donahue, 23

Eden, 65, 71, 82, 99, 100–101, 190, 217, 223, 225–232, 320; "rowing in Eden," 185, 223, 229–230, 233

Edwards, Jonathan, 55, 84
Eliot, George, 30, 114, 291, 321
Emerson, Ralph Waldo, 24, 25, 30, 43, 47, 48, 49–51, 53, 61–62, 67, 97, 108, 159, 234, 258, 279, 285, 288, 310, 321; *Nature*, 7, 48, 51, 282, 302; *Poems*, 48, 251, 317; "Self Reliance," 46–47
Emmons, Henry, 103
eroticism, 101, 104, 106, 188; in ED's poems, 3, 35, 86, 100, 134, 146, 223–225; in letters to Sue, 100, 101, 121. *See also* sexuality
eternity, 144, 146; as theme, 6, 8, 13, 45, 54, 56, 78, 98, 150, 234, 247–248, 255. *See also* immortality; infinity
Evergreens, the, 119, 141, 146, 149, 156, 157, 172, 179, 256

face(s): hidden, 16, 23, 30, 31, 46, 278; as image, 15–16, 30–31, 43–44, 45, 60, 62, 65–66, 68, 112, 287–293; of Master, 190, 219–220, 244
Faderman, Lillian, 101
fame, 49, 60, 157, 315–316, 317, 322
Farley, Abbie, 176
Farrer, Thomas, 266, 270, 271
fascicles, 131, 147, 180, 183, 189, 225, 257, 328, 375n13; early, 31, 179; later, 122, 133; no. *1*, 55, 79, 139; *2*, 109, 119, 183; *3*, 80; *5*, 133; *6*, 81; *7*, 195; *9*, 135, 179; *10*, 81, 152, 196, 225, 227–228; *11*, 228–229, 232, 233, 269, 327 (illus.); *12*, 31–32; *13*, 180; *14*, 31, 32–33, 150; *15*, 31; *16*, 159–160; *22*, 51–52, 60, 61, 62, 67; *26*, 141; *29*, 160; *33*, 195–196; *35*, 55; *36*, 143, 180–181, 311
Fitzgerald, Edward, 89
flowers, 227, 228, 275–286; daisy, 194–195, 209, 283, 285, 324, 325; jasmine, 225–226; lilac, 285–286; lily, 36, 38–39, 40, 168, 275–280; rose, 126, 157, 168, 170, 285
Ford, Emily Fowler, 25–27
Fowler, Emily. *See* Ford
Franklin, R. W., 199, 200, 217, 228, 326
Freeman, Margaret H., 183–184
French, Daniel Chester, 314–319

Gelpi, Albert, 241
Gifford, Sanford, 235, 242, 304, 352n36
Gilbert, (Thomas) Dwight, 112, 113
Gilbert, Frank, 114, 118
Gilbert, Martha, 113
Gilbert, Sandra, 40, 203, 206
Gilbert, Thomas (father), 36, 112
Gillett, Sara Colton, 29
Gladden, Washington, 66
God, 23, 43–44, 67–68, 260. *See also* Christ; religion
Grahn, Judy, 354n3
Graves, John, 103, 104
Gubar, Susan, 40, 203, 206

Hale, Edward Everett, 251
Harnett, William Michael, 273
Harper's Magazine, 42–43, 58, 70, 89, 141–142, 297
Hawarden, Clementina Viscountess, 101–103, 109
Hawthorne, Nathaniel, 11, 13, 25, 161, 192, 266
Heade, Martin Johnson, 162, 227, 229, 248, 269, 297, 301, 312
Heger, Constantin, 198, 203, 204, 209
Herbert, George, 59, 62, 326, 328
Higginson, Col. Thomas Wentworth, 1, 2–3, 4, 11, 24, 46, 48–49, 89, 111, 115, 134, 175, 243, 321–322; and *Atlantic*, 24, 48, 282–283, 299; as critic of ED's work, 49, 52, 250; as editor, 44, 226, 329, 330; ED's meetings with, 2, 38, 285; letters to, 11, 17–20, 21, 48, 49, 66, 82, 95, 175–176, 216, 249–251, 316, 317; poems sent to, 3, 49, 216, 249–250; as preceptor, 1, 49, 111, 175, 316; mentioned, 16, 32, 46, 52
Hill, John Henry, 266, 271, 273
Hill, John William, 272, 273
Hill, May Brawley, 273
Hitchcock, Edward, 1, 17, 66
Holland, Elizabeth, 3, 16, 22, 58, 95, 298, 318
Holland, Dr. Josiah, 22, 27, 79, 89, 205, 208, 291, 316, 318
Holland, Sophia, 4–5
Holt, Dr. Jacob, 63–64, 65, 66

home, as image, 25, 28, 134, 149
homoeroticism, 43, 102–103, 161, 166, 223. *See also* eroticism; lesbianism
honor, quest for, 30, 49, 60, 172, 315, 320
Howe, Julia Ward, 69, 175
Howe, Susan, 367n60, 374n13
Hudson River School, 35, 37, 55, 57, 58, 75, 82–83, 162, 185, 229, 235, 256, 262, 266, 297, 299, 302, 304, 312
Humboldt, Alexander von, 35, 226, 231, 274
Humphrey, Jane (Jenny), 103–104, 107, 125, 197
Hunt, William Holman, 222, 232, 266–269; *The Light of the World*, 266–269. *See also* plate 7

immortality, 7, 30, 46, 322. *See also* eternity
impressionists, 262–263, 265
infinity, 78, 101, 291, 298. *See also* eternity
Inness, George, 162, 262, 265
Irving, Washington, 235

Jackson, Helen Hunt, 11, 313, 316, 366n57
James, Henry, 13, 221, 298–299, 302
James, William, 25
Jameson, Anna, 37, 174
Jarves, James Jackson, 89, 371n27, 372n34
Jenkins, Rev. MacGregor, 1, 248
Jesus. *See* Christ
jewels and riches, as images, 59, 133, 138, 141–142, 167, 182, 190–191, 233. *See also* pearl
Johnson, Thomas H., 29, 79, 107, 123, 199–200, 220, 255, 326

Kensett, John F., 256, 297, 352n36
Khnopff, Fernand, 103
Klimt, Gustav, 301
knee image, 222–223
Knight, Charles, 54, 175

landscape poems, 59, 82–83, 90, 263–265, 285, 287–290, 294–303. *See also* nature poems
Lane, Fitz Hugh, 229
Lathrop, Clara, 127
Leighton, Frederick, 365n32
Leonardo da Vinci, 287, 302
lesbianism, 101, 103, 161, 163, 197. *See also* homoeroticism
Letters: (1894), 109, 199, 213; (1931), 107, 109; (1955), 199; (1958), 199, 255
Leyda, Jay, 25–26, 27, 255
light, as image, 56, 57, 58, 245–246, 248, 251–252, 254–255, 261–262, 303–305, 308–313, 325
Lindberg-Seyersted, Brita, 303
Longfellow, Henry Wadsworth, 104
Longsworth, Polly, 112, 154
Lord, Judge Otis Phillips, 3, 30, 109, 110, 115, 176, 191, 224
loss, as theme, 83, 126–127, 182
love, 35, 42, 131, 213, 247–248; ED's view of, 42, 151, 319–320
love poems, 3, 94, 108, 201, 252, 290, 297, 304–312; for Sue, 103, 119–170 passim, 182, 228; 308; for Master, 132, 144, 155, 179, 188, 189–198, 224–244, 283–284, 290, 308–309
Luminists, 35, 37, 50, 55, 60, 75, 162, 229, 235, 262, 296, 297, 299, 302, 304, 309, 310–311, 312
Lyman, Joseph, 53–54, 170, 177
Lyon, Mary, 66, 70–71, 103

Madonna figure, 36–38
Maher, Maggie, 36, 189
"Malay," the, 147–151
Marlowe, Christopher, 308
Martin, John, 230
Mary Lyon's Female Seminary, 4, 63, 66–67, 70–71, 107, 113, 257
Masque of Poets, A, 316
Master materials, 80, 109, 110–111, 138, 160, 177, 178–244, 246, 251; and identity of Master, 28, 183–184, 186, 200, 212, 218; letters, 39, 40, 85, 111, 129, 138, 184, 188, 195, 197,

Master materials (*cont.*)
198–224 passim; poems, 132, 144, 155, 179, 188, 189–198, 210, 211, 213–214, 221, 224–244, 283–284, 290, 308–309; riddles in, 239–244
Merriam, George, 180, 184, 188, 197, 205–207, 208
Millais, John Everett, 35, 105, 266
Miller, Ruth, 366n59
Milton, John, 225, 232
mirror images, 30–31, 161, 190
Mitchell, Donald Grant (Ik Marvel), 104
morning, 53–60, 78, 83, 144, 183, 231
Morris, Adelaide, 358n48
mortuary themes, 14, 104, 113, 124. *See also* death
mountains, 37, 231. *See also* volcano imagery
Mount Holyoke Female Seminary, 113
Munch, Edvard, 283

nature, 68, 227, 250, 258, 272, 291
nature poems, 274–286, 294–303. *See also* landscape poems
needlework, 257–258, 328
Newton, Benjamin Franklin, 251
Niles, Thomas, 246
Norcross, Frances and Louise (cousins), 6, 170, 177, 243, 244, 250, 255, 270, 314
Novak, Barbara, 89, 262–263, 302
nun imagery, 33–42, 44, 45, 276, 306; ED as nun, 24, 31, 36–37, 39, 40, 42

Oxford movement, 35

Paglia, Camille, 253n9, 258, 353n54
Patmore, Coventry, 12, 121, 130
Patterson, Rebecca, 147, 194, 361n81
pearl imagery, 147–153, 160, 228
photography, 2, 5, 16–20, 21–22, 290, 291
Pierpont, John, 14, 15
Poe, Edgar Allan, 88, 93
Poems: (1890), 26, 28, 44, 92, 93, 115, 182, 226, 262, 263, 309, 318, 322, 331; *Second Series* (1891), 262; (1896), 33

Pollack, Vivian, 148, 150, 218, 354n3
Porter, David, 369n2
Pre-Raphaelites, 37, 38–39, 161, 162–163, 250, 265–275, 290; American, 248, 266, 269–278, 281; British, 266–269
punctuation of poems, 326–328

red, as symbol, 39, 144, 249
Redon, Odilon, 91
religion, as theme, 30–31, 35–36, 124–126. *See also* Christ
resurrection images, 8–9, 91, 183, 210, 214
Revelation. *See* Bible
Rich, Adrienne, 241
Richards, William Trost, 266, 271
Roman Catholicism, 35–37
Root, Abiah Palmer, 4–5, 104–107; letters to, 4–5, 6, 67, 104–105, 106–107, 120, 127, 282
Rosa, Salvator, 71, 265
Rosenthal, Tobias, 93
Rossetti, Christina, 124, 269, 309
Rossetti, Dante Gabriel, 38, 162, 266, 290
royal images, 59, 134, 138, 142–143, 189, 221
Rudisill, Richard, 17
Ruskin, John, 51, 62, 183, 263, 267, 268, 271, 274, 288, 290; *Modern Painters*, 82, 227, 250, 266
Ryder, Albert Pinkham, 88–89, 92, 297, 367n65, 375n22

St. Armand, Barton Levi, 70, 256, 263–264
Sand, George, 30, 174, 321
Sapphism. *See* lesbianism
Scribner's Monthly, 89, 141, 318
sea, as symbol, 150, 151, 190, 192, 202–203, 230, 297
sentimentality, Victorian cult of, 4, 63–64, 101, 109, 139
Sewall, Richard B., 15, 105, 107, 156; *Life*, 105, 183–184
sexuality, 101–102, 138, 184, 211–212, 221, 222, 225, 226; in ED's poems, 37, 43, 86, 100, 122, 134, 138–139,

161, 162, 197, 222–223, 230; in Master material, 138, 191–192, 212, 226, 242–243, 283–284; in Sue cycle, 138–139, 145, 148, 149, 150, 158, 197
Shakespeare, William, 54, 101, 171, 246; *Antony and Cleopatra*, 101, 115, 170–176, 243, 269, 286–287; sonnets, 132, 167, 182
ships, shipwrecks, 79–80, 253
Shurr, William H., 199n37
Sigourney, Lydia, 282
Single Hound, The, 108–109, 120
Smith, Martha Nell, 345n13
snow, 41, 180, 291, 322
soul: body and, 15, 329; as theme, 6, 79–80, 83–88, 290
South or Latin America, 141–142, 297; imagery, in art, 185, 190, 226, 227, 231
Spilka, Mark, 221
"Spriggins's Voyage of Life," 70, 72–73 (illus.)
Springfield Republican, 2, 9, 22, 26, 27, 178, 179, 214, 238, 316
Stamm, Edith Perry, 326
Stillman, William James, 38, 265, 266
Strong, Abiah Root. *See* Root, Abiah
sublime, the, 82–85, 254
success, 318–319. *See also* fame
Sue cycle, 110–112, 119–170 passim, 182, 184, 188, 228, 251, 308
sun imagery, 190, 195, 196, 197, 209, 234, 236
surrealism, 83, 313
Sweetser, Catherine (Aunt Katie), 279, 280
Sweetser, Cornelia, 278
Sweetser, Joseph A. (Uncle), 128
Swinburne, Algernon Charles, 100

Tanguy, Yves, 313
Tate, Allen, 329
Tennyson, Alfred Lord, 39–40, 44, 54–55, 105–106, 161, 185, 190, 260, 331–332; *Idylls of the King,* 193, 332; *Maud,* 115, 121, 157, 168–170, 171, 192; *In Memoriam,* 331, 332; *The Princess,* 114, 168, 224, 331
Thomas à Kempis, 31, 46

Thomas, Heather Kirk, 347n43
Thoreau, Henry David, 25
titles for poems, 44, 226, 246–247, 329
Todd, Mabel Loomis, 1, 2, 27, 28, 107, 127, 128–130, 176–177, 265, 274; and Austin, 11, 27, 109, 117, 127, 129–130, 167–168, 173; as editor, 33, 44, 107, 109, 139, 199, 226, 262, 263, 264, 309, 322, 326, 329, 330, 331; and Sue, 127, 129–130, 176–177
Tractarian movement, 35
Transcendentalists, 17, 50, 60, 298–299
transitus, 6, 39, 76, 255, 310, 329; ED as poet of, 7, 36, 83, 84, 93, 310, 329. *See also* death
trees, 293–298. *See also* landscape poems; nature poems
triangulation, 108, 132, 150, 239
Turner, Clara Newman, 11
Turner, Joseph Mallord William, 79, 82, 250, 263, 265, 288

Van Dyke, Anthony, 259
Vasari, Giorgio, 287
Vedder, Elihu, 89–90, 91–93, 98, 329. *See also* plate 5
Victoria, Queen, 93, 97, 134, 191, 331
volcano imagery, 146, 163, 185, 190, 213–215, 297

Wadsworth, Rev. Charles, 16, 28–29, 66, 109, 216; as Master, 187, 200, 212, 218
Walsh, John Evangelist, 365n40, 367n59
Ward, Samuel, 69
Ward, Theodora Van Wagenen, 147
Warner, Marina, 34
Warner, Mary, 14, 15
Weisbuch, Robert, 111, 148
Wharton, Edith, 69
Whistler, James A. M., 39, 229, 297
white, the color, 29, 33–41, 309; ED's wearing of, 17, 29, 34, 37, 38, 39, 40, 219, 220, 276
Whitman, Walt, 13
Whitney, Josiah, 207
Whitney, Maria, 81, 95, 145, 278; and Bowles, 198, 206, 207–209, 244, 278
Wilbur, Richard, 224

Wilde, Oscar, 38
Williams, Dr. Henry, 170
Williams, William Carlos, 260
Wilmerding, John, 299
Wilner, Eleanor, 148

Winthrop, Theodore, 235–236
Wolff, Cynthia Griffin, 160–161, 295, 321, 346n20
Wordsworth, William, 76, 253; *The Prelude,* 51, 53, 56, 67, 76–78